Dyslexia – Successful Inclusion in the Secondary School

Edited by Lindsay Peer and Gavin Reid

Foreword by
The Rt Hon David Blunkett MP

David Fulton Publishers
London

Published in association with the British Dyslexia Association

David Fulton Publishers Ltd
Ormond House, 26–27 Boswell Street, London WC1N 3JZ

www.fultonpublishers.co.uk

First published in Great Britain by David Fulton Publishers 2001

Note: The right of Lindsay Peer and Gavin Reid to be identified as the editors of this work has been asserted by them in accordance with the Copyright, Designs and Patents Act 1988.

British Library Cataloguing in Publication Data
A catalogue record for this book is available from the British Library

ISBN 1–85346–742–1

The publishers would like to thank John Cox for copy-editing and Sheila Harding for proofreading this book.

Typeset by FiSH Books, London
Printed by The Cromwell Press Ltd, Trowbridge, Wilts.

Contents

Foreword

This book is very timely and I endorse its publication. I am committed to inclusive schools as part of the journey towards a fully inclusive society. Pupils with dyslexia are among those who very often feel excluded from the education system or from society as a whole, owing to lack of confidence and self-belief that their dyslexia can engender. I want to tackle this problem for the benefit of these pupils, remembering always to consider the individual needs of each child – one size doesn't fit all.

The broad thrust of our approach has rightly been on the early identification and assessment of dyslexia and we have put in place a number of measures including baseline assessment to help primary schools do this. Nevertheless, the fact remains that too many of our pupils are disadvantaged when they reach secondary school due to their dyslexia and poor literacy skills generally. This means they are unable to exercise their right to access a curriculum which is as broad and balanced as it should be.

It is therefore crucial to focus on the early years of secondary education and ensure that we build on the success of the National Literacy and Numeracy Strategies to continue to raise standards for all children including those with dyslexia. Last September we introduced pilot projects in 17 Local Education Authorities involving over 200 schools. These projects were designed to transform standards at Key Stage 3 by focusing on English and mathematics with an extension of the literacy and numeracy strategies. We are implementing this nationally in 2001 and all pupils will be able to benefit.

Teachers and others should ensure that pupils with dyslexia have the same opportunities as their peers. I hope this book will help to give them this by offering practical advice on how pupils with dyslexia can be enabled to succeed across the curriculum.

The Rt Hon David Blunket MP
Secretary of State for Education and Employment

The Editors

Lindsay Peer is Education Director of the British Dyslexia Association, and is a widely recognised authority in the field of dyslexia and mainstream education. She regularly appears at national and international events, and has published a considerable body of material, both theoretical and practical. Her field of experience covers teacher training, research and the teaching of both mainstream students and those with Specific Learning Difficulties/Dyslexia from preschool through to adult education. She is Vice Chair of the British Dyslexia Association's Accreditation Board, and works closely with Higher Education Institutions. She also has considerable experience of educational needs assessment and counselling. She is particularly interested in the teaching of English as an Additional Language, and specific skills relating to the educational development of bilingual students with learning problems. She is co-editor of *Multilingualism, Literacy and Dyslexia: A Challenge for Educators* (David Fulton Publishers, 2000).

Her work involves close liaison with various government departments both in the UK and abroad, including the Department for Education and Employment, the Teacher Training Agency and the Qualifications and Curriculum Authority. Among the committees of which she is a member is the National Literacy and Numeracy Strategy Group. She has lectured internationally in the USA, Israel, India, Sweden, Belgium, Finland, Iceland and Norway.

Dr Gavin Reid is a senior lecturer in the Faculty of Education at the University of Edinburgh. He is an experienced secondary school teacher, educational psychologist, university lecturer and researcher. He has made over 150 conference and seminar presentations on dyslexia throughout the UK, Norway, Denmark, Germany, the United States, New Zealand, Hong Kong, Poland, Hungary, Bratislava and the Czech Republic.

He has written and edited key course textbooks for teacher training in the field of dyslexia and literacy – *Dyslexia: A Practitioner's Handbook* (Wiley, 1997) and *Dimensions of Dyslexia* (vols 1 and 2) (Moray House 1996) and is co-author of *Dyslexia in Adults: Education and Employment* (Wiley, 2000). He is the co-author of *Learning Styles: A Guide for Teachers and Parents* and *Dyslexia: A Resource Guide for Parents and Teachers* (Red Rose Publications 1999 and 1997) and also co-editor of *Multilingualism, Literacy and Dyslexia: A Challenge for Educators* (David Fulton Publishers, 2000) and co-author of a group test 'Listening and Literacy Index' published by Hodder and Stoughton (2001).

He is a consultant to a number of national and international initiatives in dyslexia and is a member of the British Dyslexia Association Accreditation Board.

Comment from the Editors

This book is intended for a wide readership. It was born from the recognition that there is a dire need for support for those working with adolescent dyslexic learners in a mainstream educational framework. We are constantly being asked to provide information that will benefit all those involved with the process. This we hope we have achieved. We hope the book will be useful for subject teachers, psychologists, support assistants, school management, researchers and indeed all involved in the meeting of student and staff needs within the policy and practice of inclusion.

We appreciate the efforts of all those who submitted chapters for this book. One common element among all the contributors is that each one is exceptionally busy with many and varied demands on their time. We appreciate that they were able to give up some of that time to prepare a chapter for this book.

We have organised the book in a manner which we feel will be useful to its potential readership. We commence with two chapters as an introduction to the area of dyslexia within the context of inclusion in secondary schools. After these introductory chapters there follows a section on inclusion, highlighting many issues relating to principles and practices; we feel this section will engender considerable interest and debate.

Section 3 is called The Subject of Success. Here teachers provide firsthand accounts and perspectives on how dyslexic students' needs can best be met in their own subject areas. This section is deliberately practical and we hope it will be welcomed by all subject teachers.

Inclusion is essentially a whole-school issue and therefore Section 4 consists of chapters all relating to cross-curricular aspects including provision, self-esteem, EAL, examination arrangements and staff development.

The last section of the book relates to professional and personal perspectives including the views of an educational psychologist and a careers adviser.

The final chapter of the book is essentially dedicated to all parents. In this chapter a parent's perspective and experiences are outlined and we feel this represents what the book is all about – ensuring effective communication, facilitating equality for all and providing a voice for students, teachers, management and parents. This may ensure that all dyslexic people fulfil their rightful potential in education and adulthood.

Lindsay Peer and Gavin Reid
March 2001

Notes on the Contributors

Fernando Almeida Diniz teaches in the Faculty of Education at the University of Edinburgh. He has a background in educational psychology and has been a teacher, researcher and lecturer in England and Scotland. Fernando has held academic positions of Reader and Head of Department and has an international reputation for his work in social justice and inclusion, with a particular focus on disability and race. He is currently leading a national project on the 'Social inclusion of black/minority ethnic disabled children and their families'.

Chris Ashton works for Lancashire LEA as a Specialist Educational Psychologist (SpLD). He previously worked for Sheffield LEA and was a tutor on Sheffield University's Postgraduate Diploma in Severe Reading Difficulties and Dyslexia.

Isobel Calder is Lecturer in the Department of Educational Support and Guidance at the University of Strathclyde. Her research interests include dyslexia in Higher Education and also 'non-teacher' support to children with learning difficulties.

Steve Chinn is Founder and Principal of Mark College, a secondary (Beacon status) school for dyslexic boys. He lectures worldwide on maths and dyslexia and is author of several books, worksheets and a diagnostic test.

Doreen Coventry is a member of the Mathematics Department at George Watson's College, Edinburgh.

Victoria Crivelli is a Senior Specialist Teacher for the ICT and Resources Learning and Behaviour Support Service Worcestershire. She is also Vice Chair Elect of the BDA Computer Committee.

Margaret Crombie is currently manager of the special educational needs support team of teachers in East Renfrewshire. She has researched into the effects of dyslexia on the learning of modern languages in school.

Richard Dargie was formerly Principal Teacher of Social Subjects at Portlethen Academy in Kincardineshire and is currently Lecturer in History Education at the University of Edinburgh. He is a prolific writer of history resources for primary and secondary schoolchildren in Scotland with over 60 textbooks, radio and television programmes, web sites and teaching packs to his credit.

David Dodds has been a Principal teacher at Support for Learning, Boroughmuir High School since 1987. He was also a part-time tutor in the University of Edinburgh Modular Masters programme from 1996–9.

Diana Ditchfield studied piano and theory with singing at the Royal Irish Academy of Music and Music Education with English Education at the University of Warwick. In addition, she has an MA (Ed) from the Open University and a PG Certificate in SpLD from the University of Edinburgh. She has taught instrumental and class music in schools in England and Ireland.

Adele Fairman is a specialist teacher employed by the local authority and has run a Special Unit for Dyslexic students as part of a mainstream school. She now works in a number of secondary schools advising on Inclusion.

Angela Fawcett is a psychologist at the University of Sheffield. Her research with Rod Nicolson has led to screening and intervention from cradle to grave.

Robin Gray has spent 40 years in education as teacher and director, as well as a performer. He is currently Director of Art and Drama at Edington and Shapwick School, Somerset.

Gerald Hales is an independent Chartered Psychologist and Therapist. Widely experienced in assessment and diagnosis of dyslexia and similar difficulties with children and adults, he is particularly concerned about psychological effects on self-esteem and confidence. He has extensive research and teaching experience from Reception to PhD.

Pam Holmes has been a Specialist Teacher since 1992. She worked for seven years within Warwickshire LEA's Support Service and has been Learning Support Coordinator/SENCO for Rugby School since November 1999.

Christine Howlett has two dyslexic sons. She has been a teacher of dyslexic/learners for 24 years and is developing and teaching on a new programme for them at Wolverhampton Grammar School.

Vicky Hunter has been a learning support teacher for 17 years. For the last eight years she has been Principal Teacher in the Learning Support Department at James Gillespie's High School.

Mike Johnson is a Senior Lecturer in Special Educational Needs at the Institute of Education, Manchester Metropolitan University.

Jane Kirk is Dyslexia Advisor at the University of Edinburgh. In addition, she is a part-time lecturer in Moray House, Faculty of Education, University of Edinburgh and was formerly principal teacher of learning support in a secondary school.

John Landon is Senior Lecturer in the Department of Equity Studies and Special Education in the Faculty of Education, The University of Edinburgh.

Colin Lannen is the principal of the Red Rose School for dyslexic children, in St Annes on Sea, Lancashire.

John Lewis is a senior teacher and SENCO at Ercall Wood Technology College. He developed the provision for dyslexic pupils at this school. Children with this specific learning difficulty still form the majority of 75 pupils with statements of SEN at the school.

David Lumsdon is an Educational Psychologist in Northumberland. He has a specialist interest in Dyslexia and coordinates the County's courses on Specific Learning Difficulties.

Neil MacKay is a freelance consultant and trainer working primarily on dyslexia-related issues and is the originator of the phrase 'dyslexia friendly schools'. He is currently working with Flintshire LEA to spearhead their Dyslexia Friendly Schools Initiative.

Hilary McColl, a former teacher with a particular interest in modern languages and special educational needs, now works as consultant, trainer and writer on these and related topics.

Carol Orton is a parent of two dyslexic sons. She has supported parents, helplines and worked as a school governor and local magistrate. She joined the BDA in 1994 and was appointed BDA Policy and Local Services Director in 2001. She is editor of *Dyslexia Contact* and was responsible for publishing the resource pack, *Achieving dyslexia friendly schools.*

Nick Peacey is coordinator of SENJIT, Institute of Education, University of London, formerly Principal Manager for Equal Opportunities and Access for The Qualifications and Curriculum Authority. He is a member of the Curriculum IT support for the SEN steering group (managed by BECTA and DfEE) and is also a member of the National Advisory Group on Personal, Social and Health Education.

Maggie Pringle is a member of the Mathematics Department at George Watson's College, Edinburgh.

Sandie Reed gained extensive teaching experience in both secondary and special schools in London after graduating with degrees in sociology and psychology. She is currently a Learning Support Teacher in one of Scotland's largest primary schools, in Edinburgh. She is an executive member of the NASUWT and serves on its Education Committee.

Madeleine Reid has been a careers adviser for 20 years. Her role is in special needs but primarily she works with dyslexic pupils from mainstream and independent special schools. She also deals with students in training and post education.

Hilary Rifkind is a member of the Mathematics Department at George Watson's College, Edinburgh.

Janet Tod is a Reader in Education at Canterbury Christ Church University College. She is a chartered educational and clinical psychologist and has managed two DfEE-funded research projects, one concerning Individual Education Plans, the other Dyslexia. She is actively involved in research, publication, initial teacher training and INSET.

Elizabeth Turner is the Teacher in Charge of Flintshire's County Dyslexia Provision/Resource based at Hawarden High School. She is also the County Training Provider on Dyslexia and has co-authored *Dyslexia: A Parents' and Teachers' Guide.*

Janice Wearmouth has many years experience of working in the area of special educational needs in schools. She is currently employed as a lecturer in special and inclusive education at The Open University.

Charles Weedon is Head of the Dyslexia Centre and Learning Support at George Watson's College, Edinburgh.

Fionnuala Williams worked for a number of years at Ercall Wood Technology College supporting children with SEN across the curriculum. She currently works as a Learning Support Tutor with a special interest in dyslexia at Telford College of Arts and Technology and also teaches at the dyslexia workshops run at the college.

Ann Van Wrenn is an SpLD teacher at Red Rose Independent Day School, Lytham St Annes, Lancashire. She has 31 years teaching experience, ten of those as a Deputy Head Teacher and six as Special Educational Needs Coordinator. She is also a mother of three sons, one of whom is dyslexic.

SECTION 1: Introduction

CHAPTER 1

Dyslexia and its Manifestations in the Secondary School

Lindsay Peer

This chapter aims to:

- describe dyslexia and look at the affects across the curriculum
- discuss recommended policy changes within a framework of Inclusion
- make recommendations for levels of training for providers.

Introduction

The teaching profession is a hard working and caring one, but teachers have to work continually under constraints of time and resources...However we all know that success motivates. A student with unacknowledged learning difficulties will not be successful, so he is unlikely to be motivated to learn. The sooner his difficulties are pinpointed and addressed, the sooner he will be successful and motivated to progress. Instead of diminished self-esteem, with its associated behavioural difficulties, his self-esteem will grow with his achievements. Therefore time spent initially solving those difficulties will lead to less disruptive behaviour, fewer long-term problems for the student and a significant saving in time for the teacher.

And time is at a premium for the secondary school teacher.

(Peer 2000a)

My opinion relating to the position of teachers has not changed since writing the first edition of *Winning with Dyslexia* some years ago. Having spent many years in secondary schools as a mainstream English and Drama teacher and Head of Department before going into the area of special needs, I am fully aware of the pressures under which mainstream teachers find themselves. The stress of having yet more responsibilities and paperwork placed upon them with every new educational initiative can be frustrating to say the least. Currently we are in a phase of 'Inclusion', which means that today more demands than ever are being placed upon teachers. They find themselves in the position of having to possess expertise in a range of areas that previously were not within their remit – and for which in many cases they have no training.

Schools find themselves under the microscope of the media as well as the usual channels of inspection. It is not unusual to hear parents discussing 'failing schools'; asking whether their children are reaching the 'expected targets'; discussing 'league tables'. This is a new world – one in which parents demand to know far more about systems and outcomes than ever before. Many parents are empowered and become involved with the running of the schools.

The special needs debate is ongoing. The Human Rights Act and the Disability Commission are highly significant in a world where equal opportunities are valued. 'Inclusion' of those with special needs in any system as a principle, can only work when issues have been recognised, systems put in place and each learner is provided for according to need. Giving the same to all is not appropriate when we look at the broad range of special needs. We need to ensure that what is done differently for an individual means that each is provided with an effective way forward – allowing them to be on a level playing field with peers.

Contentious issues are being raised.

- Possibly due to funding limitations, Statements of Educational Need are being removed: this was seen as a protection for many children with special needs. In principle I would be happy to support this change of direction, provided that resources are put in place and teachers are trained so that SEN children still have their needs met. Parents are very concerned that their children might be placed in a seemingly inclusive situation but without the relevant support. As such, it might be said that *in such circumstances, inclusion by definition would mean exclusion*. Parents are not willing to accept the excuse that there is insufficient funding to support their children, unfortunately this is still happening in some places.
- There is debate as to whether or not specific children should be placed in mainstream or special schools.
- There is discussion as to whether or not groups of adolescents should be disapplied from specific studies.
- National Literacy and Numeracy Strategies are being introduced into secondary schools. This then begs the question as to who will be responsible for the success of the SEN children across the curriculum?

The issues with which any education system needs to deal are endless.

It is perfectly clear to everyone involved with the education system that there are currently massive changes in the air at every level. However the mainstream teacher working within this current of change has to override the pressures and continue the daily toil, working hard to ensure success for all members of their class every day of the week. This includes those who are dyslexic and those others who experience a range of literacy and/or numeracy difficulties.

What we have not mentioned are the young people themselves – the people for whom these changes have been designed to support. Who are dyslexic learners? How do we recognise them? What are the implications for teaching them?

What is dyslexia?

There are several descriptions of dyslexia, one of the specific learning difficulties. I find the following useful:

Dyslexia is best described as a combination of abilities and difficulties which affect the learning process in one or more of reading, spelling, writing and sometimes numeracy. Accompanying weaknesses may be identified in areas of speed of processing, short-term memory, sequencing, auditory and/or visual perception, spoken language and motor skills.

Some children have outstanding creative skills, others have strong oral skills, yet others have no outstanding talents; they all have strengths.

Dyslexia occurs despite normal intellectual ability and conventional teaching; it is independent of socio-economic or language background.

(Peer 2000b)

So what does this mean in practice? It has been estimated that approximately four per cent of any given population are severely affected by dyslexia, with a further six per cent moderately so. We are therefore referring to a population in school of about 300,000 at any one time, this raises issues of consideration of equal opportunities for educators in every institution.

Internationally there is much research and practice that is being carried out in the field of dyslexia and information on any aspect is easily found. From genetics to teaching, from self-esteem to auditory and visual processing, there is information for those who require it. We know from years of experience that dyslexic learners can go on to do extremely well in their chosen careers provided they are understood and appropriately supported. Inclusion in the right circumstances will be of great benefit to them. However very often they are not identified; this as a consequence leads to mishandling and poor outcomes. The hard-working brightest may be told that they 'should try harder'; the average might be led to believe that they are learners with moderate learning abilities. There is still too much 'misdiagnosis' in the system due to a genuine lack of knowledge of the aspects which can identify dyslexia.

The two most obvious groups of dyslexic learners are:

- those with visual and creative ability – but are less proficient orally;
- those who are orally proficient but are less competent with visual, spatial and hand skills.

There are those who have a mixture of the two, but their abilities do not shine as clearly. What is significant is that (a) they are all competent in some areas if given the opportunity to show their ability, but (b) that they all have problems with the processing of language leading to specific weaknesses in aspects of literacy and/or numeracy that will affect the learning process.

We know that some dyslexic students have weaknesses in aspects of the reading process, but all have problems when writing. If the learner exhibits a cluster of the difficulties listed below, it would be worth investigating further. As you can see from the lists, the weaknesses will affect learning across the curriculum. Do bear in mind however, that we are dealing with learners who despite their difficulties may indeed be extremely able and are as frustrated by their struggles as are their teachers! (See Handy Hints Poster for Secondary School Teachers (BDA 2001).) *General* areas that are affected include:

- processing at speed;
- misunderstanding complicated questions although knowing the answer;
- finding the holding of a list of instructions in memory difficult, although can perform all tasks;
- occasionally, name finding.

The types of problems experienced in *reading* might be:

- hesitant and laboured reading, especially out loud;
- omitting or adding extra words;
- reading at a reasonable rate, but with a low level of comprehension;
- failure to recognise familiar words;
- missing a line or reading the same line twice;

- losing the place or using a finger or marker to keep the place;
- difficulty in pinpointing the main idea in a passage;
- finding difficulty in the use of dictionaries, directories, encyclopaedias.

The types of problems in *written work* might be:

- poor standard of written work compared to oral ability;
- poor handwriting with badly formed letters;
- good handwriting but production of work extremely slow;
- badly set out work with spellings crossed out several times;
- words spelled differently in one piece of work;
- has difficulty with punctuation and grammar;
- confusion of upper and lower case letters;
- writing a great deal but 'loses the thread';
- writing very little but to the point;
- difficulty taking notes in lessons;
- organisation of work and personal timetable difficult;

The types of problems found in *mathematics* have actually very little to do with mathematics! They are to do with the same problems that appear in other subjects across the curriculum:

- difficulty remembering tables and formulae;
- finding sequencing difficult;
- confusing signs such as $+$ and $\times$;
- thinking at a high level in mathematics, but needing a calculator to remember basic facts;
- misreading questions that include words;
- confusing directions – left and right;
- finding mental arithmetic at speed very difficult.

As a result of the sheer frustration, perceived misunderstanding on the part of teaching staff and sometimes parents, and often exhaustion from the concentration expended in order to perform adequately in each class, there are sometimes behavioural problems too. It is clearly *imperative* to find ways of working efficiently with these children in order for all to benefit.

There is a further problem too; that is of dyslexic learners who have a bi- or multilingual background.

Teachers and psychologists have tended to misdiagnose or ignore dyslexia experienced by multilingual students because of the multiplicity of factors that seem to be causes for failure. Reasons cited include home background, different or impoverished language skills, inefficient memory competencies, unusual learning profile, emotional stress, imbalanced speech development, restricted vocabulary in one or all languages, leading to reading, spelling and writing weaknesses; sometimes numeracy is affected. However, educators are often aware that these students are very different from others who experience difficulty, as they are often bright and able orally or visually. The difference between their abilities and the low level of written work is very obvious. There are similar concerns regarding pupils who have specific difficulties while attempting to acquire a modern foreign language.

(Peer and Reid 2000)

There are schools that have many of these children in them and of that group a proportion will be dyslexic. Dyslexia is not limited to those who speak only one language! I was recently talking to the head of a large comprehensive that had over 70 languages spoken in her school. They had never considered dyslexia as an issue for anyone in this group. It is highly significant that there are very few of these multilingual learners nationally who have been identified. It may be because educators and psychologists have little experience with this sub-group of learners or it may be because it has never been considered. In our recent book, *Multilingualism, Literacy and Dyslexia: A Challenge for Educators* (Peer and Reid 2000), we have dealt with these very issues which so keenly manifest themselves in the secondary school sector where success in public examinations is so critical.

One of the main problems in a large secondary school is just that...the size. There is an unrealistic expectation that the SENCO and the English teacher are the ones responsible for supporting all dyslexic children and others with literacy difficulties! The truth is that even if qualified, there are simply too many students, their teachers and their parents with whom to deal and nowhere near sufficient resources to answer that demand. It is therefore absolutely vital that *all* teachers should see themselves responsible for supporting and helping develop the dyslexic children in their classes and within their subject frameworks. They need to understand the weaknesses as well as recognise the strengths to see where the problems are likely to lie in their particular part of the curriculum and how best to deal with them. They should then begin to consider ways of adapting that which they are doing, to give access to the dyslexic learner – in an inclusive way. Whether it is the geography teacher who works on sense of direction or the PE teacher who helps develop hand skills and balance. Whether it is the maths teacher reinforcing techniques to replace rote learning of facts or the history teacher finding ways to work with sequencing of time lines and so on. All the skills and strategies automatically will transfer from one class to another, allowing for greater access to the curriculum. As with a recognition of the value of Learning Styles and Study Skills, the *good news* is that we know that what is good for the dyslexic learner is good for all learners – encouraging everyone to achieve at a level higher than would normally be expected. The only note of caution is that while other learners can cope without this support, the dyslexic ones cannot.

Hyperactive or hyper-reactive: EBD or not?

Frustration leads very often to antisocial or even deviant behaviour. There is no doubt that the strain placed on a child to 'do better' when they are trying to the best of their ability is unreasonable. The problem is that often the child's problems are attributed to emotional issues, sometimes with a background of problems at home, rather than anything to do with a struggle with the education process. We need to look for the root causes of the stress; after all, even the best counselling will not help the child whose underlying difficulties have not been identified and addressed. There is much reported evidence that many children displaying significant behavioural problems related to frustration seem to improve dramatically when the situation that is inappropriate is replaced by something more suitable. On an everyday basis we see that there are children who may be extremely difficult in some classes, yet not in others. We do not consider them to be hyperactive, but we do ask ourselves what is happening. Is it the subject matter, the mode of teaching or possibly a personality clash with the teacher that is causing the trouble? They are simply 'reacting' to the situation in which they find themselves.

It is thought that approximately 25–30 per cent of dyslexic children are also hyperactive. Genuine hyperactivity may well start before the child enters school; everyone is aware of it! Sleepless nights and unacceptable behaviour are often part of the report that parents give. For this there are a variety of treatments, which are often a combination of both educational and medical interventions. However there are also children who seem to develop similar behavioural patterns to those who are genuinely hyperactive, but the symptoms only start when things begin to go wrong in school.

Interventions in these circumstances need to be totally different. I have seen that many children displaying these behaviours calm down dramatically when taken out of the system in which they find themselves. When placed in a 'dyslexia friendly' environment, with staff who are knowledgeable and understanding, the hyperactivity seems to disappear. That is because it was never there in the first place! As teachers and parents in secondary schools, we need to ask questions which search for information way back before the child reached the age of 11 years and entered our schools. We will often be amazed at the answers. Worryingly, there are a growing number of reports of children being sent away to schools for children who are suffering from emotional and behavioural difficulties (EBD). It is critical that we identify the aetiology of the problem before we misdiagnose and wrongly place them. The return to mainstreaming in these cases at a later date is extremely difficult if not impossible. We have a great responsibility to ensure that within the framework of inclusion, these children are truly included.

Motor skills weaknesses and dyslexia: a touch of bullying

There are groups of dyslexic children who also experience weaknesses in areas of fine and/or gross motor skills. Experience from working in this field for many years has highlighted the fact that if dyslexic children are going to be bullied, there is a strong tendency for it to be those who have weaknesses in the area of motor skill control. In the past we might have described these children as being 'clumsy'. These children are the ones who fall over things, are not wanted in the sports teams, who will turn right when the instruction was left and so on. There is a great need to keep an eye out for these children as they are more vulnerable than many others. The PE teacher is an ideal person to be working with young people like this, encouraging control over muscles of their bodies and some training in body language and self-esteem. All staff need to be made aware of the areas in which the child particularly needs to be made to feel confident. There are many exercises that should be done with children in the PE class that will reinforce what is happening in other classes. For example, no one can hold a pen effectively and make the fine motor movement so necessary for the writing process if they do not have control over the gross motor skills. A useful book is *Take Time* (Nash-Wortham and Hunt 1990), which is full of exercises that can be carried out at home and at school to improve control of the body.

Stress, giftedness and dyslexia

We also need to recognise that stress can have a significant impact on all dyslexic learners. As Susan Hampshire (1995) states in her Foreword to *Dyslexia and Stress* by Miles and Varma.

> One of the worst aspects of being dyslexic is the viscious circle caused by stress. As soon as I make a mistake I panic, and because I panic I make more mistakes.

Gifted dyslexic people have their share of anxiety and tensions too:

> I believe that the vast majority of gifted dyslexic children are still unidentified in schools today and those few who have been identified are in the main not receiving appropriate

provision. There is a great need to highlight the existence of this group and make provision for them at local and national level. The worst thing for them is to place them in classes with underachievers as this is bound to cause severe stress in an already difficult situation.

(Peer 2000c)

One interview that remains in my mind took place with a PhD university lecturer in mathematics...who takes his calculator to the supermarket as he cannot work out his bill in his head! His short-term memory is particularly weak, but his IQ is particularly high. His description of the way he was treated at school and the impact that has had on his life defy belief. So traumatised was he that he wishes never to have children so that they will not have to undergo the same stressful times that he did.

There is a real issue about the non-recognition of varying groups of dyslexic learner, causing much difficulty for all concerned. Thus becoming a 'dyslexia friendly teacher' will benefit all. The ability to identify, then ask for a diagnostic assessment that will give guidance and direction for appropriate support may well be the answer in many cases. A classroom geared up to the needs of children with mild–moderate dyslexia will also alleviate many of the stresses and support other children with a range of difficulties concurrently. The situation will truly become *win-win* for teachers, pupils and parents alike.

How to become 'dyslexia friendly'

In the Foreword to the Dyslexia Friendly Schools Resource Pack (BDA 1999), David Blunkett, Secretary of State for Education and Employment, stated:

> As I know from first hand experience, dyslexia is not something a child grows out of and when it goes unrecognised, it can be the source of much misery, frustration and under-achievement.

> It is equally important that we recognise that the effects of dyslexia can be alleviated by using appropriate teaching strategies and committed learning. Teachers need to know how to identify children who have special educational needs and how to provide for such children effectively once they have been identified.

Of the Dyslexia Friendly Schools Resource Pack, he goes on to say:

> I hope it is spread as widely as possible and catches the imagination of all those in a position to help dyslexic pupils.

It certainly has! The challenge for local education authorities is to provide the leadership and to focus the resources necessary to ensure the development of dyslexia friendly schools. The model of good practice that I am giving is that of Swansea LEA. Having made the decision to alter direction in an attempt to raise standards and reduce the number of Statements of Special Educational Need, they went through a process of change as outlined in the Dyslexia Friendly Schools Resource Pack. They met with parents, head teachers and psychologists. They are currently in the process of training one specialist dyslexia teacher to be placed in every school so that expertise can be spread in-house. There has been a dramatic improvement. Schools have looked for ways for their managers, heads of department, teachers and classroom assistants to become dyslexia friendly. They now have very few complaints and standards are rising.

So effective was this seen that other education authorities are in contact with Swansea and with the British Dyslexia Association looking to change their systems too.

Where schools have implemented the dyslexia friendly schools charter on a planned basis it has quickly become clear that there are wider benefits, including improvements in literacy across the curriculum, better teaching of literacy for all pupils, greater awareness of individual learning needs and the use of more varied teaching strategies.

(Warwick LEA, in Resource Pack (BDA 1999))

Being an effective school and being dyslexia friendly are two sides of the same coin. Effective schools enjoy strong leadership, value staff development and pay close attention to the quality of instruction and learning. These are schools in which all children are important regardless of ability or difficulty. Dyslexia in schools like this needs to be seen to have status within the school. This can be achieved by ensuring that the governors and senior managers are firmly committed to supporting dyslexic children across the curriculum. The most effective way would be through the School Development Plan, the document used by OFSTED to evaluate the management of any school. The next step would be to translate policies in to practice by:

- offering comprehensive training;
- formulating a common approach;
- setting targets based on National Curriculum descriptors;
- putting in place monitoring and evaluation systems.

Head teachers need to take the responsibility of ensuring that the ethos of the school is dyslexia friendly. This might relate to attitudes and actions held by teachers, support staff and even the dinner ladies. All staff need to be aware that although children might have weaknesses with specific parts of curriculum access, they are likely to be at least of average ability if not a great deal higher. Parents need to be brought into the changing set up, their concerns heard and their cooperation sought where possible.

Whole-school approaches to issues such as marking should be put in place – where children can receive a high mark for content and knowledge rather than always being marked down due to poor presentation skills, spelling, punctuation and grammar. The child should be getting help in these areas of weakness and should be motivated to keep trying by having his thoughts, ideas and knowledge valued. If we cannot do this, one might ask that we discuss the philosophical question as to what is education? As Neil Mackay, a SENCO, says in the DFS Resource Pack:

In a dyslexia friendly school, weak basic skills are not a barrier to achievement.

This pack is full of ideas on to how to put into good practice strategies that will be of value to young people across the curriculum. I would commend them to you as models of good practice. They have all been tried and tested by the authors and have been shown to provide excellent results.

We are now left with a consideration of the issues of teacher training on a national basis. I strongly believe that dyslexia should be mentioned in the course of Initial Teacher Training through work on the National Literacy and Numeracy Strategies. Dyslexia should be placed on both Mainstream and Special Education curricula. I cannot accept the excuse from some institutions that there is no time to deal with SEN or with dyslexia specifically; there are always ways of finding a small space to at least raise some awareness of the condition. For every year that a teacher is untrained in recognising and adapting to suit the learning styles of the dyslexic children in their classroom, so it is another year of those children's lives that are wasted – or worse.

Within schools there is the necessity for a range of training needs to be carried out with relevant staff. Whereas it would be ideal to have a dyslexia-trained specialist in every school, so too do we need mainstream teachers and knowledgeable learning support assistants in the classroom to help the child on a regular basis. In addition it would be highly useful for head teachers and governors to attend awareness-raising sessions on the needs of the dyslexic child and the benefits to the school of dyslexia provision. As Reid (1997) says of teacher training:

> it is important that classroom teachers receive some training in dyslexia offering both theoretical insights and practical experience.

Pumfrey (1997) acknowledges that 'establishing a resource allocation decision-making model that is "explicit, open, fair and thoroughly defensible", requires considerable professional knowledge'. Whatever the theoretical debates, what matters is that children in secondary schools are at a critical place in their lives. It is large, confusing – yet it is vital that they get on well if they to have any sort of future. We have seen in Swansea that the training model can work and that dyslexia friendly schooling can work.

When given the right support across the curriculum, dyslexic learners do well. I believe that it costs very little indeed to make a school 'dyslexia friendly' and to provide extra support for those who have a significantly greater need than would be expected. The cost to society and to teachers' nerves(!) is not worth the price of not doing it. It is in everyone's interest to make it work.

References

British Dyslexia Association (1999) 'Dyslexia Friendly Schools Resource Pack'. Reading: British Dyslexia Association.

Hampshire, S. (1995) 'Foreword', in Miles, T. R. and Varma, V. (eds) *Dyslexia and Stress*. London: Whurr Publishers.

Nash-Wortham, M. and Hunt, J. (1990) *Take Time: Movement exercises for parents, teachers and therapists of children with difficulties in speaking, reading, writing and spelling*. Stourbridge: The Robinswood Press.

Peer, L. (2000a) *Winning with Dyslexia: A Guide for Secondary Schools,* 2nd edn., 5. Reading: British Dyslexia Association.

Peer, L. (2000b) 'What is dyslexia?', in Smythe, I. (ed.) *The Dyslexia Handbook 2000*, 67. Reading: British Dyslexia Association.

Peer, L. (2000c) 'Gifted and talented children with dyslexia', in Stopper, M. J. (ed.) *Meeting the Social and Emotional Needs of Gifted and Talented Children*, 77. London: David Fulton Publishers.

Peer, L. (2001) 'Handy Hints Poster for Secondary School Teachers'. Reading: British Dyslexia Association. www.bda-dyslexia.org.uk

Peer, L. and Reid, G. (2000) 'Multilingualism, literacy and dyslexia: a challenge for educators', in Peer, L. and Reid, G. (eds) *Multilingualism, Literacy and Dyslexia: A Challenge for Educators*. London: David Fulton Publishers.

Pumfrey, P. (1997) 'Practical issues', in Reid, G. *Dyslexia: A Practitioner's Handbook,* 2nd edn. Chichester: Wiley.

Reid, G. (1997) 'Practical issues', in Reid, G. *Dyslexia: A Practitioner's Handbook,* 2nd edn. Chichester: Wiley.

CHAPTER 2

Biological, Cognitive and Educational Dimensions of Dyslexia: Current Scientific Thinking

Gavin Reid

This chapter

- provides an overview of current research in dyslexia
- relates this to educational factors.

Introduction

In recent years the area of dyslexia has undergone significant change accompanied by considerable scientific and educational research. Research has focused on a number of different dimensions including biological, cognitive and educational. This chapter will therefore describe these developments and assess the impact they may have on teachers, schools and the dyslexic student.

Definitions

When undertaking staff development in secondary schools the question one is most often asked is simply 'What is dyslexia?'. While there are a number of definitions that are used, many of these are not entirely helpful to the class teacher. The class teacher is essentially asking for a working plan – not necessarily a definition. That is, the cluster of difficulties, range of severity, examples of the difficulty, teaching suggestions and sources of further help in relation to dyslexia.

One of the difficulties regarding definitions is that dyslexic children are first and foremost individuals and while they may share some common difficulties there are individual differences. The British Dyslexia Association suggests a broad description which clearly displays the range of difficulties which can be experienced by dyslexic people. This is described in the previous chapter and to reiterate the following definition is useful because it is both comprehensive and broad in scope. The definition indicated in the previous chapter describes dyslexia as 'a combination of abilities and difficulties which affect the learning process in one or more of reading, spelling and writing. Accompanying weaknesses may be identified in areas of speed of processing, short-term memory, sequencing, auditory and/or visual perception, spoken language and motor skills. It is particularly related to mastering and using written language, which may include alphabetic, numeric and musical notation.'

It is also useful to consider the definition used by the Adult Dyslexia Organisation which suggests that

Dyslexia may be caused by a combination of phonological, visual and auditory processing deficits. Word retrieval and speed of processing difficulties may also be present. A number of possible underlying biological causes of these cognitive deficits have been identified and it is probable that in any one individual there may be several causes. Whilst the dyslexic individual may experience difficulties in the acquisition of reading, writing and spelling they can be taught strategies and alternative learning methods to overcome most of these and other difficulties. Every dyslexic person is different and should be treated as an individual. Many show talents actively sought by employers and the same factors that cause literacy difficulties may also be responsible for highlighting positive attributes – such as problem solving which can tap resources which lead to more originality and creativity'.

(Schloss 1999).

These definitions essentially support the view that dyslexia relates to a broad range of difficulties associated with literacy and learning, that individual differences will be present and that some students with dyslexia can have positive attributes and that any difficulties are only part of the overall picture.

A recent working party report on Dyslexia, Literacy and Psychological Assessment (BPS 1999) opted for a working definition of dyslexia because they felt that a working definition did not require any causal explanation. The working definition they opted for was as follows:

Dyslexia is evident when accurate and fluent word reading and/or spelling develops very incompletely or with great difficulty. This focuses on literacy learning at the 'word level' and implies that the problem is severe and persistent despite appropriate learning opportunities. It provides the basis for a staged process of assessment through teaching.

(BPS 1999: 18)

While this provides the teacher with a starting point it does requires further explanation. In fact the report goes on to suggest a number of hypotheses which can be associated with dyslexia which include: Phonological Deficit Hypothesis; Temporal Processing Hypothesis; Skill Automatisation Hypothesis; Working Memory Hypothesis; Visual Processing Hypothesis; Syndrome Hypothesis; Intelligence and Cognitive Profiles Hypothesis; Subtype Hypothesis; Learning Opportunities Hypothesis and Emotional Factors Hypothesis. These hypotheses each refer to different or overlapping theoretical approaches expounded by academic researchers to explain dyslexia from a causal perspective. The authors of the report suggest that the phonological deficit hypothesis provides the main focus because of the 'broad empirical support that it commands' (p. 44) and because of the impact of phonology on the other hypotheses, particularly temporal order hypothesis, skill automatisation and the syndrome hypothesis. This view is supported by Snowling (2000) who suggests that although dyslexia can manifest itself in many ways there may be a single cause – a phonological deficit. She asserts this is the 'proximal cause of dyslexia' (p. 138).

It is important therefore that teachers obtain a practical working plan. Yet due to the nature of dyslexia and its associated difficulties and the range of research studies and views it is also advisable that teachers obtain some theoretical background to allow them to understand the nature of the difficulties and how these may influence actual classroom approaches.

Biological dimensions

Genetic factors

There have been considerable efforts to identify the genetic basis for dyslexia. Gilger, Pennington and DeFries (1991) estimate that the risk of a son being dyslexic if he has a dyslexic father is about 40 per cent. Much of this work has been focused on the heritability of reading sub-skills and particularly the phonological component. Castles *et al.* (1999) found a strong heritability element among 'phonological dyslexics' and Olson *et al.* (1994) found also a strong heritability component both for phonological decoding and orthographic skills.

Gene markers for dyslexia have been found in chromosome 15 (Smith *et al.* 1983) and more recently in chromosome 6 (Fisher *et al.* 1999). Stein and Monaco (1998) suggest they may have found a possible site of dyslexic genes in chromosome 6 and significantly they may be in the same region as the genes implicated in autoimmune diseases that have been reported to show a high level of association with dyslexia (Snowling 2000). In a longitudinal study Gallagher, Frith and Snowling (2000) found at age six more than half of the at risk group scored below average compared to a control group on literacy tasks. Clearly therefore genetic factors are associated with dyslexia and this of course can lead to early identification or at least some very early warning signs of a child being at risk of being dyslexic.

The dyslexic brain

New technology such as positron emission tomography (PET) and magnetic resonance imaging (MRI) are increasingly being used to observe the active processes within the brain as well as the structure. As a result studies have shown that in phonological and short-term memory tasks the dyslexic sample displayed less activation across the left hemishere than the control group. Brunswick *et al.* (1999) reported that the PET scans of young dyslexic adults while reading aloud and performing word and non-word recognition tasks showed less activation than controls in the left posterior temporal cortex. These findings suggest that there may be processing differences indicating some deficits in left hemisphere processing among children and adults with dyslexia.

Hemispheric symmetry

According to earlier influential research (Geschwind and Galaburda 1985) these differences are due to structural differences between the hemispheres and this probably develops in the prenatal period. This view has received considerable support and a study by Leppanen *et al.* (1999) reported that at birth children at genetic risk of dyslexia show different patterns of brain activity compared to a control group.

This can have implications for teaching and learning to read. Bakker (1990, 1998) proposes a 'balance model' of reading which has been replicated in different countries (Robertson 1997). Bakker identifies different types of readers – 'perceptual' and 'linguistic' each with a different hemispheric preference and each having implications for teaching. The perceptual has a right hemisphere processing style and may have good comprehension but poor reading accuracy. On the other hand the 'linguistic' reader utilises the left hemisphere and reads accurately but in some cases may be over-reliant on the left hemisphere and may not show the comprehension level of the 'perceptual' reader.

Wood (2000) suggests that reading is concerned with translating stimuli across all modalities and that fluency is the key factor in reading acquisition. He cites the role of the visual cortex in reading which he asserts is multi-modal as it will accept input from both auditory and visual modalities. The brain he argues is high in visual-spatial skills and this also aids the understanding of information with high phonetic complexity. Since reading is essentially mapping across modalities according to Wood, then alternative languages such as music and visual graphics are helpful. In short Wood suggests that our brains are better equipped for reading and more adaptable than we have given them credit for.

Visual factors

There is also evidence of visual factors relating to dyslexia. Eden *et al.* (1996) show how dyslexic children can have abnormalities associated with the magno-cellular sub-system of the visual cortex. Stein (1994) has highlighted convergence difficulties and binocular instability and Wilkins (1995) has shown how some dyslexic children and adults may benefit from coloured overlays due to difficulties in some visual processes.

Cognitive and processing dimensions

While the teacher may be limited in dealing with the deficits discussed above in relation to biological factors associated with dyslexia much can be done to improve the processing skills of dyslexic students and particularly their phonological skills.

Phonological processing

Hagtvet (1997), in a Norwegian study, showed that a phonological deficit at age six was the strongest predictor of reading difficulties. Other studies have shown speech rate to be a strong predictor of dyslexic difficulties and this is reflected in the development of the Phonological Abilities Test (Muter *et al.* 1997).

Wolf (1996) highlights the 'double deficit' hypothesis indicating that dyslexic individuals can have difficulties with both phonological processing and naming speed. It is interesting that speed of processing and semantic fluency are included in some of the popular tests for dyslexic children. Badian (1997) in a further study shows evidence for a triple deficit hypothesis implying that orthographic factors involving visual skills should also be considered.

Metacognition

The role of metacognition in learning is of great importance as this relates to the learner's awareness of thinking and learning. Tunmer and Chapman (1996) have shown how dyslexic children have poor metacognitive awareness and this leads them to adopt inappropriate learning behaviours in reading and spelling.

Automaticity

Similarly difficulties in automaticity (Fawcett and Nicolson 1992) implies that dyslexic children may not readily consolidate new learning and therefore find it difficult to change inappropriate learning habits. Fawcett and Nicolson (1994) in fact propose the twin hypothesis that dyslexic children incur both Dyslexic Automatisation Deficit and Conscious Compensation Hypothesis. This means not only do they have difficulty in acquiring automaticity but in many cases they are able to mask this deficit by working harder. Deficits, however, will still be noted in situations where compensation is not possible.

Motor factors

Motor integration programmes have also been developed from research programmes (Dobie 1998).

Nicolson and Fawcett (1999) have shown how cerebellar impairment may be implicated with dyslexia viewed from a broader framework and may be involved in acquiring language dexterity as well as movement and balance. Factors such as postural stability, bead threading and naming speed are therefore represented in the Dyslexia Screening Test (Fawcett and Nicolson 1996). There have been many studies reporting on fine motor and gross motor difficulties experienced by dyslexic children (Augur 1985, Denckla 1985, Rudel 1985, Flory 2000, McCormick 2000). Some of these relate to dyspraxia but it is likely that some of the approaches advocated for dyspraxic children can benefit dyslexic children who may have some motor difficulties. Similarly with dysgraphia, Stracher (2000) suggests that writing problems manifest themselves in three stages which include motor factors relating to legibility, spelling difficulties and organising writing and syntactic structures. This pattern can also be seen in some dyslexic children.

Educational factors

Phonological awareness and multisensory programmes

In educational settings there has been considerable activity in the study of phonological awareness in relation to dyslexia. This is reflected in the development of assessment and teaching materials such as the Phonological Abilities Test (Muter *et al.* 1997), the Phonological Assessment Battery (Fredrickson *et al.* 1997) and many phonological teaching approaches such as Sound Linkage (Hatcher 1994), the Phonological Awareness Training Programme (Wilson 1993) and the Multisensory Teaching System for Reading (Johnson *et al.* 1999). This particular area of research is highlighted because of its direct impact on teaching and classroom practices. The authors (Johnson *et al.* 1999) conducted a research study into the use of the programme and found, as well as the above, it also encourages independent learning and improves self- esteem.

Wise *et al.* (1999) conducted a large-scale study using different forms of 'remediation' and found that the actual type of phonological awareness training was less important than the need to embed that training within a well structured and balanced approach to reading. Adams (1990) argues that combining phonological and 'whole language' approaches to reading should not be seen as incompatible. Indeed it is now well accepted that poor readers rely on context more than good readers (Nation and Snowling 1998). Language experience is therefore as vital to the dyslexic child as is a structured phonological awareness programme. This is particularly important in the secondary education sector where it may be inappropriate to provide a phonological-based programme for a dyslexic student. Here the priority may be on language experience, print exposure and comprehension activities.

It is also important to note the current interest and research in the area of multilingualism and dyslexia (Peer and Reid 2000, Cline and Shamsi 2000) which indicates the need to obtain accurate measures of screening, identification and curriculum materials to ensure that the needs of multilingual dyslexic children are met within mainstream provision (see also Chapter 4 'Inclusion – The Issues').

Right hemisphere processing

West (1997) has utilised Galaburda's research to show that dyslexic people who are right hemisphere processors can actually be at an advantage in some situations. This emphasises the positive side of dyslexia. Additionally West suggests that the transmission of knowledge and understanding is increasingly becoming visual and that those with well developed visual skills can be at an advantage in acquiring the visual language of knowledge.

Policy

It is encouraging that research is impacting on practice. Education authorities' policies on dyslexia, staff development, classroom-based assessment, computer programs and curriculum materials focusing on differentiation all facilitate access to the full curriculum for dyslexic children. Early identification and early intervention are seen as priority areas and recent research and materials help to support this (Reid 1998).

Concluding comment

Research in dyslexia can be viewed from different perspectives. It is important to recognise particularly the cognitive aspects of dyslexia because with timely and adequate intervention these can be dealt with effectively. Therefore the process of learning is of considerable importance. Despite the biological factors described in this chapter much can be done to advance the literacy and learning skills of dyslexic students through awareness of training programmes, identifying the range of difficulties and acknowledging the strengths often shown by dyslexic students. Awareness of learning styles (Given and Reid 1999) and of metacognitive strategies which can enhance the learning process throughout the full curriculum is of great importance. Together these factors provide a sound basis for staff development and assessment, teaching and classroom practices which can enhance the opportunities for success for all dyslexic children in the secondary school. In summary, it is essential that despite the advances in scientific thinking and research we do not lose sight of the individuals, their needs and their strengths. Brooks (2000: 19) summed this up very succinctly when he suggested 'Adolescents may begin to perceive the world as a place where their strengths rather than their weaknesses are spotlighted. If this shift in perception occurs, then when they are expected to assume the tasks of adulthood, they will do so with increased comfort, confidence and success.'

References

Adams, M. J. (1990) *Beginning to Read: Thinking and Learning about Print*. Cambridge, Mass.: MIT Press.

Augur, J. (1985) 'Guidelines for teachers, parents and learners', in Snowling, M. (ed.) *Children's Written Language Difficulties*, 147–71. Windsor: NFER Nelson.

Badian, N. A. (1997) 'Dyslexia and the double deficit hypothesis', *Annals of Dyslexia* 47.

Bakker, D. J. (1990) *Neuropsychological Treatment of Dyslexia*. New York: Oxford University Press.

Bakker, D. J. (1998) 'Balance model'. Paper read at the 13th All Polish Conference, Polish Dyslexia Association, University of Gdansk, Poland.

British Psychological Society (BPS) (1999) *Dyslexia, Literacy and Psychological Assessment. DECP Working Party Report*. Leicester: BPS.

Brooks, R. B. (2000) 'The learning disabled adolescent: a portrait', in *The International Dyslexia Association, Houston Branch Resource Directory*, 16–19. Texas: International Dyslexia Association.

Brunswick, N. *et al.* (1999) 'Explicit and implicit processing of words and pseudowords by adult developmental dyslexics: a search for Wernicke's Wortschatz?', *Brain* 122, 1901–17.

Castles, A. *et al.* (1999) 'Varieties of developemental reading disorder: genetic and environmental influences', *Journal of Experimental Child Psychology* 72(73).

Cline, T. and Shamsi, T. (2000) *Language Needs or Special Needs? The Assessment of Learning Difficulties in Literacy Among Children Learning English as an Additional Language: A Literature Review*. London: DfEE.

Denckla, M. B. (1985) 'Motor coordination in dyslexic children: theoretical and clinical implications', in Duffy, F. H. and Geschwind, N. (eds) *Dyslexia: A Neuroscientific Approach to Clinical Evaluation*. Boston, Mass.: Little, Brown.

Dobie, S. (1998) Personal correspondence.

Eden, G. F. *et al.* (1996) 'Abnormal processing of visual motion in dyslexia revealed by functional brain imaging', *Nature* 382, 67–9.

Fawcett, A. J. and Nicolson, R. I. (1992) 'Automatisation deficits in balance for dyslexic children', *Perceptual and Motor Skills* 75, 507–29.

Fawcett, A. J. and Nicolson, R. I. (eds) (1994) *Dyslexia in Children: Multidisciplinary Perspectives*. Hemel Hempstead: Harvester Wheatsheaf.

Fawcett, A. J. and Nicolson, R. I. (1996) *The Dyslexia Screening Test*. London: The Psychological Corporation.

Fawcett, A. J., Nicolson, R. I., and Dean, P. (1996) 'Impaired performance of children with dyslexia on a range of cerebellar tasks', *Annals of Dyslexia* XLVI 259–83.

Fisher, S. E. *et al.* (1999) 'A quantitative-trait locus on chromosome 6p influences different aspects of developemental dyslexia', *American Journal of Human Genetics* 64, 146–56.

Fredrickson, N., Frith, V. and Reason, R. (1997) *Phonological Assessment Battery*. Windsor: NFER-Nelson.

Flory, S. (2000) 'Identifying, assessing and helping dyspraxic children', *Dyslexia* 6 202–14.

Gallagher, A., Frith, U. and Snowling, M. J. (2000) 'Precursors of literacy-delay among children at genetic risk of dyslexia', *Journal of Child Psychology and Psychiatry* 41, 203–13.

Geschwind, N., and Galaburda, A. M. (1985) 'Cerebral lateralization. Biological mechanisms, associations and pathology. IA hypothesis and a program for research', *Archives of Neurology* 42, 428–59.

Gilger, J. W., Pennington, B. F. and DeFries, J. C. (1991) 'Risk for reading disability as a function of parental history in three families studies', *Reading and Writing* 3, 205–18.

Given, B. K. and Reid, G. (1999) *Learning Styles – A Guide for Teachers and Parents*. St Annes on Sea: Red Rose Publications.

Hagtvet, B. E. (1997) 'Phonological and linguistic-cognitive precursors of reading abilities', *Dyslexia* 3(3).

Hatcher, P. (1994) *Sound Linkage*. London: Whurr Publishers.

Johnson, M., Philips, S. and Peer, L. (1999) *Multisensory Teaching System for Reading*. Special Educational Needs Centre, Didsbury School of Education, Manchester Metropolitan University.

Leppanen, P. H. *et al.* (1999) 'Cortical responses of infants with and without a genetic risk for dyslexia. II: Group effects', *Neuroreport* 10, 969–73.

McCormick, M. (2000) 'Dyslexia and developmental verbal dyspraxia', *Dyslexia* 6, 202–14.

Muter, V., Hulme, C. and Snowling, M. (1997) *Phonological Abilities Test*. London: Psychological Corporation.

Nation, K. and Snowling, M. J. (1998) 'Individual differences in contextual facilitation: evidence from dyslexia and poor reading comprehension', *Child Development* 69, 996–1011.

Nicolson, R. I. and Fawcett, A. J. (1999) 'Developmental dyslexia: the role of the cerebellum', *Dyslexia* 5 155–77.

Olson, R. K., *et al.* (1994) 'Measurement of word recognition, orthographic, and phonological skills', in Lyon, G. R. (ed.) *Frames of Reference for the assessment of Learning Disabilities: New Views on Measurement Issues,* 243–77. Baltimore, Md: Paul H. Brookes Publishing.

Peer, L. (1999) 'What is Dyslexia?', in *The Dyslexia Handbook 1999*, 61. Reading: British Dyslexia Association.

Peer, L. and Reid, G. (eds) (2000) *Multilingualism, Literacy and Dyslexia: A Challenge for Educators*. London: David Fulton Publishers.

Reid, G. (1998) *Dyslexia: A Practitioner's Handbook*. Chichester: Wiley.

Reid, G. and Kirk, J. (2000) *Dyslexia in Adults: Education and Employment*. Chichester: Wiley.

Robertson, J. (1997) 'Neuropsychological intervention in Dyslexia', Paper read at the 25th Anniversary Conference, British Dyslexia Association.

Rudel, R. G. (1985) 'The definition of dyslexia: language and motor deficits', in Duffy, F. H. and Geschwind, N. (eds) *Dyslexia: A Neuroscientific Approach to Clinical Evaluation*, 33–53. Boston, Mass.: Little, Brown.

Schloss, D. (1999) Personal communication.

Smith, S. D. *et al.* (1983) 'Specific reading disability. Identification of an inherited form through linkage analysis', *Science* 219, 1345–7.

Smythe, I. (1997) 'World Dyslexia Network Foundation', in *The International Book of Dyslexia*. London: World Dyslexia Network Foundation.

Snowling, M. J. (2000) *Dyslexia,* 2nd edn. Oxford: Blackwell.

Stein, J. F. (1994) 'A visual defect in dyslexia? in Nicolson, R. I. and Fawcett, A. J. (eds) *Dyslexia in Children – Multidisciplinary Perspectives*. Hemel Hempstead: Harvester Wheatsheaf.

Stein, J. F. and Glickstein, M. (1992) 'Role of the cerebellum in visual guidance of movement', *Physiological Review* 72, 972–1017.

Stein, J. and Monaco, T. (1998) *Times Educational Supplement* 27 February.

Stracher, D. A. (2000) 'Dysgraphia', in *The International Dyslexia Association, Houston Branch Resource Directory,* 20–21. Texas: International Dyslexia Association.

Tunmer, W. E. and Chapman, J. (1996) 'A developmental model of dyslexia – can the construct be saved?', *Dyslexia* 2(3), 179–89.

Weedon, C. and Reid, G. (2001) *The Listening and Literacy Index*. London: Hodder and Stoughton.

West, T. G. (1997) *In the Mind's Eye*. Buffalo, New York: Prometheus Books.

Wilkins, A. J. (1995) *Visual Stress*. Oxford: Oxford University Press.

Wilson, J. (1993) *Phonological Awareness Training Programme*. University College London, Educational Psychology Publishing.

Wise, B. W., Ring, J. and Olson, R., (1999) 'Training phonological awareness with and without explicit attention to articulation', *Journal of Experimental Child Psychology*, 72, 271–304.

Wolf, M. (1996) 'The double deficit hypothesis for the developmental dyslexics' Paper read at the 47th Annual Conference of the Orton Dyslexia Conference, Boston, Md.

Wood, F. B. (2000) 'Surprises ahead: the new decade of dyslexia, neurogenetics and education. Keynote lecture, 51st Annual Conference International Dyslexia Association, Washington DC, 8–11 November.

SECTION 2: Inclusion: Issues, Principles and Practices

CHAPTER 3

Inclusion and the Revised National Curriculum

Nick Peacey

This chapter:

- examines the revised National Curriculum and its commitment to inclusion
- discusses the notion of the citizenship curriculum
- analyses the dimensions of the Inclusion Statement
- describes elements of a successful school environment.

The values, aims and principles of the National Curriculum

The introduction to the revised National Curriculum, which came into force in September 2000, is unequivocal. There are values underpinning the School Curriculum which are about how education influences and reflects the values of society. Education is seen as a route to equality of opportunity for all and a healthy and just democratic state. In particular the enduring values that contribute to these ends are those of valuing ourselves, our families and other relationships, the wider groups to which we belong and, particularly, the diversity in our society and the environment in which we live.

When you look further, you find two interdependent aims for the curriculum. The first one – the school curriculum should aim to provide opportunities for all peoples to learn and to achieve – perhaps could be seen as unexceptional but important. The second makes clear that the school curriculum is also explicitly seen – in law – as promoting pupils' spiritual, moral, social and cultural development.

There follows a key passage: these two aims reinforce one another. 'The personal development of pupils, spiritually, morally, socially and culturally, plays a significant part in their ability to learn and to achieve.' In other words, if we want pupils to attain satisfactorily we have to look very hard at the spiritual, moral, social and cultural environment in which they grow up. Schools, authorities and governments which take a naive view of how people learn and how they achieve – a view which, somehow, manages to separate these two aims – are not going to see the success for all learners that they seek.

The curriculum's strong commitment to inclusion becomes even clearer when we look at the PSHE and citizenship frameworks. The PSHE framework will not be statutory for the foreseeable future. It is explicit about the need to develop pupils' confidence and responsibility, to move them towards a healthy and safe lifestyle and to foster the development of good relationships and respect for differences between people.

The Citizenship curriculum, which will become statutory in Key Stage 3 and 4 from September 2002, has several strands. Of them all, for those committed to inclusion, the most important is the third: the insistence that pupils should develop skills and understanding for participation in responsible action. This is where PSHE, Citizenship and the whole business of inclusion in schools are woven together. As we know, youngsters with dyslexia are not passive learners, any more than are other pupils. They take responsibility for their own learning as they grow up and go through school. They are planning; they are looking ahead. They are looking out particularly for those skills which will enable them to make sense of their lives. If what they find when they look ahead is that there are barriers to their learning, they are not always going to be able to assume that those barriers will be lifted by others. They need that ability to participate and take responsible action on their own behalf. Equally, of course, respect for others means that they will be, through their perception of their own difficulties and what they have overcome, well-placed to take responsibility for others and to support them when they are discriminated against and find themselves in a corner not of their making.

There is an issue here which should be addressed by all pressure groups, whether created around concerns about dyslexia or anything else. It has become clear, as work on inclusion has proceeded, that those institutions which are most successful, both academically and socially, are those where the entire school community looks after itself and looks after others. That is why the interrelationship between Citizenship and PSHE in relation to inclusion is so important. We can see this if we look at the National Healthy Schools Standard (they have a web site you can pursue: www.wiredforhealth.gov.uk). The National Healthy Schools Standard stresses things like healthy eating, diet and so on, as you would expect, but it also stresses the issue of emotional well-being for pupils – all pupils, including those with disabilities or impairments of one sort or another. It also stresses the health and well-being of staff. I have been working on teacher health over the last year or so. It was clear from conferences supported by the DoH and the DfEE that there were many misunderstandings amongst educators about stress. Sometimes the assumption seems to be that, because stress can follow pressure, pressure is something to avoid. A truer model is rather different to that. We all, in our working lives, have to put pressure on others. Whether we are teachers, parents or managers, it is an appropriate part of our role to put pressure on for the right things to happen. The issue is not whether or not we should be putting pressure on – but the appropriateness of the support that comes with it. We all need to take notice of this, because if we do not make sure the appropriate support for forward movement is available when we apply the pressure we are creating stress. If we supply that appropriate support in terms of materials, ideas, cultures which enable people to build and grow, then of course we will all achieve success. So it is vital that the health and well-being of staff in schools is looked after as carefully as that of the pupils. Indeed, it is no accident that concern for the well-being of both groups goes hand in hand with high attainment in schools.

The general Inclusion Statement

The aspect of the National Curriculum which has attracted most attention in relation to inclusion is, of course, what has become known as the general Inclusion Statement. This has been widely welcomed by campaigners for disability rights all around the country. It is not surprising – it is probably one of the most powerful statements for inclusion that has been issued by any government anywhere.

I see it as having two dimensions. The first amounts to a statutory demand on teachers to have regard to the basic principles of inclusion in their planning and teaching. The second suggests substantial flexibility to allow teachers to do the job effectively. In other words, it offers pressure – 'you must look at these things' – but at the same time it offers substantial support in terms of the ability of teachers to vary programmes and plans.

Setting suitable learning challenges

The first principle of the Inclusion Statement concerns 'Setting suitable learning challenges'. The first sentence, 'Teachers should aim to give every pupil the opportunity to experience success in learning and to achieve as high a standard as possible', applies as much to those who are seen as having difficulties in learning as to those who are seen as among the most gifted in the country. A related point (which is rammed home later in the Statement) is that an analysis by strength as well as areas of concern is absolutely critical if young people and children in schools are to feel assured of success. The discussion of the principle also introduces the idea that teachers can choose from earlier or later Key Stages in a curriculum to allow the progress of individual pupil to be maximised. Teachers are also encouraged to consider the possibilities of moving, horizontally as it were, across the curriculum in their search for appropriate material to allow pupils to go as far and as fast as they can. Very often the curriculum is seen only in terms of vertical movement–vertical progression. This is not only a problem for those seen as having learning difficulties. It is also a problem for all pupils, including those with the greatest gifts and talents. If pupils are encouraged to progress too far and too fast up the curriculum, they will often miss out on the richness of thought and ideas that come from a thorough study of the many and varied aspects of a subject.

Responding to pupils' diverse learning needs

The second principle of the curriculum introduces an unequivocal commitment to proper teaching for the whole range of diversity of our school populations. Nobody can be left out of this campaign for inclusive learning.

The discussion following the principle points out that teachers must know about the range of equal opportunities legislation now covering race, gender and disability. Indeed, this is particularly appropriate at the time of writing (November 2000): the SEN and Disabilities in Education Bill is coming through; the Race Relations Amendment Act is now on the statute book and, of course, the Human Rights Act has come into force. Professional development will support teachers in being fully aware of, and proactive in relation to, their responsibilities to those they care for. (For example, the Inclusion Statement draws attention to the need to consider differences in the achievement of boys and girls. To be proactive on this area, school teams must understand how to run their results through a sieve which includes comparison of gender, race and other dimensions: only through this process will really useful patterns emerge.)

This section of the Inclusion Statement contains one of its most important elements. 'Teachers should take specific action to respond to pupils' diverse needs by creating effective learning environments.' This brings us to the heart of many of the discussions on special educational needs and inclusion taking place at the moment. The evidence from research is absolutely clear, as indeed I think is the evidence from the work on the National Literacy and

Numeracy Strategies. A collective improvement model, rather than an individualistic, needs-led model of disability and difficulty has to be in place if we are going to make real progress in moving all pupils forward. Often models which are too much based on individual needs neglect the possibilities of removing barriers to learning and work from the needs of a very few – thereby distorting resource allocation and failing to support high expectations, and high quality learning. The emphasis needs first to be on quality teaching and learning environments for all. For example, where researchers such as Morag Stuart of the Institute of Education in London or Jonathan Solity of the University of Warwick have brought in ways of teaching classes which are based, in their view, on the very highest research standards, perceptions of the numbers of pupils seen as having literacy difficulties seem to drop dramatically. So we have a very sound reason for looking at the total context – the whole-school environment and the quality of teaching as the absolute basis of any work on dyslexia or any other perceived difficulty. An example can be drawn from the field in which Lindsay Peer has done some recent work: the question of what one does about intermittent hearing loss, such as that caused by glue ear, which affects a substantial number of youngsters, particularly in infant classrooms and particularly during winter months.

It is necessary of course to provide for those youngsters the individual care that will ensure that an intermittent problem does not develop into something more serious. However, it is equally important to realise that if we make provision in the classroom, either by using improved acoustic design in the architecture or by using something like a sound field system (which is essentially a high quality but relatively inexpensive quad speaker system), the experience of all pupils in the class would be improved and the students with glue ear will have the best possible chance of learning. (All this becomes doubly relevant where classrooms are situated in places such as alongside busy main roads or under flight paths.)

The other element of the creation of effective learning environments that should not be ignored is the need to challenge stereotype. One of the critical things is to challenge those stereotypes about cleverness and stupidity that can easily grow up where the discussion of learning, how one learns to learn and how one thinks about learning are not a part of the classroom and school environment. Where such discussions do not take place, it is immensely easy for those pupils who find it harder to make progress (through dyslexia or anything else) to feel lost and out of touch – and, indeed, to downgrade their own ability. Of course, where that happens it is sad from the individual's point of view. It is also a collective failing – a failure of the school to ensure that all its students understand that it is a form of discrimination when they find themselves in camps where one group is called clever and the other group is called stupid, even if those divisions exist under the surface and are not part of the overtly acknowledged school culture.

The second section of the Inclusion Statement also deals with 'securing of motivation and concentration'. One of the key elements here has to be the valuing of appropriate balance between writing and talk in the classroom. Writing in all forms is a very vital and important medium for learning. But if the school experience of pupils is over-balanced in favour of writing (sometimes perhaps as a means of control), you will not only find pupils who are less happy and confident about writing quickly becoming bored and failing to respond but will also find that important aspects of the curriculum are simply not being covered. A full reading of the National Curriculum makes clear that the role of language and questioning, discussion, argument and so on is at its centre. Such neglect allows pupils to miss a very important part of the learning that is statutorily their right, as well as failing to permit those whose strengths are in those areas to enjoy success.

The Statement also draws attention to the need to use appropriate assessment approaches. It underlines the importance not only of ensuring that appropriate special arrangements are in place for those with dyslexia as well as everybody else, but also of ensuring that whole-school systems are geared towards coping with this need. This means, for example, that when a youngster comes into secondary school, the question of what special assessment arrangements they may need in the Key Stage 3 National Curriculum tests should be on the agenda from Year 7. For this reason, the QCA has been working with the Teacher Training Agency to devise the specification for a short module of training to ensure that all those reporting on pupils' needs for special arrangements start from a common base across the country.

Finally, this section of the Statement includes useful advice on setting targets for learning. 'Teachers set targets for learning that build on pupils' knowledge, experience, interests and strengths to improve areas of weakness and to demonstrate progression over time, are attainable yet challenging and help pupils to develop their self-esteem and confidence in their ability to learn.'

Potential barriers to learning and assessment

The final section of the Inclusion Statement directs teachers to consideration of the potential barriers to learning and assessment. It addresses the needs of 'A minority of pupils who have particular learning and assessment requirements which go beyond the provisions described in sections A) and B) (the first two sections) which, if not addressed, could create barriers to learning.' In other words, the school is to consider barriers to learning, rather than over-emphasising an individual needs-led approach. Probably this section covers the area which is most familiar to those concerned with dyslexia. It points out that action necessary to respond to individual requirements will very often be met through greater differentiation of tasks and materials, and notes that a smaller number of pupils may need access to specialist equipment and approaches and external specialists.

Significantly, it also considers the need for teachers to take specific action to provide access to learning by helping individuals to manage their emotions, particularly trauma and stress, and to take part in learning. Those who face barriers to their learning often go through very substantial stress and those who have been through trauma will very often find their minds are entirely elsewhere rather than on learning tasks. (Of the increasing number of packs to help with emotional development in schools, it is well worth looking at that produced by Bristol City LEA, *The Emotional Literacy Hour*, about the work that they have been doing across their schools.)

The Statement makes a distinction between pupils with special educational needs and those with disabilities and draws attention, very clearly, to the fact that not all pupils with disabilities will have special educational needs. 'Many pupils with disabilities learn alongside their peers with little need for additional resources beyond the aid they use as part of their daily life, such as a wheelchair, hearing aid or other equipment.'

Part of this section describes the importance of planning appropriate amounts of time to allow pupils to complete tasks satisfactorily. Parents of children with dyslexia will not need telling how vital this is in terms of classroom tasks and those relating to homework and self-organised study. Perhaps, as time goes on, we shall find schools using their web sites to post homework on or, alternatively, using an e-mail to deliver and support self study tasks. Whether or not those are good ideas, what is clear is that issue of pace, ensuring that everybody has both the time to complete a task and yet is challenged to do it at a reasonable speed, is a priority for professional development in any inclusive school. Finally, the Inclusion Statement has a section on pupils learning English as an additional language. It makes careful points on monitoring a pupil's progress in the acquisition of English language skills and draws attention to the need to think about factors, such as the pupil's age, length of time in the country, previous educational experience and, of course, particularly skills in another language. But, equally and wisely, it emphasises the need for review if things do not seem to be proceeding along the normal process of English language acquisition, to examine the possibility that the young person or child has a special educational need.

Inclusion: individual subject advice

The general Inclusion Statement has become well known. It is, perhaps, less well known that all subjects of the curriculum also include a short section on the implications of the Inclusion Statement for that particular area. These little sections are only included in individual subject booklets of the curriculum. It is important that teachers and parents and everyone else recognise their existence and take a look at them.

Threads for development

As we reach the end of the Inclusion Statement, we can perhaps draw some conclusions if we are to implement the agenda to which it aspires?

First, we must adopt an evidence-based approach to moving matters forward. We need to know the best way to do things so that we do not waste our energies and pupils' time. For example, one of the best statements that I have read on matching tasks to pupils' needs comes from work done for the Scottish Education Department by Mary Simpson and Jenny Ure of Northern College, Aberdeen, which was published in 1993. They found that teachers who effectively manage the match

- share the management of learning with pupils;
- promote the belief that things can improve by demonstrating that agreed learning strategies work;
- use a wide range of sources of information;
- give and receive continuous feedback in terms of how pupils are getting on.

Such teachers do not let pupils flounder or believe that things are going better or worse than they are.

Second, we need to be aware of the importance of using an approach based on high expectations. All our knowledge suggests that high expectations and imitation can carry all learners, including all children seen as having special needs, much further than has often been believed, particularly when those high expectations are backed with appropriate support. It is not the case that different SEN always require different teaching approaches. What is necessary is that the school employs, or the teacher employs, the best possible teaching approaches based on what has been seen and known to work. Part of this, and there is an implication here for those working in special provision, means that schools should be alert to the professional development needs of those teaching subjects where they are not specialists. At a time of teacher shortage, this is critical. It is all too easy to forget, when considering the needs of youngsters with special needs, that good subject teaching is the rock on which everything else has to be based.

I have written above about the importance of good *talk*, high quality questioning and listening. High quality listening may be a skill which is harder to adopt than others in the classroom. But if we cannot listen, we will not hear the concerns of children and young people clearly: we will not hear that a situation, that might be turned to advantage for all teachers and all pupils, is affecting an individual. That is sad: not asking a pupil can be the slowest way of finding out about their individual needs. Part of listening is of course looking out for non-verbal clues: here there has been some interesting American research into what makes a good class teacher (the work has led to the development of a screening system for entrants to the profession). It seems that, perhaps not surprisingly, where teachers are acute at perceiving the non-verbal signals given out by pupils, their teaching is highly effective. The good news is that these skills can be taught.

Overwhelmingly though, as one looks back across the whole Inclusion Statement one is struck by the need for a vision of inclusion which is actually about teamwork. We need teamwork within school communities, teamwork within local authorities, and other systems of management and, indeed, teamwork supported by government ministers. We know a lot about good teamwork. We know about the importance of whole-system commitment; we know about the need for clear aims; we know about the need to audit progress towards those aims. Indeed, many of the devices now with us in relation to special needs, such as the Inclusion Index, are tools to help school teams develop self-audit and to look at the progress they are making. We know that in teamwork, the quality of the environment, the way that everybody feels about the place in which they work, has real importance. This is where the advice now being prepared by the Architects and Buildings Branch of the DfEE in relation to the creation of a whole-school environment for inclusion is important.

The other vital element of a successful school environment, however, is the school culture. That culture needs to foster trust. Trust is important to any team because you need the ability to admit mistakes. If mistakes are not admitted they cannot be learned from. I think we have some way to go in education before we have built systems which will actually allow people to learn from their mistakes. If we cannot acknowledge that in this challenging process of promoting inclusion we are sometimes going to get it wrong, we are not going to move forward as fast as we should do.

This takes us to the underpinning of the whole exercise: the need for us to pass information around so the appropriate support for the process is in place. If we can give appropriate support in terms of information about individual needs and preferences, emotional support and best practice and if pupils, parents, teachers and support staff see that information as the right support for the right challenge, then the mental health and well-being of all pupils will be at a high level and they will feel able to commit themselves to persevere with learning which they may not find easy.

After I had been discussing these matters with a group of teachers and other professionals, an LEA inspector made an interesting comment. He said that, whenever he visited a school which was achieving successfully, he found a school culture dedicated to the development of the community for everyone working in it. This encouraged its educational and academic success. This, of course, brings us back to where we started: it embodies those two inclusive aims for the curriculum, the interdependence of the need to learn and to achieve within a culture which develops pupils' social, moral and cultural learning at the same time.

CHAPTER 4

Inclusion – The Issues

Fernando Almeida Diniz and Sandie Reed

This chapter:

- questions the extent to which discourses in 'dyslexia' connect with other areas of 'social exclusion' that are affecting schools
- proposes a set of key principles for the development of ethical and inclusive professional practice
- offers some suggestions for institutional policy and practice in schools.

Introduction

Competing sites of struggle?

It is commonplace for teachers to be asked where they stand on the issue of 'Inclusive Education', for head teachers to seek to assure parents, schools inspectors and the local community that the institutions they lead are 'inclusive schools' and for textbooks to address this topic. So why is it happening? On coming to power, the Labour government heralded its 'social inclusion' strategy for securing 'equality for all', expressing its commitment to tackle the barriers experienced by socially excluded communities. The prime minister's chant of *'Education, Education, Education'* was seen to mark the central role that education is intended to play in making Britain an inclusive and socially just society. What is of interest here is that while the current political climate is one in which the language of 'social inclusion' dominates every area of national public policy, school managers are facing demands from the same government for school improvement, higher academic standards – measured by league tables of examination results – target setting, parental choice and greater accountability. These conflicting political pressures represent the first dilemma for head teachers, that of walking the tightrope between being in the 'top league of achieving schools' and being an 'inclusive school for all' (Gillborn and Youdell 1999; Clarke *et al.* 1999).

Another source of pressure for school managers is how to command the confidence of the wider community by guaranteeing 'equitable treatment for all', while not succumbing to the demands of powerful lobbies. In an age of consumerism, central government is no longer the sole player in determining educational policy, for schools are increasingly being challenged by a succession of competing voices who claim the right to determine the way schools are run and how children are educated. Disparate advocacy groups, campaigning on behalf of disabled children (including dyslexia), racial and ethnic minorities, religious communities, linguistic minorities and those who seek selective schools for academically able pupils, all see themselves as equally deserving of a say in decision making and the allocation of resources. Neither can they be ignored given their willingness to resort to the law to achieve their 'entitlements', in the light of high media interest and of Human Rights and other anti-discrimination legislation now in force in the United Kingdom.

Policy makers seeking guidance from educational researchers are likely to be frustrated by the conceptual confusion that characterises much of the academic discourse on 'Inclusive Education'. Mainstream teachers might be forgiven for concluding that the current vogue for 'inclusion' is nothing more than an updated version of earlier debates about the 'integration' of pupils from segregated special education, for a disproportionate amount of literature is dominated by issues concerning educational provision for children with disabilities/SEN and is authored by leading academics from this field. Teachers may have a point, for there is little evidence to assure schools that the serious social inequalities experienced by other vulnerable children, as a consequence of global ethnic conflict and xenophobia, mass migration, poverty, drugs, the restructuring of labour and child abuse policy, are reflected in the above discussions on 'Inclusion'. What we have in effect are a series of fragmented discourses conducted in separate 'fora' by competing groups whose professional identities and loyalties are seen as distinct (Richardson and Wood 1999). Take, for example, the thorny question about the educational attainment of minority ethnic pupils, where notions of 'underachievement', 'school exclusion', 'bilingualism/EAL', 'learning difficulties' and now 'institutional racism' are regarded as integral to competing discourses on antiracist education and/or multiculturalism and/or multilingualism, with tentative links to special education (Diniz 1999). The same might be said about academic discourses conducted in separate journals on dyslexia, disability, gender or sexuality. The problem is one of each group wishing to claim 'its space' in the broad struggles for social justice.

It should be apparent to the reader that we regard the notion of 'Inclusion' in education and society as inherently contentious in nature and problematic to resolve. Any secondary school wishing to attain the accolade of *an inclusive school* cannot underestimate the degree of conflict that it will encounter in its endeavours, given the wide range of political expectations, competing voices and conceptual ambiguities alluded to above. It is a dilemma that we, as 'non-specialists', have experienced in writing this chapter. We start by questioning the extent to which debates in dyslexia connect with other significant problematic areas of 'social exclusion' that are affecting schools, mindful of the danger of creating a hierarchy of 'deserving cases'. Next we propose a set of key principles as a basis for the development of ethical professional practice and offer some suggestions for institutional policy and practice in schools.

Dilemmas in 'dyslexia and social exclusion'

There are a number of significant problems of social exclusion that have challenged schools for over two decades, many of which are gaining attention in recent education policy and research. All of these raise common issues of equity, social justice and inclusion. They include: the education of disabled children; school exclusions; low attainment of boys; the impact of institutional racism on black pupils, including travellers and refugees; children's rights and protection against bullying and abuse. We refer to some of these issues and question the extent to which the field of dyslexia has connected with them.

'Equality' in the academic world of dyslexia?

The seminal work by Cline and Reason (1993) was the first published article that debated questions about 'equal opportunities and dyslexia' and offered a framework for change. It is worthy of comment that no prominent work of this type has emerged in subsequent years. Moreover, once published, it failed to stimulate any meaningful discussion in the journal in which it was published or other specialist periodicals. Given the broad shift of public sector education policy in the intervening years towards models of inclusion, it is both curious and alarming to note the paucity of sociological analyses of the fundamental concerns raised by the authors. Diniz (1999) has made the same criticism of the field of special education as a whole for neglecting long-standing questions of discriminatory practices that are endemic in its own practices. Peer and Reid's (2000) edited collection is a valuable contribution in addressing the comment by Cline and Reason (1993) that it was 'extraordinary that the research traditions on SpLD and on social and cultural differences have remained in separate compartments' (p. 32). We hope that institutional and structural barriers to social justice will gain further visibility in dyslexia research, for while research in the social and natural sciences purports to be objective, it is the very prioritisation or omission of a topic for research or of the parameters along which its investigation is conducted that implies the value system under whose rubric that research is accomplished. Gray and Denicolo (1998) argue that 'all researchers need to be aware of the potentially political nature of their position' (p. 140). Some areas for research are highlighted below.

Are some more unequal than others?

Factors such as race, gender, class and poverty mediate most strongly in determining access to welfare and education provision that exists; yet a number of these constructs are either underrepresented in terms of dyslexia provision or else eerily invisible in the research literature.

Cline and Reason (1993) analysed the basic parameters of 27 research reports appearing over a 15-year period and found that 'ethnicity' was considered briefly in only three of the works; we suggest that this 'invisibility' still exists in special education research in Britain. Thus, as some racial groups experience high levels of economic discrimination and are overrepresented in some SEN categories, they are as resolutely invisible as participants in the dyslexia discourses as they are in the pages of special educational research journals (Diniz 1999, Deponio et al. 2000, Reed 2000). There are two main explanations for why this is happening: the first relates to the reality that British education provision has failed to take account of the bicultural and multilingual backgrounds of minority ethnic children; the second is that 'institutional racism' permeates research, policy and practices that determines the nature of statutory and voluntary service provision and the barriers that minority ethnic families experience in gaining access to these (Diniz 1997, Macpherson 1999). The first of these issues has gained greater attention, particularly in relation to the assessment of bilingual learners (Usmani 1999), although there is relatively little if any contemporary work on the relationship between dialect and dyslexia. The second issue has barely been acknowledged; serious attention is yet to be given to the much more difficult question of 'institutional racism' in educational research and practice (CERES 2000).

Referring to the controversy about gender effects on low attainment, Biggart (2000) suggests that this issue is far more complex than portrayed in the media. Whereas social background and area characteristics were the strongest predictors of low attainment in both sexes, some schools fared better than others with the same intakes of pupils. He found limited evidence for the view that low-attaining young people, particularly males, had very negative attitudes to education, or that disaffection was a principal cause of low attainment;

furthermore, low attaining females, while fewer in number, represented a group particularly at risk and in need of specific types of education and training provision. Boys have traditionally been disproportionately overrepresented in special education provision, including schools for emotionally disturbed children (Daniels *et al.* 1999); the converse of this is that girls are underrepresented. We think that the research reported by Kirk and Reid (2000), of 50 young males in a Scottish institution for young offenders, raises serious questions concerning possible relationships between social processes of dyslexia and deviant behaviour. It is far from clear whether dyslexia is the determining factor, for apart from the possible interface between gender-ethnicity-class-dyslexia-delinquency, the study did not consider the effects of institutional discriminatory practices in the criminal justice system (Macpherson 1999).

Medical explanations of dyslexia have a powerful pull for some parents but do not tell the whole story. For example, if dysfunction of the central nervous system processing is considered as the cause, it must be emphasised that poverty is associated with a significantly higher degree of risk during pregnancy, birth, childhood malnutrition and increased jeopardy to neurological development. A recent Scandinavian study, investigating four generations of a Norwegian family, has isolated a genetic component of a particular manifestation of dyslexia but the researchers nevertheless stress the importance of environmental factors in its complex aetiology (Fagerheim *et al.* 1999). The sub-text is that context is paramount in dealing with dyslexia at any level, be it for research purposes or in everyday school life. Schools in economically depressed areas may feel themselves unable to prioritise dyslexia because of the gruelling daily round of fire-fighting social and emotional exigencies. Wallace (2000) describes one such school in an English seaside town, in a catchment area that included a small, stable population of local poor, traumatised refugees/asylum seekers, DSS multi-occupation housing and refuges: 'Children are brought to school sick because the parents believe they are better off there than at home. They vomit over staff, have diarrhoea, arrive in the knickers they wet the night before...' (p. 14). The head teacher cannot be blamed for her honest statement that 'something simple like dyslexia never gets to the top of the list' (p. 14). This is Britain at the start of the twenty-first century.

Assessment, identification and 'Who gets a slice of the cake?'

The public face of the dyslexia debate in the press and on the Internet emphasises access to current resources for those who have been identified as dyslexic, igniting the passions and energies of those parents with the social capital to seek a 'medical diagnosis' through psychological assessment as a means of securing additional resources (Riddell *et al.* 1994). Dyslexia is possibly the only area of SEN in which there is a private sector of assessment services for parents. It is not belittling the valid concerns of these parents by broadening the debate to ask who does or does not get to be considered eligible for recognition as 'dyslexic' in the first place. Bookbinder (1988) questioned the then extant discrepancy theory that typified dyslexia as an IQ-attainment mismatch and warned of 'a kind of apartheid divide between dyslexic people and the mass of poor readers'. Though recent thinking by educational psychologists (BPS 1999) has attempted to move the emphasis away from focusing on causal explanations, deficit-theory remains a powerful force in the age of genetic science. Such reservations should not obscure the reality that children within the mainstream system who have been recognised as dyslexic are often at a disadvantage in terms of access to appropriate teaching, particularly so in the light of the pedagogic strictures of the literacy hour imposed on English and Welsh schools (Smith 2000). The inequities faced by some recognised dyslexic pupils in mainstream education are but the tip of a great iceberg of social injustice affecting a wider range of vulnerable children.

Assessment resources are drained by a high transience factor exacerbated by the problem of the transfer of records across LEA boundaries and the cumbersome procedures for assessment of SEN. Children who cross the border between England and Scotland are particularly vulnerable to process delays because of different legal systems and, on occasion, professional rivalries.

Promoting institutional change in school policy and practice

The discussion this far suggests that theoretical explanations of 'social exclusion' based on single category discrimination (e.g. SEN/dyslexia) are unlikely to fundamentally impact on institutional barriers to social justice in schools. What is desired is a shift away from past practices that see 'difference' in terms of categories, needs, deficits and theories of assimilation, normalisation and mainstreaming towards an explicit commitment to 'social justice for all', based on principles of 'equity and human rights'. This should not be read as a call for a return to the generic mantra of 'equal opportunities' policies of the past decades. We need to construct new models for ethical institutional practice that acknowledge the commonality of the human experience while tackling the unique social inequalities experienced by particular groups in society. Such a stance may provoke cynicism about an 'utopian world', far from the realities of schools and teachers (Croll and Moses 2000). In order to minimise this, we suggest how a school might proceed to frame its policy and review some of its strategies in its journey to becoming socially inclusive by setting principles and developing support models.

Establishing principles of 'inclusive practice'

An essential starting point is to determine a set of principles that the school and its community are committed to. We regard the four principles, listed below, as fundamental to ethical and inclusive institutional practice. Recent support materials that might be useful to look at are available in Scotland and England (SOEID 1999, CSIE 2000).

- 'Inclusion' is a human rights issue founded on the principle of social equity and justice, as enshrined in international legal conventions. It represents a positive valuing of the immense difference and diversity that characterises human experience in terms of gender, disability, class, race and other distinguishing factors.
- The main roots of 'social exclusion' are to be found in interpersonal and systemic discrimination, frequently exerted via unexamined habitual institutionalised practices as well as the conscious misuse of power, rather than in individual deficits, dysfunctional lifestyles and prejudice. Reforms based on single category discrimination (e.g., dyslexia) are unlikely to be effective on their own.
- 'Discrimination' of various types is socially constructed, context-specific and multifaceted. 'There must be an unequivocal acceptance of the problem of institutional racism and its nature before it can be addressed, as it needs to be, in full partnership with members of minority ethnic communities' (Macpherson 1999, 6.48). The same would apply to discrimination on other grounds.
- The development and delivery of inclusive education requires insightful leadership, strategic policies, collaborative institutional cultures and equitable resource allocation, based on principles of social equity and human rights.

Developing an inclusive model for 'support for learning'

All secondary schools would claim to have some form of support system. The questions that are relevant to ask are:

- What are the underlying assumptions that underpin the support system?
- Who gets support and who does not?
- What are the operational strategies in providing support?

Central to our discussion is the distinction that we argue must be drawn between three organisational support systems based on notions of 'segregation', 'integration' and 'inclusion'. As we have indicated earlier, much of the discourse on 'including' children with special educational needs in mainstream schools is erroneously predicated on 'integration' assumptions. We believe that discrimination and social exclusion are institutionally and systemically created and necessitate a holistic transformation of education support systems if 'inclusion' is to be achieved. Such thinking is rare in dyslexia practice but there may be signs of change (BPS 1999). An inclusive framework that we recommend was developed by McGregor (1998), in an action research Project 'Addressing Specific Learning Difficulties', undertaken by CELT in partnership with Scottish Education Authorities and St Andrew's College in Glasgow. Three models of 'Support for Learning' were evaluated in schools:

- *(Model 1) 'Segregationist':* a traditional system of offering individual support to children with particular learning difficulties; parents of dyslexic pupils tend to value this most.
- *(Model 2) 'Integrationist':* the most common current system of offering support to individuals and groups of pupils who have various special educational needs, in England (SENCO) and Scotland (EPSEN/Learning Support). The focus may be on providing support for children in class, but the assumptions are that the 'problem' lies wholly in the child and not in the overall curriculum or organisation.
- *(Model 3) 'Inclusive':* a system of providing support for the individuals, classes and teachers in a holistic way, as part of a systems approach to more effective learning and teaching for all, i.e., in partnership with pupils, staff and parents.

In justifying her choice of Model 3 (see Table 4.1), McGregor makes two key points:

If the model described as inclusive or transformational were to be widely adopted along the lines developed in this Project, it is hypothesised that this would lead to a transformation in children's attainments, as well as in ways which support for learning is developed . . .

A number of significant changes would need to take place in schools, in the provision of staff development, and in the Authorities' and national policies for a fully inclusive model to be implemented throughout the system.   (1998: p. 14)

Changing practice in schools

What might an inclusive and more socially just reality mean to policy makers, parents of dyslexic children and 'chalk face' practitioners?

Note that, within our conception of an 'inclusive approach', the multisensory approach appropriate for dyslexic pupils with its emphasis on the systematic, the structured and the cumulative is a general approach beneficial to all learners. Changing the very geography of many a classroom to optimise its dyslexic-friendliness, the positioning of its desks, work trays

Table 4.1 Alternative models of support for learning for children with specific learning difficulties (dyslexia) (spldd)

Features of provisions	Segregationist (traditional)	Integrationist (transitional)	Inclusive (transformational)
Support teaching (location)	Centre/Units either Education Authority or private/voluntary/body.	Limited classroom based/extraction.	Mainly/exclusively classroom based.
Support teaching (organisation)	One-to-one or small group with similar difficulties.	One-to-one or small group with similar difficulties.	Mainly in group/class with/without similar difficulties.
Roles for support for learning staff (sfls)	Direct teaching outwith class by sfls. May develop metacognitive strategies for individuals and small groups.	Provision of 'package' of advice/materials by sfls to class teacher and/or parents for individual children. May develop metacognitive strategies for individuals and small groups.	• Partnership working with class teacher to support children with spldd, and all children in 5–14 curriculum. • Use of peer tutoring and cooperative learning strategies. Emphasis on metacognitive strategies in all children.
Assessment procedures	Undertaken by sfls. Parents may be involved. School/teachers very limited involvement. Often referral by psychologist in Education Authority provision. Children may be rejected on grounds of limited intellectual ability.	Mainly undertaken by sfls. School/teachers may refer to sfls, who offer advice. Some referrals on to psychological services using EPSEN (staged process). Parents involved at some stage.	Undertaken jointly by class teacher and sfls. Parents involved/class teacher and schools centrally involved. Children partners in own learning. All children work together to set and achieve targets. Staged process used for persistent difficulties including referral to Psychological Service.
Features of diagnosis	Usually child aged 8+. Typically gap of two years+ between chronological age, reading age and intelligent quotient (in Education Authority Provision).	Usually child 8+. Typically, gap of two years+ between chronological age, reading age and intelligence quotient. Wider range of children supported, with literacy and other difficulties.	Emphasis on early identification of difficulties, at or before five years. Support for children with any literacy difficult/prerequisites of literacy. Assumption that all children in mainstream education can and should be literate (unless *major* cognitive/physical difficulties).
Curricular emphasis	Focus on child's basic language difficulties. Little or no opportunity to relate the work to general 5–14 class language work.	Focus on child's basic language difficulties. May be different programme from the rest of the class.	Childrens specific difficulties and programmes to address these integrated with overall class work. Emphasis on multisensory methods for all children.

(reproduced from McGregor 1998 with permission)

and resources, would have positive knock-on effects for pupils and staff. The clear layout of worksheets to minimise perceptual and directional difficulties would be advantageous to all and simplify classroom management. This is the practical end of inclusive classroom teaching.

In a real world of scarce resources, demystifying the 'specialness' of dyslexia provision would have a positive knock-on effect in freeing assets so that more children could gain access to appropriate teaching and the current lack of training for students and qualified teachers could be addressed. Furthermore, the professional time which would be saved in not having to 'reinvent the wheel' at school level would be cost-effective and morale-boosting in freeing that most precious resource, teachers, for their intended purpose.

Meeting the needs of those who have a transient and more vulnerable life situation would require considerable institutional restructuring and administrative flexibility on the part of the Government and the health and social services so as to provide appropriate, localised resource bases. Whoever thinks about including teachers? 'Teachers cannot offer their pupils the experience of ownership until they have experienced it themselves.

Conclusion

The principal message that we convey is that dyslexia cannot be viewed in isolation and apart from much wider social justice issues. Working together can bring benefits to all. We wish to see a more holistic approach in which connections are made between the field of SEN and other equally pressing areas of social exclusion. When this happens, we can claim to have the beginnings of a coordinated national strategy for 'Inclusion' in education.

References

Biggart, A. (2000) *Gender and Low Attainment*. www.hmis.scotoff.gov.uk/riu

Bookbinder, G. (1988) 'One person's dyslexic is another's poor reader – Reading, the dangers of creating a new form of apartheid in school', *Guardian Education*, 22 November.

British Psychological Society (1999) *Dyslexia, Literacy and Psychological Assessment*. DECP Working Party Report. Leicester: BPS.

CERES (2000) 'A year on from the Lawrence Inquiry Report: lessons for Scottish Education'. *Conference Report*. Edinburgh: Centre for Education for Racial Equality in Scotland.

Clarke, C. *et al.* (1999) 'Theories of inclusion, theories of schools: deconstructing and reconstructing the inclusive school', *British Educational Research Journal* 25(2), 157–78.

Cline, T. and Reason, R. (1993) 'Specific learning difficulties (Dyslexia): equal opportunities issues', *British Journal of Special Education* 20(1).

Croll, P. and Moses, D. (2000) 'Ideologies and Utopias: education professionals' views of inclusion', *European Journal of Special Needs Education* 15(1), 1–12.

CSIE (2000) *Index for Inclusion*. Bristol: Centre for Studies on Inclusive Education.

Daniels, H. *et al.* (1999) 'Issues of equity in special needs education from a gender perspective', *British Journal of Special Education*, 26(4), 189–95.

Deponio, P. *et al.* (2000) 'An audit of the processes involved in identifying and assessing bilingual learners suspected of being dyslexic', *Dyslexia: International Journal of Research and Practice* 6(1).

Diniz, F. A. (1997) 'Working with families in a multiethnic European context', in Carpenter, B, (ed.) *Families in Context*. London: David Fulton Publishers.

Diniz, F. A. (1999) 'Race and special educational needs in the 1990s', *British Journal of Special Education* 26(4), 213–17.

Fagerheim, T, *et al.* (1999) 'A new gene (DY X3) for dyslexia is located on chromosome 2', *Journal of Medical Genetics* 36(9), 664–69.

Gillborn, D. and Youdell, D. (1999) *Rationing Education: policy, practice, reform and equity*. Buckingham: Open University Press.

Gray, D. E. and Denicolo, P. (1998) 'Research in special educational needs: objectivity or ideology?', *British Journal of Special Education* 25(3), 140–44.

Kirk, J. and Reid, G. (2000) 'An examination of the relationship between dyslexia and offending in young people and the implications for the training system', Scottish Dyslexia Trust, *News and Views*, 7, Spring.

Macpherson of Cluny (1999) *The Stephen Lawrence Inquiry*. London: Home Office.

McGregor, J. (1998) *Addressing Specific Learning Difficulties (Dyslexia)*. Glasgow: Centre for Effective Learning and Teaching.

Peer, L. and Reid, G. (eds) (2000) *Multilingualism, Literacy and Dyslexia: A Challenge For Educators*. London: David Fulton Publishers.

Reed, T. (2000) 'The literacy acquisition of Black and Asian "English-as-an-Additional Language" Learners', Peer, L. and Reid, G. (eds) *Multilingualism, Literacy and Dyslexia: A Challenge for Educators*. London: David Fulton Publishers.

Richardson, R. and Wood, A. (1999) *Inclusive Schools, Inclusive Society – race and identity on the agenda*. Stoke on Trent: Trentham Books.

Riddell, S. *et al.* (1994) 'Conflicts of policies and models: the case of specific learning difficulties', in Riddell, S. and Brown, S. (eds) *Special Educational Needs Policy in the 1990s*. London: Routledge and Kegan Paul.

Smith, K. (2000) 'Dyslexics "lose in literacy hour"', *Times Educational Supplement*, 13 October, 14.

SOEID (1999) *The Manual of Good Practice in Special Educational Needs*. Edinburgh: Scottish Office Education and Industry Deptartment.

Usmani, K. (1999) 'The influence of racism and cultural bias in the assessment of bilingual children', *Educational and Child Psychology* 16(3), 44–54.

Wallace, W. (2000) 'Just passing through', *Times Educational Supplement*, 13 October, 14.

CHAPTER 5

Inclusion: The Challenges

Mike Johnson

This chapter:

- presents the argument that inclusion is a human rights issue
- analyses the socio-political context for that argument
- suggests that discussion should now focus on reducing and preventing exclusion rather than discussing reasons for and against inclusion.

Introduction

When a group of otherwise rational, professional, hardworking and basically caring people act, in one particular way, in defiance or disregard not only of informed opinion but also documented evidence it presents a pretty formidable challenge.

This is certainly the case with inclusion in general and dyslexia in particular. In part this is because our schools have become somewhat isolated from, while still being crucially affected by, the communities they serve. The challenge can be seen at many levels. Here we discuss the personal, the organisational and the political. Certain common threads run throughout all three levels, but each also have a measure of distinctiveness.

'Inclusion' – 'exclusion'

We will try to avoid the inherent danger of seeming either over-critical or depressed about the current situation. Until recently the debate was between integration and inclusion. That of inclusion versus exclusion has now joined it. The dramatic rise in the number of pupils excluded or expelled from schools suggests there is some agreement with the Rev. Tuckerman from Boston in the 1920s:

> An authority should exist to dispose of lads who are known to be profane, intemperate, dishonest and, as far as they may be at their age, abandoned to crime.
>
> (Hawes 1991: 80)

Again, in search of advancement up the 'League Tables', in spite of all the evidence to the contrary (e.g., Harley and Malcolm 1999) 'setting by ability' is propounded as the way forward, certainly for secondary schools. Again, this has firm historical roots:

Now that we are able to discover in the early years of the elementary school through the use of tests which is pure silk and which sow's ear we as educators shall so apply the educational process so that the silk shall be made into a silk purse and the sow's ear into a pigskin purse.

(Tildsley 1921)

Davies (2000) has detailed in vivid, journalistic clarity the effects of the 'marketing' of education. In particular he points to the stubbornness with which both minister and officials have defended their contention that because poverty is not the only factor determining success in school, the school shall bear the full weight of responsibility for pupils' achievement. He has the evocative analogy of 'a man furiously pumping up the tyres on his car to make it drive more smoothly when actually it has run out of petrol' (p. 20). Hardly surprising then that Tony Booth, who has been one of inclusion's main protagonists for many years, writes:

> I regard inclusion/exclusion, essentially, as a political process. Possibilities for, and barriers to, inclusion are shaped by all aspects of education and social policy. Inclusion/exclusion is only part of an endeavour to reduce exclusion within society more generally... In relating inclusion and exclusion to issues of equality I would prefer to give them more active meanings (inclusion) as the 'reduction of inequality' and (exclusion) as the 'increase of inequality'.
> (Booth 2000: 79)

He also sees the current political situation as inimical to inclusive education. The casting of school education in an increasingly instrumental stance ignores completely the social consequences both inside and outside schools.

> Thus we have a policy of 'naming and shaming' failing schools and teachers, identified during school inspections, that rivals the excesses of the Chinese Cultural Revolution.
> (p. 79)

Booth claims that arguments about inclusion need to be divorced from their traditional context of 'special educational needs' or 'disabilities' and we will return to this. However, even within those confines there are some powerful challenges to be met.

The Salamanca Declaration proclaims that:

- Every child has a fundamental right to education, and must be given the opportunity to achieve and maintain an acceptable level of learning.
- Every child has unique characteristics, interests, abilities and learning needs.
- Education systems should be designed and educational programmes implemented to take into account the wide diversity of these characteristics and needs.
- Those with special educational needs must have access to regular schools which should accommodate them within a child-centred pedagogy capable of meeting these needs.
- Regular schools with this inclusive orientation are the most effective means of combating discriminatory attitudes, creating welcoming communities, building an inclusive society and achieving education for all. Moreover, they provide an effective education to the majority of children and improve the efficiency and ultimately the cost-effectiveness of the entire education system.

(van Steenlandt 1998)

Article 2 of the EU Convention on Human Rights states:

> No person shall be denied the right to education. In the exercise of any function which it assumes in relation to education and to teaching, the State shall respect the right of parents

to ensure such education and teaching in conformity with their own religious and philosophical convictions.

Article 14 reinforces this:

The enjoyment of the rights and freedoms set forth in this convention shall be secured without discrimination on any ground such as sex, race, colour, language, religion, political or other opinion, national or social origin, association with a national minority, property, birth or other status.

These principles might appear to form a major plank of current Government intentions.

The ultimate purpose of SEN provision is to enable young people to flourish in adult life. There are therefore strong educational, as well as social and moral, grounds for educating children with SEN with their peers. We aim to increase the level and quality of inclusion within mainstream schools...

(DfEE 1997: 43)

However, the paragraph does not stop there. It goes on:

While protecting and enhancing specialist provision for those who need it, we will redefine the role of special schools to bring out their contribution in working with mainstream schools to support greater inclusion.

One is tempted to remember the comment made about Brighton Pier – it was an impressive piece of architecture but a lousy way to get to France!

Similarly a year later:

For most children [with SEN] placement in a mainstream school leads naturally on to other forms of inclusion. For those with more complex needs, the starting point should always be the question, 'Could this child benefit from education in a mainstream setting?' For some children a mainstream placement may not be right, or not right just yet.

(DfEEa 1998: 23)

The essential point here is that mainstream education is seen to be a 'given', in the mathematical sense. The question relates to whether pupils with SEN will fit into it, not how the system needs to alter. The same 'reversed thinking' can be seen in relation to speaking of 'extra resources' for pupils with SEN, not what is their fair share of all existing resources.

This line of argument resolves itself into a need to refocus the debate on exclusion not inclusion.

Booth and Ainscow (1998) present the 'Dimensions of Difference' between the two perspectives:

Definitions
1. Are inclusion and exclusion seen as unending processes or as states of being inside or outside the mainstream, or of being either 'fully' or not included?
2. Are some exclusions taken for granted and only some examined and contested?
3. Are inclusion and exclusion seen as separate processes, affecting different groups of students, or are they seen as necessarily linked?
4. Are inclusion and exclusion applied to a limited group of categorised students or are they applied to all students whose participation in mainstream cultures, curricula and communities might be enhanced?

Responses to diversity

5. Are some students seen as 'other', as 'them' rather than 'us'?
6. Are difficulties in learning or disabilities attributed to defects or impairments in students or seen as arising in relationships between students and their social and physical environments?
7. Is the response to difficulties experienced by students seen only as individual and technical or as also a matter of values and philosophies, policies, structures and curricula, affecting all students?
8. Is diversity celebrated as a resource to be valued or seen as a problem to be overcome?
9. Is participation within a local mainstream school seen as a right or as dependent on professional judgement?
10. Is there an emphasis on a common curriculum for all or on special curricular for some?

Recognising differences of perspective

11. Are inclusion and exclusion in school connected to wider social and political processes?
12. Are the concepts used to discuss inclusion and exclusion seen as universal or as embedded within a social and cultural context that makes translation complex and hazardous?
13. Are approaches to inclusion and exclusion seen as common within a country amounting to a national perspective or as reflecting particular perspectives, voices and interests?
14. Are differences in perspective on inclusion and exclusion among and between staff and students explored or ignored?
15. Are the differing voices within groups of researchers revealed or obscured?
16. Are forms of presentation and research methods seen as part of the approach to inclusion and exclusion or as distinct from it?   (p. 15)

One important force operating to maintain the emphasis on SEN and inclusion is that of the discourse used by those involved.

> Policy is the product, whether written (laws, reports, regulations) stated or enacted (e.g. pedagogical practice), of the outcomes of political states of play in various arenas. In these arenas there are struggles between contenders of competing objectives, either about objectives or how to achieve them: in these struggles discourse is deployed as tactic and theory.
>
> (Fulcher 1989: 11–12)

She goes on to say that discourses articulate the world in particular ways. They not only 'identify' problems but also perspectives on those problems and therefore solutions. She postulates five main discourses on disability: medical, lay, charity, rights and corporate. The medical discourse is the most pervasive and links impairment with disability. It assumes that objects correspond with the term usually used to describe them. This can be seen in common parlance in the use of the definite article: the dyslexic child. It implies that disability is an objective attribute rather than a social construct. This discourse depoliticises and individualises disability. The approach to it is technical and therefore professional. This is where challenge arises. A professional such as an educational psychologist or speech therapist has a training that involves the development of a body of knowledge and the skills to apply that knowledge. Some of that knowledge and skills will be based on research, some not.

School level

Regarding the school level, Tom Ravenette, writing in 1999 about dyslexia, presented four propositions:

1. It is a reality that some people believe dyslexia to be an entity and that a diagnosis of dyslexia entitles a child to special educational provision.
2. To those people who believe in dyslexia, dyslexia is a reality.
3. The construction of reality is personal, subjective and not easily transferable to another. The communication of reality is even more personal and subjective.
4. The assumption that realities, and their associated prescriptions for action, are unilaterally transferable is a major source of interpersonal and inter-professional hostility.   (Ravenette 1999: 83–4)

Seen in this way the inclusion of pupils with dyslexia becomes an argument about the nature of reality, the locus of control, the use of power. The pupil with dyslexia and his or her parents have a clear view of the contexts within which success and failure may occur. The school can readily view many of the features of dyslexia as something else entirely. Vivid examples are in the pack, *Teaching Today: Staff Development* – 'Dyslexia in the Primary Classroom' (BBC 1997). Recognising that disorganisation, forgetfulness, 'clumsiness' may be a part of the dyslexia can be difficult for both teachers and pupils, even frustrating. Particularly as, equally, at any particular time they may not be. A teenager with dyslexia is still a teenager.

Moving away from preconceptions is a real challenge. In a recent study of the effects of epilepsy (Johnson and Thomas 1999) we observed that pupils with 'absence seizures', where the child loses consciousness for only a split second, were practically impossible for teachers to cope with. However much they were told about the condition, shown the diagnosis, consulted with parents, there was still a tendency to complain that the pupil was daydreaming and should concentrate more.

Ravenette is clear that an educational psychologist 'Needs to be equally skilled in dealing with the teacher's problems that a referral reflects' (p. 177). He recognises four categories of teacher referral that tell us much about the school level challenge to inclusion:

The first category reflects a failure in understanding a child and this failure represents a threat to the teacher's sense of knowingness about children.

> *'I can't understand J. I need someone to come and look at him.'*

The second category reflects the teacher's inability to make a difference to what the child does; the child continues not to learn and continues with behaviour that is disturbing for the teacher. It is a challenge to the teacher's sense of competence.

> *'I've tried everything and it's no good.'*

The third category relates to those whom the teacher says have special educational needs.

> *'It's not my job to teach him. I wasn't trained to do this.'*

The fourth category is from a teacher who feels she can cope but is concerned about others.

> *'I don't know what will happen when she/he gets to secondary.'*

In each of the four categories there is a sense that the referral is actually, for that teacher, the solution. Underlying them all is an assumption that there is an alternative pedagogy only available to some teachers, but vital for this child. Brahm Norwich addresses this issue in his recent writings referred to below.

We said earlier that DfEE and NLS publications suggested that while there was, broadly, a common curriculum and pedagogy that would benefit all pupils with 'minor difficulties in learning', that would be 'generally overcome through normal teaching strategies', these guidelines also recognise 'another, smaller group [whose] difficulties need to be addressed through different teaching strategies' (DfEE 1998b). However, in a major survey of the evaluative literature today, Lewis and Norwich (1999) conclude that an analysis of their evidence:

> Rejects distinctive SEN teaching strategies and accepts that there are common pedagogic principles which are relevant to the unique differences between all pupils, including those designated as having SEN. (p. 3)

And in the section discussing dyslexia:

> Specialist approaches have much in common with teaching literacy to any pupil, though there is a tendency to bottom-up approaches (e.g. Synthetic Phonics). Other differences include the degree of structure, detail, continuous assessment, record keeping and overlearning. (p. 39)

> Pupils with specific learning difficulties also generally require more practice than other pupils and practice that is well designed. They need, like other pupils to be actively engaged in managing their learning, though they tend to have difficulties in applying learning and performance strategies. However, evidence has shown that such pupils can be taught to use and apply such strategies. (p. 41)

Lewis and Norwich conclude that:

> The notion of continua of teaching approaches is useful as it enables us to distinguish between the 'normal' adaptations in class teaching for most pupils and the greater degree of adaptations required for those with more severe difficulties. These are adaptations to common teaching approaches which have been called 'specialised adaptations' or 'high density' teaching. (p. 3)

This is not to say that all teachers need to do is 'try harder'. 'High density' teaching needs professional development opportunities and, often, particular resources and sometimes equipment. Nevertheless, it is the same pedagogy and therefore far more flexible in conception. Both teacher and pupil can move along the pedagogical continuum, with both learning as they go.

Approaching the issue from a completely different stand point OFSTED (1999) conducted a survey of pupils with specific learning difficulties in mainstream schools. They noted that success in secondary school resulted from early identification and help at the primary stage. That help consisted usually of highly structured programmes using multisensory approaches. They also noted that:

> Pupils who had learned keyboard skills were more successful at using word processing programmes to assist them in their writing.

In other words, if a pupil cannot do something, the first question to ask is 'Did somebody try to *teach* them how to do it?' However, in relation to the pedagogy argument, Finding 22 is most relevant:

> The teaching strategies devised for those pupils with specific learning difficulties were often used effectively with other pupils who had more generalised learning difficulties.

Again, this is an endorsement of the need for more intensive application of a general pedagogy.

However, there are other elements of secondary school practice that are relevant to reducing exclusion. At the time of writing, the 'League Tables' referred to earlier were announced. The clearest common factor relating to those at the top of each list was additional funding. However, the state school standing out most was the Thomas Telford School in Shropshire where 100 per cent of the pupils taking GCSE gained passes at A* to C grade. The significance of this is that while it does have additional funding and autonomy through being a City Technology College (CTC) it is a non-selective school and, because of its CTC status, must draw from inner urban areas and maintain a social balance which reflects it catchment area.

What is different about it is organisation. Many UK schools have short days, short breaks and many lessons per day. Telford begins at 8.30 a.m. and does not finish until late in the evening. Pupils and staff work and eat together, there is no staffroom and only two three-hour lessons per day with breaks in between for self-directed work. Contact with parents is by ten reports per year but no 'parents' evenings! What is particularly interesting about this is the parallels with the Pacific Rim countries. Some years ago now, after James Callaghan initiated the 'Great Debate' about education in his Oxford speech, a delegation went to visit these countries because they were thought to attain higher standards of pupil progress. About the only noticeable result was the current emphasis on 'whole-class' teaching.

I do not wish to enter that debate here. However, what was singularly ignored about education in these countries is detailed in Stevenson and Stigler (1992). Firstly, there is an emphasis on getting good teachers and paying them well: 'Elementary school teachers and corporation employees with comparable degrees of education receive equivalent salaries' (p. 133).

However, more significantly (though possibly achievable because of this) there is both a longer school year and school day. On average 240 days per year are spent in school. A school week can consist of six not five days. School lessons start at 8.30 and finish at 4.00 on weekdays, noon on Saturdays. Formal classes are mixed with extracurricular activities that also continue after 4.00. Recesses between classes are long (as in Telford). Lunch can be an hour and a half. So the picture we get is of school being the place in which the children spend most of their time, both during the day and during the year. There are short weekends and short holidays. During the holidays pupils and parents work on assignments to enhance the work of the previous term.

Thus, like work for adults, the school is the significant centre of their lives where they also receive an education. In the UK one sometimes gets the feeling that for many children it is incidental to their main activities – particularly if they are not 'mainstream' (preferably high achieving mainstream). One might argue that the UK obsession with uniforms is a desperate attempt to induce some group feeling where natural forces have failed. (To be really cynical, if it matters that much why don't teachers wear it and why are sixth formers often exempt? If it is seen as an effective measure, why do I see the boys at my local secondary tuck their shirts in only as they enter the school gates?) In Telford each teacher has one day per week free from classes for preparation and marking. Stevenson and Stigler report Pacific Rim teachers teaching no more that three hours per day (in Japan, by law) so that they can both work together, plan together and mark and also help pupils with special needs.

Mittler 2000 summarises the core elements of inclusion at school level:

- All children attend their neighbourhood school
  – in the regular classroom
  – with appropriate support.

- All teachers accept responsibility for all pupils
  – receiving appropriate support and
  – opportunities for professional development.

- Schools rethink their values
  – restructure their organisation, curriculum and assessment arrangements
  – to overcome barriers to learning and participation and
  – to cater for the full range of pupils in their school and in their community.

(pp. 113–14)

Conclusion

So to summarise the challenges.

- At governmental level there is the challenge to change from the macho, confrontational style of management to a no less demanding but cooperative enterprise which seeks to emphasise the contribution of all to the success of the whole. Even in the infant school rewarding the class is always more effective than rewarding the individual. There is the challenge to recognise education as a right, not a commodity and also that a major part of the means to access that right lies in the alleviation of poverty in the community.
- At the school level there is the challenge to recognise responsibility for each pupil, not just some generalised 'all pupils'.
- At teacher level the challenge is in part pedagogic, in part attitudinal. Recognition that there is a common underlying pedagogy removes any mystique and enables a wider range of strategies to be offered to all pupils. Recognition that general pedagogy has a continuum of intensity of delivery means that professional development can focus on how it relates to the teaching of particular subjects, groups or pupils. This also implies a readiness to have recourse to evidence, not exhortation, in deciding what is or will be effective.

In attitudinal terms it means recognising that the language you use to talk about pupils determines the way you think about them. To talk of 'the' dyslexic child puts him or her in a group with assigned group characteristics. It is as offensive as talking about 'the women'. But more than this, to talk about 'diagnosing' difficulties is medical discourse, 'making special arrangements' is charity discourse, asking whether we can include a child 'because of the effects on the others' or asking 'what will the other parents say' is lay discourse. Making provision either for individual or group needs dependent on 'getting extra resources' rather than considering it as part of transparent, overall budget strategy is to use a corporate discourse. All four discourses lead to exclusion from the rights of each and every child.

The final challenge, then, is to recognise that:

No man is an island, entire of itself; every man is a piece of the continent, a part of the main. Any man's death diminishes me, because I am involved in mankind; and therefore never send to know for whom the bell tolls; it tolls for thee...

(*Norton Anthology of English Literature*. 5th edn. W. W. Norton, 1962, vol. 1, p. 1107)

References

AEP (2000) *Children are Unbeatable.* AEP Circular 085/00.

BBC (1997) 'Dyslexia in the Primary Classroom', in *Teaching Today: Staff Development.* London: BBC Learning Support in association with the British Dyslexia Association.

Booth, T. (2000) 'Inclusion and exclusion policy in England: who controls the agenda?', in Armstrong, F., Armstrong, D. and Barton, L. (eds) *Inclusive Education: Policy, Contexts and Comparative Perspectives.* London: David Fulton Publishers.

Booth, T. and Ainscow, M. (1998) *From Them to Us: An international study of inclusion in education.* London: Routledge.

Davies, N. (2000) *The School Report.* London: Vintage.

DfEE (1997) *Excellence for All Children.* London: The Stationery Office.

DfEE (1998a) *Meeting Special Educational Needs: A programme of action.* London: DfEE.

DfEE (1998b) *The National Literacy Strategy: Additional guidance. Children with Special Educational Needs.* London: DfEE.

Fulcher, G. (1989) *Disabling Policies? A comparative approach to education policy and disability.* Lewes: The Falmer Press.

Harley, W. and Malcolm, H. (1999) *Setting and Streaming: A Research Review.* Edinburgh: Scottish Council for Research in Education.

Hawes, J. M. (1991) *The Children's Rights: A history of advocacy and protection.* Boston, Mass.: Twayne Publishing.

Johnson, M. and Thomas, L. (1999) 'Schools' responses to pupils with epilepsy,' *Support for Learning* 14(1), 13–22.

Lewis, A. and Norwich, B. (1999) *Mapping a pedagogy for special educational needs.* Exeter: Universities of Warwick and Exeter.

Mittler, P. (2000) *Working Towards Inclusive Education: Social Contexts.* London: David Fulton Publishers.

OFSTED (1999) *Pupils with specific learning difficulties in mainstream schools.* London: OFSTED Publications Centre.

Ravenette, T. (1999) *Personal Construct Theory in Educational Psychology: A practitioner's view.* London: Whurr Publishers.

Stevenson, H. W. and Stigler, J. W. (1992) *The Learning Gap: Why our schools are failing and what we can learn from Japanese and Chinese Education.* New York: Summit Books.

Tildsley, J. L. (1921) 'Some possibilities arising from the use of intelligence tests', *Fifth Yearbook of the National Association of Secondary School Principals,* 45–54.

van Steenlandt, D. (1998) *UNESCO and Special Education.* Brussels: Inclusion International.

CHAPTER 6

Inclusion – Changing the Variables

Janice Wearmouth

This chapter:

- examines factors which influence the implementation of policy developments towards the inclusion of dyslexic pupils
- suggests ways in which they might be addressed in order to facilitate that inclusion.

Recent years have witnessed central government support for the inclusion in mainstream schools of all pupils, including those who are dyslexic, wherever possible. In the past, policy change in education has often failed to effect change in practice. Fullan (1992) has suggested that a number of factors contribute to this failure:

- the complexity of the issues is often poorly understood;
- policy makers may be interested only in immediate results;
- solutions which rely on modifications to the curriculum and assessment ignore their implications for teacher development;
- the resources required to support policy initiatives are not always provided.

The complexity of the issues

Meeting the special learning needs of dyslexic pupils within the context of 'inclusion' implies that teachers can address a number of intrinsically complex challenges. To put the principle of inclusion into operation, policy makers are faced with the fundamental dilemma of how to make educational provision for all pupils, which takes full account of 'sameness' and, at the same time, pays due regard to 'diversity' amongst individuals (Norwich 1996). The revised National Curriculum for 2000 (QCA 2000) in England and Wales, for example, contains a statutory 'General Statement on Inclusion' which refers to 'providing effective learning opportunities for all pupils' and which sets out three 'key principles for inclusion':

- setting suitable learning challenges;
- responding to pupils' diverse learning needs;
- overcoming potential barriers to learning and assessment for individuals and groups of pupils.

However, it also enjoins educators to identify and address individual pupils' 'special educational needs' in order to meet the requirements of the law.

Recent years have seen a growing awareness of the so-called 'interactive' model of difficulties in learning (Wedell 2000) and a broader concept of what specially 'needs' to be done to address these. In this model the barriers to pupils' learning arise as a result of the interaction between the characteristics of the child and what is offered through the pedagogy and supporting resources. The complex challenges facing those planning programmes to address dyslexic pupils' learning needs are therefore:

- to focus on ways in which the learning environment potentially creates barriers to, or facilitates, literacy development;
- to consider how most appropriately to assess the characteristics of the individual pupil from the perspectives of those with an interest in the pupil's progress – professionals, parents/carers, the pupil;
- to plan programmes which take account of the perspectives of all concerned and, in an inclusive school, can be embedded into the whole-school curriculum.

Learning environment

Understanding how the learning environment can produce barriers to pupils' learning implies a thorough grasp of the school context. Salmon (1998), cited in Wearmouth (2000), feels that a number of factors make schools as institutions incapable of responding to the learning needs of all pupils:

- regimentation of pupils;
- lack of individuality and personal recognition;
- chronological age grouping;
- inappropriate model of child-as-learner;
- within-school power relationships;
- authoritarianism.

While all these factors have a potential significance for the inclusion of dyslexic pupils, it is probably at classroom level that the most important interactions affecting pupils occur (Florian and Rouse 2000).

Support for learning: in-class and withdrawal

There is no single clear-cut way of ensuring the inclusion of dyslexic pupils. Lewis (1995) notes that the withdrawal group work which focused on the teaching of specific skills for pupils who experienced difficulties in certain areas that was common practice in the 1970s and early 1980s has now largely fallen into disfavour because:

- apparent gains made in the small group situation could not be sustained and/or generalised in the context of the classroom;
- students lose the continuity of classroom activity and instruction;
- the teaching methods used in the withdrawal groups may conflict with those in the main classroom;
- class teachers had less incentive to take an interest in examining how teaching for all pupils, including those with difficulties in literacy, might be improved.

Using support staff is common practice in many classrooms, but there seems to be little consensus among teachers, parents and pupils about what exactly the role ought to be. In-class support is often something imposed on the class teacher to accompany the 'integration' of pupils 'with' difficulties. Potential clashes may occur in a situation where, conventionally, one professional is in control and another professional is working in the same place. Support teachers may lack status in the eyes of staff and pupils, lack authority and subject-specific knowledge (Lovey 1995). Often, support teachers find themselves propping up the system by helping pupils through inappropriate lessons, thus, unwittingly, contributing to pupils' problems in the long run (Allan 1995). In this context, even the best qualified, most experienced support teacher can be humiliated by lack of definition of role, being treated like one of the pupils, and not being able to act in the familiar capacity of authoritative adult (Best 1991, Thomas 1992).

It is hardly surprising, however, that many teachers would still support withdrawal group work in the area of literacy. Moss and Reason (1998) note that the explicit teaching of literacy may have suffered where in-class support is always used to facilitate access to the curriculum.

Some schools have adopted a much more flexible and creative use of support teaching (Clark et al. 1997). For example, individual teachers or subject departments might be asked to put in a bid for in-class support to develop differentiated strategies and schemes of work for all pupils. Partnerships might be drawn up requiring class and support teachers to plan lessons together. Support teachers might be regarded as full members of a subject department.

Assessment

Professional perspectives

There are two important issues about which professionals must be very clear in their assessment of dyslexic pupils. The first relates to what they are trying to achieve in the assessment process, and the second to the underlying assumptions of particular forms of assessment. In relation to the first, for example, the distinctions in kind and purpose between formative and summative assessment are crucial (Harlen and James 1997). Ongoing formative assessment is carried out by teachers to collect information and evidence about a pupil's literacy development and to plan the next step in his/her learning. It combines the assessment of skills required for specific tasks, and pupil-referenced (ipsative) techniques where the same pupil's progress is tracked across time. Summative assessment takes place at certain intervals when achievement has to be recorded and is intended to provide a global picture of the learner's literacy development to date. It requires a high degree of reliability, and may involve a combination of different types of assessment, for example the measurement of individual pupil progression in learning against public criteria.

Regarding the second, underlying the formulation of assessments for statutory purposes there are assumptions which intrinsically contradict notions of inclusion. In the first place, available resources have often dictated the provision made for individual pupils (Cline 1992). In order to decide who is eligible for additional services, special educational provision depends on norm-referenced assessment designed solely to indicate a learner's achievement in comparison with others and, therefore, identify some students who are 'different'.

Furthermore, it is obvious that norm-referenced tests of ability and attainment carry the power to 'determine selectively the way in which issues are discussed and solutions proposed' (Broadfoot 1996). The influence of psychometric thinking leads to deterministic views of ability and achievement which limit what we expect from certain students, and restrict developments in assessment. Norm-referenced tests typically produce measures in terms of ranks, for example standardised reading scores. They do not indicate appropriate intervention strategies because 'the scores do not provide details of what the child knows or does not know, nor do they elucidate the processes that are involved in the child's difficulty' (Dockrell and McShane 1993: 34)

If such systems are to be inclusive then, as Dockrell and McShane (p. 35) note, they need to be criterion-based, using task analysis, and result in such measures as developmental profiles and checklists to 'help identify whether or not an individual possesses some particular skill or competence . . . allow for the analysis of error patterns . . . provide a clear indication of what a child can and [indicate] what skills should be taught next.'

Finally, identification of what needs to be measured is not simple (Beard 1990). It may be possible to break the development of awareness of sound–letter correspondence down into measurable objectives. Assessment of enjoyment of reading and aspects related to the finer points of the meaning of text is much more problematic.

Pupils' perspectives

One of the major challenges facing those responsible for the progress of dyslexic pupils is that of engaging with pupil perspectives in a positive and meaningful way. Garner and Sandow (1995) have identified philosophical and practical problems surrounding pupil self-advocacy. Among these are that the model of pupil as participant and self-directed learner rather than empty vessel to be filled implies that the traditional role of the teacher as purveyor of wisdom and transmitter of knowledge must change to that of facilitator. This development in the teacher's role may be uncomfortable. Self-advocacy may run contrary to the traditional behaviourist model of learning adopted in some schools which relies on learning programmes designed to reinforce desired behaviour and inhibit undesired behaviour. Additionally, some pupils may be seen as undeserving of the right to self-advocacy; others, even at secondary level, may be perceived as incapable of contributing rationally to decisions about their own lives. Pupils, especially teenagers, may openly verbally challenge teachers' authority as well as the structure and organisation of the school. Self-advocacy involves a transfer of power from teacher to pupil in the degree of legitimacy accorded to pupils' opinions.

Gersch (2000) notes that progress made in involving children more actively in their education over the past 20 years 'has been patchy, unsystematic and slow'. However, without exploring pupil perspectives it is impossible to understand anything of the 'competing values and expectations stemming from internal idiosyncratic processes or from differing family and sub-cultural values' (Ravenette 1984) that pupils may experience which lead them to rejection of everything associated with school.

Gersch (2000), reporting on a project which aimed to enhance pupil active participation in school through encouraging self-evaluation and advocacy, encountered a number of dilemmas:

How does one deal with other colleagues who might feel that children should be seen and not heard?

Are some children not mature or capable enough to participate?

How does one deal with parent–child dislike?

What about scope needed for children to negotiate, try things and change their minds?

How do adults distinguish what a child needs from what he or she prefers or wants?

What if the SENCO comes into conflict with the head teacher over ways of meeting a child's needs? What then happens to the child's views?

Clearly there are no easy solutions to these dilemmas which represent, essentially, conflict between the roles of the participants.

Gersch (2000), quoted in Wearmouth (2000: 118)

The nearest Gersch himself comes to offering an answer is to point to 'the importance of a trusting, listening, open, non-judgemental relationship' between teacher and pupil.

Parents' perspectives

There are a number of contentious issues that must be addressed if parents' perspectives on their children's learning are to be taken seriously. Firstly, there may be a big difference between what is perceived as fair and necessary by different groups of parents. Competing or conflicting parents' voices may be irreconcilable within the walls of one school. For example, parental concern about replacing withdrawal from class and individual tuition in literacy with in-class support assumed great significance in a research project at 'Downland', an urban comprehensive school attempting to move towards an inclusive approach (Clark *et al.* 1997). This particular school was finally forced to recreate special forms of provision for some pupils as a result of pressure from parents of those pupils with Statements who regarded generalised in-class support as insufficient to meet specific literacy needs.

Additionally, exercising parental rights requires a high level of determination as well as, sometimes, access to legal representation and financial resources. Research suggests that resources are unfairly allocated to children whose parents are more literate, persistent and articulate (Audit Commission 1992). Some writers, for example Gross (1996), support the notion of formula funding in the interests of 'fairness' for all children. However, others, for example Simmons (1996), conclude that the solution to the problem is not to remove entitlement from learners, but to persuade local authorities to fulfil their obligations towards every child.

Planning

Planning to meet the learning needs of secondary dyslexic pupils must incorporate assessment of learning needs, a global view of the learner together with future career possibilities and also the overall curriculum structure that relates to all pupils in a school (OFSTED 1996). It is essential to consider the implications of curriculum differentiation for future life chances as well as ways of embedding individual plans into the whole-school curriculum.

Whatever alterations teachers make to enable dyslexic pupils to engage more fully in any aspect of the curriculum might solve some problems but create others (Norwich 1994). Solutions commonly adopted include:

- reducing the content coverage of the curriculum to release more time for literacy development;
- enabling some pupils to access the curriculum through alternative means, for example through the use of information and communications technology;
- providing different pedagogy, materials or specialist teaching for some pupils.

At secondary level few years of compulsory schooling remain. There is a very fine line between constricting curriculum choices so that they impact adversely on future life chances, and not offering sufficient support to encourage the competence in literacy necessary for independent, successful life as an adult.

An inclusive approach means that planning for pupil learning should be embedded into the whole-school curriculum. Cowne (2000) notes a number of important tasks for teachers planning programmes for individual pupils:

1. Relate the principal curriculum objectives for pupils to the overall school schemes.
2. Consider the way in which the principal objectives and key concepts are to be assessed in each subject area, the criteria which indicate a satisfactory level of skills and how to record the outcome of the assessment.
3. Identify the prerequisite skills for the principal objectives, and the prior level of knowledge required to understand key concepts in each subject.
4. Be aware of the extent to which all pupils, including those identified as dyslexic, have the prerequisite skills and prior knowledge for lessons in different subject areas in order to arrange any necessary 'pre-teaching', or differentiated resource.
5. Cross-reference relevant skills and knowledge from all curriculum areas.
6. Consider ways in which various kinds of group work, with or without additional assistance from adults, might assist learning.
7. Consider the extent to which those pupils with the greatest needs might be expected to fulfil the principal objectives and grasp all key concepts in every subject area and lesson.

Fulfilling these tasks demands flexibility and a thorough grasp of the National Curriculum structure and its underlying principles, in addition to the strengths and needs of individual pupils.

The interests of policy makers

School practices in relation to pupils who experience difficulties are heavily constrained by national and local authority policies. Schools must be accountable to the general public for the quality of education they provide for the nation's children. However, where national policies attempt to promote the majority interest through setting normative targets to be achieved within the lifetime of one parliament, and through establishing league tables of academic achievement, as in England and Wales since the 1988 Education Act, the problems created for many pupils with difficulties such as dyslexia are very hard to resolve. How far the effect of imposing additional pressure on schools to improve their overall academic standards will result in squeezing some dyslexic pupils out of the system remains to be seen. In response to the Green Paper *Excellence for All Children* (DfEE 1997) one parent wrote:

> We live in an area containing many high quality mainstream schools which are oversubscribed. These schools are very competitive and strive to achieve high measures in success rates primarily measured by the number of GCSE and A level passes gained by each pupil. Such measurements are meaningless as far as our son is concerned, except to say that the more competitive and academic the classroom, the less likely it would be able to educate our son effectively because he would not be able to cope with ... the situation and would hold the rest of the class back.

> (Wearmouth 2000: 72)

Change and its implications for teacher development

The ability of a school to improve the quality of education for all the pupils who attend, that is become more inclusive, as Hopkins and Harris (1997) argue, is dependent on a school's capacity for continuous reflection and development. For any school there is a challenge in thinking through the way in which change might be developed and implemented, while simultaneously harnessing sufficient support throughout the school for it to be sustained.

Initiatives designed to bring about change in pedagogy must take account of the teacher's purpose in his or her work (Fullan and Hargreaves 1996). Change which either cuts across what teachers feel is in the best interests of those they teach or which appears impractical is likely to be resisted and/or resented.

One of the reasons why dyslexic pupils in schools find themselves in difficulties in relation to the delivery of the National Literacy Strategy may be that this Strategy is, in some ways, in opposition to research findings from projects into what effective primary school teachers of literacy know, understand and do. For example, *Effective Teachers of Literacy* (Exeter University (1998), sponsored by the TTA) concluded that teachers' personal philosophy, awareness and understanding of literacy are the factors which guide pedagogy and predispose to effective teaching. 'Knowledge and understanding of literacy development consistently and coherently informs [effective] practice'. This contrasts with a system of practices imposed by the National Literacy Strategy, and has different implications for teacher professional development based on personal knowledge, reflection and analysis.

Availability of the necessary resources

In their research into school policies on special needs, Tarr and Thomas (1998) found 'little or no information on budgets for SEN' and, consequently, less chance of transparent accountability for the use of monies assigned to the school for this purpose. The corollary of this is that local education authorities are much less likely to assign additional funds to schools because it is difficult to justify. Clearly it is in the interest of those supporting dyslexic pupils to request 'transparent procedures that describe how funding comes to the school and how it is thereafter spent' (Tarr and Thomas 1998).

Whenever there is a question of allocating additional, or 'special' resources to particular pupils, inevitably the issue of equality of opportunity arises. Ostensibly, planning provision to fulfil 'need' conveys a sense of benevolence. In practice, however, the concept is 'deeply problematic' (Salmon 1995). There is often an assumption of agreement between all the interested parties about what is 'needed' which ignores the implied value placed on pupils by the kind of special or additional provision which a pupil is deemed to 'need' – or deserve. Particular approaches to provision for pupils seen as 'dyslexic' may often be interpreted as reflecting the dominant values of an educational institution. Elsewhere (Wearmouth 1997) I have reported on an initiative in an upper school where a special needs coordinator introduced laptop computers to assist pupils who experienced difficulty in expressing themselves in writing. The upper school concerned had maintained its very strong academic traditions from its days as a grammar school and an expectation of a stratified model of pupils' ability. When the pupils using the new laptops began to produce written work of a higher standard than some other pupils, their unexpected achievement was received by many staff in a similarly negative manner to that reported by Rosenthal and Jacobson (1968). This disruption to the anticipated hierarchy of achievement appeared to cause considerable feelings of discomfort. The following year pressure to maintain equilibrium in the school system resulted in considerable resistance to the learning support coordinator working in the same way.

In a climate of increasing accountability and recourse to litigation, it is vital that those responsible for requesting, or overseeing the allocation of, additional or special resources are very clear in their procedures and practice, which must be open to scrutiny. Making appropriate provision for dyslexic pupils requires a flexibility of approach in incorporating and embedding additional and/or unfamiliar resources into the curriculum in ways that address identified needs. It also requires a thorough understanding of what resources are available, human, physical and financial, how they are allocated and how they might be reallocated to improve educational outcomes for pupils.

Conclusion

Past experience of failure to effect educational policy change in practice indicates that moves towards including all pupils in mainstream schools are unlikely to succeed unless, (Fullan 1992), sufficient account is taken of the teachers who are expected to put the change into operation. The complexity of the issues must be teased out, policy makers must understand the long-term nature of embedding change, the implications of the change for teacher development must be taken seriously, and necessary resources and technology must be made available.

Those supporting the introduction into schools of any new initiative or resource for dyslexic pupils would do well to pay regard to the checklist for introducing information and communications technology that was produced by NCET (1995: 8–9):

Context

- What evidence is there to support the need for IT?
- Why isn't the present provision adequate?

Purpose

- What does the learner need to achieve?
- What else, apart from IT, is needed to meet the learner's needs?
- Is the IT provision linked into the learner's Individual Education Plan?

Resourcing

- Is the IT already available in the school/classroom being fully utilised?
- Is the provision appropriate for the learner's age and stage of development?
- Is any proposed equipment compatible with the IT already available in the school?

Support

- Is the learner familiar with any proposed resources?
- Can all adults working with the learner use the equipment appropriately?
- Do staff know where to find help?

Expectations

- Have the learner's views been taken into account?

- Have the parents been involved in the discussion over provision?
- What are the class teacher's expectations?

Management

- Are all staff committed to supporting a learner with IT provision in the classroom?
- Who will take responsibility for ensuring that the equipment is functioning correctly?

Monitoring

- What criteria will be used to monitor the effectiveness of the provision?
- What criteria will be used to monitor the learning targets?

Transition

- What planning is in place for considering the changing needs of the learner?
- What planning is in place to consider changing needs, both in school and beyond school?
- What planning is in place to consider developments in technology?

This checklist has a generic value in that it can be applied to any other form of initiative or resource.

References

Allan, J. (1995) 'How are we doing? Teachers' views on the effectiveness of co-operative teaching', *Support for Learning* 10(2), 127–31.

Armstrong, D. (1995) *Power and Partnership in Education*. London: Routledge.

Audit Commission (1992) *Getting in on the Act: provision for pupils with special educational needs*. London: HMSO.

Beard, R. (1990) *Developing Reading* 3–13. London: Hodder.

Best, R. (1991) 'Support teaching in a comprehensive school', *Support for Learning* 6(1).

Broadfoot, P. (1996) *Education, Assessment and Society*. Buckingham: Open university Press.

Clark, C. *et al.* (1997) *New Directions in Special Needs*. London: Cassell.

Cline, T. (ed.) (1992) *The Assessment of Special Educational Needs*. London: Routledge.

Cowne, E. (2000) 'Inclusive curriculum: access for all – rhetoric or reality?', in *E831 Professional Development for Special Educational Needs Co-ordinators*. Milton Keynes: Open University.

DfEE (1997) *Excellence for All Children: meeting special educational needs*. Sudbury: DfEE.

Dockrell, J. and McShane, J. (1993) *Children's Learning Difficulties: a cognitive approach*. Oxford: Blackwell.

Dyson, A. (1997) 'Social and educational disadvantage: reconnecting special needs education', *British Journal of Special Education* 24(4).

Exeter University (1998) *Effective Teachers of Literacy*. Exeter: Exeter University/TTA.

Florian, L. and Rouse, M. (2000) *Investigating Classroom Practice in Inclusive Education: final report*. Cambridge: University of Cambridge, School of Education.

Foucault, M. (1980) *Power-knowledge: selected interviews and other writings, 1972–1977*. Brighton: Harvester Press.

Fullan, M. G. (1992) *The new meaning of educational change*. London: Cassell.

Fullan, M. and Hargreaves, D. (1996) *What's Worth Fighting for in Your School?* New York: Columbia Press.

Garner, P. and Sandow, S. (1995) *Advocacy, Self-Advocacy and Special Needs*. London: David Fulton Publishers.

Gersch, I. (2000) 'Listening to children: an initiative to increase the active involvement of children in their education by an educational psychology service', in *E831 Professional Development for Special Educational Needs Co-ordinators*. Milton Keynes: Open University.

Gipps, C. and Gross, H. (1987) 'Children with special needs in the Primary school', *Support for Learning* 2(3).

Gosling, P., Murray, A. and Stephen, F. (1996) 'Planning for change', in Clarke, D. and Murray, A. *Developing and Implementing a Whole-School Behaviour Policy*. London: David Fulton Publishers.

Gross, J. (1996) 'The weight of the evidence', *Support for Learning* 11(1).

Harlen, W. and James, M. (1997) 'Assessment and learning: differences and relationships between formative and summative assessment', *Assessment in Education* 4(3).

Hopkins, D. and Harris, A. (1997) 'Improving the quality of education for all', *Support for Learning* 12(4), 162–5.

Lewis, A. (1995) *Primary Special Needs and the National Curriculum*. London: Routledge.

Lovey, J. (1995) *Supporting Special Educational Needs in Secondary School Classrooms*. London: David Fulton Publishers.

Merrett, F. (1998) 'Helping readers who have fallen behind', *Support for Learning* 13(2).

Moss, H. and Reason, R. (1998) 'Interactive group work with young children needing additional help in learning to read', *Support for Learning* 13(1).

NCET (1995) *Access Technology: making the right choice*. Coventry: NCET.

Norwich, B. (1994) 'Differentiation: from the perspective of resolving tensions between basic social values and assumptions about individual differences', *Curriculum Studies* 2(3), 289–308.

Norwich, B. (1996) *Special needs education, inclusive education or just education for all?* London: London University Institute of Education.

OFSTED (1996) *Promoting High Achievement for Pupils with Special Educational Needs in Mainstream Schools: a report of the Office of Her Majesty's Chief Inspector of Schools*. London: HMSO.

Qualifications and Curriculum Authority (QCA) (2000) 'General Statement on Inclusion', in *National Curriculum for 2000*. London: QCA.

Ravenette, A. T. (1984) 'The recycling of maladjustment', *A.E.P. Journal* 6(3), 18–27.

Rosenthal, R. and Jacobson, L. (1968) *Pygmalion in the Classroom*. New York: Holt, Rinehart and Winston.

Salmon, P. (1998) *Life at School*. London: Cassell.

Simmons, K. (1996) 'In defence of entitlement', *Support for Learning* 11(3).

Tarr, J. and Thomas, G. (1998) 'Compiling school policies for special educational needs', in Davies, J. D., Garner, P. and Lee, J. *Managing Special Needs in Mainstream Schools*. London: David Fulton Publishers.

Thomas, G. (1992) *Effective Classroom Teamwork – support or intrusion?* London: The Falmer Press.

Tomlinson, S. (1982) *A Sociology of Special Education*. London: Routledge.

Wearmouth, J. (1997) 'Pygmalion lives on', *Support for Learning* 11(3).

Wearmouth, J. (2000) *Special Educational Provision: meeting the challenges in schools*. London: Hodder.

Wedell, K. (2000) Personal interview (unpublished).

SECTION 3: The Subject of Success

CHAPTER 7

Dyslexia and the Teaching of Modern Foreign Languages

Margaret Crombie and Hilary McColl

This chapter:

- addresses the notion of inclusive education for all by highlighting the misplaced assumptions which often prevail in relation to dyslexic students and Modern Foreign Languages
- illustrates with examples how dyslexic students can deal with phonological difficulties in relation to language learning
- emphasises factors relating to presentation of materials
- discusses learning and memory strategies
- comments on policy issues particularly relating to examinations and curriculum access.

Introduction

The notion of inclusion and inclusive education carries with it an assumption of entitlement for all those included in the education system. Those who have a physical presence in the school are therefore entitled to be included, as far as they are able, in the whole programme of education which is taking place there. In relation to the learning of a modern foreign language for dyslexic students, this has not always proved to be the case. Dyslexic young people, for whatever reason, have been, and still are, on occasions removed from the modern languages classroom to work elsewhere, being considered unable to benefit from the work taking place. This assumption however is often misplaced, and fails to take account of a multitude of factors which all affect whether and how a young person will learn effectively. Access to the modern languages curriculum through use of appropriate strategies, including technology, is at times denied the dyslexic student. This is a situation where no blame should be attached, as teachers have lacked appropriate guidance on what to do and how to do it.

Dyslexia and the teaching of MFL

Dyslexia has historically been an area shrouded in a mystique regarding appropriate teaching and what works for the dyslexic person. Teaching has been seen as highly specific, and the preserve of a few who have completed specialist modules or diplomas. Modern language teaching too has gone through a series of stages characterised by ever-changing recommendations with regard to appropriate methodologies for learning and teaching modern foreign languages. The 1960s saw the introduction into schools of Skinnerian techniques using language laboratories, audio-lingual courses and precision teaching with remedial worksheets. By the time these became commonplace in schools, psychology had begun to discredit the theory on which such approaches had been based. Skinner, it seems, was to be displaced by Chomsky's theories on language learning (Johnstone 1999). By the 1980s, the emphasis had moved to real life language for real life situations. Emphasis for those who seemed less able language learners (and this must have included the dyslexic population) was now on speaking and listening. Reading and writing tended to be regarded as less important for the less able. This assumption was not based on any form of research or on national guidelines (SOED 1993), but on the assumption that if you weren't good at something, then omitting that something would help. In fact omitting that something was denying the dyslexic student channels of learning which could have aided the learning process. The benefits of multisensory teaching which most dyslexia specialists now regarded as standard practice were not adequately communicated to modern language teachers. Although Scottish national guidelines still recommended that all four areas should be developed in a balanced and progressive manner, and writing was seen as having 'an important function in supporting language acquisition' (SOED 1993: 2–3), the assumption that dyslexic students should be spared the possible distress which reading and writing might cause was prevalent at the time.

The last decade however has seen a new light dawning on teaching professionals. With the introduction of a modern foreign language as a core element in the curriculum throughout the UK, modern language specialists and support for learning specialists are seeing the benefits of collaborative working, and the sharing of expertise which promises to make foreign language learning a real possibility for the vast majority of young people, including those who are disadvantaged in their learning by dyslexia. For the dyslexic student, language learning will still not be easy, but with the appropriate understanding, curriculum, techniques and support, it can prove possible.

It will still not be easy! The difficulties which dyslexic individuals have in learning their native language will impact to some extent on the learning of a foreign language. Factors such as phonological processing, working memory, auditory discrimination, auditory sequencing and confusion over grammar and syntax are liable to cause similar difficulties in foreign language learning as they have in the learning of the first language (Crombie 1997a, 2000, Ganschow et al. 2000, Simon 2000). On the other hand, this parallel between first and second language learning also means that modern language teachers do not have to start from scratch. As Schneider (1999) has shown, many of the strategies which have proved effective in helping dyslexic students to improve their handling of their mother tongue provide pointers to what might work in second-language learning. With sufficient understanding of the difficulties facing dyslexic learners, and the assurance that some success is possible, the modern language teacher can devise appropriate strategies to facilitate the learning of dyslexic students. Teachers should not be unduly concerned about the effects which these strategies might have on the rest of the class, as many of the routines and techniques will help all students. Although not all will require the same volume of overlearning and multisensory practice, strategies which build up phonological awareness and adopt a systematic approach to grammar for example will be of benefit to all.

Research into first and second language acquisition indicates that students' capabilities in their first language form the basis for success in the foreign language, and that the difficulties they are already experiencing in acquiring competence in their first language are likely also to affect second language acquisition (Sparks *et al.* 1989, Sparks and Ganschow 1993). Since dyslexic students experience most difficulty with phonological coding – converting symbols to sounds and sounds to symbols and forming a representation in memory – this is likely to have far-reaching effects on their foreign language learning. Students may struggle to discriminate between different sounds, may fail to appreciate how the sounds produced by letters and groups of letters blend together, may be unable to remember sounds for long enough or clearly enough to repeat them accurately, and may have difficulty understanding the relationships between letters or groups of letters and the sounds they make. All this will make it difficult for the student to sustain concentration on spoken language, to pronounce written words correctly and to spell accurately (Simon 2000). Listening, speaking, reading and writing will all, directly or indirectly, be affected. It is therefore incorrect to assume that dyslexic students have difficulty with reading and writing only and that the solution lies in avoiding these. On the contrary, when all four activities are allowed to interact, failure becomes much less likely.

It is worth reiterating at this point that 'difficult' does not mean 'impossible'. Dyslexic students, like others, will vary in the degree of difficulty they experience with different activities. Worth noting too, is that difficulties of this sort are not confined to dyslexic students. What is important for all learners, is to identify the specific strategies and techniques which can make learning easier.

Dyslexic students have areas of strength as well as weaknesses. Figure 7.1 summarises some of the problems which might be encountered by dyslexic students in the modern languages class and some strategies which might be employed to assist them. The strategies summarised emphasise the dyslexic student's strengths, give additional practice in areas of weakness or provide additional support. Some of these strategies can be incorporated relatively easily into normal classroom practice and will be of benefit to all students; however, the dyslexic student's need for frequent repetition and additional learning time may require some extra planning. Occasionally, the availability of an additional resource can make the difference between success and failure. These additional support strategies are listed separately. The summary is not intended to be definitive, but it is hoped that it will provide a framework for further discussion between modern language teachers and support staff.

Much of the work done in the modern language class, based as it generally is on text, will highlight weaknesses of which the student is all too well aware. To counteract this, every opportunity can be taken to enrich the language learning experience by offering additional channels of input and output which will exploit students' strengths. By undertaking tasks which combine all the activities of seeing, hearing, speaking and writing as closely as possible, the student can capitalise on stronger channels of input while at the same time exercising the weaker ones (Crombie 1997b). The reading (if reading aloud) and writing elements offer kinaesthetic, oral and auditory input supported by a visual image which might otherwise be denied through merely speaking and listening.

A variety of ways of making use of multisensory techniques must be found to minimise the boredom which can result from constant repetition of the same elements. The Language Master for example is a piece of equipment which enables the teacher to provide a model pronunciation for the student to emulate without the need for the teacher always to be present or give direct input. The machine uses cards with a strip of magnetic audio tape. The teacher can record in the target language a word or phrase to be learned along with the translation in the home language. In addition to the written word or phrase, the card could also have a picture to aid visual imagery. Students pass the card through the machine which will play the teacher's recorded voice. They can do this as many times as they wish while listening and looking at the printed card. When

Factors to take into account Characteristics of some dyslexic learners which will affect learning	Effect on FL learning Learners may have difficulties with the following	Strategies Incorporating these strategies into normal class teaching may help	Additional support Examples of additional support which may be needed
Phonological processing • Poor grasp of sound/symbol correspondence • Lack of awareness of individual sounds within words	• Pronunciation, even of frequently encountered words • Recognising familiar words and phrases and confusion of similar sounding words • Reading, especially if asked to read aloud	• Early introduction to phonic system of the new language • Introduce new material in a multisensory way – show it, listen to it, look at it, hear it, say it, write it, etc. • Ask student to read aloud only if she/he volunteers	• Use practice cards for reinforcement • Provide tapes to accompany printed materials • Use Language Master/PALE • Pair student with a good reader
Memory • Working memory is limited; if overloaded, information may be lost • There may be inaccurate representations in long-term memory	• Remembering and carrying out instructions (in either language) • Remembering recently learned vocabulary • Repeating multisyllable words • May know the answer but be unable to 'get it out'!	• Present new information in bite-sized chunks • Set limited but realistic targets • Make use of additional channels of learning – music, actions, graphics • Allow extra time for recall	• Provide materials for further revision at home or with additional support
Auditory discrimination/perception • Unsure of the sound which has been heard • Difficulty in perceiving the difference between similar sounds • Difficulty in knowing where a spoken word ends and a new word begins	• Knowing whether a sound is being pronounced correctly (e.g. repeating after the teacher) • Ability to recognise the difference between two words containing similar sounds in either language • Listening tasks • Answering oral questions	• Provide text to accompany sound • When speaking to dyslexic students, exaggerate word separation at first, then let them hear it as it would be spoken normally	• If student has a choice of language, opt for one which is phonically similar to home language, e.g. Italian or Spanish may be better for English-speaking student than French
Sequencing • Getting things in order, e.g. alphabet, word order in sentences or letter order in words, etc.	• Accessing words from dictionary • Ordering days in a week, months in a year, numerical data, etc.	• Provide frequent practice using variety of strategies – rhyme, rhythm, games, songs, etc. • Have lists/diagrams, etc., on the wall for reference	• Make use of technical aids, such as foreign language spelling and word checker • Encourage the use of mnemonic strategies
Writing • Handwriting may be painfully slow and the result inaccurate and difficult to read	• Copying from the board • Committing to paper what can be produced orally • Spelling may follow English phonic code ('mother tongue interference')	• Limit the amount of writing required for classwork, but do not eliminate it • Avoid assessing written work if very poor	• Accept assessments in forms other than writing – taped, word processed, etc. • Provide photocopied notes with tapes which can be used for practise at home

Figure 7.1 Problems which might be encountered by dyslexic students (continued overleaf)

Factors to take into account Characteristics of some dyslexic learners which will affect learning	Effect on FL learning Learners may have difficulties with the following	Strategies Incorporating these strategies into normal class teaching may help	Additional support Examples of additional support which may be needed
Speed of processing information • Tendency to be slower in responding to incoming information	• Responding to information or instructions given verbally in either language • Responding to a continuous flow of information	• Slow down speed of presentation to allow extra time for processing information • Be prepared to allow student extra time to answer questions and to complete work	• Apply for extra time and other special arrangements for external examinations
Difficulty with directionality • Tendency to confuse left/right, up/down, etc.	• Following and giving directions • Responding accurately to instructions which rely on prepositions	• Provide pictures, arrows, etc., as well as text • Give visual clues when speaking	• Pair student with another who has no difficulties in this area and who can help
Grammar and syntax • Poor understanding of grammar and syntax in first language	• Forming accurate sentences • Rules of grammar	• Teach rules and reinforce daily • Use diagrams, cards and other language building blocks, etc. to demonstrate linear sequences and patterns of language	• Write rules onto revision cards for students to use as reference in class and at home
Visual discrimination/recognition • Poor ability to discriminate and/or differentiate between words in and between words	• Differentiating between similar looking words (in either language or between languages) • Differentiating between accents, and therefore assigning correct pronunciation • Confusion between languages, e.g. pain (bread) in French confused with the English word	• Use picture cues for association. • Use practice cards for daily revision of common words with accents • Highlight accents in colour	• Use Language Master to aid learning of common words to help with accents and to reinforce easily confusable words

Figure 7.1 (continued)

happy that they can remember, the student records his/her own voice which can then be compared with the model pronunciation. When satisfied that they can do this, the phrase can then be written while simultaneously repeating the phrase. In the classroom, this can be subvocalised to avoid disturbing others. Headphones too are available so that listening can be done without distraction. Additional strategies might include the following:

Presenting new language:

- When introducing new language use charts and diagrams to show the bigger picture so that the student sees where the learning fits in with what has been learned previously.
- Add mime and gesture to words.
- When introducing or practising long words, try clapping the rhythm.
- Add pictures to text.
- Demonstrate how language works by calling attention to patterns of language, using charts, grids, card sequences, etc. – whatever is needed. Figure 7.2 is an example of how sentences are constructed in French to make language patterns visible and comprehensible to the student.
- Group words in logical ways (by similar letter patterns, by gender, etc.).
- Use colour to highlight gender, accents, etc.
- Create wall charts which show language in non-linear relationships (e.g. labelled diagrams and pictures).

Making language patterns visible and comprehensible to the student

Making statements about pets

			Examples
j'	ai	un chien un chat	
tu	as	un poney un hamster	J'ai une souris
il elle on	a	une souris une tortue	Nous avons un chien et une tortue
nous	avons	une perruche	Elle a un poney
vous	avez	deux......s	Sam a deux perruches
ils elles	ont	trois......s	

Asking questions about pets

			Examples
qui	a		Qui as une tortue?
tu	as	..................?	Tu as un chat?
vous	avez		Vous avez un chien, madame?

Figure 7.2 Example of how students might be helped to understand how sentences are put together to achieve a given purpose

Practising the language

- Use games and attractive resources to consolidate vocabulary and language patterns. Stile materials and Miniflashcards are useful examples.
- Make up a pack of cards for practice. Students' practice cards should be pocket sized, approximately 32 × 22 mm (3 × 2 inches). Different colours can be used for different purposes, e.g. blue for vocabulary, red for rules of grammar, pink for sounds. If being used for a whole group of students, then the teacher would wish to have a matching set which are large enough to use as flash cards. A modern languages assistant or classroom assistant could help give daily routine reinforcement practice.
- Make use of any form of ICT which the student finds helpful. Many computer programs are multisensory and allow the students to work at their own pace.
- Give opportunities for brief dictations. Allow the student to respond in writing, then provide correct version on photocopied sheet. Student then corrects in coloured pen, analyses where they went wrong and rewrites correctly. Teacher checks the corrected version.

Working with foreign language texts

- Combine listening and reading by providing text and tape. Slow speech, where possible, to a speed which the student can follow.
- Use Mind Maps (copyright), spidergrams, writing frames, etc. to help the student to plan oral and/or written work.
- Allow student to produce a tape rather than having to always write out work if this will result in a better standard.
- Use charts and diagrams to show 'the bigger picture' so that the student can see where this learning fits in with what has been learned previously.

Foreign language learning makes intensive use of memorisation. In order for words and phrases to be memorised they first have to enter short-term working memory, so they can then (hopefully) be transferred to long-term memory. At a later stage they will require to be recalled into working memory to be assembled into coherent messages. Dyslexic students are likely to have difficulty at all stages, so each stage will require consolidation:

1. Input to short-term working memory
Present and model new language in small amounts by a variety of means, with frequent opportunities for repetition and regular revision. Use any mnemonic strategies which might help. Use students' own ideas about what works best for them.

2. Transfer to long-term memory
Provide opportunities to practise hearing, saying, reading, writing the limited amount of new language. Include opportunities to use different examples within carefully delineated language patterns. Carefully chosen games can provide the stimulus for extended practice.

Repeat stages 1 and 2 many times in as wide a variety of ways as possible.

3. Recall from long-term to working memory
Students will need time and opportunity to bring back into working memory the words and phrases they will need to use in an output exercise. Assist recall by providing cues where

necessary – pictures, rhythms, rhymes which were used to assist input – as well as reference to the word in English. Using the same picture or labelled diagram may be the cue or link required to bring the stored information back from long-term memory. Playing the same language games again may also remind students of key structures.

4. Assembling the message
Stimulate recall before initiating output in order to make the output task easier for students. Provide outlines or other cues for organising written work.

The dyslexic student often needs detailed explanation. Rules and other important information should be provided in written form for further study and future reference. There are times however when questioning the logic of something is unhelpful and time wasting. The logic of why certain nouns in other languages have a specific gender often defies explanation, therefore there are times when the dyslexic student simply has to be told, 'Here is a strategy. Try it! Colour all the le's/der's in green, and the la's/die's in brown, and the das's in blue. Can you think of a better way?' Charlann Simon, herself dyslexic, considers that 'perseverance can compensate for a lack of natural potential in a number of academic areas' (Simon 2000). A sense of humour and positive outlook on life can also help students to reframe negative experiences in terms of what has been learned.

The challenges and opportunities

The challenge for teachers of modern languages – whether as the modern language specialist or the support teacher – is to make the language as motivating as possible. The student needs a reason to learn, and that needs to be more than the passing of an exam. Give an interest in the country by showing films, and introducing aspects of the culture, foods, pen pals or better still e-pals where messages sent can be very brief and to the point with a limited vocabulary. Ask students to share their study strategies, and if they find a particularly helpful one, demonstrate it to the whole class. A number of Charlann Simon's recommendations have been included here. Perhaps the most important ones for the language teacher are to make the language seem 'doable' by providing the supports necessary, and by respecting the students' wishes – such as calling on them only when they volunteer (Simon 2000).

It is important for dyslexic students to be given every encouragement and to be reassured that success, however limited, *is* possible. However, it must be acknowledged that dyslexic students have to work harder than others in order to achieve success. Even assuming that all the appropriate strategies are in place and that the classroom is generally 'dyslexia friendly', there may be occasions, even in the most inclusive of environments, where dyslexic students and their parents may decide that what can be achieved through inclusion in foreign language learning through endless hours of additional study is simply not worth the struggle. Pressure to succeed in other subjects which the student hopes to pursue at university level for example may be more important and considered to be more of a priority than a modern foreign language which may have proved a tortuous exercise. The question then is whether the dyslexic student should aim to achieve a modified target or abandon foreign language learning altogether. Given that many dyslexic adults have regretted their loss of foreign language learning opportunity, in the days when it was 'all or nothing', it may be worthwhile considering the other options available today.

The importance of reconciling students' learning needs with their entitlement to access to foreign language learning is stressed in previous work by McColl (2000). Research carried out with American students suggested that by reducing the amount of content to be covered, and by teaching the remainder in a highly structured way, dyslexic students were able to achieve a reasonable standard of work (Downey and Snyder 1999). It may be, therefore, that some of the alternative forms of certification currently available in the UK could offer a more amenable pathway to some dyslexic students. In Scotland, for example, the new Higher framework offers students the possibility of studying for individual units which are internally assessed instead of a full course with external certification (individual units have a value which contributes towards an overall Scottish Group Award).

The situation elsewhere in the UK is more complex, but a number of examining boards now offer alternative syllabi leading to some sort of Certificate of Achievement. These offer the possibility of more flexible provision organised in graduated steps which might be easier for dyslexic students to negotiate, while at the same time allowing them to claim recognition for what they have been able to achieve. For schools, modular arrangements provide an alternative means of ensuring that as many dyslexic students as possible can receive their entitlement to the full curriculum, including a successful language learning experience.

Decisions about modified courses or total withdrawal can be taken only after discussion with all involved, and the repercussions such as the difficulty of trying to 'pick up' the language again later should be fully discussed with the student. What is most important is that the foreign language learning experience should not be allowed to go on to the point where the student finds the subject or the whole school experience intolerable, and where the student's disaffection spills over into other areas of the curriculum. Dyslexic students should feel that their difficulties are understood, their efforts appreciated and that every effort has been made to meet their needs.

As speakers at the BDA's 1999 First International Multilingual Conference made clear, we have moved beyond the question of entitlement. It is now generally accepted that dyslexic students are entitled to be included in foreign language learning. The question now is one of access to the curriculum. Equality of opportunity is not enough. We must strive for equality of outcome. This can be achieved by the removal of barriers to learning, and by the promotion of understanding of the effort required by both staff and students. The question of curricular access is not just important for students and their teachers, but should be seen as a whole-school issue and a challenge for the whole community. The resolution to the challenges presented lies in a collaborative venture where all parties – management, modern language teachers, support for learning staff, assistants, parents and the students themselves – can all work together and educate one another so that barriers can be removed, and foreign language learning can be a worthwhile experience for all.

Resources

Language Master
Scottish Learning Products, Greenacres, Highfield Road, Scone, Perth PH2 6BR.
Miniflashcard Language Games
MLG Publishing, PO Box 1526, Hanwell, London W7 1ND.
Stile
LDA, Duke Street, Wisbech, Cambs. PE13 2AE.

References

Crombie, M. A. (1997a) 'The effects of specific learning difficulties (dyslexia) on the learning of a foreign language in school', *Dyslexia* 3, 27–47.

Crombie, M. (1997b) *Specific Learning Difficulties: Dyslexia – A Teachers' Guide,* 2nd edn. Belford: Ann Arbor Publishers.

Crombie, M. A. (2000) 'Dyslexia and the learning of a foreign language in school: where are we going?', *Dyslexia* 6, 112–23.

Downey, D. and Synder, L. (1999) 'College students with dyslexia: persistent linguistic deficits and foreign learning'. Paper presented at the First British Dyslexia Association International Conference on Multilingualism and Dyslexia, Manchester.

Ganschow, L., Schneider, E. and Evers, T. (2000) 'Difficulties of English as a foreign language (EFL) for students with language-learning disabilities (dyslexia)', in Peer, L. and Reid, G. (eds) *Multilingualism, Literacy and Dyslexia: A Challenge for Educators.* 182–91. London: David Fulton Publishers.

Johnstone, R. (1999) 'Modern Foreign Languages', in Bryce, T. G. K. and Humes, W. M. (eds), *Scottish Education,* 527–30. Edinburgh: Edinburgh University Press.

McColl, H. (2000) *Modern Languages for All.* London: David Fulton Publishers.

Schneider, E. (1999) *Multisensory Structured Metacognitive Instruction: An approach to teaching a foreign language to at-risk students.* Frankfurt: Peter Lang.

Scottish Office Education Department (1993) *Modern European Languages 5–14, National Guidelines.* Edinburgh: SOED.

Simon, C. S. (2000) 'Dyslexia and foreign language learning: a personal experience', *Annals of Dyslexia* 50,

Sparks, R. and Ganschow, L. (1993) 'The effects of multisensory structured language instruction on native language and foreign language aptitude skills of at-risk high school foreign language learners: a replication and follow-up study', *Annals of Dyslexia* 43, 194–216.

Sparks, R., Ganschow, L. and Pohlman, J. (1989) 'Linguistic coding deficits in foreign language learners', *Annals of Dyslexia* 39, 179–95.

CHAPTER 8

Dyslexia and English

Elizabeth Turner

This chapter:

- examines the difficulties experienced by dyslexic students in English
- discusses different types of reading literature
- highlights the use of oracy for written language, handwriting and expressive writing
- discusses spelling strategies
- shows how the English teacher can support dyslexic students in the mainstream classroom.

Aims

This chapter is concerned with supporting dyslexic students in the mainstream English classroom. It aims to explain what problems these students present to their English teacher and how their difficulties may best be ameliorated and strengths utilised. It notes that the approaches, which succeed for dyslexic students, are frequently the best for all students in the class. There need not be a massive increase in the English teacher's workload. Teaching dyslexic students may make the teacher think harder about the teaching approach. Good dyslexic teaching practice is good teaching practice.

Introduction

The ability to communicate via the written word is traditionally an area of difficulty for dyslexic learners and never is this more apparent and exposed than in the English classroom. The very word 'English' has associations for the dyslexic student. It demands and expects accuracy in reading, writing and spelling and examines a competence in written language skills. Some dyslexic learners, especially at the secondary phase, have emotional hang-ups about the curriculum term 'English' precisely because of these connotations and this can be compounded when there has been an accumulated history of struggles and difficulties in acquiring basic literacy skills at Key Stages 1 and 2. Singleton (1992) defines dyslexia very simply as an unexpected difficulty in acquiring literacy skills: Thomson and Watkins (1990) definition of dyslexia emphasises the incongruity, which can frequently exist between written language skills and intellectual ability.

Developmental dyslexia is a severe difficulty with the written form of the language independent of intellectual, cultural and emotional causation. It is characterised by the reader's reading, writing and spelling attainments being well below the level expected based on intelligence and chronological age. The difficulty is a cognitive one, affecting those language skills associated with the written form . . .

(Thomson and Watkins, 1990: 3)

When considering how to support the dyslexic student in the English classroom it is first necessary to look at the curriculum term 'English' and see what the components are and then examine how these correspond to strengths and weaknesses in the dyslexic profile.

Reading

For the public at large, the term Dyslexia is usually restricted to reading difficulties.

(West 1991: 79)

There is a popular misconception amongst lay people that dyslexia simply means a problem with reading. There are of course some dyslexic people, appearing on the severe end of the dyslexia continuum, who do have significant problems with reading which can last a lifetime. What is also important to remember is that there are many others who can read, who have mastered the mechanics of reading and who present themselves as confident and fluent readers in the classroom. There are others who read, but read slowly, decoding word for word, 'barking at print', and frequently losing meaning in the process. Payne and Turner (1999) suggest that fluent and experienced readers adapt their style of reading to suit their purpose in reading. This is a fundamental issue and should be taught explicitly. Do not assume or presume that students 'know' what style of reading to use for a given task. For efficiency and effectiveness, reading is adapted according to the need and the purpose of the task. Thus the reading for examination questions and instructions is detailed; the reading for gleaning facts, specific information and reference is scanning; the reading for getting a general overview or impression is skimming and the reading of novels for enjoyment is simply pleasurable and a combination of all three. Supporting students means teaching them exactly what type of reading to use and giving them practice in that skill. English in secondary schools is geared to the eventual climax of sitting GCSE examinations in Language and Literature. GCSE Language is a highly sought after and well-regarded certificate, valued and desired by employers, colleges and universities alike. It is important that dyslexic students do not waste precious time and effort in decoding words in an inappropriate manner when preparing for these important examinations.

Literature

The study of English Literature is an area, which deserves special consideration. Many dyslexic students derive great enjoyment from studying the great literary works, and accessing age and ability appropriate literature. It needs careful and sensitive handling by the teacher to maximise the inclusion of dyslexic pupils who may not have a wealth of reading experience behind them. Teaching the language of Literature is important. At the start of GCSE there is a whole range of vocabulary associated with Literature that needs to be taught explicitly. All students in a class need this type of support but especially dyslexic students. Poetry, novels, prose can be tackled with greater confidence when students are armed with this knowledge about Literature. The use of ICT, video and cover-to-cover audiotapes also helps to support the dyslexic learner and to ease the bulk of reading which may be required. They are not short cuts or easy options because a student cannot be bothered to read something, but a real and worthwhile alternative and enrichment allowing inclusion, in its fullest sense, to be accessed. Other strategies such as pointing out underlying themes, encouraging the use of mind maps to plan and see the overview and interrelationships of characters are support techniques that the English teacher can use, remembering that these also help and support all students in the group.

Oracy

As explained by Jayne Pughe (*BDA Handbook 2001*), the use of oracy as a preparation for written literature tasks cannot be overemphasised. This is where many dyslexic learners have great strengths, which should be utilised to their advantage. In Literature exploration of character, plot, theme and atmosphere are essential skills. Dyslexic students are able to do this more successfully if they have been allowed to discuss their ideas and contribute both in an informal and formal situation. Drama activities develop empathy and a deeper moral understanding of a piece of literature. Tasks are numerous and can lend themselves to any text. Even less confident students gain from watching others or having an instrumental role in the planning of a piece. Oral planning is beneficial for many reasons. Students are willing to invest time and energy into planning a task because they are talking and this does not threaten their confidence as writing might. As they have invested in their planning and received positive feedback from the teacher and peers they feel empowered and a sense of ownership of the work (Pughe 2001).

Spelling

Spelling for dyslexic students tends to be a difficulty, which carries on in many cases for life, and certainly long after early reading difficulties have been ameliorated and addressed.

> Although reading has always been given more prominence than spelling in the early days at school, spelling in fact poses the greater problem for dyslexic children, and this difficulty can continue long after the reading difficulty has been greatly improved. Poor spelling is usually a lifetime's embarrassment.
>
> (Pollock and Waller 1994: 39)

From his research, Miles (1993) supports the view that dyslexic children often have greater difficulties with spelling than with reading and Thomson's (1984) research also suggests that many dyslexic children, particularly the more intelligent ones, have often overcome earlier reading problems but spelling still remains a serious concern. This is because spelling and reading although interrelated involve quite different skills. Reading is a decoding skill where a pupil can be helped by clues to work out the word to be read. Spelling on the other hand is an encoding process, which involves the total recall of words, which then have to be reproduced accurately from memory. The skills a competent speller requires are good visual recall of words involving accurate mental imagery, good auditory discrimination and an awareness of sound symbol correspondence. Frith (1981) indicates that spelling skills are directly related to the student's metalinguistic awareness – that is the acquisition of language skills in relation to the development of language, to talk about language. This has important implications for classroom English teaching. Improvements and accuracy in spelling can be helped by explicitly teaching the reasons why words are spelt the way they are to all students – dyslexic and non-dyslexic. Spelling then becomes more predictable and logical when dyslexic students have an understanding of how letters relate to each other and why. Instead of trying to grasp a whole word image, which relies on weak sequential memory, the student armed with this knowledge, can work out what is the most probable way to spell a word and use their higher level thinking skills to help them. Students therefore need to have knowledge about Language. They need to know what consonants and vowels are, and their functions, the use of short vowels and how they affect letters following them, the work of long vowels, the different ways of spelling a sound and the part that syllables play in both reading and writing. Goswami (1991) notes that

> Children's knowledge about the linguistic structure of the syllable plays an important part in what they learn about spelling patterns.

Knowing about and using diacritical marks helps illustrate spelling/sound differences between long and short vowels, which is crucial when teaching spelling.

Therefore, for competence in spelling, students need to have an awareness of alphabetical knowledge, the importance of vowels and their sounds, rhyming ability, phonemic awareness, a knowledge of segmentation, clear articulation, legible cursive script and good visual brain imagery. These skills however, which are necessary for spelling, are the ones which tend to be areas of weakness in a dyslexic profile, hence the spelling difficulties which are apparent in so many dyslexic's written work. Unfortunately because of the age we live in, parents, teachers, employers and the students themselves regard spelling weakness as a major handicap at the secondary level and tangible evidence of a learning difficulty. This spelling weakness can, especially when it is unexpected, result in work being undervalued and restrictive to the student's spontaneous outflow. Difficulty in spelling as Moseley (1990) points out is manifested both in what is written and what is not written for fear of error.

At secondary level the dyslexic student may benefit from the following strategies:

1. If the student is strongly visual then some sort of association or 'peg' is useful to utilise the strength of the right hemispherical mode of thinking which is often a dyslexic strength. Mnemonics are a good technique to employ especially if students devise their own – the more personal and rude the mnemonic the more likely it is to stay in memory and the personal lexicon.
2. The student should also use associative clues looking at the visual structure of words. Work that involves word derivations, roots of words, prefixes, suffixes are useful tools to support spelling. The use of a highlighter is strongly recommended to help spelling. Often a student 'knows' how to spell accurately part of a word and can easily identify the section of letters or letter that is causing confusion or difficulty. Highlighting that area and learning using visual clues does help to reduce the overload on memory. There is no point in learning what the student already can spell accurately. Visual inspection using the 'look–say–cover–say–write–say–check' routine is a useful one to encourage. Other helpful techniques are SOS (Simultaneous Oral Spelling) and NLP (Neurolinguistic programming).
3. Moseleys ACE (Aurally Coded Dictionary 1995) gives many dyslexic learners access to a spelling dictionary through aural means and allows them independence and freedom in finding words at speed. This can be easily taught in three lessons and from personal experience in teaching how to use this dictionary, students do grasp it quickly and gain success in finding words without the frustrations that a conventional dictionary can bring.

In a survey of research on ways to improve spelling Moseley (1990) suggests there are many ways to teach spelling but the most successful are the ones that combine a number of features. Thomson and Watkins (1990) in their *Dyslexia: A Teaching Handbook* support the teaching of spelling principles and rules to dyslexic pupils.

> Spelling rules are a collection of short sentences that aim to give children a logical strategy which, when mastered and applied, allows them to spell hundreds of words. The advantages are that they allow the dyslexic to apply logic. (p. 125)

They point out that these principles give a simple structure and logical approach to building words, which is not reliant on rote learning and uses the strengths of good reasoning skills, which many dyslexic people possess. However a word of caution, rules or principles must not be learned in isolation as memorised sentences – they must be used and rooted firmly in habit, understood and transferred to all written work across the curriculum.

The English mainstream teacher can best support dyslexic students in the classroom by encouraging and accepting logical spelling, if accuracy is not possible. They can support by not covering a student's written work with red corrections identifying each and every spelling error. (If a student is weak at spelling, they already lack confidence in personal spelling ability and do not need to be further demoralised by having red marks or 'sp' scrawled all over work.) Spelling is an emotive issue. Marking, whenever and wherever possible, should be within a framework of a whole-school policy on spelling which takes account of dyslexic difficulties and gives consistency of expectations. The dyslexic student then has a structure within which to operate.

Handwriting

Dyslexic individuals can find the actual task of writing itself difficult. This may be due to a variety of reasons which include poor writing style, difficulty with gross and/or fine motor control and a difficulty with the actual formation and orientation of letters. Weak spelling can also exacerbate the problem. If the work is illegible then the spelling errors cannot be identified and corrected. Correct letter production is important in the secondary school for examinations and confidence. The student does not enjoy having work regarded as immature and not reflective of their emerging adolescent self-image. A weak and illegible script provides evidence to parents, teachers, peers and employers that there is a problem and can in some instances give a wrong impression of the student's innate ability. If the student is having significant problems with legibility then clearly written work should be accepted and submitted in word-processed form. At university/college all work has to be submitted word-processed. The dyslexic student can sit GCSE examinations using a word processor if appropriate, if special arrangements are applied for and permission granted by the relevant examination board.

Written work

Some dyslexic students may have such significant difficulties with written work that the work they produce has to be presented in alternative forms. With the increase in technological aids, audio visual equipment, the use of word processors, speech recognition, text help with reading and voice centres which allow 'voice to text', the student really does have a variety of these aids to choose from. This should be encouraged and alternative methods of presenting work, that allow the innate ability of the student to shine through, accepted.

GCSE Language papers usually require students to write essays, comprehend what they have written and generally show on paper, their knowledge about Language. To support this in the classroom it is necessary to give all students the tools of the trade. It would be no good teaching somebody the rudiments of joinery if there was no explanation of the terminology or identification of tools and what they are used for. Similarly, it is no good telling students to write in sentences or paragraphs if they have no idea what one actually is! A technique that benefits all students in a class is to draw the concept. For example when teaching about paragraphs and their use, the fundamental concept of what a paragraph is can be explicitly taught through a drawing. (A picture, as the old song goes can paint a thousand words.)

Students can then see the shape of a paragraph, which allows them to understand exactly what a paragraph is. With this in mind, it is unproductive telling a student to use punctuation in sentences if the student does not know what a sentence is. They may be able to tell you that sentences start with a capital letter and end with a full stop, but if they have no idea of what a sentence is, there will be full stops and capital letters sprinkled at random. It is therefore worthwhile teaching in a structured, cumulative way, building up the concepts of words, sentences, paragraphs to illustrate how they interrelate and are dependent on each other. Teachers should also include parts of speech and figures of speech so that students know how to play with words, use words descriptively and are adventurous with their language. For instance, dictation of notes to dyslexic students is not an effective way of imparting information. Having a photocopy of the dictated work that they then could highlight would support them; marking for content and not always for accuracy is another way. The English teacher needs to be well prepared and offer alternative ways of accessing the Literature and Language curriculum for dyslexic students using technology. For example there are some excellent CD-ROMs on English Literature and Language that operate in a multisensory manner and are ideal ways to support the English curriculum.

Breaking work down into manageable chunks so that students understand the task and giving sequences of instructions with a maximum of three will also support the dyslexic student. For example 'turn to page 22 and look at exercise 3' is enough, pause and then when everyone has done this ask them to 'look at Section A and Question 1'.

With comprehension, students have to read and understand what they have read. Many dyslexic students find this difficult because of weak short-term memory – by the time they get to the bottom of the passage, perhaps struggling with decoding certain words, the meaning is lost. A strategy, which can be employed here, is to explicitly teach how to go about answering questions. Here are some useful tips taken from practical teaching experience with severely dyslexic students. First of all answer what the question wants: if it asks for two examples give two, not one or three! This is where detailed reading comes into play. It is important that the student aurally rehearses the question and tries to give the type of answer required. Practice in this skill is good for examination comprehensions.

Secondly encourage students to 'look' as opposed to 'see' what clues can they glean from the written question paper. For example pictures, diagrams, graphics, captions, headlines, sub-headings – can all give an impression of what the passage is about. It is rather like being a detective – trying to piece together without reading lengthy passages of print. Finally read the questions first and ask what type of answer is being sought. Many comprehension passages, especially the ones which have recently been part of the SATS in English, do have numbered lines and direct students in their questions, to those lines to look for answers. Dyslexic students need to be taught how to do this explicitly and given practice in this skill before examinations are sat.

Planning and drafting

These skills must also be explicitly taught to GCSE students. Scaffolding is an excellent technique to use. In scaffolding the teacher and learners work together on a task several times and in different situations. It is a real task and initially the teacher does most of the planning and the more difficult parts with the students helping. The teacher reveals what they are all doing and why – the explicit element. The students gradually practise and take over more and more as they become more proficient and confident. The importance of this approach is that the teacher not only shows by action how to do a task but also reveals the thinking process, which goes with it. Because this is a partnership, the task is always completely successful. As Pughe (2001) points out, modelling good practice is a useful exercise. Looking at successful pieces of coursework from a previous year on a different text and deciding what each paragraph consists of, can be a starting point. Then the class can produce a group scaffold for their own text.

Another extremely useful technique is to look at examination style questions and plan answers for homework on a regular basis. Sharing these plans reinforces the skill for those who are successful but again provides extra modelling for those, such as dyslexic students, who are still developing their ability to plan.

Finding quotations that reinforce certain points is another crucial part of the planning process. This can be an extremely daunting task and therefore when planning and preparing coursework group 'searches' can eliminate a great deal of stress. Make sure that students look for a number of alternatives for each point and encourage debate about who has the stronger quotation. This will ensure that students develop an interest in dissecting Literature and Language and it fosters the idea that many alternative interpretations are valid in this subject area.

Drafting is always a difficult area to approach especially when dyslexic students have spent a long time writing the first draft. The use of a word processor is ideal here as the dyslexic student can revisit, quickly and efficiently, to improve spelling and does not have to worry about legibility. Making sure that students are aware of the marking criteria for both Language and Literature is a helpful stimulus for redrafting – many dyslexic learners are dissatisfied with their own work and knowing what they are being marked for does help to encourage them upwards and onwards. By offering the criteria in more concrete and accessible terms it is possible to help students look at their work and the work of their peers in order to set achievable and relevant targets for improvements (Pughe 2001).

Conclusion

Inclusion means being included, being part of and having access to. Inclusion for dyslexic students in the English mainstream classroom can be achieved by using a variety of strategies to support their learning. This chapter has emphasised the importance of these strategies in Reading, Writing, Spelling, Handwriting, Language and Literature. It has shown that explicit teaching is required to support dyslexic students so that they can maximise their innate learning potential and access the English curriculum. It has recommended the use and support of technological aids, word processors, text to word, word to text recognition, to support dyslexic students. It has looked at the components of the curriculum term 'English' and how these components are compatible with the strengths and weaknesses of a dyslexic profile. Finally, this chapter has stressed that the approaches necessary to support dyslexic students in the English classroom are appropriate to use for all students. *Good dyslexic teaching practice is good teaching practice.*

References

Frith, U. (1981) *Cognitive Processes in Spelling.* London: Academic Press.

Goswami, U. (1991) 'Recent work on reading and spelling development', in Snowling, M. and Thomson, M. (eds) *Dyslexia, Integrating Theory and Practice.* London: Whurr Publishers.

Miles, T. R. (1993) *Dyslexia, the Pattern of Difficulties.* London: Whurr Publishers.

Miles, T. R. and Miles, E. (1983) *Help for Dyslexic Children.* London: Routledge.

Moseley, D (1990) 'Suggestions for helping children with spelling problems', in Pumfrey, P. D. and Elliott, C. D. (eds) *Children's Difficulties in Reading, Spelling, and Writing.* London: The Falmer Press.

Moseley, D. (1995) *ACE Spelling Dictionary,* 7th edn. Wisbech: LDA.

Payne, T and Turner, E. (1999) *Dyslexia, A Parents' and Teachers' Guide.* USA: Multilingual Matters Ltd.

Pollock, J. and Waller, E. (1994) *Day to Day Dyslexia in the Classroom.* London: Routledge.

Pughe, J. (2001) 'Teaching literature to dyslexic students', *BDA Handbook 2001.* Reading: BDA.

Singleton, C. (1992) 'The patient teacher', in *Special Children,* September.

Thomson, M. E. and Watkins, E. J. (1990) *Dyslexia: A Teaching Handbook.* Whurr Publishers.

Thomson, M. E. (1984) *Developmental Dyslexia. Its Nature, Assessment and Remediation.* London: Edward Arnold. (3rd edn, 1990, London: Whurr Publishers.)

West, T. G. (1991) *In the Mind's Eye.* Buffalo, NY: Promenentheus Books.

CHAPTER 9

Dyslexia and History

Richard Dargie

This chapter:

- offers practical advice to History teachers in secondary school
- examines assessment in history
- provides strategies for pupils and teachers to make history accessible to all
- provides a positive and inclusive view of the subject of history in schools.

This chapter begins by considering the particular challenges which the study of history presents for the dyslexic learner in the secondary classroom. Successful learning in history requires confidence and dexterity in talking, reading, writing and thinking. These depend to a considerable degree upon the learner's ability to recall complex narrative and explanatory sequences of information, and to comprehend, sort, classify, analyse and present material which may be encoded in archaic and certainly unfamiliar linguistic registers. The chapter offers practical advice to secondary teachers of history who wish to maximise the attainment of dyslexic learners in terms of:

- talking, listening and thinking in history;
- reading and writing in history;
- and assessment of dyslexic learners in history.

Dyslexia remains a contested and controversial term in the field of educational observation and research. However, most currently authoritative definitions of dyslexia generally agree that dyslexic learners tend to present a number of commonly identifiable symptoms (Reid 1999: 2–3, Poustie *et al.* 1997: 16–26). These include :

- persistent difficulties in reading which hamper the acquisition of fluency;
- the inability to acquire proficiency and confidence in writing and spelling;
- weak or erratic skills in processing textual information;
- difficulties in retaining and recalling information from memory;
- low self-estimation of ability and potential attainment.

History therefore presents a considerable challenge to the dyslexic learner and his/her teacher, for as Burston (1963: 41) noted, 'in History teaching we are dependent to a quite exceptional degree on ordinary language as our medium of communication. History, more than any other school subject, depends upon literacy in its pupils as a prerequisite to success, and increased literacy is perhaps its most important by-product.' In order to talk and think effectively in history, pupils must acquire and develop the ability to understand and utilise the rich, conceptual vocabulary that underpins the subject.

In order to read effectively in history, learners must be able to decode, contextualise and analyse a range of types of text such as diaries, letters, recorded oral testimony, press journalism, posters, leaflets, official documentation, e.g. Acts of Parliament, government reports. Each textual genre comes with its own obstacles to comprehension such as format and convention, and may be couched in an alien or archaic linguistic register. Moreover, history courses often additionally require learners to be comfortable with this variety of textual types across a range of chronological and cultural contexts. Thus an S3 (Year 10) pupil on the Scottish Standard Grade History course might be required to make sense of primary sources as diverse as a letter written by a tenant farmer in the eighteenth century Scottish Highlands in Term 1, a telegraphic communication sent in 1914 from the British Admiralty to Kaiser Wilhelm's Secretariat in Berlin in Term 2, and a rhetorical speech by Lenin, Goebbels or Ghandi in Term 3. Other pupils may be following mediaeval and early modern syllabus options which pose additional linguistic problems for the reader. A further complexity for the dyslexic history pupil lies in the fact that historical debate relies in large part upon historiographical interpretations and evaluations of abstract ideas as well as upon understandings of the different values and assumptions held by people in the past (Hoodless 1998: 5).

In order to write effectively in history, pupils must be able to select, organise and shape discursive text in order to address a specific argument or issue. Assessment in history is commonly undertaken through the medium of lengthy, if not extended, pieces of writing. Thus the Extended Response is a key instrument of assessment even for lower ability candidates following the Scottish Intermediate Two syllabus. Essay writing is the predominant assessment vehicle in history at Higher and A level. History teachers have frequently been discouraged by the apparent inability of lower attainers to make progress in producing pieces of explanatory and/or discursive writing (Counsell 1997: 7), leading many to question whether such learners should pursue the study of the subject at all.

Prima facie it would seem that history is an unsuitable field of study for dyslexic adolescents given the potentially unfortunate mapping between the characteristics of the dyslexic learner and the demands of the subject discipline, contemporary concern for curricular inclusion notwithstanding. Indeed, until quite recently, professional discussion about the value of history for weaker learners was dominated by a pessimistic 'deficit model' which prescribed very limited goals for such learners in the subject (Cunnah, 2000: 113–17). In recent years however a radically more positive and inclusive view of the power of history as an educational vehicle has evolved, as History teachers have perhaps been readier to look beyond the traditional confines of the subject, and have adopted perspectives and practices gleaned from colleagues in more generic fields such as cross-curricular literacy. Current approaches stress the value, the relevance and the accessibility of history for all pupils including those who have learning difficulties such as dyslexia. Effective teachers of history also now accept more readily the need to think comprehensively and strategically (SCCC 1996, Reid 1999: 140) about the range of preferred learning styles implicit in any class of History pupils, and to adopt teaching approaches which can enable all pupils 'to make progress in history if taught in an appropriate manner' (Cunnah, 2000: 121–2).

Indeed the very dependence in history upon literacy which was formerly seen as a barrier to the progress of lower attaining pupils, is now heralded as the key benefit which the subject can offer to pupils seeking to address their learning needs. Effective history teaching which seeks to motivate all pupils via a wide repertoire of language-based approaches and activities can also empower dyslexic pupils by increasing their communication and thinking skills: 'words, for both teachers and pupils, are the most potentially powerful tools we have' (Husbands 1996: 97).

Talking, listening and thinking in History

All learners, and dyslexic learners in particular, need opportunities to talk extensively in the History classroom. This can allow learners to engage in 'print-free' debate and frequently to capitalise upon their strengths in oral argument and exposition of narrative with consequent benefit to their self-estimation of their ability in the subject.

Talking through an issue can help pupils to rehearse the separate components within an 'argued case', a strategy of benefit to dyslexic learners who may have difficulty in sequencing information. Contributing successfully to a discussion exercise, a class debate or a group presentation can have positive consequences for the dyslexic learner's self-esteem as well as helping him/her identify elements of a preferred learning style. Practice in discursive talking also clearly has a direct impact upon the pupil's ability to question, infer, deduce, propose, estimate, guess, judge – that is, to think.

Learning to talk well about history is a fundamental corollary of learning to read, write and think well in the subject. History exercises which are effective in generating talk in S1 and S2 (Year 8 and 9) classes include:

- Group investigations of photographs of typified families between 1880 and 1960 which require pupils to pool their collective knowledge of British social history in order to identify the key features of the family's background. Exercises of this kind utilise the latent historical knowledge of children who may be visually literate and articulate, yet reticent to transfer their knowledge into written form. Typically this exercise provokes a great deal of discussion and encourages pupils to generate their own elaborate hypotheses: 'I think this is a working class family because there aren't many photographs of them before 1930 and most working people were too poor then to waste money on having their picture taken.' Just as usefully, it prompts pupils to formulate their own sequences of questions: 'Did women do their hair like that during World War 1 or World War 2? Is that an army truck she's driving? That looks like wings on the badge – is it an RAF truck maybe?'

- Card-matching games which can be used to engage reluctant readers with substantial amounts of historical content, acting as an alternative to teacher-led transmission of content. Groups are given a set of cards bearing key dates in a historical period and required to match them to the correct description. This requires the participants to draw upon their collective recall and understanding of the topic. The clue cards can be structured so as to encourage pupils to draw appropriate inferences and conclusions from the given historical material. This exercise can be used to establish the basic chronology and/or sequence of the topic and can provide a helpful reference point or memory trigger for dyslexic learners in subsequent lessons.

- Card puzzles and games designed to enhance pupil familiarity with key historical vocabulary and concepts from a given topic. In one variant, groups of six S1/S2 pupils play a version of 'Call my Bluff' to establish the true meaning of unfamiliar words relating to a study of the church in mediaeval Europe. In another, Higher Level pupils studying the Cold War are required to provide both American and Soviet definitions for ambiguous period terms such as 'nuclear deterrence', 'imperialism' or 'communism'. In another, S4 pupils studying the reasons behind Hitler's rise to power play a simplistic form of poker which requires them to collect a flush hand of social, political or economic reasons.

- A simple board game replicates the discipline, financial hardship and physical pain suffered by workers in a textile factory circa 1800. S2 players begin the week with a full wage and a full set of limbs displayed upon graphic cards. Landing on chance squares requires the pupil to read out his fate and surrender cash and/or relinquish a limb. Subsequent testing has revealed a high internalisation of specialised period vocabulary and a clear understanding of key concepts by all participating pupils.

- Paired homework with an emphasis upon pupils having to check that their partner can readily explain topic vocabulary and concepts such as change, cause, etc. This was helpful in encouraging pupils to incorporate unfamiliar historical vocabulary within their own subsequent class talking and writing.
- Examining well-selected examples of contradictory primary sources and/or secondary interpretations can also be an activity accessible to the student with dyslexia. One example for S1 and S2 pupils might be to contrast the facts about Macbeth known to modern historians with the key elements of the fictional representation offered by Shakespeare (Dargie 1995: 36).
- Progressive pupil participation in structured role play and limited pieces of semi-dramatisation can be used to promote thinking skills (Goalen 1995).
- Ensuring that pupil comprehension of historical material is repeatedly tested by extracting extended oral responses to sequences of persistent teacher questioning.
- Listening skills in history can be enhanced by providing dyslexic pupils with topic content in audio cassette form for individual use in Walkman-type players. Many excellent audio resources exist for most history courses, particularly those broadcast by the BBC. Admittedly, less than 30 per cent of the school age population have auditory learning strengths (Milgram *et al.* 1993: 17) and fewer teachers now use audio resources for whole-class purposes. Nevertheless they can still be valuable in helping individual learners rehearse topic vocabulary before a lesson, or for reinforcement purposes.

Several of the activities above are particularly effective for dyslexic learners because they involve the pupil almost immediately in decision-making and problem-solving processes without the need to read lengthy print instructions (Reid 1999: 130).

Reading in History

In order to ensure that all pupils have the opportunity to develop into successful readers of history, subject departments need to plan a reading strategy which seeks to create 'more self-aware' readers who understand the purpose of their reading and who appreciate how and why the text in front of them is shaped in the way that it is. An effective reading strategy in history might include features such as:

- Consistent teacher pre-checking of text material and calculation of reading age to ensure pupils encounter historical text in a planned, progressive way.
- A focus upon concept vocabulary and upon discursive connectives which develop historical argument.
- The selective use of word-processing functions such as emboldening and/or increasing point size to highlight the way historical text works.
- The planned reading of material as homework to increase pupil familiarity with the demands of the text using scissors and highlighter pens to analyse how different kinds of historical text are constructed.
- Highlighting photocopied text to given criteria, e.g. in search of key phrases.

- Persistent teacher questioning to accompany pupil reading to check comprehension. This is particularly important when working with dyslexic readers who may only have partially automatised the decoding of print, and who may not yet be self generating questions as they read.
- Teacher awareness of the different preferred reading styles of pupils, and of the interactive nature of effective reading.
- Teacher awareness of the difficulties posed by 'weasel words' in history such as class, state, party, church, which have an abstract historical usage in addition to their more familiar common concrete meaning.
- Teacher alertness to the difficulties posed by subject-specific conventions such as c. for circa, IV for fourth, C. for century.
- Teacher awareness of the need to structure their own text to meet the needs of different learners, e.g. by avoiding long, multi-clausal sentences, avoiding over use of passive voice constructions; planning ways of explaining unfamiliar vocabulary and ideas, e.g. word boxes and marginal scaffolding, keeping text concrete where appropriate rather than abstract, minimising the use of metaphorical language, being alert to the range of tenses used in history to describe actions in the past.

Writing in History

Recent years have seen an increased awareness among history practitioners of the technical reasons for difficulties encountered by dyslexic and other weaker writers, a development in large part due to the work of Christine Counsell (1997). Thinking about how learners write in history, and encouraging them to write in an extended manner, lies at the heart of helping dyslexic learners address their needs, for as the British Dyslexia Association has noted, the condition is particularly related to mastering written language (Reid 1999: 2). Writing by dyslexic pupils frequently exhibits aspects of the following organisational symptoms (Counsell 1997):

- difficulty in appreciating the relative importance and relevance of information/ideas;
- difficulty in sorting and arranging historical information into an appropriate textual format;
- difficulty in distinguishing between general and particular pieces of evidence and in judging their relative importance;
- the possession of a relatively restricted vocabulary of discourse with relatively few temporal and/or causal connectives at their disposal.

Strategies to address these difficulties include:

- graphic sorting and classifying methods to help pupils organise and prioritise historical material such as keyword concept maps, spider diagrams, continuum diagrams;
- Chinese Squares, ripple diagrams, Venn diagrams, etc.;
- organisational frames for note-taking and for planning, sorting and arranging material for inclusion in written text;
- differentiated writing frames which provide the learner with suggested paragraph openings, sentence stems and suitable connectives;
- card layout games to strengthen pupil ability to assess the relative relevance of material to a specific historical question such as 'Why did the Scots win the Battle of Bannockburn in 1314 ?';

- text reconstruction exercises where pupils are given the constituent sentences of an essay printed on separate strips of paper and are required to reconstruct the whole. This is a particularly useful exercise for helping weaker writers develop an appreciation of how successful paragraphs are constructed and how different kinds of paragraph such as introductions and conclusions have different functions within a piece of writing. Presented as a puzzle, it helps solve the motivational difficulties which dyslexic pupils can frequently present when required to undertake critical textual analysis;
- displaying appropriate paragraph and sentence stems, and similar prompts and cues, on the classroom wall or board;
- providing pupils with good and bad models of pupil performance in different kinds of writing task and getting pupils to identify their strengths and weaknesses;
- organising peer-help in planning and drafting different kinds of written work;
- providing schematic support to alert pupils to possible difficulties when introducing them to unfamiliar historical writing styles such as academic, journalistic, bureaucratic, reminiscent;
- setting clear, high expectations of technical accuracy as regards structure, grammar, punctuation and spelling in finished work while providing support by explaining demands precisely, planning-in sufficient time for drafting and amendment processes;
- displaying hints about common errors, e.g. its/it's, on classroom walls, judiciously alerting dyslexic learners to errors and either offering correct alternatives or the reference means to establish these;
- planning a writing in history strategy for all pupils in the department from S1 to S6 which ensures pupils acquire practice in a range of writing tasks, and in which pupils gradually develop their own autonomy as planners, organisers and presenters of historical material.

Implications for assessment in History

Internal school-based assessment in History should take account of the cognitive and emotional difficulties which the dyslexic pupil can face when being tested. One model adopted by a school in Kincardineshire for its S1 (Year 8) History pupils was designed to provide a range of assessment activities in order to structure the amount of reading and writing required of pupils in a suitably progressive way. The test consisted of six short tasks which focused upon the previous month's work on the topic of The Early People of Scotland. As this was the first History test experienced by these Term 1 'new arrivals' in the secondary school, bolstering the self-esteem of less confident learners was a key principle underlying the design of the test. Learners who had been previously identified by primary colleagues as experiencing difficulties in reading, writing and information processing were provided with a differentiated degree of support in three of the activities.

The first section of the test consisted of four relatively simple tasks which required little writing and which were intended to remind pupils of the work covered throughout the unit:

- Completing a simple cloze passage with provided answer box which clued up the unit content featured in the rest of the test.
- Matching a table of names to pictures of specific artefacts used by Early People.
- Listing things from the prehistoric period found by archaeologists in the school's local area. The test papers used by dyslexic learners contained a memory trigger in the form of a copy of the local map used by the teacher in the lesson on this aspect of the topic.

- Completing five sentence stems such as 'We know the Skara Brae people in Orkney were shepherds because . . . . . .'. This fourth exercise required pupils to apply recalled subject knowledge to complete the sentence appropriately. However, three of the five sentence conclusions had been clued up by triggers in the first exercise to provide assistance for pupils with memory difficulties. Line indicators were used in the test paper to encourage pupils to write as fully as possible. This fourth task also acted as a bridge from the deliberately simple initial tasks requiring a short response to the second section of the test which consisted of two extended writing activities.
- Writing a brief paragraph about the work of archaeologists at Skara Brae. Dyslexic learners were assisted by a five stem writing frame.
- Explaining the method by which Skara Brae people built their houses. The scaffolding for dyslexic learners consisted of five thumbnail versions of textbook illustrations showing the process of building a prehistoric Skara Brae dwelling. Pupils had encountered these illustrations when working through the unit.

This test had a limited set of aims. Principal amongst these was the desire to ensure that all S1 pupils felt they had made a successful start to their secondary education in History. The mark allocation was structured to ensure that pupils recorded as positive a score as possible. Consequently the marks attained by all pupils were high and recorded across a relatively narrow band between 75 and 100 per cent. Learners with characteristics of dyslexia frequently recorded scores in excess of 85 per cent.

Although designed to examine a wider range of outcomes and skills such as historical evaluation and interpretation, further testing of S1 and S2 in this department embodied the above principles of a judicious use of confidence-boosting starter items, progression of task, scaffolding and differentiation. Thus an S2 test on the theme of Life in A Factory Town in 1840 used a set of progressively complex visual images (timegraph–line drawing–cartoon from an Early Victorian magazine) as stimuli, rather than textually based contemporary source extracts, in order to assess pupil understanding of required historical concepts such as bias and perspective. The varied range of assessment tasks deployed in this department generally mirrored the variety of teaching and learning approach encountered by pupils throughout their History course. Pupils in the department were interviewed at the end of S2 and generally characterised themselves as being 'good' or 'very good at history'. Not surprisingly, the uptake for Standard Grade certificate history in S3 and S4 was significantly above the (Scottish) national average of 34 per cent of the year cohort.

The official agencies which supervise national certificate examinations for the middle and upper school age range in History have generally adopted a range of procedures designed to assist candidates with learning difficulties such as dyslexia. Thus the Scottish Qualification Authority organises scribing, modification of exam paper print format, the provision of exam papers in audio format and time extensions for recognised poor readers and slow writers. However individual History departments need to consider a strategy for study skills and exam candidate preparation which takes the needs of dyslexic candidates into account. Elements of such a strategy might include:

- Providing systematic instruction in note-taking which encourages dyslexic learners to devise their own preferred formats of signs, symbols, word contractions and abbreviations (Coate and Simkin 1986: 12).
- Providing schematic frames to encourage extended note-taking.
- Providing dyslexic students with concise revision notes which incorporate a high degree

of information in diagrammatic, rather than prose, format. Flow charts are an especially useful way of contracting complex historical narratives, e.g. the impact of Bismarck's policies upon Prussia 1860–1890, into a manageable form.

- Providing pupils with 'Everything you need to know about......' topic sheets which incorporate all characters, dates, events, vocabulary, policies, etc., on one single A4 sheet.
- Peer-testing of pupil understanding of concepts and events by flash card games.
- Encouraging pupils to devise their own mind maps and mnemonics for historical topics.
- Encouraging pupils to use presentational software such as MS Powerpoint as an aid to organising and reducing note information.
- Providing pupils with examples of good and weak practice in study skill areas such as note-taking and getting pupils to reflect on these critically.
- Liaison with SEN staff, the school librarian and with staff in subjects such as English and Art and Design to investigate ways of reinforcing learning gains made in History in other parts of the curriculum.
- Incorporating multisensory teaching into the daily practice of the History department.

Conclusion

History can be a difficult subject for dyslexic and weaker learners. The complexity of the subject and the unfamiliarity of its terminology can be daunting. Dyslexic pupils' difficulties in handling text and ideas place an obligation upon the History teacher to re-examine his/her practice to ensure that the classroom experience in history addresses these specific needs. However, in school departments where activity and enquiry are at the heart of the learning, the study of history can be motivating, challenging and inspiring for all learners. The best provision for dyslexic learners is to be found in such departments where innovative and energetic learning and teaching are normal practice and planned as an experience for all.

References

Burston, W. H. (1963) *Principles of History Teaching*. Methuen: London.

Coate, L. and Simkin, D. (1986) *A Guide to Project Work*. Brighton: Tressell Publications.

Counsell, C. (1997) *Analytical and Discursive Writing at Key Stage 3*. London: The Historical Association.

Cunnah, W. (2000) 'History teaching, literacy and special educational needs', in Arthur, J. and Phillips, R. (2000) *Issues in History Teaching*. London: Routledge.

Dargie, R. (1995) *Scotland in the Middle Ages*. Fenwick: Pulse Publications.

Goalen, P. (1995) 'Teaching history through drama', in *Mitteilungen der Internationale Gesellschaft fur Geschichtsdidaktik* 16(2).

Hoodless, P. (1998) *History and English in the Primary School: Exploiting the Links*. London: Routledge.

Husbands, C. (1996) 'What is history teaching? Language, ideas and meaning', in *Learning about the Past*. Buckingham: Open University Press.

Milgram, R., Dunn, R. and Price, G. E. (1993) *Teaching and counselling gifted and talented adolescents*. Westport, Conn.: Praeger Press.

Poustie, J. *et al.* (1997) *Solutions for Specific Learning Difficulties: An Identification Guide*. Taunton: Next Generation Press.

Reid, G. (1999) *Dyslexia: A Practitioner's Handbook*, 2nd edn. Chichester: Wiley.

SCCC (1996) 'Teaching for Effective Learning: a paper for discussion and development'. Dundee: SCCC.

CHAPTER 10

Dyslexia and Geography

Fionnuala Williams and John Lewis

This chapter:

- discusses the role of Geography within the National Curriculum
- discusses some barriers which confront dyslexic students in Geography and shows how these can be dealt with in the classroom and in examinations.

Background

Most secondary school classrooms contain pupils with a wide variety of special educational needs. A school's register of special needs may indicate the presence of children with Asperger Syndrome, Attention Deficit Hyperactivity Disorder, sensory impairment, mild and moderate learning difficulties, physical disabilities and of course dyslexia. Recent educational trends have moved away from attaching labels to children in acknowledgement of the uniqueness of each pupil and the understanding that attaching labels to people can often lead to misleading assumptions.

A wide variety of strategies are employed in the classroom to deal with pupils with learning difficulties. This has benefited many other children. Multisensory teaching is now employed with a wide range of pupils and is not regarded as only for the dyslexic student. Therefore when writing about teaching methods and arrangements for the dyslexic student in the Geography classroom many of the strategies and techniques could be regarded as good practice for several other pupils.

Geography and the National Curriculum

The importance and role of Geography in the National Curriculum is clearly defined:

> It [Geography] develops knowledge of places and environments throughout the world, an understanding of maps, and a range of investigative and problem solving skills both inside and outside the classroom. As such it prepares pupils for adult life and employment.
>
> (DfEE and QCA 1999)

Geography is seen as having relevance across a wide range of interest areas and educating and informing students in the broadest sense about the world we live in. At its best the study of geography can:

Inspire them to think about their own place in the world, their values, and their rights and responsibilities to other people and the environment.   (DfEE and QCA 1999)

The curriculum lays emphasis on the enquiry approach in developing geographical knowledge and understanding. Rider and Rider (2000: 2) state that 'the requirement is for children to develop a range of skills encouraging them to both ask questions about the world around them and suggest and evaluate answers'. At Key Stage 3 the students must be encouraged to develop and use a variety of strategies including asking geographical questions, suggesting appropriate investigations including field work, collecting, recording and presenting data and evidence and analysing and evaluating this evidence. There is great emphasis on cultivating awareness of the environment and environmental issues and of other societies and cultures and their values and attitudes. Fundamental to this learning process is the ability to communicate this knowledge and understanding using a wide variety of resources including ICT.

The ability to communicate this information requires that the student 'progresses through the language skills of naming, identifying, locating, describing, explaining and predicting.' (Rider and Rider 2000: 2). The inability of a student to express themselves within the recognised code of language can undermine their success as geographers. By KS3 the type and range of skills required includes:

The ability to use extended geographical vocabulary, to use atlases and globes and maps and plans... select and use secondary sources of evidence... to draw maps and plans at a range of scales, using symbols, keys and scales.   (DfEE and QCA 1999)

Many of these skills are not ones that come easily to the dyslexic student and the demands placed on them could exclude all but the most dedicated and persistent pupil. The accurate knowledge of place names, geographical features, map reading and specialised vocabulary can prove, as Stirling (2000: 69) so aptly puts it, 'an unwelcome load for the dodgy dyslexic memory'.

Demonstrating knowledge and understanding

The major barrier to success for dyslexic students is their inability to communicate knowledge and understanding in written form. In Geography, as in many other subjects, alternatives to the written answer need to be employed whenever possible. The skilful use of questioning by the teacher is an important technique involving either the whole class or on an individual basis. An atmosphere of trust within the class needs to be present allowing children to answer incorrectly without being ridiculed by other pupils. An alternative to the teacher asking the questions is for the pupils to be allowed to ask them. The rule that a student can ask the class a question only if they know the answer themselves can result in the more able dyslexic demonstrating their knowledge to everyone by learning to ask the most difficult questions. A reward for the best question can also be given.

When written answers cannot be avoided alternative arrangements need to be employed. Many secondary schools employ learning support assistants to support pupils with special educational needs. Often they work alongside the subject teacher in mainstream classes and, because of the amount of reading and written work involved, Geography is a subject that is often timetabled for support. LSAs enable pupils to receive assistance with reading, note-taking, map reading, recording homework accurately and other writing tasks.

Exam provision

In order to allow the dyslexic pupil to demonstrate what he or she has learned in geography it may be appropriate to read questions or allow dictated answers for examinations and tests. Examination boards permit a variety of special arrangements to be made for dyslexic students providing a report from a psychologist or specialist teacher demonstrates the student fits the criteria for the arrangements requested. Boards also stipulate that the dyslexic student has been in receipt of the special arrangements as the 'norm' throughout their secondary school careers. Therefore additional adult support will be necessary in the Geography lessons whenever testing takes place. This is particularly important when a scribe is deployed for individual students. Reading questions to the class or individuals may be feasible for the class teacher alone but may prove to be difficult without distracting other pupils.

Written work

Written work in most secondary school subjects is unavoidable. Many strategies used to help the dyslexic student to produce written work in the Geography classroom are equally valid in other subjects.

Many dyslexic pupils favour the use of word processors to produce their written work. Small laptop computers can be useful to many students, although secondary schools with networked computer systems allows the student to store and access work in a variety of locations. Writing frames can aid the layout and organisation of a piece of written work. Pictorial versions such as the one illustrated in Figure 10.1 can be useful in helping the pupil to write a description of a river.

Spelling is of course a weakness for nearly every dyslexic. The specialist language in geography is quite complex and preferably needs to be learned by the student. Ercall Wood Technology College (where the authors of this chapter have worked) has 'Starspell' available on all its computers linked to the networked system. This program is designed to teach spelling using the 'look–cover–type–check' method. It contains spelling lists for each subject and the geography section contains a comprehensive list of 103 words under the headings of natural hazards, ecological terms, climate, weather, ecosystems, population, European lands, farming and natural hazards. The program has the facility to add and edit individual words or add a completely new heading. Ercall Wood provides two further means for pupils to access Geography spelling lists. The homework and study diary given to each pupil provides lists of words and specialist vocabulary for each subject needed during each year. Additionally a separate GCSE spelling booklet is provided for all pupils at Key Stage 4, not only listing words needed for coursework and examinations but also with suggestions about how to learn to spell unknown words.

Differentiation

The National Curriculum for Geography, as with other subject areas, states that:

> Teachers should teach the knowledge, skills and understanding in ways that suit their pupils' abilities. This may mean choosing knowledge, skills and understanding from earlier or later key stages so those individual pupils can make progress and show what they can achieve.
>
> (DfEE and QCA 1999)

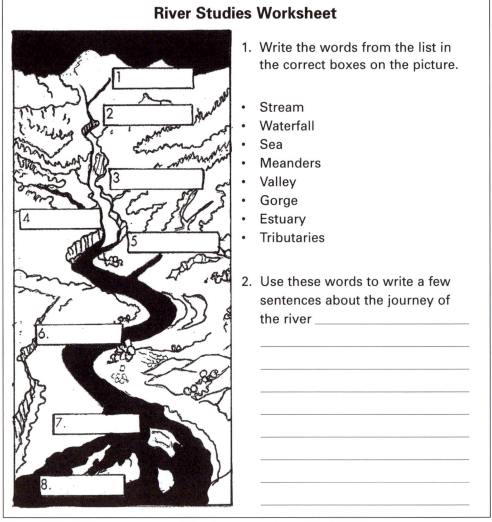

Figure 10.1 EWS worksheet (modified from worksheet SCAA 1996)

Therefore teachers have the flexibility to work within the various Key Stages at a level that suit the learning needs of their pupils. However they also have a responsibility to:

> Plan appropriately challenging work for those whose ability and understanding are in advance of their language and literacy skills. (DfEE and QCA 1999)

This is one of the key points that needs to be reinforced to those involved in educating the dyslexic student – weak literacy skills are not an indicator of intelligence. Where they occur in a student whose intellectual capacity is on a par with, or exceeds that of his peers, access to the curriculum has to be targeted at the intellectual capacity of the pupil. The main way this is achieved is through differentiation.

Differentiation is described as the 'action necessary to respond to the individual's requirements for curriculum access' (DfEE and QCA 1999) and may take a number of forms. As Smith (1996: 45) states:

Differentiation can affect the way the teacher delivers the curriculum, the materials used, the organisational structure within the learning situation and the way the individual is able to access what is being taught and expected of him or her.

Examples of the most commonly used types of differentiation include differentiation by resource, by task, by outcome and by support. Differentiation by resource does not necessarily mean writing worksheets with reduced content. Rather, resources for the dyslexic student should be selected for appropriate readability levels and readability of text should be matched sensitively to the needs of the pupil, with perhaps better readers supporting those less able. Reading levels can be assessed using 'Fogg's Test of Readability'. This provides a quick and convenient way of identifying the levels of reading difficulty of any written material that is more than 100 words long (see Klein 1993: 66). Resources should be well designed and clearly laid out with instructions clearly identifiable from the rest of the text. The provision of printed maps can greatly aid the dyslexic student in the Geography classroom, as tracing is often a problem. The use of structured response sheets targeted at the appropriate level for the dyslexic student can eliminate the need for copious amounts of writing and note-taking. Access to copies of the teacher's notes, particularly for those students taking exams, can enable the dyslexic student to listen and concentrate on what is being said in lessons instead of struggling to copy from the board or making notes that will probably be unintelligible an hour later. The provision of key word and specialised vocabulary spelling lists can be invaluable for the student doing course work and revision. The substitution of textbooks with other media such as tape recordings of key passages, videos and CD-ROMs will provide the dyslexic student with opportunities for multisensory learning and positive reinforcement.

Differentiation by task is when the teacher provides a variety of tasks matched to the student's abilities and interests or when the element of choice is introduced whereby the student chooses from a range of tasks. Again care must be taken to ensure that the tasks are pitched at the right level for the dyslexic student and that the content matches their intellectual ability as well as their literacy skills.

Differentiation by support refers to the provision of Learning Support Assistants whose role within the classroom may be pupil orientated or task orientated. Within that framework the LSA may work with groups, individuals or around the classroom as the need arises and provide support in a variety of ways as described earlier.

Differentiation by outcome involves the provision of a common task with a variety of possible responses or outcomes. In many ways this form of differentiation is most valuable to the dyslexic student. Used effectively, it enables them to show what they know, to demonstrate their knowledge in a way that is not limited by their weak literacy skills. Encouraging students to present their work in a variety of ways using multi-media, including tapes, videos and most importantly ICT, enables them to communicate their knowledge of geography effectively. It also fulfils the requirements of the National Curriculum where appropriate use of ICT underpins geographical knowledge, skills and understanding. Differentiation by outcome also enables the teacher to move away from preoccupation with getting students to learn in the same way, to looking at the results of their learning and rewarding those results. A recurrent theme in our informal discussions with dyslexic students who studied geography was the lack of opportunities to show their knowledge. The emphasis was placed on traditional forms of presentation, which inevitably are literacy based and penalise the dyslexic student. The use of video, tapes and ICT software like PowerPoint and desktop publishing packages were identified as being particularly suitable for Geography course work, assignments and presentations.

For the dyslexic students we spoke to who studied Geography at Key Stage 3 and Key Stage 4, Geography was a source of interest and enjoyment. Because geography as a subject is based on looking at the world around us and the issues facing that world, they felt they could bring their own personal experience to bear in a way that is not possible in many other areas of the curriculum. The practical skills and hands-on aspect of geography also appealed to them as well as the fieldwork and provided opportunities for learning that were not literacy based. The use of a variety of media and in particular ICT were identified as being crucial to their learning. The range of geography software available was helpful not only as a source of information on environmental studies, development issues, economic development, etc., but with map reading skills, using grid references, atlases, studying tectonic activity and so on. The problem areas were identified as note-taking and recording information and here the use of Dictaphones to record lessons, support from an LSA or access to teacher's notes could have been invaluable. While there was access to differentiated resources these were not always felt to reflect the knowledge of the dyslexic student. Differentiation by presentation was also discussed as a way for the student to present their work in an appropriate and suitable way that shows what they can do without dwelling on their weaknesses.

Extension work

The able dyslexic pupil at Ercall Wood Technology College is able to demonstrate their knowledge and understanding of Geography by being chosen to take part in the school's Able Pupil Extension Programme. Pupils are selected using a combination of SATs results, verbal and non-verbal reasoning scores and a variety of teacher assessments. Approximately 15 per cent of the cohort are chosen to be part of the projects in groups of approximately ten pupils. They have eight one-hour sessions in school along with an unlimited amount of their own time to work on the project. The task they are given is quite simple. They must research a country of their choice, obtain basic background information and then investigate in depth a particular aspect that interests them most. At the end of the eight weeks they are required to give a presentation to someone from outside school such as a member of the governing body. They are allowed to make their presentation using an overhead projector, hand-outs, posters or a computer program such as PowerPoint. Interestingly the dyslexic students often favour a PowerPoint presentation as their chosen tool. Pupils are encouraged to be original. This has resulted in pupils preparing food from various parts of the world, dressing in a national costume, performing the New Zealand All Blacks' Haka and several other imaginative presentations.

Over the years the Able Pupil Programme has been running several dyslexic pupils have been selected for the project. Feedback from the students suggests many benefits, including a huge boost to confidence and self-esteem.

Fieldwork

An important part of the secondary school Geography curriculum and a necessary requirement of the syllabus is the requirement to carry out fieldwork. In the five years a student attends Ercall Wood, visits for fieldwork would include Church Stretton to study settlements, Dovedale to look at a National Park, Mid Wales to investigate coastal features, Birmingham for the study of an urban residential area and The Long Mynd for river profiles. The dyslexic student needs not only to absorb the information from the field trip but also to record it for future use. A Dictaphone can be a useful tool for many dyslexic learners but the problem of transferring the information to paper afterwards still exists. A support assistant working with the dyslexic student on the visit could be a valuable asset, acting as a scribe and helping with organisational difficulties. Dyslexic pupils will benefit greatly from the direct experience gained from fieldwork. As mentioned elsewhere, acquiring and reinforcing knowledge in this way is a favoured means for these pupils.

Conclusion

Geography is a highly visual and immediate subject in that it relates to the study of phenomena, people and activities in the world around us. It also relates to things we see, talk about and do everyday without thinking: planning a journey, planning a holiday, shopping, sport, changes in the weather, etc. The local area we live in is part of a larger region that is ultimately part of an international and global system that in one way or another affects the life we lead. This ability to see the global picture and the interrelationships between the physical, economic, social, political and cultural is not something that comes naturally to all of us. West (1997: 39) states that:

> This sense of the whole also is often seen to characterise the thought of the dyslexic and learning disabled children. They are quite often described as being global thinkers who have a heightened sense of the whole but make frequent errors in details.

West also suggests that dyslexic pupils often have greater strengths in visual thinking, pattern recognition and learning than they do in the linear progressive type of learning favoured by the education system. Geography as a subject is more amenable to this type of learning in that it looks at geographical processes and patterns and the interdependence of places and environment. The range of options available, for example England, World Sport, Rivers, Shopping, Tourism, Volcanoes, National Parks, should ensure there is something of interest for everyone and these topics lend themselves to multisensory teaching strategies that will benefit all pupils. However, 'the tendency of the system to be preoccupied with quick verbal responses and vast amounts of testable facts' (West 1997: 40) can effectively exclude those who learn in a different way. The responsibility for avoiding this lies with the classroom teacher and the SEN department using a wide range of strategies and resources and is clearly defined in the National Curriculum.

Perhaps the time has come for those involved in education to acknowledge that, 'the complex of traits referred to as learning difficulties or dyslexia may be in part an outward manifestation of the relative strength of a different mode of thought' (West 1997: 19).

The way forward according to West is (p. 11) 'that we should be more concerned with results than with trying to get everyone to learn things in the same way'.

References

DfEE and QCA (1999) *The National Curriculum for England: Geography*. London: DfEE and QCA.

Klein, C. (1993) *Diagnosing Dyslexia: A Guide to the Assessment of Adults with Specific Learning Difficulties.* London: Basic Skills Agency.

Rider, C. and Rider, M. (2000) 'Standards: Homework 8: Geography', *Special Children* (129), 2.

School Curriculum and Assessment Authority (SCAA) (1996) *Consistency in Teacher Assessment: Supporting Pupils with Special Educational Needs, Key Stage 3.* Hayes, Middlesex: SCAA.

Smith, D. (1996) *Spotlight on Special Needs: Specific Learning Difficulties.* Tamworth: NASEN.

Stirling, E. G. ((2000) *Help for the Dyslexic Adolescent*, 11th edn. Sheffield: E. G. Stirling.

West, T. G. (1997) *In The Mind's Eye.* New York: Prometheus Books.

CHAPTER 11

Dyslexia and Physics

Pam Holmes

This chapter:

- examines factors relating to the subject of Physics and shows how it can be presented in a dyslexic friendly manner
- looks at obstacles which can present difficulties for dyslexic students
- offers suggestions for dyslexic students to develop personal coping strategies
- discusses whole-school initiatives in meeting the needs of staff and students in making physics accessible.

The aim of the chapter

That dyslexic people can succeed in life in the long term has been well documented. On the British Dyslexia Association's web site's list of successful dyslexic individuals there are several who have made a name for themselves in Science and associated occupations.

However, being successful in life and achieving in school are not the same thing. For most of our school lives we are expected to demonstrate our abilities mainly by showing prowess in the use of secretarial skills. The ability to read accurately and with understanding, and be able to write things down in a logical way applying vocabulary and language effectively, often within the constraints of a limited time, are accepted as being the essential tools for the successful student. Many dyslexic people will have struggled to acquire the basic literacy skills from an early age. The feelings of failure and decline in confidence and motivation that can result are likely to affect and depress their academic performance, culminating in feelings of frustration and/or resignation that can remain throughout their school years. Even the most promising students can find themselves severely challenged.

For some, it seems, the Sciences can offer an opportunity to succeed. The aim of this chapter is to look at the teaching of Physics and to discover what it is in the Physics classroom that can help dyslexic students to do well. Some pointers to good practice should emerge which it is hoped can be used as a basis for advice and recommendations for Physics teachers and learners.

Can dyslexic pupils do well in Physics at school?

Any inquiry into which factors help dyslexic pupils achieve in Physics must necessarily involve a look at the dyslexic students who do achieve in an attempt to establish what it is within their learning environment that helps them to do well.

To inform this writing some informal research was conducted in a medium sized co-educational public school where intake is by examination and interview. The majority of students board, although there are a small number of day pupils. As for other subjects, students are placed in sets for Science, and there are six sets, set 1 being the highest achievers. With very few exceptions all students have a measured IQ of average or above, and several of the dyslexic students have very high scores for verbal ability as measured on the Wechsler scale. Most students take the three separate sciences (triple award) while a few take dual award science (Edexel).

The GCSE results of 22 dyslexic students, 7 girls and 15 boys, all of them having been fully assessed by educational psychologists and all having examination provisions of one sort or another, revealed interesting data (see Table 11.1).

Table 11.1 GCSE results of 22 dyslexic students

Grade	Physics		Biology		Chemistry		Maths	English	
		Dual		Dual		Dual		Eng	Lit
A*	4		2		5		3	2	2
A	7	3	7	3	5	3	10	10	3
B	4	3	4	3	5	3	7	7	11
C		1	2	1		1	2	3	2
Total A grades	14		12		13		13	12	5

Contrary to what had been expected the dyslexic pupils had fared better in Physics than in any of the other core subjects listed. Of the 22 dyslexic students 11 achieved their highest grade for Physics. Only five students got their lowest grade for Physics. Four of the students did better at Maths than Physics, seven students did better at Physics than Maths, and 11 got identical grades for both subjects. (*Note.* The sample was very small and confined to one school, and therefore the information it provides should not be regarded as representative of dyslexic individuals' performance overall.)

What Physics offers dyslexic learners

The subject content in Physics, being concerned with the natural physical laws which govern our planet and beyond, is very 'tangible'. There is an emphasis on the acquisition and application of knowledge and the use of it to make predictions and to solve problems. Thinking and understanding are at a premium, and these are two areas in which dyslexic pupils can do well. Although the body of knowledge in Physics is sometimes added to, and/or modified, it is not open to the differing interpretations and subjective comments found in many of the arts subjects.

In the Physics classroom, diagrams, charts and demonstrations are often used to provide a visual backup to what is being taught. There are also opportunities for practical experience to be gained from laboratory practical sessions. The nature of the subject allows attention to be drawn to the practical applications of what the pupils are studying, thus providing 'concrete' examples. This 'tell–show–do' approach which typifies many Physics lessons is the essence of multisensory teaching – something which has long been advocated as good practice for teaching dyslexic pupils. The 'Accelerated Learning' lobby also regards multisensory teaching and learning as an essential feature of an effective learning programme. This style of teaching should be suited to not only dyslexic students, but most students, whatever their cognitive style and learning preferences.

Understanding, which is often a strength for dyslexic learners, plays an important and essential role in effective learning. In some subjects they are hampered in demonstrating their knowledge since it frequently depends on the secretarial skills, including accurate spelling and grammar, which are involved in essay writing. Dyslexic learners often comment that despite understanding and 'knowing' a subject they cannot get it down on paper. The majority of those interviewed for this study cited 'good understanding' as being essential to success in Physics. Apart from being a very desirable outcome of the learning process, understanding contributes towards resolving sequencing and memory problems.

Links can be made between the different topics in Physics that help to reinforce the basic principles, and assist in providing opportunities for 'overlearning', something which is strongly recommended for dyslexic learners.

Literacy skills are not a prime concern in the subject. As one teacher put it, there is an emphasis on 'substance over style'. Students are not laden with notes. Examinations do not require long written answers that can put a strain on processing, handwriting and organisational skills. In Physics large numbers of marks can be gained for calculations and single word answers. Very few marks are lost for poor spelling, which is always an area of anxiety for dyslexic students. Reading is limited, although it has to be acknowledged that the language, vocabulary and terms used are very specialised and need practice, particularly when preparing for examinations.

What prevents dyslexic learners from achieving in Physics?

The accurate recall of formulae was considered to be the most essential and demanding part of the subject by most of the dyslexic students interviewed. Accurate recall of names, terms, facts and formulae is required whether answering questions verbally or on paper, so that there is a heavy reliance on good memory skills, for verbal responses and for spelling. The number of subject-specific words to learn is a challenge to anyone with poor organisational and memory skills. Physics uses many words that have different meanings in other parts of the school curriculum and in everyday life, e.g. 'force', 'charge', 'conducting', 'transformer'. Sometimes words sound the same but the spelling is different (synonyms), e.g. 'currant'/'current'; sometimes words sound so similar that they can be confused, e.g. 'reflection'/'refraction'. Some words can be represented by symbols (e.g. for charge the symbol is Q), thus there is a language, together with a symbolic shorthand to learn. In turn, these terms may be associated with standard units (e.g. the standard unit for a charge is coulomb, C) and then there are also formulae ($Q = I \times t$, where I is the current and t is the time). Mathematical symbols are also involved, as are topic specific symbols, such as the circuit symbols for electricity. All of this adds to the memory load, although dyslexic learners with visual strengths might find symbols easier to remember than words alone, since they are very visual. The mixture of letter and number symbols in formulae can be particularly confusing to those who have problems with maths or for students who have symbol/number visual perception/confusion problems.

Students who have difficulties with word-finding (sometimes termed 'Dysnomia') may encounter problems with the accurate recall of subject-specific words, particularly when under stress. (It is worth commenting here that most dyslexic students said they found Biology to be the most difficult science and cited difficulties in learning the essential vocabulary as the reason.)

Success in Physics seems to be closely associated with ability in maths, especially in arithmetic and algebra. This obviously presents problems for those students who experience difficulties in maths, and more particularly those for whom maths is the major problem, including dyscalculics.

The organisational skills required for practical work and for managing materials and equipment can place a burden on dyslexic learners. It is essential to keep an efficient and accurate record of work covered, revision for tests and exams can be made impossible if work has not been filed appropriately. There is a need to be able to manage time effectively, particularly for revision.

Although those interviewed said they did not rely on them a great deal, some Physics textbooks are very uninspiring. They are often monochrome with small diagrams and lots of dense text.

Dyslexic students are often not statemented, sometimes not on the school's SEN register, and the variety of difficulties which they display prevents them from being regarded and dealt with as a single group. Dyslexia can sometimes be masked by able students who employ successful compensating strategies, and for some, their learning problems are only an issue when time constraints are involved, or when access to dictionaries and other study aids is restricted, i.e. in exams. Such students are usually reliant on their teachers to identify their needs and to ensure that these are met appropriately, including application for examination concessions, if necessary.

What dyslexic students say

Views of dyslexic students were sought to try to establish what factors they thought were essential to success. An analysis of their responses follows.

Interviews/questionnaires with dyslexic students

Views of 16 students were sought. These ranged from Year 9 to Year 12.

Table 11.2 Difficult topics in Physics

Difficult topics
- These areas were mentioned as being difficult:
  Remembering formulae
  Remembering words
  The mathematical side
  Remembering formulae was most often mentioned, even by students who say they understand the subject
- They also mentioned difficulties in learning and understanding these topics: Forces, Pulleys, Gravity, The Solar System, Pivots, Waves

How easy/difficult do they rate the subject?
Students (Years 9 to 11 only) were asked to rate the subjects they studied in order of how easy they found them – not necessarily how successful they are:

- None of the students rated Physics as the easiest subject
- Two rated it as the hardest
- Nine of the 14 students placed Physics in the easy end of the range, while five placed it at the harder end
- All but one of these five also rated maths as being a hard subject
- Only two said they thought they are good at Physics, three said they are not, one declined to answer. The remainder said they are 'average' or 'OK'

Table 11.3 Strategies for learning and revising, key factors, what teachers can do

---

Strategies for learning and revising:

- Only three of the 16 students use 'Mind-Mapping' (copyright) to help them to learn or to revise
- Most use colour and highlighting
- Most said they read and make notes, often using colour to emphasis key words
- Only one mentioned tape-recording – he uses a Dictaphone for self-testing
- They mostly lack structured learning strategies – typically, 'I just read over and over and try and get it in my head'

What students consider to be key factors to success

- Understanding
- A reasonable ability in maths
- Good organisation of files
- Being methodical, logical and organised
- Asking questions – being curious

Their views of what teachers do to enhance learning

- Offer advice on making and keeping an organised file
- Give tips, e.g. 1. dating work; 2. using an index – to help with organisation
- Conduct periodic file checks
- Provide good, concise notes, with diagrams
- Use diagrams and pictures to support teaching
- Explain diagrams
- Give good, clear demonstrations
- Provide opportunities for practical work following teacher demonstration
- Explain how a formula has arisen to aid understanding
- Check understanding before moving on
- Give lots of tests – allowing revision for previous homework/prep
- Provide a clear syllabus
- Use colour to emphasise and highlight key words
- Teach and encourage 'mapping' or use of 'spidergram' as a strategy
- Teach and encourage application of mnemonics – e.g. learning the names of the planets
- Make it clear that it is OK to say, 'I don't understand'

Table 11.4 Advice to dyslexic students

Advice they would give to dyslexic students who wish to succeed

- Listen in class; concentrate
- Keep tidy, arranged, clear notes; highlight important formulae, keywords, etc.
- Go over work done in lesson not too long afterwards
- Read through notes at night and type them out, it *really* helps you to understand; it helps most when you read the previous notes
- Look frequently at the notes of things you struggle on
- Be organised
- Learn formulae
- Do thorough revision for tests
- Set aside time for learning and revision, do not be distracted
- Always go to the test/exam with a calculator
- Use your logic
- Use mnemonics if you can to help your memory
- Do not be afraid to ask for help from Support Teachers
- Do homework or preps on time
- Work hard

Teacher responses

Views were gathered from only a small number (4) of Physics teachers.

Table 11.5 Views of teachers

Qualities needed to achieve in Physics	Areas benefiting from focused support
Curiosity Perseverance Aptitude for maths Ability to relate and apply theory in practical situations Logical thinking	Mathematical work Conceptual work – velocity, acceleration, etc. Study skills Astronomy – difficult vocabulary Drawing diagrams Knowledge of technical terms
Factors contributing to poor achievement in the subject	**Successful strategies used by teachers**
Disorganisation Difficulties with the language of Physics Difficulties in maths Conceptual confusion	Clear instructions relating to organisation, notes, etc. Visual demonstrations Structure and order Use of visual aids Explanations in basic English Summary notes on OHP

Practical solutions and suggestions

Whole-school initiatives

- A school special needs policy should be in place and responsibilities should be made clear. All maintained schools must show regard to the DfEE Code of Practice for Special Educational Needs and be aware of their statutory obligations as regards meeting the needs of the pupils within their care.
- A whole school awareness of dyslexia and its associated problems, will enable teachers to handle the subject sensitively and with some insight, including playing a part in the identification of vulnerable students. Teachers should share good practice and show a willingness to collaborate with colleagues in order to maximise the learning of all students. They should be aware of, and should give regard to, advice from professionals, including that provided by Educational Psychology reports.
- The school should formulate a policy in regard to making decisions about which students should have entitlement to additional arrangements for examinations. The Joint Council for General Qualifications issues annually (usually in October) a booklet entitled *Examinations and Assessment for GCSE and GCE, Regulations and Guidance relating to Candidates with Special Requirements*. For the past two years schools, through their Heads and Principals of Centres, 'are empowered to grant additional time up to a maximum of 25 per cent of examination time, and/or rest breaks, to examination candidates with special requirements, having seen appropriate evidence of need' (p. 8). Applications for using alternative forms of recording should be considered, if this is an issue. For Physics exams word-processing is not usually helpful, since responses are usually written in exam

booklets and diagrams are often required. Use of an amanuensis may be appropriate for students with major problems. Applications need to be made to Examination Boards for this provision, at an early stage of the GCSE course.

- Awareness should extend to the protection and nurturing of confidence and self-esteem for all pupils. Support and counselling should be made available for needy students and access should be facilitated.
- Whole-school policies on spelling and grammar can help to assure some consistency of approach within which allowances or variances can be made for those who are struggling.
- Each department should have a teacher with responsibility for special needs issues and for disseminating information to other staff.

Recommendations for the Physics classroom

Problems particular to Physics

- Teachers should be alert to which topics in Physics commonly cause problems for dyslexic pupils; this may vary according to school, teacher expertise, etc. Departments should build up a bank of support materials to cover vulnerable areas.
- Difficulties with maths may mean that some students need additional support and practise to develop expertise and confidence in coping with the mathematical demands of the subject. There should be liaison with the Maths and Learning Support Departments to ensure consistency of approach. There is a growing body of work on maths and dyslexia. Teachers should work with individuals to attempt to identify the root of the problem and find solutions.
- Some students will find calculators intimidating and may need advice on suitable models, e.g. there are 'talking' calculators and ones with coloured symbols. Students with problems are likely to need some modelling on how to use the calculator, with perhaps a 'crib' sheet to support independent use, especially for those with sequencing problems.
- Careful thought should be given to the type of GCSE course to be followed, double or single award, (or separate subject Sciences), and to the tier of entry. Choice will usually depend on predicted grades with an eye to A levels/career plans.

Organisation

- Encouragement and training should ensure that students bring the correct equipment to lessons, e.g. calculators. This is especially important for exams and tests. Provide classroom spares so that work is not disrupted when items are mislaid or forgotten.
- Most dyslexic students will benefit if the organisation and presentation of Physics work folders is standardised, particularly at first. Clear and detailed instructions about indexing and filing, with frequent reminders, will be invaluable to students experiencing problems with organisational skills.
- Use structure and routine in the classroom to encourage automaticity – without being so predictable the classroom becomes boring.
- A routine should be established for the setting of homework, such as always using a part of the blackboard or a display board to which pupils have access. Submission dates should always be specified. Allow time for students to write down homework instructions, or allow alternative methods, such as Dictaphone. Use of technology such as posting homework on

e-mail or putting messages on answering machines can help to minimise excuses about forgetting.

- Students who are very badly affected by poor organisational skills may need a classroom 'buddy' to provide advice and help.
- For routine tasks a checklist to which the student can refer may be useful. Where possible break things into numbered steps, using colour to help them to learn and remember.
- Give overt praise and reward for improved organisation.
- Teach goal setting and encourage students to set own realistic goals. Teachers can help by providing a realistic range – within which students can achieve and improve their own learning.
- Teachers should work with individual pupils to devise effective time management systems that promote efficiency and independence.

Vocabulary

- New words or terms should be explained *and* written out to avoid confusion. When possible provide an illustration/diagram/picture to assist memory.
- Pupils will benefit from having access to a subject-specific word list. Opportunities should be provided for learning and practising spellings. Teachers should ensure that students can apply new vocabulary appropriately.

Presentation

- Use of mapping such as Tony Buzan's 'Mind-Mapping' (copyright) helps students to demonstrate their thinking in a pictorial way. Mapping can help to show how the different themes in Physics are linked, and are effective used as wall charts. Lots of colour should be used. Lots of practice is needed to develop confidence in mapping skills. It is a useful 'tool' but is only effective if it helps.
- Clear advice should be given about how to set out mathematical working and answers to avoid confusion when marking.

The promotion of learning

- The provision of a departmental booklet with formulae, essential diagrams, laws, etc., will be useful for revision. It could be posted on the school's Intranet system where one exists.
- Prompt notes or 'thinksheets' can help to direct pupils to ask themselves the right questions.
- New learning should be associated with something that has gone before. Relationships between and within topics should be explained and demonstrated, where possible, using practical activities and diagrams/pictures/charts which should be large enough for details with legible labels. Colour can enhance understanding and make different aspects clear.
- When the student fails to grasp information the teacher should be prepared to explain in a different way, rather than reiterating what the student has already failed to understand. Ensure comprehension with 'show and tell' sessions. Use this formative assessment to inform planning for the future.
- Cater for a variety of learning styles, allowing flexibility as pupils become more aware of their own learning preferences, e.g. allow a choice in presentation method – mapping,

linear notes, etc., according to strengths/preferences. In demonstrations teachers should use of a variety of graphic organisers to show students the possibilities available. Encourage pupils to try mapping software and other tools.

- Allow plenty of practice, reinforcement, review for new skills, new strategies.
- When introducing new topics provide students with 'the big picture' so that they have an idea of the content and the way the topic is moving, how it relates to other topics and the learning objectives involved. End each lesson with a plenary, allowing students to demonstrate what they have learned.
- Encourage an atmosphere of inquiry – value everyone's contribution. It is useful to include some negative examples to promote thinking. Getting students to make negative and positive statements to which other students have to respond can be effective. Promote thinking skills through the use of open-ended questions.
- Challenge students, and encourage them to share successful, creative, and perhaps innovative ideas and strategies for learning and presenting information.
- Teach a variety of learning/memory tools, e.g. mnemonics, listening to own voice tapes, using examples within the subject to encourage appreciation of the possible benefits.
- Avoid dictating notes, although this tends not to be an issue in Physics. Where practical, provide notes so that the available time can be used for highlighting relevant points, picking out important stages in a process, etc.
- It may be useful to provide taped versions of explanations so that pupils can access them in their own time.
- To allow access for all students teachers should give consideration to 'differentiation of approach', tuning the task to the pupil's capacity and progress, when necessary reducing content to concentrate on mastery. This can be achieved by actively planning for and using a balanced mixture of visual, auditory and kinaesthetic presentation, as recommended for teaching dyslexic learners and by proponents of Accelerated Learning.
- Students often need guidance in planning a practical and manageable revision timetable. Sorting out work to be learned into MUST learn, SHOULD learn, COULD learn categories can help disorganised students.

Teacher awareness

- Individual teachers should know which of their students have identified special needs. They should read, and act on, advice given in Educational Psychology reports and by other professionals as regards differentiating their teaching approach to meet the pupil's needs. Liaison with the SENCO, the departmental special needs representative and other staff who teach the pupils is important.
- By becoming involved in the identification of pupils with problems, teachers should ensure that students have the exam concessions that are appropriate to their needs. Not all students need extra time – but it may reduce stress if they know they have it.
- Exam provisions need to be practised, indeed the Examination Boards require this to happen: exam technique, highlighting, using time wisely, familiarity with the exam format, necessary equipment; looking at the exam papers – what is required? Encourage thinking skills. Lots of practice is needed to help students to become familiar with exam conditions and the stresses of performing under the constraints which are an accepted part of the exam ethos. The aim is to encourage automaticity and boost confidence.
- Dyslexic learners confidence can be very fragile. Even comments that are meant to be

tongue in cheek can hurt and offend. Use praise and encouragement and beware of being over-critical. Recent research seems to indicate that confidence can be a bigger contributor to success than ability (Feinstein, *Observer*, 24 October 2000).

What the pupil can do

- The more pupils know about their own learning – metacognition – the more effective they are likely to be in academic terms. 'Metacognition is the jump-lead which can spark a dyslexic student's academic ignition when conventional learning methods fail' (Mary Flecker, 'Learning to Study', *Dyslexia Review*, Spring, 1999). Teachers should encourage metacognitive awareness so that students take on more responsibility for managing their own learning. If students understand what the task is and what they are trying to achieve it helps them to visualise and build a schema for themselves as a 'hook' to facilitate their learning.
- Rewriting notes or typing on a word processor can help to enhance understanding. This can be more easily managed in Physics than in other subjects since the note-making/note-taking burden is minimal in comparison to History, for example.
- Students should be prepared to ask questions in the classroom, challenge what they are being told.
- Students benefit from having familiarity with successful strategies for learning and retaining information. Good ideas include visualisation, use of tape recorders, mapping techniques, flow charts, highlighting significant words/phrases, etc.
- Students themselves should ensure that they access any support that is available, when and if necessary.

Conclusion

Clearly it is possible for dyslexic learners to succeed, and even excel in Physics. This is more likely to happen within a learning environment which encourages students to take responsibility for their own learning. The setting of targets, so that there is always a goal to achieve, can help in ensuring positive progress. Believing in their own worth and having the confidence to say they don't know and to ask questions is an important step towards achieving adult independence. Students should feel comfortable in accessing whatever support is available to make their lives easier.

One dyslexic learner studying Physics at University now listens, and is able to respond to lectures, rather than try to make notes. He has discovered that all lectures are posted on the University Intranet and he can print them, so that he has an excellent set of notes. He now feels so confident with his learning, and is doing so well that he is considering staying on to do a Master's degree.

Useful resources

- Software
  Inspiration – has received good reviews in dyslexia magazines. Especially useful for dyslexic learners who find 'mapping' too demanding of artistic skills or too time

consuming. It contains a variety of different mapping templates – not just for Physics. The program also has an added facility for changing diagrammatic notes into linear notes – thus changing the 'map' into an almost instant essay plan.

- *Redshift* – mentioned by one of the teachers interviewed as providing a very visual means of exploring the solar system. Both programs are available from TAG, telephone 0800 591 262.
- Tape recorders and/or Dictaphones for auditory back-up.
- A subject-specific wordbook, either produced by the department or purchased. *Subject Spellchecks – Spelling for Exams* by E. G. Stirling, available from Better Books, 01384 253276 (contains spellings for all curriculum areas).
- Charts and posters.
- Careful consideration of textbooks used. *Physics for You*, Johnson (1996) Stanley Thornes, Cheltenham, is recommended as having colour illustrations, and summaries and helpful advice are given on revision, exams, etc.
- Internet resources for revision – some of these are interactive.
- Good web site for information on teaching strategies and techniques, not exclusively for Physics: http://www.Idonline.org/ld_indepth/teaching_techniques/strategies.html
- A very useful book on numeracy and dyslexia is *Mathematics for Dyslexics: A Teaching Handbook,* Chinn, S. J. and Ashcroft, J. R. (1993), London: Whurr Publishers.
- Dyslexia Institute web site: http://www.dyslexia-inst.org.uk
- British Dyslexia Association web site: http://www.bda-dyslexia.org.uk
- Calculators – 'talking' calculators, ones with coloured keys – a variety of suppliers.
- Interactive whiteboards – expensive, but highly recommended for visual demonstrations.

References

Black. P. (1996) 'Formative assessment and the improvement of learning', *British Journal of Special Education* 23(2).

Dryden, G. and Vos, J. (1994) *The Learning Revolution.* Aylesbury: Accelerated Learning Systems.

Jensen, E. (1996) *Brain Based Learning.* Del Mar, Calif.: Turning Point Publishing.

Joint Council for General Qualifications (1999) *Examinations and Assessment for GCSE and GCE, Regulations and Guidance relating to Candidates with Special Requirements 2000.* Joint Council for General Qualifications.

Hill, G. (1997) *Revise GCSE Science.* London: Letts Educational.

Holmes, P. (1996) 'Specific learning difficulties and mathematics', M.Ed. Dissertation, University of Wales.

Ott, P. (1997) *How to Detect and Manage Dyslexia.* Oxford: Heinemann.

Peer, L. (1996) *Winning with Dyslexia.* Reading: British Dyslexia Association.

Reid, G. (1998) *Dyslexia: A Practitioner's Handbook,* 2nd edn. Chichester: Wiley.

Rose, C. and Goll. L. (1992) *Accelerate Your Learning.* Aylesbury: Accelerated Learning Systems.

Smith, A. (1996) *Accelerated Learning in the Classroom.* Stafford: Network Educational Press.

Smythe, I. (ed.) *The Dyslexia Handbook 2000.* Reading: British Dyslexia Association.

CHAPTER 12

Dyslexia and Biology

Christine A. Howlett

This chapter:

- discusses the nature of dyslexic difficulties in biology
- describes some possible approaches for acquiring the knowledge and skills for biology
- describes the implications of this for practical work in biology.

Problems biological studies pose for dyslexic learners

The difficulties

Difficulties characteristic of dyslexia which have implications in Biology lessons are: accurate learning and recall of 'names'; accurate pronunciation and spelling of words; rote-learning of facts; assimilating ideas presented in an abstract form; orderly and tidy organisation of work, whether written or physical; slowness in writing/copying; lack of confidence hindering the asking of questions and making observations.

The implications for Biology

Compared with many other subjects, Biology may well seem to involve a massive amount of factual details, often labelled by technical words, rarely used in everyday speech. They are often long words with Latin or Greek style spellings and being unfamiliar, may readily be confused when visually similar, e.g. cerebellum/cerebrum. This makes copying, for example from the board, accurately and fast enough especially difficult. Many of the ideas or concepts may seem abstract and outside everyday experience, e.g. homeostasis, ecosystem, respiration. Diagrams should be used a great deal, as they are particularly useful for dyslexic children who are often helped by the visual presentation of information.

Slowness, untidiness and inaccuracy in writing can have serious consequences when recording observations in practical investigations. Difficulty in assimilating and recalling detailed instructions can also produce problems in such practical assignments, made more difficult if the students are afraid of asking and appearing stupid before their peers. The ability of many dyslexic students to engage in lateral thinking and form a holistic view may enable them to have illuminating and useful insights, which their lack of confidence hinders them from offering.

It is perhaps worth noting that there are aspects of biology studies which are helpful to dyslexic students in particular: although somewhat abstract concepts may be involved, there is much information which, to be fully appreciated, requires to be understood in visual and kinaesthetic modes.

Summary of the problems

- Remembering and recalling 'names' accurately, for text and diagrams.
- Spelling of technical words.
- Learning of many factual details.
- Assimilating abstract concepts.
- Drawing and labelling of diagrams.
- Practical work: remembering and following instructions accurately and fully; recording observations/data accurately, in orderly manner and fast enough.
- Having confidence to: ask about anything not understood; offer original questions and comments.

Some solutions and helpful approaches

Spelling

- It is useful to compile an **alphabetically arranged biology spelling book** – ideally having one for each year, each new year having all that has gone before plus the new words likely to be encountered that year. A relatively disposable photocopied format has advantages – with the master copy on computer, it is easy to update/amend; it is less expensive to replace if lost and each pupil can highlight in their own copy, the words they personally find troublesome.
- Such a spelling checklist can have other useful information in it, such as **definitions**, e.g. of respiration, ecosystem, osmosis, immunisation. Valuable for spelling knowledge would be a table showing **singular and plural endings of Latin/Greek words** (see Figure 12.1). If spaces are left, words can be added by the pupil as they are come across.

Singular	Plural
....................................**um** e.g. bacteri**um**, ov**um**	....................................**a** e.g. bacteri**a**, ov**a**
....................................**us** e.g. vill**us**, bronch**us**	....................................**i** e.g. vill**i**, bronch**i**
....................................**a** e.g. vertebr**a**,	....................................**ae** e.g. vertebr**ae**
....................................**on** e.g. mitochondri**on**, spermatoz**on**	....................................**a** e.g. mitochondri**a**, spermatoz**a**
....................................**is** e.g. test**is**	....................................**es** e.g. test**es**
odd ones stom**a**, stigm**a**, cotyled**on**,	stom**ata**, stigm**as**, cotyled**ons**

Figure 12.1 Singular and plural endings of Latin/Greek words

- As no one willingly does anything as boring as learning spellings, it is helpful to the pupil if the **teacher provides the impetus for regular learning of words**, though each pupil could select the words they personally find most troublesome. **Starspell and Wordshark computer spelling programs could be customised** to enable both practice and testing for individuals. There may be a place, for two or three minutes each lesson, being given to **all pupils rhythmically chanting the most difficult spellings currently needed**, then each few weeks, forming small groups to compete in chanting spellings correctly in unison. It would not then matter if a lone dyslexic pupil could not quite keep up, they would still have a useful auditory experience.
- The Biology teacher should be aware of the multisensory and visual methods of learning spellings, hopefully taught to the dyslexic pupils by special needs teachers. However, with words specific to Biology, which have unfamiliar letter combinations, e.g. ae, ch = k sound, psy-, or are visually similar to other words, e.g. cerebrum/cerebellum, it can be helpful to gradually **build up a collection of master sheets which can be photocopied, to practise** such words at home. This can be done in a mechanical manner, but taking only a few minutes each day, so encouraging automatic recall. For each word there can be two types of practice, both to be done as fast as possible:
  - (a) A vertical row of words (in handwriting size font) with the correct version at the top, then each successive word with a different letter missing, then increasing the number of letters missing until all are missing. It is helpful in the top one, to indicate how the word may be broken up into easily recognisable sections (e.g. syllables or morphemes).
  - (b) A grid of 30 to 50 words, with some, arranged at random, spelled correctly and the rest with letters missing, added, misplaced, etc., as near as possible to likely misspellings, and the correct ones have to be identified and ringed. This could be tried more than once, with the pupils aiming to beat their own record in seconds. This is not suitable for really poor spellers – only those whose errors are relatively minor. Avoid very small print – the example shown in Figure 12.2 is to illustrate the principle only.

Clearly, it is laborious to build up such a bank of materials, but this should not prevent one making a start – if it is added to each year, it will eventually be a most useful resource. If dyslexic students are provided with alternative means of recording notes from the board other than slow and inefficient copying, once the material on the board has been read and assimilated the remaining time that the rest of the class spend in copying, could be usefully used practising with such sheets, otherwise such sheets could be used at home.

imm uni sa tion	immunisation	imunisation	immunsation	imminisation
- - - unisation				
imm - - - sation	imunisaiton	immuisition	iminisation	immunisation
immuni - - tion				
immunisa - - - -	imnisaiton	immunisation	imnisation	immunision
i- - uni - ation				
- mm - ni - at - on	immunisation	imunisation	immunisation	immunissition
im - uni - - tion				
- m - u - i - a - ti - -	immunnisation	immunisation	immunisition	immunisation
- - - - - - - - - - -				

Figure 12.2 World grid

Drawing and labelling diagrams

Biology teachers have been familiar with biology diagrams for so many years, it often does not occur to them **to give instructions about the purpose of these, how to go about producing them and the best ways of labelling them.** As in so many areas, dyslexic students do not 'pick up' ideas or conventions easily and it is **often necessary to make things explicit to them** that others seem to just absorb without effort.

Many dyslexic students have excellent visual skills and can copy shapes well. Some but by no means all are also artistic. It needs to be pointed out that you do not need to be artistic to produce good diagrams and that 'diagrams' are as different from 'drawings', as good cartoons are from a detailed, realistic portrayal of some object.

Diagrams are to give specific information and, as such, must be as simple, clear and unambiguous as is possible to fulfil that aim. Some information is given or clarified more efficiently in a visual than in a purely verbal form. This can be quickly demonstrated by putting pupils into pairs, and giving each two or three objects to describe for their partner to guess – no gestures or drawings or clues are allowed, only words describing the shape, colour, size, etc., of the appearance.

It is useful to spend a little time on the mechanics of producing diagrams, since ability to do this well will be of benefit for years to come. Before *writing* in detail, it is often quicker to make a plan, then rough draft first, to avoid wasting time constantly crossing out and amending. Similarly, taking time to plan diagrams before drawing them in detail can actually save time overall and produce a more accurate result:

- decide how much of the page is to be used (usually better to aim at more rather than less!);
- then hold a pencil loosely and with light, sketchy lines, indicate the rough proportions of the diagram, gradually adding more detail, still very lightly if necessary, the light planning lines can be erased with a soft rubber later;
- then, with a sharp, HB pencil, draw the permanent lines firmly, leaving no incomplete joins;
- use shading or colour if, and only if, it will make the meaning of the diagram easier to see and understand.

See example (Figure 12.3).

Once the diagram is complete, care needs to be given as to the **labelling**. There should always be a *main label*. By custom, in texts, this is often beneath the diagram, but it is probably less likely to be forgotten if it is *placed above the diagram and printed in capitals*.

Ideally **labels should be** (see Figure 12.4):

- in pencil;
- printed (not in cursive script) in lower or upper case, whichever can be done most neatly;
- always written horizontally;

and **labelling lines** should:

- be ruled in pencil;
- end *clearly* at the point being labelled (with or without a small arrowhead);
- long, so the labels do not clutter up the diagram, but can be read as easily as possible;
- in a radiating (or occasionally, on long thin diagrams, parallel) pattern, rather than at conflicting angles, so the eye can most easily glance along without distraction.

It is helpful to have a poster on display for reference, listing the above 'rules'.

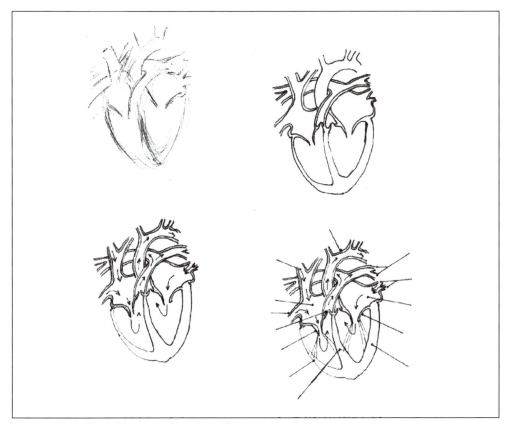

Figure 12.3 Planning and drawing diagrams

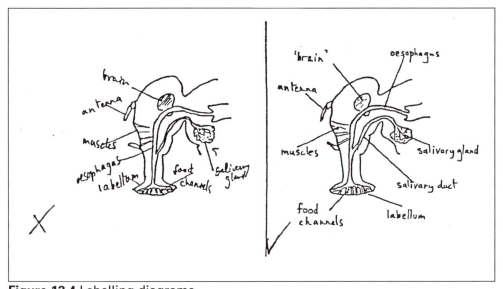

Figure 12.4 Labelling diagrams

Accurate recall of 'labels'

As well as having problems with spelling, dyslexic students tend to have difficulty in learning and retrieving 'naming words' accurately. They may know the related group of words to which it belongs, but easily confuse the members of the group and may, therefore retrieve the wrong one, as in younger dyslexic students there is so often confusion of: left/right, yesterday/tomorrow, ask/answer. Thus, a child may know the set of words to be used as labels, but use them incorrectly. It is useful again, to have home practice sheets with diagrams to be labelled. There should be one correctly labelled version for reference, then ideally, three versions of the diagram, each with labelling lines in a different arrangement, so that it really is the items being learned and not just the position of the labels. If the diagram is complex, or the spellings have not yet been mastered, one could provide an alphabetical list of the labels needed, each designated by A, B, C, etc., so only the letter needs to be put on. For repeated practice at home, the pupils could put the labels on slips of paper, to be arranged as quickly as possible and then checked by a parent.

Learning facts/concepts

Because of weakness in short-term memory and 'naming', dyslexic pupils have difficulty in assimilating information at the same speed as peers, whether reading or listening, so may at times be slow to grasp the concepts involved, 'not being able to see the wood for the trees'. Then, an attempt to learn the facts involved, would be predominantly by rote-learning, an activity notoriously difficult for them. As with learning about English spelling, the load on the memory is greatly reduced if the 'rules' and patterns are appreciated and can be applied. If the concepts and patterns are emphasised, it enables them to find *meaning* in the array of facts, thus facilitating learning. The main ones could be on permanent display as large slogans on a poster, and referred to whenever possible (examples are shown in Figure 12.5).

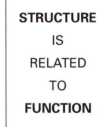

| **STRUCTURE** IS RELATED TO **FUNCTION** | COMPETITION > SELECTION > ADAPTATION

 for resources   of favourable   and <br> food, mate   VARIATIONS   EVOLUTION | 3 MAIN NEEDS

 INPUT OF MATERIALS AND ENERGY

 AVOIDANCE OF WHAT WOULD HARM

 MATE/MEANS OF REPRODUCTION |
| | INTERACTIONS INTERDEPENDENCE

 BALANCE | |

Figure 12.5 'Slogan' diagrams

Many if not most dyslexic students seem to have strong visualising abilities and are easily able to see the 'whole picture' and scan over it. It is helpful if they can be given and also shown how to construct for themselves, **summaries of topics**, which use *as few words as possible* and have a *strong visual aspect*, e.g. Mind-Maps (copyright), flow diagrams, tables (see Figures 12.6–12.10).

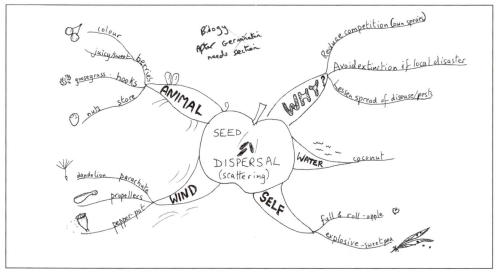

Figure 12.6 Simple example of a mind-map

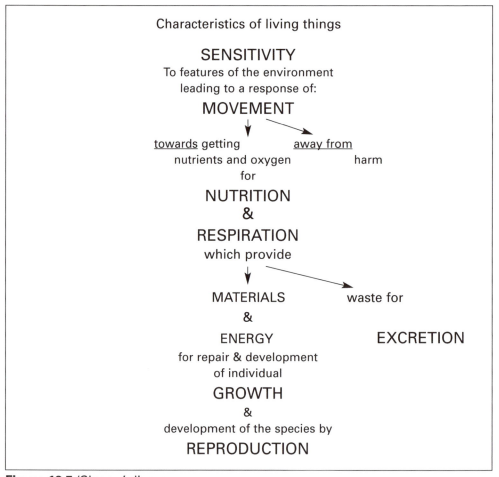

Figure 12.7 'Slogan' diagrams

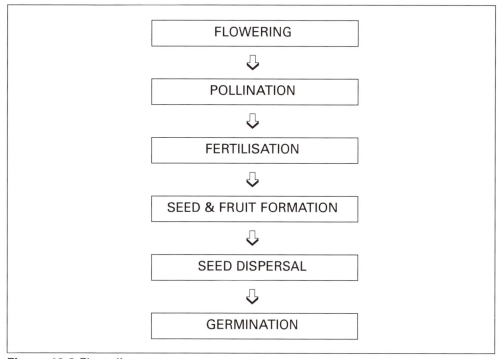

Figure 12.8 Flow diagram

After Fertilisation	
petals	Shrivel
Stamens	and die
Ovary >	Fruit
Ovule >	seed

STRUCTURE OF SEED	
testa	Protective outer coat
cotyledons	Embryo leaves storing food
epicotyl	Stalk between cotyledons & plumule Lengthens to bring above ground
radicle	Embryo root. Produces side roots > root hairs
plumule	Embryo shoot – begins photosynthesis
hilum	Scar where seed joins fruit (pod)
micropyle	Pore through which water can be absorbed

Figure 12.9 Example table

CHAPTER 13

Dyslexia and General Science

Vicky Hunter

This chapter:

- examines the obstacles that can impede learning for dyslexic students
- emphasises the role of the classroom teacher in developing dyslexia friendly materials
- describes some strategies the dyslexic student can utilise for organisation, memory and comprehension
- discusses the use of technology, target setting, learning styles
- considers the role of parents in the learning process.

Introduction

For many dyslexic students the Science subjects are areas of the curriculum where they can excel. Because the need for extended writing is much less than in English or social subjects they are able to focus on content to a greater extent without finding the secretarial demands overpowering. Dyslexic learners often have good practical skills and they enjoy the opportunity to offer oral answers to interesting and relevant questions. Assessments are often multiple choice or short answers rather than lengthy essays. There are however a number of obstacles that can impede learning for dyslexic students and teachers can do a great deal to overcome these. This chapter therefore aims to look at some of these obstacles and to offer practical strategies for overcoming them.

Information to teachers

As with all subjects in the secondary school the first imperative is that the Science teacher is notified of the pupils needs. It is not just enough to say that he/she is dyslexic, the individual strengths and weaknesses must be explained. Does the pupil use a laptop or should they be given access to a computer in the classroom? How well do they cope with technology? Is reading very limited or perhaps adequate although slow? Is spelling very poor or is it fine until the pressure of time or assessment causes it to break down? What about handwriting – does it also tend to break down under pressure? How does the pupil respond to the help available? How is their self-esteem affected by the specific learning difficulty? What support can home offer? The teacher can then implement the strategies that are most appropriate for the individual's needs.

The role of the classroom teacher

As always, most of a dyslexic pupil's needs have to be met by the class teacher. There is rarely enough staffing in school to give individual support in every subject and it is therefore vital that class teachers are willing to accept and support dyslexic children and that specialist advice and support is available to enable them to do this. One of the functions of learning support staff is to act as advocates for pupils to communicate with classroom teachers and to ease any difficulties.

It may be possible to allocate a learning support teacher to the class or, certainly in junior classes, to recruit sixth year students to assist. For assessments where readers and/or scribes are required older students or sometimes parents can be drafted in. However the main burden of enabling the dyslexic pupil to achieve success lies with the classroom teacher. It has been the writer's experience that, in general, Science teachers are comfortable in recognising the difference between dyslexia and ability in their subject. Perhaps this is because the pupil's ability to demonstrate understanding is not impeded by the lengthy essays demanded elsewhere. In addition, many opportunities are available in the laboratory setting to demonstrate initiative and an inquiring mind. It might also be an interesting topic for research to discover how many Science teachers are themselves dyslexic as against the number of dyslexic English or social subjects teachers.

The difficulties

The first hurdle that affects dyslexic students is the layout of the Science classroom – the lab. In their first year children love this different environment and the opportunities for active practical group work. This is fine until it comes to reporting back on the findings of the experiment. If pupils are sitting round lab benches, many of them with their backs to the teacher, board and overhead projector it makes it difficult for a dyslexic pupil to cope with copying or oral to writing tasks. At this point it is important that the needs of the dyslexic pupil are recognised and addressed.

One common practice is for pupils to have a booklet in front of them in which they are going to complete a table with the results of an experiment (see Figure 13.1). If this exercise is conducted purely orally the dyslexic student may have a number of difficulties. The first problem may well be in locating the booklet which has been hastily pushed aside while all the apparatus for the experiment was being set up. Next, the pupil may not catch what was being said and is unable anyway to translate the spoken word into a written word, particularly if it is new vocabulary. He cannot keep track of where each word is to go because of the difficulty in reading quickly the other elements of the table. And sadly he is unable to demonstrate his own success in conducting the experiment because he is so busy trying to figure out how to complete this written exercise. All this is then compounded at assessment time because the notes are incomplete or illegible and the opportunity for consolidation supposedly afforded by the whole-class oral exercise was denied to the dyslexic child who was struggling just to keep up.

Liquid	Colour in water	Colour in acid	Colour in alkali
A			
B			
C			
D			

Figure 13.1 Grid for results of experiment

Strategies

When it comes to written exercises the dyslexic pupil must always have opportunities to see as well as hear the word. The teacher should have the table drawn up either on the board or an overhead transparency. The dyslexic pupil must face this source. Too many pupils sit in Science (and other classrooms) purportedly doing group work when in fact the task involves copying from a board. They are sitting in some cases with their backs to the written source and to copy have to repeatedly turn round. For a dyslexic pupil, by the time they have turned round, they have forgotten which letter they were supposed to be writing.

Teachers should ensure that all pupils can see the source clearly but it is fundamental for dyslexic pupils. It is important that the key words are explicitly taught and that time is allowed for every pupil to have complete usable information.

Copying

Science is often taught through the medium of booklets where the first part of a lesson involves copying something from the booklet into an exercise book. For dyslexic pupils these booklets should simply become disposable, write in booklets. Contrary to what some teachers think, other students do not perceive this as an unfair advantage particularly if the climate in the school and the classroom is one of accepting and understanding all individual difficulties.

Another technique often employed is that of dictated notes. Again this is extremely difficult for dyslexic pupils. Solutions include giving the pupil a copy of the teacher's notes or asking a buddy to lend the pupil good notes so that they can be copied or photocopied. For younger pupils the teacher may have to select the buddy – someone whose note-taking and handwriting can be relied upon – as the pupil may not feel comfortable approaching such a member of the class. The happiest solution is when a dyslexic's best friend also happens to be the neatest and quickest writer in the class! Teachers are often anxious at dyslexic pupils doing nothing during dictation if they are to get copied notes. They should be encouraged to listen carefully to the dictation and ideally make their own Mind-Map© or bullet points. This is a technique that must be learned but it is important that class teachers encourage pupils to use methods like this that have been taught by learning support staff.

Technology

Many dyslexic pupils benefit from the use of technology. If they have a laptop it is important that access to a power point is made easy and matter of fact and that appropriate use is made of the equipment. Often, if photocopied booklets are made available as described above, the need for writing is minimal and using a computer is not in fact helpful.

Teachers have to be sensitive to this and not insist that a pupil uses his laptop when it is not in fact the best solution at that time. One of the most successful recent innovations in the ICT field has been the networking of schools so that pupils can access their own file on a classroom computer anywhere in the school. This means that pupils can start something in the Science lab and then complete it either with a support teacher or in the library. Very soon they will even be able to access it from home. This should help to overcome a lot of the difficulties of laptops, particularly the problem when teachers are concerned that they are not receiving printouts on time and therefore cannot mark work or assess understanding before the next lesson.

Wordbar

All the benefits of technology apply in the Sciences but in particular the program Wordbar can be of great help. In this program the teacher can make up lists of the key vocabulary in the particular subject and the student uses it alongside a word-processing package. All the pupil then has to do is recognise the correct word and select it. It is also useful to use these lists as a basis for key word lists to learn. One of the coping strategies that some dyslexic pupils have decided to use is that of making their handwriting even worse than it might be in order to disguise poor spelling. They have found it preferable to be ticked off for poor handwriting than be told to write out a word ten times – knowing in their hearts that they still will not be able to spell the word the next time. This strategy tends to come a bit unstuck in science when it is important to differentiate between particular words, e.g. chlorine and chloride, or sulphate and sulphide. Use of key word lists, ICT and Wordbar can go some way towards tackling this.

Organising notes

Because dyslexic youngsters have poor organisational skills they need help in keeping Science notes in order. This may not be too great a problem in junior years when most of the work is done in exercise books but in Standard grade work is often stored in loose leaf binders. Dyslexic learners do not instinctively know where one topic ends and another starts and if they do not set off on the right track the task of organising their notes can seem insurmountable.

Sometimes they just give up, either bringing every single scrap of paper with them to every lesson and spending inordinate amounts of time looking for the right page or mysteriously losing everything that ever leaves the classroom. Time invested in setting up binders with labelled dividers and polythene pockets, and discarding unnecessary pieces of paper, is time well spent and liberates the student from the burden of overpowering paperwork. For those of us interested in Feng Shui this clearing out of the clutter enables the chi to flow smoothly!

Basic number

For many dyslexic students tables and number bonds are not well established. They may understand the problem they are being asked to address but the supposedly simple arithmetic holds them back. Obvious answers are to allow them to use calculators, addition and multiplication squares. Additional help can be given by support staff or at home on the specific skills required. Overlearning of some of these may make a difference, particularly if the student is motivated by an interest in Science and acknowledges the relevance of the topic. This, however, may not be enough, as the processing will still take them longer than most pupils. It is therefore essential that time allowances are made. It is also important to separate out this particular problem from the pupil's general competence if decisions are being made about which discrete Science is to be studied at exam level. This is an area where support staff must discuss with their Science colleagues which difficulties are due to dyslexia and the strategies that could be employed in examination subjects to enable dyslexic students to achieve their full potential rather than be placed in less demanding academic classes inappropriately.

Reading comprehension

In some topics in Science, the task is to put certain events in the correct order. There may be a list of six or seven events labelled A to F etc. which have to be placed in order, e.g. 1–6. Dyslexic students find it difficult to hold this information in their heads and have to be taught simple strategies. They should write down the letters A B C D E F and cross each one off as they use it. They also need practice in reading such lists and identifying the key discriminating word or words. Sometimes the essence of answering the question depends on spotting fine differences which a pupil with poor decoding skills may miss. In Biology Standard Grade assessments there are often questions which are fundamentally exercises in reading comprehension. Dyslexic students need a great deal of practice in order to tackle such exercises effectively. They need to be taught skills such as highlighting key words with highlighter pens in order to become more skilled at identifying crucial points.

DARTs type activities such as noting in the margin what they understand the topic of each paragraph to be and reorganising the information in note form can help students to become more proficient at interpreting the information. By actually attacking the passage, processing the information and writing on it with highlighters students become more in control of the work. Often dyslexic students seem almost frightened of text and reluctant to engage with it. By giving them permission to assume ownership of text teachers give such students confidence. A minor practical difficulty that arises from this approach in school is that pupils are often expressly forbidden from writing on hand-outs such as past papers because of the cost implications. This is where the Learning Support Department or school management must be prepared to subsidise approaches that enable dyslexic students to achieve their potential.

EXAMPLE

Passage from 1996 General Biology paper
9. *Read the passage below.*
(Adapted from *The Trials of Life,* by David Attenborough)

Spiny lobsters are found on the coral reefs of Florida and the Bahamas. In the autumn, **storms disturb the water** around the reefs. The lobsters gather in large groups and **begin** walking in single file, **each animal touching the one ahead with its long antennae.** They **migrate** towards deeper water where they will escape the buffeting of the winter storms. The lower temperature in deep water will slow down their body processes so **they use up less energy at a time when food is scarce.** Their navigation system may simply detect cooler water. They may also be able to detect the direction of wave movements.

Moving in single file **reduces the drag of the water on all but the leader.** Moving this way also allows them to respond quickly if they are attacked by trigger fish. They form defensive circles with their pincers pointing outwards.

Answer the questions based on the passage.

(a) What makes the lobsters **begin** to migrate?
(b) Describe how each lobster **keeps its place** in the migrating group.
(c) Give one reason why moving into **colder water** is an **advantage** to the lobsters.
(d) State an **advantage** to the lobsters of moving in **single file.**
(e) The passage describes an **example** of rhythmical behaviour – migration in spiny lobsters.

Describe **one other example** of rhythmical behaviour and state the external trigger stimulus.

Rhythmical behaviour ....

Trigger stimulus ....

The bold words and phrases indicate how a student would have been taught to tackle such an exercise. They need to look at the question, establish the key word or phrase in it and then locate the right part of the passage for the answer. They also need to have made explicit several other aspects that other students seem to pick up. They may well be thrown by the word 'state' and have to be taught it. They need to be taught that generally speaking the answers are to be found in the passage in the same order as the questions. Finally they have to learn to recognise when the questions are not in fact based on the passage and instead call for their own knowledge as in (e) above.

Clear targets

Dyslexic students need clear, logical learning, with short achievable targets. It is therefore important that at the beginning of a topic the learning outcomes are clearly stated and at the end of a topic there are opportunities for structured revision. Exercise books with learning outcomes for each topic pasted into them and constantly referred back to enable dyslexic students to follow the course. Regular and rigorous marking and grading of class work also helps them to keep on top of things. It also means that the class teacher can quickly spot if huge chunks of work are missing, incomplete or illegible and can put in place strategies, such as copying from a buddy, to rectify this. Dyslexic students are often very adept at disguising their difficulties and are anxious to be seen as the same as everyone else. Because of this close, discreet monitoring and gentle, subtle implementation of assistance, is essential.

Learning styles

Use of Mind-Maps (copyright), mnemonics and bullet pointed revision sheets to help recall will capitalise on the differing learning styles of many pupils in the classroom and will benefit not only the dyslexic pupil. Opportunities for group discussion and presentations to the class will enable all students to process information themselves and therefore achieve deeper learning. As is so often the case, good methods for teaching dyslexic pupils are those that also benefit all children.

Parents

Parents can help their dyslexic children by encouraging them to put into words what they have been doing in Science and what they have therefore learned. Children will often describe in great detail the process of boiling something up or the different colours of indicator but need help to make the final connection as to why they did these things and what was therefore proved. Of course many adolescent children are reluctant to tell parents about their school day, revealing as little as possible or conceding only that they got on OK. However, if parents can try to adopt a light touch and encourage children simply to talk, this in itself helps them to clarify their thoughts and ideas. Parents can help at home by reading and scribing homework (after discussion and agreement with school), helping with keyboarding skills if possible, and encouraging and supporting high standards in class exercise books.

Most of all they can, as always, value their children for who they are no matter how difficult they find school. They could also remind their children that Einstein was dyslexic!

Conclusion

Science is a part of the curriculum where dyslexic students can achieve very well provided their needs are met sensitively and appropriately. Self-esteem can be engendered through their ability to conduct experiments with their peer group and to offer oral answers on the same footing as others. The problems in dealing with recording, remembering and assessing should not overshadow these positive benefits of studying Science. The practical strategies outlined above should enable dyslexic students to achieve their potential in Science.

CHAPTER 14

Learning Styles and Mathematics

Steve Chinn

This chapter:

- raises the awareness of the different learning styles in maths in a class of pupils
- increases understanding of the cognitive styles of pupils
- explains the impact of learning style and cognitive style for dyslexic pupils
- suggests ways that different learning and cognitive styles can be addressed in a mainstream classroom.

Introduction

There are many factors which affect how successfully pupils learn mathematics, for example, memory, speed of working, language skills, attitude and learning style. Often these skills interact and are interdependent, so, for example, poor retrieval memory for basic facts will affect speed of working.

The focus of this chapter is learning style and its subsidiary, cognitive style. In some respects teachers might consider that acknowledging learning style is a refinement rather than an essential of teaching, a luxury rather than a necessity, but it can be a significant contributor to failure in maths, with some particular relevance for dyslexic learners. Many aspects of learning style can be addressed in a mainstream classroom by awareness and adjustment of teaching style. The outcome should be a better learning environment, that is, more successful.

Learning style and cognitive style

Mortimore (2000), referring to Schmeck's (1988) work, explains that cognitive style is an individual's characteristic and relatively consistent way of processing incoming information of all types from the environment. Learning style is simply the application of an individual's cognitive style to a learning situation.

Riding and Rayner (1998) suggest that 'A person's cognitive style is a relatively fixed aspect of learning performance'.

Riding and Rayner and Riding and Cheema (1991) are writing about all subjects, whereas this chapter singles out mathematics. From the mathematics point of view I have reservations about their use of the word 'fixed' even if moderated by 'relatively'. Our most recent research, carried out with our Comenius partners in the Netherlands and Ireland, suggests a very strong influence of teaching programme/philosophy on pupils' cognitive styles, that is the style can be modified by teaching.

I always envisage learning style as encompassing the learning environment, the structure of learning time and the characteristics of the learner. For example, the Numeracy Strategy gives a lesson structure that broadly splits into three sections, each with a different activity. Some learners will benefit from this sectional structure. The Numeracy Strategy also structures its programme so that topics are revisited at short time intervals. Again some learners will benefit from this built in revision/overlearning structure. Others may find that they need more time to assimilate the information.

Some learners prefer oral instruction while others need visual input. Some need concrete materials, while others find them irrelevant and confusing. Some like to sit formally at a desk while others need to slump in a chair. Others can only concentrate if they are doodling or fiddling with Blutack.

In summary, learners are individuals. Much of that individuality can be managed in a classroom setting. For the included special needs pupil, awareness from the teacher and appropriate management of his/her individuality will be essential for success.

Cognitive style in Mathematics

A handful of researchers have examined cognitive style in mathematics (see Chinn and Ashcroft 1998). The common theme seems to be that there are two extreme styles and that to be a good mathematician you need to make appropriate use of both. Krutetskii (1976) described this ideal as being 'harmonious'. There are benefits and limitations with an exclusive dependence on either style, hence the need to encourage a flexible use of the appropriate style. The Numeracy Strategy, recently introduced in primary schools in England and Wales, encourages flexibility.

Let us start by looking at three maths problems and the ways pupils may solve them.

Faced with a mental arithmetic addition sum, 152 + 199, some pupils will visualise the sum as

$$152$$

+199 and will add 9 and 2

$$
\begin{array}{r}
152 \\
+199 \\
\hline
1 \\
\end{array}
$$

1 (a 'carried' 1)

They will add the tens column

$$
\begin{array}{r}
152 \\
+199 \\
\hline
51 \\
\end{array}
$$

(another 'carried' 1) 1 1

and finally the hundreds column

$$
\begin{array}{r}
152 \\
+199 \\
\hline
351 \\
\end{array}
$$

This has generated an answer of 351, but in the reverse order, 1 then 5, then 3.

Faced with the same sum, 152 + 199, another pupil will add 152 + 200 to obtain 352, then subtract 1 to reach a final answer of 351.

A pupil is told to 'find' w if w + 3 = 10
 so he remembers his teacher's instructions and writes
$$w = 10 - 3$$
$$w = 7$$

Another pupil looks at the equation and just writes w = 7.

A pupil is asked to find which stall at a fair raises £90, if the total raised is £500 and
 tombola takes   34%
 books takes   11%
 cakes takes   23%
 spinner takes   18%
 crafts takes   14% of the total

So he methodically calculates
$$\frac{34}{100} \times £500 = £170$$

$$\frac{11}{100} \times £500 = £55$$

$$\frac{23}{100} \times £500 = £115$$

$$\frac{18}{100} \times £500 = £90$$

A classmate looks at the same question and writes £90. The teacher asks, 'Where is your working out?' *'Didn't do any.'* 'So how did you do it?' *'Just knew.'* 'No working, no marks.'

How he did it was to see that among the percentages, only one was a multiple of 9. 18 is a multiple of 9, so 18%.

Is that explanation acceptable?

Now let's look at some descriptions of cognitive style.

Bath *et al.* (1986) described cognitive style in maths by tabulating the behaviours associated with two styles, which they name 'inchworms' and 'grasshoppers'. As with Krutetskii, the goal would be to make appropriate use of both styles.

Cognitive styles of the inchworm and grasshopper

	INCHWORM	GRASSHOPPER
Initial approach to a problem	Focuses on parts and detail Separates	Overviews. Holistic. Puts together
	Looks at the numbers and facts to select a relevant formula or procedure	Looks at the numbers and facts to estimate an answer or narrow down the range of answers. Uses controlled exploration

Solving the problem	Formula, procedure oriented	Answer oriented
	Constrained focus	Flexible use of different methods
	Works step by step, usually forward	Often works back from a trial answer
	Uses numbers exactly as given (takes numbers 'literally')	Adjusts numbers by breaking down, building up, relating to an easier number
	Likes to use paper and pen Documents method	Rarely documents method. Does calculations in head
Checking and evaluating	Unlikely to check and evaluate answers	Likely to appraise and evaluate answer against original estimate
	If checking is done, the same procedure/method is used	Checks by an alternate method
	Often does not understand procedures or values of numbers. Works mechanically	Good understanding of methods, numbers and relationships

Marolda and Davidson (2000) also tabulated the characteristics of Mathematics Learning Style I and Mathematics Learning Style II. By describing learning style as opposed to cognitive style they take in a broader picture, but describe similar cognitive patterns to Bath *et al*.

Mathematics Learning Style I	Mathematics Learning Style II
Highly reliant on verbal skills	Prefers perceptual stimuli and often reinterprets abstract situations visually or pictorially
Tends to focus on individual details or single aspects of a situation	Likes to deal with big ideas; doesn't want to be bothered with the details
Sees the 'trees', but overlooks the 'forest'	
Prefers HOW to WHY	Prefers WHY to HOW
Relies on a preferred sequence of steps to pursue a goal	Prefers non-sequential approaches involving patterns and interrelationships
Reliant on teacher for THE approach.	
Lack of versatility	
Challenged by perceptual demands	Challenged by demands for details or the requirement for precise solutions
Prefers quizzes or unit tests to more comprehensive final exams	Prefers performance based or portfolio type assessments to typical tests
	More comfortable recognising correct solutions than generating them
	Prefers comprehensive exams

Sharma (1989) describes two learning personalities, the qualitative and the quantitative.

A quantitative mathematics learning personality processes mathematics information sequentially, parts to whole and is procedurally oriented. They look for specific methods, 'recipes' and formulas.

A qualitative mathematics learning personality processes mathematical information preferably visually from whole to parts. They approach problems holistically and explore global approaches to solutions. This pupil is good at identifying patterns, both spatial and symbolic, and is more adept in relating and connecting different types of concepts and ideas.

With these descriptions in mind, we can return to the three maths examples at the start of this section and identify the learning/cognitive styles of the pupils as they solved the maths problems.

In the mental arithmetic problem, we can identify the first pupil who uses a procedure and a sequential approach as an inchworm and the second who adjusts the numbers and uses subtraction to complete an addition as a grasshopper.

In the algebra question, the first pupil is happy to follow the teacher's methodical procedure. The second pupil can see that the answer is 7 and sees no reason to write down steps that are irrelevant to his perception of the answer.

In the percentage question, the first pupil systematically uses a standard formula to proceed towards an answer. He would be unlikely to overview the percentages and select more probable answers. The second pupil uses the interrelationships of numbers to select an answer, and eliminate the other options.

The first example raises another important consideration. What influences the choice of a particular cognitive style?

What the pupil brings to the problem

In solving a question such as $152 + 199$, many sub-skills are used, for example, the ability to visualise $152 + 199$ in memory as

$$\begin{array}{r} 152 \\ +199 \\ \hline \end{array}$$

The pupil will have to recall that $2 + 9$ is 11 and that $5 + 9$ is 14. He will have to remember to carry 1 into the tens column and add it to the 14, remember to carry 1 into the hundreds column and add it to 2. He will have to remember that he has created 1 in the units column, 5 in the tens column and 3 in the hundreds column and produce the answer in reverse order as 351.

The sub-skills are visualisation, short-term memory, long-term and retrieval memory, sequencing and reversing a sequence. If all those skills are there then the choice of method is suitable.

Now imagine the same pupil trying the subtraction $351 - 199$ and list the steps and thus the sub-skills. Is that a harder task for the pupil?

Now imagine a grasshopper pupil doing both the addition and the subtraction and analyse his steps and sub-skills.

A pupil will be able to adapt more easily to new methods if he has the relevant sub-skills.

Grasshopper methods may offer a dyslexic a method that minimalises written work, but it does draw on a strong awareness of the interrelationships of numbers and operations, for example using 5 as a half of 10, making 9 one less than 10, seeing 1/4 as a half of a half. The National Numeracy Strategy encourages this awareness.

On the other hand dyslexic pupils, like many children with a learning difficulty, like secure and predictable consistency. Inchworm methods offer this. For example, subtraction with decomposition will always work (hopefully correctly), whereas dealing with +99 and then +96 as +100–1 and +100–4 requires a degree of flexibility some pupils find hard to achieve.

This introduces attitude as a further factor. The characteristic of seeking consistency coupled with an avoidance of risk (of failure) is a powerful restriction on learning new or alternate methods.

An analysis of the Marolda and Davidson, and Bath *et al.* tables shows the benefits and disadvantages of a pupil using one style exclusively. For dyslexic pupils, the inchworm demands of memory and sequencing can be a difficulty, while the dyslexic grasshoppers find the requirement to document can be a problem, possibly because the methods they use are more intuitive than procedural.

Cognitive style assessment in the classroom

It will be important to look at the errors the included dyslexic makes in his maths problems. Just marking it 'wrong' will not be enough. A truly useful question is 'How did you do that?'. Whatever diagnostic test you may choose, this simple question is hard to beat.

A European study

As part of a Comenius-funded study we looked at cognitive style in maths in three European countries, Ireland, the Netherlands and England. The study compared pupils from specialist schools and mainstream schools for dyslexic pupils. The age range of the pupils was 10 to 13 years, with 22 pupils from each of the three specialist schools and 22 from each of the mainstream schools. Full details will be published in a separate paper, but the summary of our results and observations showed that:

- the dyslexic pupils in all three countries showed a greater tendency to use the inchworm cognitive style;
- the Dutch dyslexic pupils showed more grasshopper tendencies than the English and Irish;
- the non-dyslexic Dutch pupils showed more grasshopper tendencies than their Irish or English counterparts;
- the Irish non-dyslexic pupils showed more inchworm tendencies than their English and Dutch counterparts.

Our main hypotheses are that:

- the Dutch Realistic Maths programme (Treffers and Beishuizen 1999) encourages a balanced, harmonious cognitive style;
- the Irish maths programme in place at the time of the study did not encourage flexibility in approach (there is a new Maths curriculum from September 1999, which may well change this situation);
- the dyslexic pupils tend to the inchworm strategies – the reason for this is security, the need for consistency and the avoidance of risk;

– both cognitive styles are used in classes by significant proportions of pupils;
– teachers cannot afford not to address both styles.

The Dutch results and our own experience and the retesting of the English pupils after six months of a specifically tailored programme for dyslexic learners suggests that pupils can develop a more balanced cognitive style if taught appropriately. This suggests that cognitive style is not habitual, at least not in maths.

The classroom

First some general points, then some specific examples to illustrate how cognitive style is a factor in the classroom.

Awareness is the first requirement. Teachers need to be aware that their pupils may have different cognitive styles and that their dyslexic pupil may not make best use of his or her preferred cognitive style for several reasons which will include the need for consistency and possibly a compliance to work in the way teacher says.

A pupil with a cognitive style at the far end of the continuum may need to achieve confidence initially by working to that style. Many dyslexic pupils have experienced failure and are reluctant to take any risk that may lead to further failures, even if it is just one maths question. Once confidence is restored it should be possible to explore the complementary strategies. (Though there may be some pupils for whom remediation is too late to consider flexibility, their cognitive style may be too entrenched.)

Teachers need to realistically appraise their own cognitive style when teaching maths and look at the pupils who sail through their lessons. Then they should look at the pupils who struggle and see if a mismatch of cognitive style is a contributing factor.

The old teaching adage of 'tell 'em what you are going to teach, teach 'em, tell 'em what you've just taught them' could infer 'supply an introductory overview, provide a detailed explanation and then review and appraise the whole process and results'. You cover the cognitive styles and teach flexibility and thoroughness in working processes.

Finally, remember that the dyslexic often likes the security of the familiar, even if the familiar is not all that successful. You may have to do the hard sell on that alternative method.

Cognitive style and the Numeracy Strategy

England and Wales have a prescribed numeracy programme, the Numeracy Strategy for pupils from Reception to Year 6 (rising 11 years). It is due to be extended into the next three Year groups. The examples below, although taken from the Numeracy Strategy, illustrate how different cognitive styles can be introduced to any Maths class.

Some examples of methods that could be classified as grasshopper include:

In Years 5 and 6 pupils are asked to find percentages by halving and quartering and halving again, as in finding 12.5% of £36,000 by halving three times and in finding 75% of £300 by halving to get 50%, halving again to get 25% and adding to obtain 75%. This is interrelating numbers, building up and breaking down numbers.

A Year 5 pupil is taught to 'see' 1.5 + 1.6 as double 1.5 plus 0.1.

A Year 1 pupil is encouraged to explore all the pairs of numbers which add to 6.

In Year 2 the mental addition $16 + 7$ is shown as $16 + 4 + 3$ and $22 - 7$ is $22 - 2 - 5 = 15$.

In Year 3 the four times-table facts are obtained by doubling the two times-table facts.

In Year 4 pupils practise responding rapidly to oral or written questions, explaining the strategy used. (Sadly there is still this need to do maths quickly, which is not so good for many dyslexic pupils).

In Year 5 to (continue) to add/subtract 9, 19, 29, or 11, 21, 31 . . . by adding or subtracting 10, 20, 30 . . . then adjusting.

Some examples that could be classified as inchworm include:

Using standard written methods for addition and subtraction in Years 5 and 6.

In Year 4 using standard written methods for short multiplication.

Knowing facts by heart in Year 1.

Using number lines for addition in Year 3.

Without doing a detailed analysis, I guess that grasshopper strategies lead over inchworm strategies in the Numeracy Strategy. With its emphasis on mental arithmetic this is not surprising. On the whole grasshoppers have a better time than inchworms with mental maths. I also feel that when it comes to understanding numbers and the four operations and the whole interrelationships of numbers and processes that the grasshopper methods are preferable, but still should not be taught exclusively. Formulae and procedures will become more frequent later in maths and the groundwork will have to be there.

Conclusion

Part of the eternal challenge of teaching is dealing with the complexity of the individual. The challenge of inclusion is to address that extra complexity in the special needs pupil in your class. This chapter has attempted to explain that pupils use different thinking and problem-solving styles and that this needs to be one of the factors considered when designing a lesson. The Dutch have achieved great success from using 'Realistic Maths' which teaches children to be flexible in their approaches.

A final thought, take comfort in the knowledge that the adjustments you make to help the dyslexic pupil will help other pupils too. Differences in cognitive style are not exclusive to dyslexic pupils, just more likely to create a problem.

References

Bath, J. B., Chinn, S. J. and Knox D. E. (1986) *The Test of Cognitive Style in Mathematics.* East Aurora, NY: Slosson (now out of print, see Chinn 2000).

Chinn, S. J. (2000) *Informal Assessment of Numeracy Skills.* Mark, Somerset: Markco Publishing.

Chinn, S. J. and Ashcroft, J. R. (1998) *Mathematics for Dyslexics: a teaching handbook*, 2nd edn. London: Whurr Publishers.

DfEE (1999) *The National Numeracy Strategy. Framework for teaching mathematics from Reception to Year 6.* London: DfEE.

Krutetskii, V. A. (1976), cited in Kilpatrick, J. and Wirszup, I. (eds) (trans Teller, J.) *The Psychology of Mathematical Abilities in School Children*. Chicago: University of Chicago Press.

Marolda, M. R. and Davidson, P. S. (2000) 'Mathematical Learning Profiles and differentiated teaching strategies', *Perspectives* 26(3) 10–15.

Mortimore, T. (2000) 'Learning style and dyslexia', in Smythe, I. (ed.) *The Dyslexia Handbook 2000*. Reading: British Dyslexia Association.

Riding, R. J. and Cheema, I. (1991) 'Cognitive styles – an overview and integration', *Educational Psychology* 11(3 and 4) 193–215.

Riding, R. J and Rayner, S. (1998) *Cognitive Styles and Learning Strategies*. London: David Fulton Publishers.

Schmeck, R. R. (1988) *Learning Strategies and Learning Styles*. New York and London: Plenum.

Sharma, M. C. (1989) 'Mathematics learning personality', *Math Notebook* 7 (1 and 2).

Treffers, A. and Beishuizen, M. (1999) 'Realistic mathematics education in the Netherlands', in Thompson, I. (ed.) *Issues in Teaching Numeracy in Primary Schools*. Buckingham: Open University Press.

CHAPTER 15

Supporting Students with Dyslexia in the Maths Classroom

Doreen Coventry, Maggie Pringle, Hilary Rifkind and Charles Weedon

This chapter:

- examines the nature and demands of mathematics
- considers the implications of mathematics for the dyslexic learner
- provides a range of strategies which can be used to support dyslexic learners.

If a child does not learn the way you teach, then teach him the way he learns.

(Chasty1989)

Aims

By looking at the nature and demands of maths in relation to some typical characteristics of the dyslexic learner, this chapter considers the consequent difficulties for these students, and how one school responds to them.

Background

The authors teach in a large, co-educational, independent, all-through school that has, for a long time, included an annual intake of students with specific learning difficulties of a dyslexic nature. These students are fully integrated and included within a mainstream environment that is not directly geared to the needs of the dyslexic. The pace may be quite demanding, and the expectation of staff, students and parents is that all students should achieve to their full potential, regardless of specific impediments. Maths classes are broad-banded in the first year of secondary school, then setted. Success in public examinations is emphasised. This applies equally to non-dyslexic and dyslexic students. For most of our dyslexic students, expectations tend to be pitched at university entrance level. Their dyslexia is at no time seen as an implied impediment to this.

Our combined experience as teachers suggests to us that we are not considering a unitary, single condition. No two students labelled as 'dyslexic' present in the same way in the Maths classroom (though there are likely to be a number of common factors). Nor are distinctions between difficulties – dyslexic, dysgraphic, dyspraxic, or dyscalculic, etc. – necessarily helpful in suggesting a way forward in teaching maths. They imply a diagnostic precision that, even if it exists, or may come to exist, is certainly not widely used. For example, it is recently reported that dyscalculic difficulties are manifested in a different part of the cortex than dyslexic difficulties (TESS 7 July 2000), that different areas of the brain are implicated in maths difficulties than in reading difficulties, and that correlations are low between the two. Neuroscientists may be able to make such distinctions – but for the foreseeable future, they are unlikely to be meaningful in the mainstream classroom.

In this chapter, the term Specific Learning Difficulties (SpLD) is preferred and will be used, and refers to students for whom there is a clear discrepancy between their apparent overall academic potential and their actual performance in specific key areas of learning. This may be confined to the areas of mathematics and/or numeracy – although far more likely, their specific difficulty will pervade and impede their learning across a number of areas.

These students present simply as students who may find maths hard in some (or many) ways – and hence there is no single set of guidelines that will allow the SpLD student to be supported effectively.

But they can be supported effectively. This chapter considers and explores how this is achieved. It sets out to reflect, from the viewpoint of practitioners who have proved successful at guiding a wide range of SpLD students through to examination success in Mathematics, what is the nature of their difficulties in the mainstream Maths classroom, and what seems to work in countering them.

The demands of learning Maths

Mathematics tends to be defined as the science of quantity and quantitative relationships. By means of numbers and other symbols, it considers both spatial and numerical relationships (Sharma and Loveless 1986).

Webster's Dictionary includes the entry (perhaps significant when considering why people might find it so hard): 'Mathematical: rigorously exact, perfectly accurate…being beyond doubt or question'. It combines rigour with abstraction, and the processes of abstracting and classifying are essential to it (Skemp 1971). The very essence of maths is that it abstracts to a stage beyond words. Mathematical thinking exists as a distinctive entity partly because it explores areas of thought beyond the easy control of words. It has developed and utilises a whole different symbol system to express ideas and relationships in a very compressed and precise way. They are ideas and relationships that cannot easily be put into words (Weedon 1992).

The purpose of maths is to solve problems (Orton 1987). It demands the acquisition, organisation and access to knowledge, rules, techniques, skills and concepts with the aim of providing solutions to novel situations. It is both an organised body of knowledge and a creative activity.

It is helpful in other ways to see mathematical thinking as having two main strands: skills versus knowledge, procedural versus conceptual. Algorithms play an essential and central part – the formal routines that we learn and depend upon so much, the rules and techniques that are often rote learned.

Successful maths draws simultaneously upon widely differing clusters of abilities: visual and verbal abilities are both implicated; spatial skills are needed in understanding shape, symmetry, and relative size and quantity, and linear skills contribute to understanding the kind of sequential and ordered symbols and representations found in the number system and algebra (Joffe 1980).

It requires that large bodies of arbitrary information be stored and retained to allow swift and automatic access and retrieval. It requires a capacious and flexible working memory.

It requires the processing of a form of English (ME – Mathematical English – as opposed to OE – Ordinary English) that is high in density and low in redundancy. It says things with utmost bareness and without repetition, in a context that supplies little semantic support, and often using everyday words in a critical role but in a way that is different from OE usage (Shuard and Rothery 1984). In fiction, for example, the poor reader may rely on context, on the fact that there are plentiful clues to the meaning of a difficult word:

> Jan sighed. Becoming an Olympic equestrienne was still possible, but the costs of keeping the horses, of the stabling, and of paying the grooms needed to exercise and care for the horses, was more than she could manage. Her childhood dream of riding for Britain was looked more distant every day…

'Equestrienne' might be a challenge to the uncertain reader, but only for a moment – the context quickly explains it. Not so in Mathematical English – consider:

> A quadrilateral whose four corners lie on the circumference of a circle is called a cyclic quadrilateral.

Full of challenges – and no support at all from the context. Mathematical text says things once, and in as bare a manner as is possible.

Even then, what is said may perplex the reader. A student may well understand the meaning of such words as 'difference', 'evaluate', 'odd', 'mean' and 'product', but then find that they have special and quite different meanings in the context of mathematics. This will present a challenge to any reader – but to the uncertain reader, doubly so.

We have, then, a subject which demands, as part of its very essence:

- linearity and sequentiality
- rigorous exactitude and precision
- a dependency upon wholly arbitrary symbols used in a way that is highly compressed
- effective storage, access and retrieval
- effective and flexible working memory
- the ability to combine creativity with rigorous mental organisation
- algorithmic competence – the ability to learn and apply rules
- the ability to process high density and low redundancy text swiftly and effectively
- the ability to draw simultaneously upon a range of learning styles and preferences.

These are not qualities that are typical of the SpLD learner, however committed and intelligent that learner may be.

The nature of the SpLD learner

As already suggested, we do not see SpLD as a unitary entity – for all practical purposes, there appear to be as many 'dyslexias' as there are 'dyslexics'. But there are common features, and, given the demands outlined above, a trawl of typical diagnostic checklists brings up a host of characteristics that might impinge directly upon performance in the secondary Maths classroom:

- reading and spelling difficulties
- copying difficulties, and losing the place on page and blackboard
- poor speed of processing, and consequent slow pace of work
- difficulty with writing and page layout/organisation
- access and retrieval difficulties: those 'tip of the tongue' experiences when the answer's there but won't come forward
- difficulty in rote memory and common sequences
- poor numeracy
- confusion of directional words, and difficulty in telling left from right, and orientation
- reversals of numbers and letters, and confusions of similar looking letters – b/d, p/q, etc.
- difficulty with coordination, hand–eye coordination, and fine motor skills
- poor spatial skills and shape recognition
- personally disorganised and untidy
- can see 'answer' but can not say how it was reached
- 'good' and 'bad' days for no evident reason
- inattention and poor concentration
- frustration and anxiety, and possible subsequent behaviour problems
- fatigue and outbursts at 'overload'
- poor auditory discrimination
- poor visual discrimination
- visual/perceptual difficulties
- easily tired
- blurring and poor visual tracking
- undue dependency upon a preferred learning style.

No student will manifest all of these – but many will manifest some of them. There are probably many more.

Some consequences for the SpLD student in the Maths classroom

Such students are likely to perform below their own potential when confronting the demands of mathematics. They may have many qualities to set against their weaknesses – a powerful conceptual grasp, a creative approach to learning, effective problem-solving techniques, and a wholistic and global understanding that moves forward through metaphor and analogy rather than sequential mastery. But overall, they have an uphill struggle.

Some features merit special attention. At a practical level, an inability simply to read the material fast enough and effectively enough may bring serious disadvantage, as does a chaotic and untidy page.

At a conceptual level, memory is central – effective storage and retrieval, and a cognitive workbench in the working memory large enough to manipulate the retrieved and incoming information, is essential. A working memory deficit is very characteristic of SpLD.

In particular, algorithms and rote learning have an important role in maths – a role that is undervalued in an educational philosophy that has for decades emphasised mastery and understanding. Often, it has been argued, dependence upon these algorithms, without understanding, leaves the learner's mind a cluttered mess of confusing rules: 'the smaller number goes on the bottom line', or 'turn it upside down and multiply'.

But in maths, it might be argued, often it seems that techniques and approaches that have been learned and used successfully but with limited understanding are understood and appreciated only in retrospect, once the student has moved on to more advanced concepts. 'It is a subject where one learns the parts; the parts build on each other to make a whole; knowing the whole enables one to reflect with more understanding upon the parts . . . ' (Chinn and Ashcroft 1998). Thus an ability to internalise a procedure, without understanding it fully (or even partially?), may be more important in maths than in other areas of learning – so for those for whom rote retention of arbitrary information is specially hard, a core maths learning skill is damaged.

Learning style may be specially important. A preference for visual, auditory or kinaesthetic learning will cause different learners to cope differently with different aspects of maths. Any imbalance of hemispheric dominance may lead to overdependence upon spatial or linear strategies. Both are needed. SpLD learners tend to over-rely upon one.

Self-esteem is important, with all these factors arrayed against them, some early experience of failure seems inevitable – and failure within a context so remorseless, cumulative and linear as the Maths curriculum is failure that reverberates and re-echoes across every aspect of maths learning. Institutional constraints reinforce this: we press on with the syllabus – increasingly, in an environment dominated by league table and political/journalistic expectations, we have no choice but to do so. Yet if we test a skill taught and practised some time ago, probably we do not expect a generally high level of competence. Given our recognition of the rigorously linear nature of maths, we teach with a remarkably high toleration, even expectation, of failure. These are students with bruising experience of failure. We compound it.

So, a picture emerges of the learner, the institution and the subject all apparently at odds with one another. Yet there is every opportunity for success. These are intelligent and adaptive learners. How can this success be achieved?

Some teaching tips

Mindful of grandmothers and sucking eggs, we tried tabulating 'problems' and 'responses'. It looked something like this.

The problem...	The response...
Poor numeracy, and no automatic access to number facts.	Encourage table squares and calculators as an immediately available fallback – don't allow it to become an impediment.
Showing working – these are not linear thinkers, and they often appear to know the right answer without knowing how they got there.	Emphasise this essential linearity – it is central to formal maths, but may be completely alien to the right brained and metaphor oriented learner struggling with it in your classroom. Make processes just as explicit as possible when teaching them – get the child to explore their own processes, making each step just as explicit as possible. Emphasise the choices of ways forward, so that they can find and

	choose the ones that work best for them: e.g. subtraction by counting on, or by formal algorithm; percentage problems by decimal multiplying, or by finding 1%, etc.
Slow pace of work, due to poor processing speed.	Ensure the work they do does focus upon key techniques and concepts, and reduce the 'extra practice' element – but at the same time help them recognise they simply have to do more work than others if they are to get enough practice.
Untidy and illegible work means they cannot read their own earlier working.	Encourage plenty of space – a whole page for each exam question, and extra time; or use a scribe if there is someone available.
Poor reading skills.	Read the questions to them, or have them audio taped, maybe – on to Dictaphone. Use magnifying devices – ask your optician. Photo enlarge the papers and texts – it makes it much easier. Encourage line markers, to help keep place: a ruler, perspex strip or piece of paper.
Similarity of textual detail – e.g. the important differences between x^2, $2x$, and $x + 2$, or between x and $+$, and $-$ and $\div$	Make them explicit, and return to them as often as is needed. Confront the difficulty – don't avoid it, or underrate it.
Too many easily confused algorithms and procedures.	Articulate them into words whenever possible, with mnemonic.
Poor concentration span.	Agree a coded signal that doesn't draw the attention of others.
Copying from board difficult.	Provide notes, even if just a photocopy of another student's notes.
Poor memory.	Keep revisiting, revising, visualising, and sharing ideas with others about the techniques that work for them.
Poor self-esteem.	Boost it by praise - these can be very bruised students, and they cannot get enough recognition and appreciation.

Figure 15.1 Teaching tips – responses to problems

Students with SpLD will benefit from good maths teaching that recognises and responds to the 'differentness' of each learner in the room. Interestingly, most of our strategies are essentially practical and organisational ones; the pedagogic ideas, the teaching tips, are no more than a restatement of good maths teaching practice that apply to all learners who encounter difficulties.

What other strategies might be helpful – practical and organisational strategies that support and facilitate the insightful teaching strategies described above?

Some practical strategies

We use Sixth Year helpers, in the classroom alongside individual learners; in the Learning Support (LS) Centre as tutors; and most important, as readers and scribes for all tests and assessments.

Parent volunteers and friends of the school act as readers and scribes for major external exams, and sometimes as in-class helpers. There's an enormous willingness to help in most communities – people are waiting to be asked.

LS staff teach cooperatively with Maths staff.

Extra time is allowed for students whose psychometric profiles allow it.

There is a facility for putting text onto audio tape – again, provided by parents and friends of the school. Studying a page of maths is made much easier if the text part is being heard as well as seen.

Where students' psychometric profiles allow it, calculators are allowed in non-calculator contexts.

LS issue Learner Profiles of SpLD students to all staff who teach them – as well as describing briefly their strengths and weaknesses, they offer suggestions for the classroom. (An example is provided as Figure 15.2.)

Staff deployment, too, is an important issue, so that no teacher is exposed only to competent mathematicians year after year. Such teaching does nothing to cause us to try to understand how a child is seeing a problem. But the baffled teacher who has struggled to bring understanding to each child in that small 'bottom set' last year is infinitely better equipped to teach that top set next year, when it includes one or more SpLD students.

Conclusion

Part of the pleasure of mathematics is to be found in its 'closure' – there is a neat and elegant solution awaiting those who persevere, a solution without loose ends, a solution that is the 'right answer', and intrinsically deeply satisfying for that very reason. The poem may never be completed; the History essay is handed in with misgivings that some parts of it could be improved; but the completed maths problem is complete.

In our opinion, there are no formulae, no neat packages of answers; and certainly no sense that one has ever completed the task of helping the SpLD learner in the Maths classroom. Perhaps a useful way forward in meeting the needs of all dyslexic students in the mainstream school, within the current climate of inclusion, is to consider the quote with which we started this chapter,

'If a child does not learn the way you teach, then teach him the way he learns.'

Student: John Smith

Learner Profile Session 00/01

Updated: August 2000

LS Year Teacher: C. Weedon

Review summary
John has a significant and clearly defined specific difficulty affecting his reading, spelling and rote memory, and he attends the Centre instead of Modern Languages.

He is an extrovert and enthusiastic student, with a swift and robust sense of humour. But as well as the exuberance, there is real perceptiveness and sensitivity. He still tends to underestimate himself – because of his dyslexic difficulty, such tasks as reading, writing and copying all require considerable effort from him, and even with this effort will still be imperfect. He had some quite difficult times during last session, and became very discouraged in some areas. He finds it hard to commit facts to memory, and becomes very anxious about tests and exams.

Suggestions for the classroom
- Let him know you are aware of his difficulty, that you are sympathetic – but that you have high expectations of him.
- Be generous with the praise and cautious with criticism – John has had some very bruising classroom experiences in the past, and his self-esteem is still quite fragile.
- Allow extra time for tests and assessments.
- Arrange a Reader and/or Scribe for all major pieces of work and assessments.
- Arrange an S6 in-class helper if he would like it.
- Don't ask him to read aloud.
- Do not expect extended and unsupported reading - if there are any course texts, or major readers, arrange in advance with LS for these to be taped.
- Encourage him to photocopy a peer's notes at the end of each lesson.
- Encourage the development of his word-processing skills for more extended pieces of work - and nag him about editing and spellchecking.

These targets, strategies and comments have been seen by and discussed with the student.

If and when there is anything you think should be changed or added, please let the LS Year teacher know so that we can update the targets and strategies.

That way they should change as the student changes, and give an up to date picture of the actual classroom needs of each student. Thanks.

Figure 15.2 Learner Profile of SpLD student

References

Chasty, H. (1989) Paper presented at the First International Conference, British Dyslexia Association, Bath, April.

Chinn, S. and Ashcroft, J. R. (1998) *Mathematics for Dyslexics: a teaching handbook.* London: Whurr Publishers.

Giles, G. (1981) *School Mathematics under Examination: Part 3 – factors affecting the learning of Mathematics.* University of Stirling, Department of Education DIME Projects.

Joffe, L. (1980) 'Dyslexia and attainment in school mathematics', in *Dyslexia Review* 3(1) and 3(2).

Joffe, L. (1990) 'The mathematical aspects of dyslexia: a recap of general issues and some implications for teaching', *Links* 15(2).

Lansdown, R. (1978) 'Retardation in mathematics: a consideration of multi-factorial determinant', *Developmental Medicine and Child Neurology* 20.

Miles, T. and Miles, E. (eds) (1992) *Dyslexia and Mathematics.* Routledge: London.

Orton, A. (1987) *Learning Mathematics: Issues, Theory and Classroom Practice.* London: Cassell.

Plunkett, S. (1979) 'Decomposition and all that rot', *Mathematics in Schools* 8(3), 2–5.

Polya, G. (1957) *How to Solve It.* Anchor: Doubleday.

Sharma, M. C. and Loveless, E. (eds) (1986) 'Dyscalculia – a special issue on the work of Ladislav Kosc', *Focus on Learning Problems in Mathematics,* Summer/Fall 8(3 and 4).

Shuard, H. and Rothery, A. (eds) (1984) *Children Reading Mathematics.* London: John Murray.

Skemp, R. (1971) *The Psychology of Learning Mathematics.* London: Penguin Books.

Times Educational Supplement Scotland (TESS) (2000), 7 July.

Weedon, C. (1992) *Specific Learning Difficulties in Mathematics.* University of Stirling and Tayside Region.

Weedon, C. (1993) 'Specific difficulties and mathematics', in Reid, G. (ed.) *Specific Learning Difficulties (Dyslexia).* Edinburgh: Moray House Publications.

Weedon, C. (1994) 'Learning difficulties and mathematics', in Riddell, S. *et al.* (eds) *Special Educational Needs Policy in the 1990s: Warnock in the Market Place.* London: Routledge.

CHAPTER 16

Drama and Art: The Experience of Learning

Drama – *Robin Gray*
Art – *Anne Van Wren*

This chapter:

- through personal accounts from experienced practitioners describes the benefits of experiential learning in drama and art
- illustrates how dyslexic children can fulfil their potential in learning, communication and self-esteem in these subject areas.

DRAMA

Introduction

Teaching drama to dyslexic pupils can be frustrating but infinitely rewarding. The teacher can experience feelings of total desperation one minute and joy the next. The fun of taking part is often a catalyst to developments in other learning areas, and subsequent improvement in confidence and self-esteem.

> I had a group working on a 25 minute version of Cinderella. They were determined to put the show on for the school but as the date for the show grew closer, it seemed to get worse and worse. Putting them in costume made a difference but I still watched from the wings in dread.
> *They were superb!* As they took their bow to the cheers of the rest of the school, the look on every face was something to behold.

Improvisation

I find one of the best ways to start off a drama group is to introduce some basic improvisation. Some helpful illustrations follow.

- Improvisation can be in the form of a game such as charades or statues. Success is the secret of continued enthusiasm so I try to keep it simple. In charades the teacher can lead the way by asking the group to guess which job they are acting. I make it nice and easy;

something like window cleaning or a policeman on point duty. When every one is guessing well, I suggest one of them have a go. It doesn't take much for most of them to be eagerly demanding a go although there is bound to be one who is more reluctant. Some will have their own ideas while others may need help.

Statues is another good game to get pupils out in front of the rest of the group. Once again the ideas should be as simple as possible to provide a successful outcome. The improvisation of conversations and situations follows on almost naturally, and much excitement can be expected. However the difference between playing and playing a part may not be as easy to deal with.

- Some marvellous improvisations can be produced from a basic starting point. For instance a short piece may be devised by the pupils working in pairs, based on a visit to a friend in hospital, and I have had really dramatic improvisations based on a visit to a friend who is in a coma!

Starting points

A starting point which stirs the emotions is always successful. The war photographs of Don McCullin may well be shocking but I have never had an improvisation session based on them that has not gone well. Why not try Picasso's *Weeping Woman*, or *The Scream* by Munch?

- Other starting points may be an object or group of objects. The student may be given an object or invited to choose from a group of objects on a table. Working in pairs or small groups often works well with this approach and some exciting, often hilarious outcomes can result. This approach takes much of the strain of reading, traditionally associated with drama studies, off the students' shoulders and helps to build enthusiasm for the subject and a trust in the teacher before scripted work is introduced. Enjoyment and fun is the key to success.

Group size

The need for small groups cannot be overemphasised. The pupils will usually have very limited concentration span and they will find it hard, if not impossible, to watch a long performance without fidgeting or interrupting. I attach great importance to their role as an audience, and repeatedly make sure everyone receives applause for a finished performance. The ability to watch and make critical judgements of others' improvisations is an essential skill for the pupils to develop. The teacher will need to develop strategies to deal with the pupils' natural wish to 'take the Mickey' and make funny comments. Small groups seem to suffer less from this problem than large groups. I find six to eight pupils to be the ideal group size.

Other successful improvisations

Thinking up an improvisation on the spur of the moment will be extremely hard for some dyslexic pupils and some improvisations may well move away from the original starting point or lose direction completely. Props, costumes, wigs and masks have proved to be successful stimulations and are essential for keeping the actors on track.

A successful improvisation can often generate excitement in both the audience and the actors. With many dyslexic pupils, this excitement can very easily get out of hand with everyone talking at once and forgetting they are in a classroom situation. This is particularly so if the piece is humorous and it is all to easy for them to forget what is appropriate behaviour.

Plays

The challenge of a scripted play is often one which pupils who have tasted success in improvised situations are keen to take up. However there is almost always one if not more who will view this new departure with reluctance and a degree of trepidation.

After much searching, I have found there are few really suitable plays for dyslexic pupils. Many of the plays which have a suitable reading age offer little in the way of an exciting story line and I find that I am constantly rewriting lines or even inventing new scripts which the students will find both interesting and not impossible to deal with.

The problems here are much the same as in other reading situations. The pupil will find difficulty with certain words, and with keeping their place. Problems with short-term memory will at times cause the pupil to forget which part they are playing and some who read everything correctly will not pick up the meaning, having worked very hard to say the words correctly. Others who are not engaged in reading can easily lose concentration. The sheets of paper with the all important words become a hindrance to the action.

The temptation to read through a new play in order to discover what is going on is I think, best avoided. I prefer to outline the entire story: make it exciting! If the characters can be seen in the imagination first, the chance of early understanding of the plot and a wish to take part can be achieved.

Having heard the story, many of the cast may be clambering to be the character that most takes their fancy. Here I try to make everyone try all the parts and this has several advantages. They all get to read all the lines and thus know the play better than if they had concentrated on just a single part. (It is possible for someone to know their lines but not know the story!) They can see different ways of playing the same part and the ones with the least reading ability hear the lines several times before having a go.

Pupil participation

Many dyslexic pupils have difficulty with short-term memory. I find it useful therefore to find out who can remember what. I often use a ten-word test with a single action and present it as a challenge. 'Who can copy this exactly?' Holding a top hat to my chest I say in a loud clear voice, 'My Lords, Ladies, and Gentlemen, welcome to Billy Smart's Circus.' Of course none of them has heard of Billy Smart or his Circus but never mind. I move the top hat from my chest to full stretch to the right and then back to its original position. Many dyslexic pupils find it impossible to repeat this simple act even after several goes!

For the non-reader it is not essential to get all the lines right. Providing the sense is maintained it is possible for a non-reader to function successfully alongside those with far greater reading ability.

For the dyslexic actor, the act of struggling their way through a script is very tiring. To take the strain away from a tiring actor a change of direction is often useful. Discussion as to the action or the placing of a piece of scenery may be all that is needed to refresh the situation.

Planning sets

Planning the sets, and designing costumes and make up, are popular ways of working from the script. The student can work through the scenes and fill out columns with lists of props, character costumes, and ideas for scenery. All this encourages the student to read through the play and thus get to know it better. The student can be quietly helped through reading problems at the privacy of their own desk. This builds confidence in their knowledge of the play before the next rehearsal.

Something I find very useful is to produce the script in a very much larger type size, either by photocopy enlargement or better still by retyping the script in a large sans serif type face. Gil Sans seems to be the most successful. It is also useful to type the script so that each sentence has its own line where possible.

Performing

Performance in front of others is a challenge which often results in great enthusiasm. A piece delivered in school assembly will usually go down well. *Revolting Rhymes* by Roald Dahl are a tremendous source of fun for audience and actors alike. Most translate into several parts and can be an hilarious and slightly subversive start to the day. Other sources to try are *Dirty Beasts* by the same author, *Works* by Spike Milligan, and much of the work of Roger McGough.

Script reading and attention

My biggest challenge is *not,* as might be expected, the ability of the group to cope with reading the script. It is the fact that many dyslexic students find it almost impossible to keep on task for more than a few minutes. Scripts are damaged and crumpled almost as soon as they are given out and a good number of replacements are required. Tapping rhythms and fiddling with chairs or what ever else comes to hand can become very distracting to those engaged in the action. The stopping of such behaviour has only short-term effects. The audience will find it almost impossible not to interrupt and will contribute ideas and thoughts as they come to mind. Most have an uncontrollable urge to be the class clown and these traits can become more troublesome as the size of the group increases. Working alongside non-dyslexic students can often make this behaviour appear consciously disruptive. It should be borne in mind that the dyslexic pupil is not necessarily being 'naughty', and will have little control over the situation until quite a lot of experience is gained.

Success through experience

As the group gains experience the interruptions become less troublesome, and some very rewarding work can result.

One of the most popular parts of the drama course for my students is when I introduce them to make up. Snazaroo and Grimace face paints have been developed to produce clear and dramatic effects and with just a little demonstration the students will work with focus and determination. I have been both surprised and delighted with the results as they take it in turns to turn each other into first monsters, and then old ladies and gentlemen. A useful addition to the make up kit is a box of Caran D'Ache Neocolor 11 crayons. These water-soluble crayons are the only ones that are non-allergic and can be used to create some spectacular make up effects. Another popular and useful skill is the creating of lifelike wounds and the boys and girls will take great pains to produce the most horrendous injuries and of course insist on wearing them into lunch! It never fails to surprise me how much better their performance becomes when they see their character come to life in a mirror. This improvement continues even when the make up is taken off, and it is well worth all the mess.

Cross-curricular aspects of drama

Drama is possibly the best of the cross-curricular activities. It can involve the production of stage sets, the design of costume or the making of masks and puppets, the use of stage lighting and sound effects, and the discovery of suitable props. All of these activities stem directly from the script and involve the students in creative thought and activity. This involves the students in discussion about what is required and makes use of any talents the students may possess. Several teachers can get involved.

Original scripts

One of the most successful types of drama lessons involves improvisation and scripts produced by the students themselves. I work on an everyday scene based on the student's own experiences. For instance, the reaction of parents to a child getting in late. I ask the class to get into groups of two or three and to work out an idea for an improvisation. They then act out the piece and the rest of the students comment on it. The piece is then worked on and performed again. Those taking part are then invited to write out the play in their own words.

I type out the plays, making all corrections, and produce enough copies for the author to choose the players and produce the piece for the rest of the class. Once again I find a simple sans serif type face easier for the players to read and I also try to keep each sentence to its own line. A larger than usual type face also seems to be helpful, 16 point is the one I favour.

Writing scripts

The students are always keen to take part in something they have had a hand in writing and are delighted to see their words in print for others to perform. I am at present working with a fairly large group who have gained quite a lot of experience over the last twelve months. They have already overcome much of the embarrassment associated with reading aloud and not getting everything right.

We started by establishing a basic story line with discussion and some improvisation. After the class finished I put their ideas down on paper so we could run through them together and agree the wording during the next class. I then went away and came back with a couple of scenes for their approval. After a few changes the first scenes were ready and ideas for sets were drawn up. They are very enthusiastic and I must admit that it is all going very well. We are now on scene five, act one, and Sir Gerald Black is about to meet his untimely end. Each student will now write the next scene: scene one, act two.

The aim is to read all the versions and to amalgamate the ideas into a finished scene. It is important that everyone who has tried to contribute gets a say and that the scene is also as good as possible. It is very exciting to note that the whole group already knows most of the words and is thus unhindered by the script. This frees us up to work on the production. It is very much their work and they are justly proud of it. We can make any changes required with ease and every one feels free to express ideas, and hopefully, to accept the decision of the group. Already the acting is less wooden and one can feel the sense of achievement and confidence that the pupils have gained.

Assessment

Assessment within the classroom situation presents few problems. It is easy for the teacher to see how practical skills and techniques develop both in performance and aspects of theatrical design. However the constraints of examinations are often an enormous hindrance to the effective teaching of drama, especially where a truly adaptive approach is necessary. The dyslexic student will sometimes make extremely slow progress and find it very difficult to evaluate their own thoughts and progress, especially on paper. They will often have a very low level of self-esteem and find it very difficult to come to terms with having been successful. This can spoil the sense of achievement and detract from the enjoyment. The teacher is often placed in the position of having to decide whether a student succeeds in drama and enjoys success and the obvious benefits of improved self-confidence, or struggles to get through the GCSE at the risk of missing the benefits of theatrical success.

Effects of Drama

The effects of dramatic success are often clearly seen in other areas of study within the curriculum. I have seen great advances in reading aloud from students eager to play a part well and this can add great impetus to their efforts. In a work experience exercise the drama students stood out by their ability to present themselves with confidence.

Some of our students may well go on to take exams and others may not. The lucky ones may even go on to greater things: to appear in theatre, television, or even films. However, it is not everyone who has the wish to tread the boards. The teaching of drama is not aimed at that. If we can give people the chance to have a go, to stand up and talk with confidence in public and most of all enjoy it, then we have been successful. And, of course, we will have a group of people who love going to the theatre. 'Break a leg'.

Acknowledgements
I would like to thank David Walker, Mary I'Anson and Sue Gray for their help and encouragement with our drama sessions at Shapwick.

ART

Dyslexia in the Art classroom

> Art and design is the freedom of the individual, the freedom of expression and the freedom to fail without retort.
>
> (Simon Waterfall, Creative Director, Deepend; quoted p. 14 National Curriculum)

This quote should give encouragement to dyslexic students included in the Art classroom of a secondary school. Art stands apart from other subject areas in that it is unrestricted by goals. In art, aesthetics and perception are qualities that make art, as a way of learning, unique within the curriculum. There are no comparisons in art, only individual interpretations and response. Therefore the main aim in an Art and Design Department should be for all children, including identified and unidentified dyslexic students, to be encouraged to reach their full potential creatively in the knowledge that the sky is the limit.

Art is a useful vehicle for learning. As Robert Clement (1993) wrote in *The Art Teacher's Handbook*, 'there are exclusive ways of operating within art that are beneficial to all children, whatever their skills or potential as artists'.

Background

In 1996 the National Curriculum provided a framework in art for *all* schools to adhere to; giving more unified aims and paving the way for easier integration and inclusion of special needs children coming from Special Education Centres following the same guidelines as mainstream schools. If a school aims to cover the programmes of study set out in the National Curriculum for Art and Design they will be providing opportunities for all students, but most importantly for the creative dyslexic. The school should aim to promote a pupil's spiritual, moral, social and cultural development. It should provide opportunities for developing key skills of communication, application of number and IT and aim to encourage thinking skills, enterprise and entrepreneurial skills and develop the students' understanding of the relevance of art and design in life, and help them to recognise the range of possibilities for employment in creative and cultural industries and for becoming involved in shaping environments.

Inclusion

Schools should not feel insecure about inclusion, but welcome it. Bruce Allen Knight (1999) wrote, 'the goal of inclusion is not to erase differences but to enable students to be valued for their individuality in an education community'. Similar, but more direct, is James Dyson's 'Insight' (Dyson 2000) 'We must encourage people to embrace difference with a sense of hope and optimism, after all, only dead fish go with the river.'

West (1991) provides an inspiring message when he suggests that

> The extent of coming change may be very great. For some four hundred years we have had our schools teaching basically the skills of the medieval clerk ... reading, writing, counting and memorising texts. Now it seems we might be on the verge of a new era ... in the future we might see the solution of difficult problems in statistics, molecular biology, materials development, or higher mathematics coming from people who are graphic artists, sculptors, craftsmen, film makers, or designers of animated computer graphics. Different kinds of problems and different kinds of tools may require different talents and favour different kinds of brains.'

This message needs to be noted and applied in an inclusive teaching environment if full inclusion is actually to be achieved.

National Curriculum – themes

Throughout Key Stages 1, 2, 3 of the National Curriculum the same key themes are identified for study:

- exploring and developing ideas
- investigating and making art, craft and design
- evaluating and developing work
- developing knowledge and understanding.

Individual teachers should aim to promote and provide opportunities for pupils to experience these throughout the year. Later in this chapter there is an account of my own personal experience of teaching a range of Art and Design topics throughout one year to dyslexic students in an Independent Day School. The approach aimed towards personal success in art for the individuals involved. It promoted these key themes and thus began preparing the way for integration and inclusion in the secondary school. To guide me throughout and to help me keep on track I produced a Mind-Map. I find this approach, advocated by Tony Buzan, invaluable – it helps me to focus on what is important, and trims down what seems at times to be a quagmire of ideas (see Figure 16.1).

Art provides a way to build a student's confidence and self-esteem, particularly that of the dyslexic student. These students, even if they have poor belief in themselves because of past experiences, can be shown how to guide their feelings, imagination, emotions and ideas into works of art and design. Educators should aim for positive encouragement for all students. Even if a student with a poor working memory may have interpreted and produced something different to the initial set of instructions, the finished product is still *art* and should be assessed as such.

The teacher can decide on a pupil's level of attainment for Art and Design and judge which level best fits the pupil's performance. The levels range from 1–8, plus one for exceptional performance level, but these can only be guidelines because they are open for individual teacher interpretation. Levels do not have much relevance. No differentiation is required in the Art lesson. For the dyslexic student the main aim in the Art lesson is to raise awareness kinaesthetically and raise trust in their ability to achieve.

The Art teacher, while promoting these aims in the classroom, may well discover the undiagnosed dyslexic and be able to liaise on his/her behalf in cross-curricular areas. This will help to provide an environment which encourages the dyslexic pupil. It will also help in the reintegration process, from 'time out' in a specialised school, so that inclusion within the Art classroom is likely to be a smoother process.

Art, Design and Craft

Art and design are by their very nature are multisensory. This is a positive factor for dyslexic pupils, who benefit from multisensory learning environments: 'Art and design is not just a subject to learn but an activity that you can practise with your hands, your eyes, your whole personality' (Quentin Blake, Children's Laureate; quoted p. 14 National Curriculum 1).

In general the right cerebral hemisphere is the visual hemisphere (Treays 1996); the left side is used for speech and language. The right hemisphere of a dyslexic student's brain is more developed than the left, allowing him/her to have more creative thoughts and impulses. This is the reason that multisensory techniques used in the teaching of numeracy and literacy for dyslexic students are more successful than more traditional methods. Teachers need to stimulate a dyslexic pupil through their senses and encourage metacognitive thoughts. It therefore follows that dyslexia in the Art classroom can be an ingredient for success and can help to promote success in other curriculum areas.

National Curriculum – Art and Design

The National Curriculum in 1996 recognised the importance of Art and Design: 'Understanding, appreciation and enjoyment of the visual arts have power to enrich our personal and public lives'. This recognition was an encouraging sign for the more creative thinking dyslexic student. A chance to succeed and feel more included in school life. Not so for some students educated previous to 1996. Richard Flint, an adult dyslexic, has recently had his expressive art displayed at the Royal Exchange Theatre in Manchester. The exhibition, entitled 'Our Lives 2000', was of new work by leading disabled artists, in Greater Manchester in July/August 2000. Richard has found expressing his frustration and anger through art helpful and also a means of expressing to others the lack of support he has felt during his school life. Richard explains that: '3 Wise (half) Asses is a new work which developed a response to my treatment in the academic environment prior to discovering at the age of 26 that I am dyslexic.' The three pieces were entitled: Get The LL Outta Here, Scratchin' 'n' Twitchin', and Poetry Motion – Merdre Avec Parole. The pieces of work were three wooden desks with three gouged holes in the scratched lids. His concern is that 'late diagnosis of adult dyslexia is far more prevalent than we might expect. Failure to recognise dyslexia/ignorance about the condition/especially in the teaching profession is a fundamental failure of our society'. Gura (1996) also states that the 'latest figures suggest that learning problems become more apparent after the age of 7 under the present system of education in the UK'.

Since the National Curriculum in 1996, dyslexia is now more widely recognised. Unfortunately, however, there will still be people like Richard who feel let down by the education system. Similar experiences of mature students are discussed by Miles and Varma (1997). He points to research that proves that for pupils to be assessed as dyslexic at a young age is more beneficial. To be recognised and included knowingly in a school environment gives these students a more positive attitude and will hopefully restrict possible deep-rooted anxieties. Within the State system since 1996, it is hoped that in the Art classroom the dyslexic will be allowed to express thoughts and feelings throughout their educative years instead of anxieties being allowed to grow and boil over in later years. In some circumstances the results may still be deep and thought-provoking like Richard's art, but getting rid of these anxieties while still in the education system must be more healthy and healing. Dyslexic students are very concerned with self-image and how others see and relate to them, particularly their peers. They have bad experiences of not being understood and they have suffered injustices. Inside they 'hurt' and if through art and design and craft they can begin to ease out their frustrations and interpret their emotional life, to solidify their feelings and their thoughts through the different mediums and textures in art, then that is a positive healing therapy and can have repercussions in other areas as other teachers begin to recognise the creative gifts these students possess. It can be a great boost to the ego.

Using skills

Howard Gardner (1993), a professor at Harvard University, talks about the seven intelligences: linguistic, mathmetical, visual/spatial, musical, kinaesthetic, interpersonal. Mitchell (1997: 162) comments that at school the dice often seems heavily loaded towards the first two intelligences but in the outside world the other intelligences are both useful and valued. They are essential to our society. Dyslexic students often have a deep-rooted low self-esteem due to their past experiences in schools where the emphasis has been on the first two intelligences (linguistic and mathematical) which are compatible with the left hemisphere of the brain. In the Art classroom, we need to place stress on the words of the National Curriculum, and encourage the dyslexic to use the right hemisphere in his/her brain to think in pictures, 'Awareness and interaction with design is part of the contemporary professional environment. Design issues enter our everyday life' (Peter Saville, Art Director and designer).

Art can be an escape from academic goals. Gura (1996) states 'if you impose too many academic goals on young children it will not change what happens at eight, nine and ten. It will simply bring failure forward'. Failure has been the experience of most dyslexic children in mainstream schools. In the Art lesson a student's self-esteem will grow through success and praise because there is 'always something in a child's art work to praise'. (Foster 1993: 9). But *remember*, make sure you mean it – you rarely feel good if you know, *and the child will know*, that someone is just saying something to make you feel better.

A personal account

The greatest change for myself in the last year working within the dyslexic classroom has not been in terms of knowing more but seeing more and becoming more aware. The words of Pat Gura, speaking about education in early childhood, echo exactly my own feelings in the Art classroom with the dyslexic child. 'Awareness for me has also developed through a more genuine openness to the children which helps me to see, hear, think and feel more of what they see, hear, think and feel. This makes me want to work *with* them rather than *for* them.' She advocates a developmental approach with younger children. I advocate a developmental approach in the Art classroom with a dyslexic pupil. Gardner (1993) also suggests there is no need to shift from a developmental to a more academic approach to learning until around the age of nine or ten. It has been my experience particularly in the last year that, as with young children, a developmental approach to their work, particularly in art, helps the older secondary aged pupil who is dyslexic. It helps their desire to know and come to terms with their immediate world. They begin to believe in themselves. It is what Davies (Davies with Braun 1994) calls 'on the job training . . . In fact, when learning is presented experientially, dyslexic people can master many things faster than the average person can comprehend them.'

This approach enriches their lives. It promotes what the National Curriculum states as the importance of art and design to pupil's education. 'Art develops spiritual values and contributes a wider understanding to the experience of life, which helps build a balanced personality.'

So, through discovery in art and design, developing awareness of the range of tactile, emotive mediums that encompass art and exposing ourselves to aesthetic and perceptual responses, my dyslexic pupils and myself as a teacher began to feel success. We shared our experiences as I worked *with* them. Motivation crept back for the dyslexic child whose lack of self-esteem and confidence had meant they no longer motivated themselves. They now become aware of reasons of their own which made it worth their while to go on learning and creating.

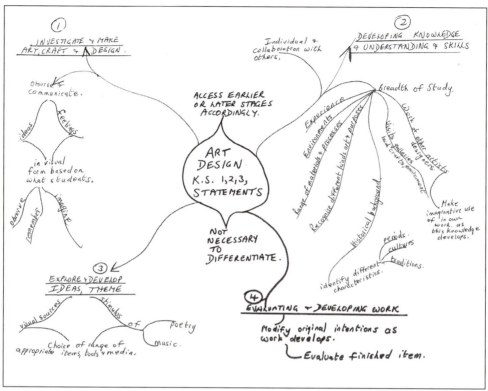

Figure 16.1 Art and Design – the four themes of the National Curriculum

Small steps led to achievable personal goals. The pleasure of completed work displayed which showed their views, their interpretation on the subject which was meaningful to them.

I approached the subject of Art and Design bearing in mind the four themes of study outlined in the National Curriculum (see Figure 16.1). I tried to ensure that investigating, designing and making in art, design and craft included exploring and developing individual choices. The pupils were of different ages and at different levels of attainment, with varied previous knowledge and understanding and experiences but aspects of art and design were developed through individual work and often through collaborative work using a range of materials and processes. We investigated the work of various artists, crafts people and designers and furthered this with visits to art galleries and local environments. We widened our knowledge and understanding as we evaluated and adapted our original views and choices.

Firstly it was essential to set the scene for success and convince *all* the pupils in the class that their artistic views were important. Their perspective of seeing an artist's work or their interpretation of a theme was personal and just as valid as someone elses. There was no right or wrong way. If it felt right for them and they followed their own instincts they would experience satisfaction and success. Circle Time provided a good opportunity to discuss these issues. Dyslexic children, if they are given the opportunity, have strong likes and dislikes and they began to discuss how they might interpret the theme or task differently. Their personal views and choices showed how everyone's approach differs but is just as relevant and important. Different details were seen as important by each individual and these were accentuated in the finished product.

We began by looking through Tony Buzan's (1993) book on Mind-Maps (copyright). We discussed how our creative thoughts blaze outwards, like petals on flowers, frost beads on a spider's web. We took these thoughts into the Art room, focused on an aspect of the season of autumn and painted our radiant thoughts. The results were to be our first art display and it looked fantastic. It also set the scene for the way the students were going to start putting down their thoughts for Creative Writing. Furthermore it paved the way for mind mapping other areas of the curriculum, e.g. Science.

Moving on to the practical sessions in Art and Design was an invaluable experience for myself. I realised that I had preconceived expectations of what the finished products would look like. I offered suggestions and expected a positive response, an 'Oh yes, I'll do it that way' – but no! I learned, as Augur (1997, p. 51) says, 'dyslexics' strengths are quick "thinker" and "doer" – but not in response to instruction' and I had already set the scene for individuality in the circle and although they listened to my suggestions they either discarded them or only adhered to part. They were using thinking skills and were able to give me a reasoned judgement for their decision. It is useful to allow the dyslexic child experiment, to develop their own aesthetics and perceptions and ways of working things out with only tentative guidance from myself but lots of encouragement. I learned not to expect a certain end-product; I waited for it to happen. Each child *did* produce a piece of work worthy of display. Displaying all their work as quickly as possible rewarded me with a more positive response next time and they attempted more and varied art work. At all costs I avoided any negative comments – it 'takes twenty positive comments to cancel out one negative one' (Arabella Hughes in *The Dyslexia Handbook 1997*: 147). In our Western society, which is so highly competitive, teachers and parents create anxiety about attainments, and the fact that children learn best when having fun is lost among this kind of anxiety. 'As teachers we need to relax and enjoy the child' (Lawrence 1996).

Cross-curricular implications

My students learned across the curriculum. Spiritual, moral, social and cultural developments, the application of number and IT skills were promoted in our Art and Design Technology lessons, as were the skills of communication, exploring sources of information, working with others, evaluating their own and each other's work and problem solving in collaboration with others. Each member of the class gained respect for the ideas and opinions of others and encouraged each other to develop work further. The students designed squares of a millennium quilt for a local church. They made puppets for a shadow play about the Hindu story *Rama and Sita*. They produced images to depict the different festivals of light within the Christian religion. While investigating the work of the artist Klimt, they experimented with shape and pattern on two- and three-dimensional decorations for Christmas and exploded shapes and patterns to marvellous effect. Another meaningful task was to design a memory game to assist them with a short-term memory task they personally had problems with, e.g. long and short vowel sounds/months of the year. They used IT to type and design a rules and instruction sheet of how to play the game. This was an invaluable lesson in self-discipline having to organise their thoughts into a correct sequence of events but their editing skills on the computer eased the frustration. These games were still being used at the end of the year and not just by the students who made them. They took great satisfaction seeing other students benefiting from their ideas. Time is a problem for dyslexic students so they each designed and decorated different shaped wooden working clocks. Making volcanoes out of chicken wire and papier mâché and testing their effectiveness to erupt with vinegar and bicarbonate of soda was a project that broadened our experience. Sculpting block and fold mountains from clay helped us to understand land formations.

Unfortunately sculpting freely in clay and other mouldable materials was an area we did not expose ourselves to, the time factor being one reason, but I have to admit I had not thought of the therapeutic effect these areas of tactile art could have for dyslexic students until I read Sylvia Hurt's explanation of how moulding metal sculptures had helped her to 'solidify feelings and thoughts with its rawness and myriad of textures held within the medium' (Our Lives 2000). This is an area the students and myself will have to develop in future. I am sure it will help some of them if not all to interpret their emotional life and the traumas they may have suffered, and maybe through their sculptures using mouldable materials, like Sylvia, they will begin to break free of the legacy of their past.

The greatest challenge of the year in design was making wall-hangings using a hessian background and coloured silks. But this was at the end of a list of rewarding and productive achievements. Sewing, particularly for the boys, was not a welcome topic but each student proved they could do it, even the dyslexic boy whose dyspraxia made fine motor movements difficult.

At the start of the year one boy did not want to join in Art or Design lessons. He would use every delay tactic he could think of. But then he realised intricate, complicated designs were only some people's way of expressing themselves and that his simple, direct way of interpreting the task was just as distinctive when he saw it displayed. There were still times when the old feelings of failure resurfaced but if encouraged and left to reflect on past achievements and watch others busily creating he would eventually come up with a distinctive slant. When we all saw his aeroplane hanging on the wall and his smile it was a wonderful feeling.

Fine Art

In Fine Art we studied skills and techniques, moods and emotions. For this we investigated artists and their work. I read to them about each artist, his life story, his personality. This set the scene to evoke interest and in some cases empathy. We looked at the paintings of each artist, identifying characteristics from different cultures and traditions and placing them within an historical context. We then used viewfinders to narrow down the perspective of a chosen painting. The students copied what they saw into black rectangles the same size as the viewfinder on white paper. With Van Gogh they studied line and movement, with Monet it was hues and shades, with Klimt it was pattern and shape, with Picasso distortion and bold colouring. The students then chose a medium to work with and copied a painting of personal choice using the studied technique. They then extended the same technique to an idea of their own and painted 'in the style of'. In the same manner we looked at self-portraiture, adding other artists such as Renoir, Rembrandt. When studying Turner we concentrated on the sea and its mood, looking at brush strokes and movement. Other means of stimuli such as poetry and music of the sea added a new dimension to our art work and to our displays. We compared Turner's violent, angry seas with those of other artists, one of whom was Lowry. It was through studying Lowry we decided to take a trip to the Lowry Museum in Salford. Lowry's way of painting people alone, even when in a crowd, fascinated the students. When we studied *The Funeral Party* and they each took one of the figures and copied it in pencil and charcoal we rearranged the order of the figures from the original and it was 'spooky' the way it still gave the same effect. The exhibitions at the Lowry Museum were all variations and different perspectives of people, their moods and personalities.

This visit to an art gallery gave us the opportunity to study contemporary art and broaden our vision and understanding of the Arts and Crafts. Lindsay Seers, with her disturbing negative images of the darker side of human nature, stimulated some strong responses. Alice Maher's *Hair*, drawn straight onto a wall in charcoal, was incredibly real and stirred deep feelings and childhood memories of Rapunzel and Lady Godiva. Adults painted acting like children by James Reilly were humourous but unsettling in their openness of intimate thoughts. Portraits by Thomas Ruff combining two faces appearing on and over each other so you cannot tell who is who, and a third identity evolves, were fascinating but thought-provoking because things were not as they seemed. Circle Time discussions about these emotions were rousing and made us admit to beginning to face our own prejudices and hidden fears, if not publicly then privately.

The visit to the Lowry Museum certainly helped the students to recognise the range of possibilities for employment in the creative and cultural industries. The hands on multisensory ArtWorks, the Lowry's interactive gallery, widened their horizons and challenged all their senses using digital technology, interactive sculpture and creative experiences. It was at this point the students discussed famous and successful people who themselves had been dyslexic. That such diverse figures as Leonardo de Vinci, Auguste Rodin, Albert Einstein and Walt Disney are all believed to have been dyslexic gives us examples of the brain structures of dyslexic people providing them with a more holistic way of viewing the world. I told the class about Charlie Paul, a successful animator. He has developed a highly unusual way of working that gives it a distinctive style. He draws an image, photographs it, and then works another image on top of the one he has already made, photographs that and so on. He feels he has an advantage over everyone else because he doesn't see things the way they do so his work reflects a totally individual technique, style and approach, so there is nothing to compare him with. This account (Osmond 1994: 5) is very encouraging for a dyslexic person to hear.

The Arts Dyslexia Trust that was set up in 1991 by twelve successful dyslexic artists and designers. They have brought more attention to the advanced visual/spatial skill in dyslexic individuals. Often severe dyslexic people display well-developed skills in the visual field and in multidimensional tasks. Susan Parkinson, the co-founder of the Trust, has been training dyslexic pupils for entry to art college for twenty years. Eight professional art and design disciplines are represented: fine art (sculpture and paintings in various media), silversmithing, set design, model-making, furniture design, graphic work, print-making and product design. Colour illustrations of the work of this group are available from the Trust, *Christies Exhibition Catalogue*, within which is a Foreword by Lord Hinlip, a sufferer himself from well-intentioned teachers who did not understand. 'It is on helping the teaching profession to understand and sympathise with dyslexics that much of the Trust's work is focused and the high standard of work shown (in the catalogue) helps that cause enormously as it shows teachers that they are not dealing with "no-hopers".' Dyslexic pupils are worthy of inclusion and should be persevered with.

To include a dyslexic student in the Art classroom of a secondary school is to include a successful ingredient into the mix, because all the basic abilities dyslexic students share are creative abilities to enrich the art environment. As Davies (1994) suggests dyslexic people can utilise the brain's ability to alter and create perceptions. They are highly aware of the environment. They are more curious than average. They think mainly in pictures instead of words. They are highly intuitive and perceptive. They think and perceive multidimensionally (using all the senses). They can experience thought as reality. They have vivid imaginations. These are powerful gifts and if included and utilised in Art can give the dyslexic student the boost to his/her ego that has been lacking in other academic areas.

References

Arts Dyslexia Trust, Lodge Cottage, Brabourne Lees, Ashford, Kent TN25 6QZ.

Augur, J. (1997) *The Dyslexia Handbook 1997*. Reading: British Dyslexia Association.

Buzan, T. (1993) *The Mind-map Book. Radiant Thinking*. London: BBC Books.

Clement, R. (1993) *The Art Teacher's Handbook* 2nd edn. Cheltenham: Stanley Thornes.

Davies, R. D. with Braun, E. M. (1994) *The Gift of Dyslexia*. London: Souvenir Press.

Dore, H. (1994) *The Art of Portraits*. Bridgeman Arts Library. Parragon.

Dyson, J. (2000) *Insights*. Arts Dyslexia Trust, Lodge Cottage, Brabourne Lees, Ashford, Kent TN25 6QZ.

Edwards, J. (1994) *The Scars of Dyslexia* (8 case studies in Emotional Reactions). London: Cassell.

Education Act 1996 *The National Curriculum Key Stages 1 and 2, Key Stages 3 and 4*. London: DfEE.

Foster, J. (1993) *Dyslexia: The Story So Far*. Farnham: Inner Sense Development Centre.

Gardner, H. (1993) *The Unschooled Mind*. London: Fontana.

Geraldine, C. (1993) *Step by Step Art School. Pastels*. London: Hamlyn.

Great Artists Collection (1969) *Their Lives, Works and Inspiration. 'Rembrandt' 'Monet' 'Turner'*, A Marshall Cavendish Weekly Collection.

Gura, P. (1996) *Resources for Early Learning, Children, Adults and Stuff*. London: Hodder and Stoughton.

Jacobson, J. (1997) *The Dyslexia Handbook*. Reading: British Dyslexia Association.

Knight, Bruce Allen (1999) 'Towards inclusion of students with special educational needs in the regular classroom', *British Journal of Learning Support. 'Support for Learning'* 14(1).

Lawrence, D. (1996) *Enhancing self-esteem in the Classroom*, 2nd edn. London: Paul Chapman Publishing.

Livewires Real Lives (1999) *Vincent Van Gogh*. London: Hodder and Stoughton.

Livewires Real Lives (1999) *Leonardo de Vinci*. London: Hodder and Stoughton.

Lowry–Art at The Lowry. 'Lowry's People' and 'The Double', April–September 2000. Salford: Lowry Press.

Miles, T. R. and Varma, V. (1995 reprinted 1997) *Dyslexia and Stress*. London: Whurr Publishers.

Milner, F. (1993) *Monet*. Leicester: Magna Books.

Mitchel, J. (1997) *The Dyslexia Handbook 1977*. Reading: British Dyslexia Association.

Osmond, J. (1993 reprinted 1994) *The Reality of Dyslexia*, Channel Four Book. London: Cassell.

Our Lives (2000) Exhibition of Art by Disabled People, Independence Festival Ltd., Royal Exchange, Manchester, 15 July to 5 August.

Peter, M. (1998) '"Good for them or what?" The Arts and pupils with SEN', *British Journal of Special Education* 25(4).

Royal Academy of Arts *Monet Postcard Book*. London: Boston and the Royal Academy of Arts.

Parkinson, S. (1995) RC (for The Arts Dyslexia Trust) 'Who's afraid of the visual arts', *Drawing Fire*, the journal of the National Association for Fine Art.

Taschen Benedikt (1990) 'Munch Edward 1863–1944'.

Taschen Benedikt (1993) 'Klimt 1862–1918', Ingo F. Walther.

Taschen Benedikt (1986) 'Pablo Picasso 1881–1973', Ingo F. Walther.

Taschen Benedikt (1990) 'Van Gogh: Vision and reality', Ingo F. Walther.

Treays, R. (1996) *Understanding Your Brain*. Usborne Science for Beginners. London: Usborne Publishing.

Waters, E. and Harris, A. (1993) *Royal Academy of Arts Painting. A young artist's guide*. London: Dorling Kindersley.

West, T. G (1991) 'In The Mind's Eye', 'Visual Thinker, Gifted People with Learning Difficulties, Computer Images and the Ironies of Creativity'. Loughton: Prometheus.

CHAPTER 17

Dyslexia and Music

Diana Ditchfield

This chapter:

- examines the implications for students in the Music class and for examinations
- provides suggestions for teachers on how any difficulties may be dealt with
- discusses the positive aspects of dyslexia and music.

> We are the music makers,
> We are the dreamers of dreams . . .
> We are the movers and shakers
> Of the world forever, it seems.
> (*We are the Music Makers*, by A. W. E. O'Shaughnessy)

Introduction

Some people may be better players or have ears more attuned to music than others but it is very difficult to find a totally unmusical person. Music means different things to different people and although the secondary school curriculum permits all children to have some formal exposure to music, there are also many opportunities for informal music making. There is no greater joy than music making since performers and listeners alike are participants. For the dyslexic in particular, this can offer a liberating avenue of expression and great rewards in raised self-confidence and self-esteem which may advantageously affect other areas of life and learning. Thus the key to inclusion in the secondary school is simply music and this is because everybody can pick and choose from music and anybody may participate. Of all curricula, the Music curriculum is perhaps the ideal multisensory medium and offers greater scope for differentiation and curriculum adaptation than many other subjects. It is possible to find ways for pupils to fit into music making and it is also possible to adapt music to fit particular students.

Difficulties

Musical notation

In music, a dyslexic learner is presented with different challenges from those he or she faces in other classes. The nature of the challenges will be affected by the individual's particular pattern of dyslexia. Some of these difficulties are described below:

- Decoding difficulties can be made worse when two clefs are used which have subtle differences between them in addition to different pitch representations.
- Visual difficulties which could be caused by unstable vision that results in apparent movement of lines and spaces, omissions, insertions and so on. All of these manifestations of dyslexia are especially relevant when reading a page of music where white or black blobs with vertical and maybe also horizontal lines are attached and are written on or between small lines and spaces.
- A keyboard or xylophone player is obliged to convert what appears to be on a vertical plane to the horizontal instrument. This conversion is a fairly frequently occurring conceptual or spatial challenge, which is not necessarily confined to horizontal instruments but also found among players of, for instance, stringed instruments.
- A dyslexic person may have eye–hand coordination difficulties or other motor complications which are compounded by the fact that the dyslexic brain usually processes information more slowly and often differently from the non-dyslexic brain.
- Sight reading can be difficult for the dyslexic as a good deal of information has to be processed and reproduced in a different format almost simultaneously and this is one of the things which is very difficult for most of them. At this point, however, some may tend to do as they might do when reading words and have a guess at what is coming next. Although the results are likely to be inaccurate, the children and the performance may well be musical.

There are many strategies that can be used to deal with these areas of difficulty. These include:

- Large stave music which can be of great benefit to the dyslexic; if necessary, a normal size score may be enlarged. Some dyslexic people find that it helps if printed on tinted paper although most do not like yellow. Coloured overlays are very helpful for some dyslexic people and specialist help from someone who specialises in the visual difficulties for dyslexic individuals may make seeing musical notation and words much better. One needs to adapt to individual needs.
- There are several ways around the problem of sight reading. The use of various mnemonics is common and may either help or confuse. It seems best to go along with whatever a particular student finds helpful or even to tailor them for a particular individual. I tend to use People in the treble clef – Every Good Boy Deserves Favour and FACE, and Animals in the bass clef – Great Big Dogs From Africa and All Cows Eat Grass.
- Although it is necessary for some students who wish to pursue music as a career to become very familiar with different clefs, for some dyslexic individuals it is easier to stick to a single clef. There is always much additional information on a page of music other than the actual notes and individuals who participate in music making with others also have to be watchful of many other things. Once a dyslexic knows what is required it is likely they will find their own way of giving themselves support.
- Of course, it is possible for music to be read and played without conventional musical notation at all, for example in steel bands or Irish music where traditionally the notation is in alphabetical form. (This latter may have the advantage of helping establish letters which have often been difficult to learn in the first place.)

Other key factors include:

- Improvisation in jazz as well as in Asian ensembles and on the church organ arises from the music itself. There may be structures around which such improvisation is built but it does not strictly follow 'written in' notes. Of course the notation may later record the improvisation, as for example in cadenzas in instrumental concertos.

- One of the advantages of micro technology is that it is possible for such improvisation, or any music which is played, to be displayed simultaneously with the playing. This would be a way of helping the dyslexic learner who has difficulty writing musical notation without inhibiting their composing. It would have an additional advantage in that the proof-reading of such a product by reversing the process and matching what has been composed with what is written down would help both checking the accuracy of the time in the playing and also give the opportunity to correct any mistakes which could hinder another player when performing such a composition.

- It is a pity to exclude singers from choirs because of poor understanding of musical notation as they may enjoy music enormously and contribute greatly. A dyslexic singer in this category may have no idea he or she is singing a difficult augmented fourth but produce the correct interval every time to the point where the music readers depend upon him or her. Of course, it is not necessary to be dyslexic in order to sing an augmented fourth! In that some have very well developed mimicking skills and, if musical, often develop good musical memories, then the augmented fourth may be sung spontaneously where a non-dyslexic may feel a need to work the difficult interval out in their head first which might lead to hesitancy and lack of confidence in performing.

- Professor Margaret Hubicki produced Colour Staff when she was teaching at the Royal Academy of Music. By using the concept of the circle of fifths in conjunction with the rhyme to accompany the colours of the rainbow, namely 'Richard Of York, Gives Battle In Vain', students are enabled to identify and work out particular notes and patterns. The use of wall charts and coloured markers on white board helps pupils to spot a red C regardless of the clef or ledger line/space in or on which it appears.

- The use of computer technology will also help some students. There are some excellent programs to help individuals learn conventional notation and other aspects of theory and practice. In that there are presently many such programs which may also be used in conjunction with keyboards, the teacher is advised to investigate and select what they think will be most useful to the dyslexic student. Indeed it is possible to dispense with traditional methods like ink and manuscript paper altogether, when recording musical scores. Thus computer technology may be used as an aid to composing or to help learn musical notation. It may be that the former may be useful for the latter.

- It is important to discover the specific difficulty of a particular pupil and here it may be helpful to discuss the perceived problems of a particular student with the special needs teacher(s). It is possible to break things down to very simple units and offer single facts at any one time. It might be useful to take out fragments such as sequences or repeated rhythmic or melodic sections and practise them for all learners alike while at the same time pointing out from the score that these are sequences, etc. It is worth stating the obvious and the pattern may not have been spotted by some. There also needs to be some thought given to how things may fit together so that there is always revision of what has gone before and that new information is added in a structured, systematic, cumulative manner.

- Dyslexic students tend to favour a particular learning style, so it is worth trying to discover the particular style and use it but at the same time offer other styles not just for other students but also, hopefully without adding confusion, to broaden the learning style of a particular student. It is possible for pupils to learn almost anything provided it is offered in an appropriate manner for a particular student.

- Dyslexic students need to be allowed to learn at their own pace and in their own way and the teacher is wise not to offer an excess of information, either at any one time or indeed altogether. It is also important that teacher and student have the same understanding, for example of a word or concept. Immense confusion may result if common ground is not present.

Writing difficulties

Some individuals find it difficult to write either musical notation or even essays about music. For the serious examination student, it is possible to find ways around this by amanuensis and tape-recording, extra time allowance or again the use of computers. If a reading difficulty is also present, with short-term memory problems and the requirement to find information from lectures or in books, a dyslexic learner is often disadvantaged and needs extra help. They often say that concise lecture/lesson notes are helpful, especially when it comes to revision. If it is possible, the tailor-made choice of a particular examination or examination board may make a difference to the outcome in terms of achievement and opportunity.

Dyslexic students with writing difficulties, sometimes known as dysgraphia, may be enabled to compose by using computer technology and there may also be financial help for such students for this purpose. Individuals who are good performers are sometimes 'put off' seeking to pursue their interest in music at tertiary level as a result of dysgraphia, especially if it occurs in conjunction with a reading difficulty. They find note-taking from books or lectures extremely difficult and could waste valuable time and energy trying to handwrite essays which could be either audio-recorded or written on the computer.

Motor difficulties

The fine motor control required to play a musical instrument can be extremely difficult for some individuals. Where this manifestation is present, clearly it is better to use large instruments where there is plenty of space, such as a double bass, or possibly a brass instrument which has only three or four valves, often uses only one clef and may also use fewer notes; a well chosen percussion instrument could be the answer. It's largely a matter of trial and error, although consideration should also be given to the preferences of an individual regarding the choice of instrument. Certainly a harp or tin whistle may cause extra stress for the dyslexic learner. Singing may help.

Many dyslexic students find the acquiring of automaticity difficult and it may help if there is less scope for error when deciding what instrument to learn. It is also worth remembering that it can be difficult to convert fingering, for example shown on a flute vertically, to the horizontal plane for playing, or to remember that cellos and basses produce higher notes as the left hand moves away from the body. Westcombe (2000) points out that 'the bassoon has a downwards-then-upwards fingering sequence whereas the sound continues to go down'.

If movement is required to complement music, it is possible that the dyslexic person will be clumsy. For example, dancers may start with the wrong foot or end up in the wrong place at the wrong time. Marchers may be out of step. These problems may be overcome to a greater or lesser degree but usually require additional practising.

Difficulties with numbers and calculations

Although many dyslexic people have an innate sense of rhythm, the actual musical calculations required may be extremely stressful. I have found that for good performers, who have perhaps learned by rote and from memory, the key to calculation often arises from their performance experience. To impose mathematical concepts such as fractions, where, frankly, music itself is the essential being considered, seems unnecessary in the Music classroom. Tapping a rhythm may lead to its conceptual understanding in terms of calculation. It is also possible to simplify the maths and also perhaps choose music which seems within the existing understanding of an individual.

Examinations

Although the performing section of state examinations may not be too difficult for dyslexic people, the paperwork sections present difficulties. Even if the dyslexic person has a very good ear, it is likely he or she will find difficulty in writing in notes from dictation within the given time span. Indeed, even the syllabus itself states that, 'The length of the Aural Perception test requires a long span of intense concentration from even the best candidates'. Where a dyslexic person has perhaps a weak aural or visual memory, it is likely that this test would present extreme difficulty for them. Miles (1993) points out that some dyslexic people need much longer than non-dyslexic people to process information regardless 'of the sense modality through which the material is presented' (Chapter 17: 137). This may be compounded if they also have poor spatial awareness.

For some it is helpful to have a special tape which permits more time for writing down information or perhaps an extra opportunity to listen. Some teachers say this does not help as they tend to lose their place. The teacher is in the best position to decide which would be most helpful for their student.

In Theory examinations, a dyslexic student may well be capable of writing the scale of G melodic minor, descending and ascending without key signature in the bass clef to the given rhythm pattern in 9/8 time and mark in the semitones – but it will almost certainly take them longer to do so. They will probably need a ritual to follow so as to be sure not to miss anything out. However, rituals can be helpful for many of us.

In addition, the essay requirement is also likely to present a difficult test in the same way that a history or English essay would. It is indeed possible to prepare dyslexic learners for such tests but it requires extra effort from the teacher and it may be more helpful if the candidate is helped to prepare for this section with the assistance of a teacher who specialises in dyslexia and is familiar with both the student's requirements and also has the specialist knowledge of how best to address their particular need. Such a teacher does not need specialist knowledge of the subject area. Rather, in conjunction with the subject teacher, the specialist teacher may be able to help the dyslexic access the information required and help the student with preparation. The endeavour therefore becomes inclusive in the sense that there is widespread support for the dyslexic from several members of staff.

Advantages of dyslexia

Frequently, dyslexic students are thought to be Right Brained (Springer and Deutsch 1984) creative individuals. They are found amongst outstanding musicians and may be extremely sensitive performers. They are often also extremely hard-working because they know they have to go over and over things to be sure of learning and retaining them. Unless unreasonably stressed, their knowledge is often very secure. In that dyslexia has no correlation with intelligence, some dyslexic people may be extremely intelligent and creative. This often means that, once understood, they often find their own very effective and novel solutions to their problems even though they may arrive at them more slowly.

In that one of the strategies used by dyslexic students is to memorise things so as to avoid the necessity of having to read, the aspect of a good long-term memory may be used to advantage. It is usually instant recall or poor short-term memory which causes difficulty but once information is consigned to the long-term memory, it can be very valuable, and the teacher may wish to use this feature to help a dyslexic person's confidence, for example in soliciting information from them which the dyslexic is likely to have retained and the non-dyslexic may have forgotten.

Backhouse (2000) points out that the dyslexic person about which she writes found 'that the way she perceived music was quite different from that of many colleagues. She saw patterns and shapes in music, of which – to her surprise – other musicians seemed largely unaware.'

Suggestions for teachers

- If somebody has forgotten their music or their instrument or is late for class, it is likely to be the dyslexic pupil. It is often difficult for them to follow sequential instructions and to remember them. It may be useful for the teacher to have spare copies of music or an alternative lesson plan. Non-dyslexic people also demonstrate similar behaviour patterns. It is best to try and permit the pupil to see the disadvantage of their forgetfulness without being negative. It really is so very important to aim for positive classes at all times.

- Many musicians need to practise small sections carefully and repetitively. This may be particularly helpful for the dyslexic person who may take longer to learn it but who will retain and reproduce it reliably in normal circumstances which is often greatly appreciated by others in ensemble work of all kinds. However some dyslexic people find it very confusing to have to 'cut in' to a piece of music which they have possibly learned from memory, including kinaesthetic memory and the practise of sectional practice is therefore cruelty. Backhouse's (2000) pianist was a person who needed to work on the 'big picture'. The teacher needs to be sensitive about this.

- As previously stated, the key for the dyslexic and non-dyslexic alike is multisensory, structured, systematic and cumulative practice with much revision and repetition. Many dyslexic students also have more difficulty than average with attention span and are unable to concentrate for any length of time. This means they may miss things. Thus it is even more important to give them the opportunity to find the gaps and this may result in apparently stupid questions which may give rise to levity from other members of the class. It really is important that the teacher simply gives the information required to enable the pupil to fill in such omissions for themselves.

- Westcombe (2000) points out that things that happen in music are often analogous to the rhyming of words, for example by using a rhythmic pattern to bring a phrase to a close and to use such a fragment on more than one occasion. It is also possible that the musical interpretation of phrases and cadences may be transferred into general reading where dyslexic learners have a tendency to rush on to the next sentence as soon as they spot a full stop, thus losing a rhythmic balance. They often need to realise that interpretation is preferable to speed, whether in reading music or words.

- It is difficult even for non-dyslexic students to keep an eye on the conductor as well as reading words or music or both and then reproduce them either vocally or on an instrument. How much more for the dyslexic? Similarly, for the inexperienced musician it is difficult to observe tacet for several bars and then be ready and come in at the correct time. In such circumstances, it may greatly help the dyslexic to sit alongside a good, experienced non-dyslexic. If motivated and feeling there is a chance of success, the dyslexic pupil will probably work very hard to pick up cues and memorise and get things correct. They then become reliable members of a choir or ensemble. Marking the score or copy in ways which mean something to the individual can be a great help to dyslexic and non-dyslexic alike.

- It is worth trying to discover what the dyslexic can do well and cash in on it both for the individual themselves and for everybody else. It is a pity to limit them for reasons of teacher time, and energy, ability and effort in meeting the needs of individual dyslexic pupils will be well rewarded. Of particular value is a wide knowledge of instruments, the repertoire and types of music making and this can be acquired by a teacher.
- It is worth exposing all students, whether dyslexic or not, to a wide range of music. School is a unique opportunity for offering music which may not normally be heard in the day to day life of some students. In that the United Kingdom is now a multicultural and multilingual society, it is worth acknowledging that aspect to enrich music making. In that dyslexic individuals are found in all societies, it may well be that they are also amongst those of who are of other cultural origins.

Conclusion

There is still scope for improvising music in the secondary school, albeit rather differently from primary school improvisation. It is also an area where there may be cooperation with other school disciplines, for example in drama or for musicals where there is usually input from many subject areas. Improvisation frequently shows a style peculiar to a composer and the dyslexic is no different here because they often establish a pattern which works for them and reproduce it in various guises. It is important to recognise that this is probably the result of much hard work by the dyslexic and is not a totally spontaneous performance even where it might seem so. A teacher may extend such ability for dyslexic students and non-dyslexic students by suggesting incorporating new strategies in certain ways. Improvisation usually follows some structure, for example in jazz, and thus it is possible for dyslexics to excel in this area where they are not required to read musical notation accurately.

It is worth commenting that there is an issue of inclusion even before you get to dyslexia. Some young people are put off music because they do not feel that the western traditional music is relevant to them. They therefore feel that unless the teacher makes lessons very participative and widely embracing, they will, even in their own popular/dance section, feel that their only role is to comment on other people's music making.

On the specific point of inclusion, it is vital that the teacher – and particularly visiting instrumental staff – know who the dyslexic pupils are so that consideration can be given to specifics such as slow sight reading. Fortunately most of the music making outside the classroom works on an incremental basis of a number of rehearsals, so the fast-reading aspect becomes of little import in the end.

It is also important to remember that some dyslexic learners slip into secondary schools without their situation being appreciated or statemented. It is also probable that such children will have drawn the attention of regular teachers and the teachers of the special needs support services. Conversation and cooperation between teachers is a normal part of secondary school education and it is particularly valuable in helping dyslexic pupils, even in specialist areas such as Music.

The Music Committee of the BDA is presently piloting a questionnaire to assist teachers and pupils to identify if there are differences between dyslexic and non-dyslexic musicians and help them find positive and constructive ways in which the pupils might include Music into their schedules and also help teachers include such pupils in school music making.

Music teachers love music and it is a great privilege to make music with others. We want to open these doors of pleasure and development as lifelong dimensions and we have the joy of transmitting our own love in addition to using more formal modes of teaching. It is however, necessary for anybody to work very hard if they are to access all that is available to them in the Music curriculum and to achieve results which are commensurate with their ability in music. It is simply more difficult for the dyslexic who has additional difficulties to overcome. Music lessons may end up being such an enjoyable relief for the dyslexic learner in the school day and it is important to try to make them such for dyslexic and non-dyslexic alike. However, learning in such lessons may be utilised in other classes, as has been shown where singing may help reading and maths.

With awareness, flexibility and care on the part of the Music teacher, there is no reason why a dyslexic pupil should not participate in secondary school Music in as full a way as any other student. In addition, since they are often very creative individuals, they may not only shine, gain great pleasure, and have raised confidence and self-esteem, but also contribute very considerably to school music making. Such advantages may be transferred into other areas of learning for themselves and may enhance the contribution of others.

Acknowledgement

The lively and diverse contributions from members of the Music Committee of the BDA and their strong unfailing support was greatly appreciated in the compiling of this chapter.

References

Backhouse, G. (2000) 'A pianist's story', in Miles, T. R. and Westcombe, J. *Music and Dyslexia: Opening new doors*. London: Whurr Publishers.

Hubicki, M. and Miles, T. R. (1991) 'Musical notation and multi-sensory learning in child language', *Teaching and Therapy* 10(1).

Miles, T. R. (1993) *Dyslexia: The Pattern of Difficulties*, 2nd edn. Whurr Publishers.

Miles, T. R. and Miles, E. (1999) *Dyslexia a hundred years on,* 2nd edn. Buckingham: Open University Press.

Miles, T. R and Westcombe, J. (2000) *Music and Dyslexia: Opening new doors*. London: Whurr Publishers.

Oglethorpe, S. (1996) *Instrumental music for dyslexics: A teaching Handbook*. London: Whurr Publishers.

Springer, S. P and Deutsch, G. (1984) *Left Brain, Right Brain*. New York: Freeman.

Westcombe, J. (2000) 'How dyslexia can affect musicians', in Miles, T. R. and Westcombe, J. *Music and Dyslexia: Opening new doors*. London: Whurr Publishers.

SECTION 4: Cross-curricular Aspects

CHAPTER 18

Cross-curricular Approaches to Staff Development in Secondary Schools

Jane Kirk

This chapter:

- seeks to demonstrate why cross-curricular approaches are essential in responding to the needs of pupils with special educational needs such as dyslexia
- analyses two established approaches to staff development
- demonstrates, on the basis of direct participation in staff development initiatives, that the most fruitful approach to staff development is one that combines features of both models.

The case for cross-curricular approaches

In a statement in 1999 the TTA issued the following challenge:

> The key to unlocking the full potential of pupils in our schools lies in the expertise of teachers and head teachers. Research and inspection evidence demonstrate the close correlation between the quality of teaching and the achievement of pupils.
>
> (Teacher Training Agency 1999)

The central premise of this chapter is that high-quality teaching requires cross-curricular approaches.

The call for the adoption of cross curricular approaches reflects a number of basic concerns about the subject-based curriculum. That mode of curriculum organisation, in which pupils are systematically exposed to a range of separate academic subjects and disciplines, rested on the assumption that each subject had a distinctive contribution to make to the education of every pupil. To fail to provide all with a systematic initiation into all of these separate fields of study was to lead to an unbalanced education and to deprive young people of access to one or more of the means by which we interpret human experience and by which we make sense of the social and physical environments.

One concern about that approach is that it can entail such a pronounced respect for the integrity of a subject's academic content that it fails to illuminate for pupils certain fundamental aspects of their lives. The introduction to the National Curriculum of a number of cross-curricular themes sought to address this difficulty. The following documents not only provided schools with information on how to tackle a particular theme but also introduced them to a different approach to teaching and learning, an approach that sought to allow transfer of skills between different subjects and disciplines. The titles, which give an indication of the breadth of study intended, are:

The Whole Curriculum (NCC 1990a)
Education for Economic and Industrial Understanding (NCC 1990b)
Health Education (NCC 1990c)
Careers Education and Guidance (NCC 1990d)
Environmental Education (NCC 1990e)
Education for Citizenship (NCC 1990f).

The modification to the National Curriculum required that schools should adjust the treatment of subjects in such a way that they could each contribute in their distinctive ways to enlarging pupils' understanding of, for example, health, the environment, and their role as citizens. These concerns were not the responsibility of any single subject: they were multidisciplinary in the sense that they drew on insights from several subjects.

A second concern was that the subject-based curriculum of the secondary school, in which subjects were pursued but in isolation, could leave pupils with a highly fragmented educational experience.

A third concern was that, unless specific steps were taken to counteract it, the subject-based curriculum did not exploit those common features which all subjects share. For example, all subjects foster the capacity to think, to communicate, to solve problems, to engage with others, and to acquire important skills of various kinds. Failure to recognise these features that are found in all subjects – that is, those features that are cross-curricular – has important consequences. It means for example that opportunities are not taken to enable study in one subject to reinforce learning and understanding in another. Even more seriously, the subject-based curriculum can be regarded as the chief aim of the secondary school rather than a means to the achievement of a range of educational objectives. Arguably, the fundamental objectives of the secondary school are concerned with the cultivation of certain skills and ways of knowing that are cross-curricular. On that basis, cross-curricular initiatives are not to be seen as mere addenda to the secondary school curriculum – which receive attention only when other important matters have been addressed – but rather of such fundamental importance that the various subjects should be tackled in a way that emphasises their contribution to the achievement of cross-curricular aims. From this standpoint the teaching of a subject does not simply involve the transmission of content that is taken for granted; but, on the contrary, it involves a careful examination of how the subjects in their different ways contribute to the wider educational and social purposes of the secondary school.

One of these wider educational and social purposes is inclusion. The commitment to education of the present Government is clear; and one of the key drivers of that policy is inclusion: the educational achievements of all learners, not simply the ablest, need to be raised; the obstacles to effective learning, whether they arise from disability or disadvantage, need to be eliminated; and all pupils need to be supported in pursuing an appropriate curriculum through which they will achieve their best potential. It is therefore appropriate to see inclusion as a major cross-curricular theme. Just as it is possible to claim that every teacher is a teacher of English, because every teacher, regardless of specialism, has an obligation to insist on higher standards of communication, so every teacher, again regardless of specialism, needs to incorporate in his/her subject teaching those techniques and strategies that nurture inclusion, by which is meant full participation in an appropriate curriculum directed towards a wide range of academic, social and personal achievements.

Dyslexia is now well established as a complex condition that can seriously interfere with pupils' educational progress and achievement. Subject teachers may need to turn to Learning Support and other specialists for help in managing the learning of pupils with dyslexia; but they cannot escape the responsibility to adapt and adjust teaching approaches to ensure that the difficulties posed by dyslexia are countered or minimised. Indeed, one of the cross-curricular responsibilities of all teachers is to incorporate strategies for supporting pupils with dyslexia within their repertoire of professional skills. The draft revised *Code of Practice on the Identification and Assessment of Pupils with Special Educational Needs* (DfEE 2000) emphasises this point by stating that 'All teachers are teachers of pupils with special educational needs' (p. 41).

Of course, it can be assumed that during their programmes of initial training all teachers will be made aware of these responsibilities and helped to acquire the relevant insight and skills. However, throughout their careers all teachers will require support of this kind and it is an important function of staff development to provide that. Indeed, staff development may be defined as the means by which schools equip themselves to respond positively to the challenge of enhancing the quality of the educational experiences they provide for all pupils.

Contrasting approaches to staff development

Building on the work of Cooper, who delivered an unpublished, innovative paper on 'Core Teams for school-focused INSET' to the Welsh Collaborative Project Conference in 1986, O'Sullivan, Jones and Reid (1988) offer two models of staff development. The first they identify 'the typical INSET scenario', which might be taken to represent a traditional approach. It has the following main features:

- fragmented approach to staff development;
- top-down needs identification;
- little institutional involvement;
- little individual teacher involvement;
- little, or no, evaluation;
- menu-led INSET courses;
- participants are volunteers.

The second model is described as 'a prototype for staff development'. This model is very different and is characterised by the following:

- balanced and coordinated strategy for INSET;
- bottom-up process for identifying staff development needs;
- curriculum-led INSET courses;
- process and learning strategies tackled as well as content;
- schools at centre of INSET process;
- systems to ensure individual teacher involvement;
- monitoring and evaluation built-in to staff development process.

By contrast with the traditional or 'provider-led' model, this progressive or 'professional autonomy' model accords well with the notion of the creative school or the school as a learning environment for staff as well as pupils, in which all members of staff acknowledge the responsibility to contribute to the revitalisation and enhancement of the school's work. Moreover, that model is based on the principle of ownership: teachers recognise the need for change and accept the responsibility for the direction that change will take. On this model teachers are not developed: through shared analysis of a school's performance and through collegial discussion on the way forward, teachers develop themselves. In this way of working the staff of a school can overcome the common barriers to educational change which Dalin had identified (Morrison 1994: 126): the value barriers, which lead to disagreement over the direction of change or the need for it; the power barriers, which threaten professional standing and control; the practical barriers, such as the threat of increased workloads or the lack of resources; and the psychological barriers which derive from the unsettling fear of change.

Perhaps the most significant difference between the models is that, whereas the first INSET scenario is disempowering and, perhaps, deprofessionalising in implying that staff development is something that is inflicted on reluctant teachers by others, the professional autonomy model affirms the importance of the right of a school staff to work out their own educational salvation. Indeed the second model is one in which the staff development reflects the school's organisational health.

The effectiveness of the professional autonomy model appears to depend on a number of critically important features. First, the school staff need collectively to be aware of shortcomings in existing provision which are identified through audit, the process by which a school assesses its performance against a policy or against a set of criteria of effective provision. The audit, in turn, leads to an action plan, a pooling of ideas on remedial development into a coherent strategy for change including staff development. Thirdly, the action plan is implemented against a time-scale with appropriate allocation of resources, Finally, the revised provision is again evaluated and the cycle of development is maintained. In other words, staff development forms an integral feature of a school development plan.

There are grounds for believing that the professional autonomy model offers a much more appropriate context for cross-curricular change than the traditional INSET model. Cross-curricular initiatives require a blurring of distinctions between subjects; they assume that what matters is the educational philosophy of the school rather than the philosophy adopted by the discrete subjects; they are facilitated when the staff of a school collectively decide to approach the teaching of subjects in agreed ways in order to achieve certain school-wide objectives. It is clear that that degree of agreement and shared commitment is most likely to be generated when staff involvement in the development of the school is established and when staff realise that the success of the school as a learning environment depends primarily on their ownership of an agreed strategy for change. The effectiveness of a school's cross-curricular teaching depends on effective staff development: effective staff development depends, in turn, on the adoption of a cross-curricular approach to the development of the school and its curriculum.

Staff development in practice

How do these theoretical approaches to staff development operate in practice? Drawing on experience of providing staff development sessions and participating in school-based curriculum development this chapter will argue that while the two theoretical models certainly are to be found, there are effective approaches which combine aspects of both models.

It is difficult for the dyslexia specialist to avoid being cast in the role of the external expert. Dyslexia currently has a high profile and schools have become only too well aware of its importance and of the need to make a response which ensures that pupils with dyslexia are given the attention their learning needs demand. Since few schools have dyslexia specialists on their staffs it is perfectly understandable that schools should call in a person with relevant expertise to offer a one-day presentation for all members of staff. Such sessions take a familiar format. There is an introductory session in which teachers are invited to write brief individual answers to the following questions as a way of focusing their attention on their own practice:

What prevents some of my pupils from achieving?
How does low achievement manifest itself in my classroom?
In which processes do I need to provide further support?
Which additional skills do I need in order to deliver this support?

There follows an explanation of dyslexia from three different theoretical perspectives: biological, cognitive, and behavioural. Throughout the explanation the staff of the school are given examples of how different aspects of dyslexia can affect learning. The session concludes by offering the following definition as a working model:

Dyslexia is a combination of abilities and difficulties which affect the learning process in one or more of reading, spelling and writing. Accompanying weaknesses may also be seen in speed of processing, short-term memory, sequencing, auditory and/or visual perception, spoken language and motor skills.

(British Dyslexia Association 1999)

The teachers are then encouraged to think about the implications for them of supporting pupils with dyslexia. The speaker offers the following list of issues:

- Identification
- Assessment
- Teaching and learning strategies
- ICT provision
- Course development.

Each issue is addressed briefly and advice offered about how to put systems in place to support the pupils who are underachieving. The remainder of the presentation focuses on teaching and learning strategies: on best methods of teaching language skills; on presenting guidelines for global learners; on offering advice on metacognition, or learning how to learn; and on appropriate study skills for pupils with dyslexia.

The INSET approach certainly can be used as a way of jolting the complacency of a school by requiring all staff to acknowledge that there is an area of provision in which their practice falls well short of the best. However, the INSET approach has many shortcomings:

- staff development is imposed upon all members of staff;
- teachers are led to adopt a passive role, only encouraged to respond individually in writing during the session;
- the external speakers are not aware of school politics, of trying to impose their solutions rather than enabling the school to develop its own response;
- there is evidence of a 'credibility' gap between experts and staff;
- the approach tends to be too general and needs follow-up, small group work so that learning can be transferred to the classroom situation;
- there is some evidence of teachers feeling threatened by a feeling of inadequacy in dealing with pupils with dyslexia.

The most fundamental weakness of that INSET model is that the day is an isolated event which is not integrated into a wider range of staff development and curriculum development activities. To respond to that difficulty the external expert has to be prepared to engage in a fuller dialogue with the school prior to the INSET event and to agree a range of follow-up activities. These discussions usually require a change of emphasis in the external expert's presentation: a key feature concerns the ways in which the school will move forward after the inservice day; it will involve the discussion of an audit of existing practice, the establishment of an interdepartmental task group, the formulating of an action plan against a time-scale, and a strategy for evaluation which ensures that dyslexia will continue to feature on the school's agenda and is not forgotten as soon as the external expert's back is turned. Indeed, in the most favourable circumstances the external specialist retains contact with the school, receives reports on progress, and becomes a critical friend who can make a strong contribution to embedding changed practice in the school.

In the same way the professional autonomy model can borrow features of the INSET approach. A school committed to the autonomy model will usually have passed through a number of phrases. First, it will have found a way, normally through ongoing evaluation of its work, of recognising that teachers are encountering difficulties in responding to pupils with dyslexia; secondly, it will have conducted an audit of provision, scrutinising pupils' work and teachers' responses through questionnaires or in other ways, leading to an agreement that there is a need for school-wide action. Thirdly, a planning group will be established including the SENCO, a member of senior management team, and representatives from the different subject domains. The group will be chaired by the staff development coordinator and its remit is to devise a whole-school plan to help teachers to support pupils with dyslexia. The plan will usually involve the development of a programme of study skills covering, for example, information-gathering, note-taking and other related skills. The unit will be discussed by individual departments in draft form before being finalised. The outcome is likely to be a unit of work taught to all first-year pupils by the Learning Support specialist with expertise in dyslexia, and the agreement by all subject teachers to ensure that these same study skills are reinforced in their specialist classroom settings. Each subject specialist is expected to maintain a log of lessons illustrating how the agreed list of study skills were exemplified and reinforced in their specific contexts. With the support of the school's senior management team time will be found in all school staff development sessions for the sharing of experience, for agreeing adjustments to the programme, and for its extension to other year groups.

In one school, as the initiative percolated into the curriculum of more senior pupils, the same key skills were emphasised but others were added to ensure that the demands on pupils were progressively increased. The project culminated in a programme for sixth form pupils that was closely related to a unit used in a nearby university on study skills for students' with dyslexia, a relationship that was established when the Learning Support teacher undertook part-time work in the university. Significantly, as teachers gained experience of the unit, they came to see even more opportunities to use their specialist subject not simply as content to be transmitted but as a vehicle for acquiring and developing skills. They came to see their subject as a context for processed-based teaching.

Of course, this exercise in cross-curricular staff development called for considerable investment of time from the Learning Support teacher, who had to convince the school's senior management of the need for action in a key aspect of the curriculum, of the value of a cross-curricular approach, and of the attractiveness of the professional autonomy model. However, the project was strongly influenced by the fact that, at planned intervals, an external specialist with expertise in dyslexia was invited to the school. That specialist's interventions had several purposes: to convince sometimes sceptical staff that the project was important; to raise morale by informing staff that they were making more substantial progress than that of the specialist's own school; to demonstrate that the problems encountered by the school in responding to dyslexia were similar to those being experienced elsewhere; and to retain the commitment of the school's senior staff, who derived satisfaction from the knowledge that their school was breaking new ground in a way that enhanced the standing of the school. The evidence of the effectiveness of this modified professional autonomy model was twofold: firstly, the impact of the project extended beyond pupils with dyslexia and strengthened the study skills of all pupils throughout the school, to the satisfaction of all staff; secondly, a school inspection report was obtained which commended the school's efforts in developing a whole-school approach to pupils with dyslexia and the effect of that initiative on teaching and learning throughout the school.

The INSET approach offers school staff an external perspective on supporting pupils with dyslexia. It assumes that new, informed ideas will provide the stimulus for teachers to look at their own practice and change. Although there is value in giving expert advice in this way it must be offered as part of a whole-school initiative and integrated into the development plan of the school. Unless such steps are taken there is a danger that teachers might feel demoralised or deskilled by academics offering theoretical advice out of the context of their particular teaching situation.

The professional autonomy model is likely to be more successful because it is a collaborative effort. From the identification of the difficulty, through evaluation and the staff questionnaire, through interdepartmental discussions, and through participation in a new programme of work, all members of staff become involved. The inclusion of all members of staff in providing practical suggestions on how to tackle the problem raises self-esteem in teachers who realise their input is valued.

Conclusion

Naturally, the two models of staff development that have been discussed are not mutually exclusive. It is perfectly possible, for example, for a school with marked organisational health and a staff committed to change, to invite the external expert or consultant to stimulate its thinking about its own educational effectiveness or to learn from experience elsewhere. Schools can be parochial: they should welcome the opportunity to test their experience against that of others. However, it seems necessary that the external consultant serves as a stimulus and accepts that the role is to energise others to take school development forward rather than to impose a ready-made solution from elsewhere. Perhaps it is the school which has taken to heart the professional autonomy model that is in the best position to benefit from external advice. On the other hand the school that is still following the traditional INSET model is likely to experience significant difficulties in applying cross-curricular initiatives. Such a school is likely to require a change of culture which forces the staff to discuss their school's provision self-critically and through that develop a willingness to act in the light of their own self-evaluation. That can be provided by the intervention of the expert consultant provided that intervention becomes integrated into the mode of operation of the whole school.

References

DfEE (2000) *Code of Practice on the Identification and Assessment of Pupils with Special Educational Needs* (Consultation document). London: DfEE.

Morrison, K. (1994) *Implementing Cross-curricular Themes.* London: David Fulton Publishers.

National Curriculum Council (1990a) *The Whole Curriculum.* York: NCC.

National Curriculum Council (1990b) *Education for Economic and Industrial Understanding.* York: NCC.

National Curriculum Council (1990c) *Health Education.* York: NCC.

National Curriculum Council (1990d) *Careers Education and Guidance.* York: NCC.

National Curriculum Council (1990e) *Environmental Education.* York: NCC.

National Curriculum Council (1990f) *Education for Citizenship.* York: NCC.

O'Sullivan, F., Jones, K. and Reid, K. (1988) *Staff Development in Secondary Schools.* London: Hodder and Stoughton.

Teacher Training Agency (1999) *National Special Educational Needs Specialist Standards.* London: TTA.

CHAPTER 19

Dyslexia Friendly Schools

Neil Mackay

This chapter:

- examines the process of becoming a dyslexia friendly school
- describes good practice and factors relating to a supportive school environment.

The concept of 'Dyslexia Friendly Schools' was developed during a presentation I made at a British Dyslexia Association Governor Training Conference some years ago. Since then it has been embraced by schools and LEAs across the UK and beyond. The power of the concept seems to lie in the fact that changes made to become more dyslexia friendly also seem to enable schools to become more effective. Also, the new Code of Practice places fresh imperatives on schools and LEAs to examine classroom practice in order to secure inclusion and equality of opportunity.

Managing the process

From a senior management viewpoint, the motivation to become dyslexia friendly is the potential for enhanced school effectiveness and better performance for all pupils in their SATS tests at Key Stages 1, 2 and 3 and at GCSE. This is the power of the dyslexia friendly approach, in that changes made on behalf of dyslexic pupils can benefit all. By the same token, changes made to make schools more effective and more empowering for all inevitably seem to make them dyslexia friendly. Criteria of effective schools include:

- attention to the quality of instruction;
- pervasive and broadly understood instructional focus;
- use of pupil achievement as the basis of programme evaluation.

(Scottish Education Office 1991)

together with:

- carefully crafting the curriculum to match differing learning abilities;
- systematically monitoring and evaluating pupil learning;
- seeing staff development as a valuable component.

(Harrison and Butler 1995)

Support for the dyslexia friendly approach is lent by Ford and Baxter (1999): 'It is important to ensure ownership of the work, if initiatives are to succeed and be effective. The positive benefits are that teachers have a wider appreciation of the demands made on pupils in different areas of the curriculum.'

Similarly, the Basic Skills Agency (1998) recognises that the integration of basic policies into school development plans was a feature of successful programmes, warning that 'programmes must impact at departmental level within schools'.

So, from a management perspective, the ideal would seem to be a situation in which all staff are committed to delivering top quality teaching which is systematically monitored through the evaluation of learning. Teachers are then supported through regular training and professional development opportunities to ensure that they have the knowledge and skills to fulfil different learning needs. Also developed, through a culture of accountability and ownership, will be an ethos of 'corporate responsibility' for securing progress across the spectrum of needs and for empowering all pupils to become the best they can be.

This approach negates a frequently voiced concern that there is 'no money' to do things differently for dyslexic pupils. The good practice described above is expected of schools as part of the OFSTED inspection procedure and therefore needs to be in place for all pupils, it being a happy coincidence that such measures will also make a school more dyslexia friendly.

Building the culture

If it is accepted that materials and methodology go hand in hand, what we are seeking is a culture or ethos of dyslexia friendliness. This culture will share some of the following characteristics.

- Empowerment – There are acknowledged to be at least seven intelligences (Gardner 1983), each of equal importance to a well-rounded individual. Although there will be inevitable strengths and weaknesses within the profile of intelligences, most people are naturally competent at two or three learning preferences and we all have the capacity to improve our performance in our weaker areas.

  An empowering culture recognises learning preferences and deliberately sets out to harness them in order to capitalise on learning. It also models a wide variety of good practice and requires learners to develop competence in most, if not all. Such flexibility of thinking is associated with lifelong learning and the ability to respond quickly, appropriately and creatively. Thus the dyslexia friendly learning environment will provide safe opportunities to use, experiment with and sometimes fail with a variety of styles of learning, information processing/presentation and so on.

  For example, processing information to achieve an objective can be done in a variety of ways, including stream of consciousness, mind-mapping, linear plans, flow charts. Even within individual learning preferences, there is an optimum situation for each style. The key is for dyslexic learners to have the tools at their disposal and the opportunity to make appropriate choices.

- Largely 'error free' in the early stages – Many teachers will recognise the burden of guilt/low expectation/poor self-image that dyslexic pupils bear. It has been suggested that 80 per cent of learning difficulties are due to stress: experience may confirm this finding. Thus, the teacher has the responsibility to make it transparently clear that it is okay to be dyslexic. Then, having brought the issue into the public domain, she/he must 'walk the talk' at all times. Empowerment implies education rather than training and so there will be times when inappropriate choices are made. If the opportunity arises to respond to inappropriate choices in the learning situation, the dyslexic is more likely to make the right choice in exams and in the workplace.

- Clear objectives about the nature of tasks, what is to be achieved and how the tasks will be assessed – If the task is to produce a handwritten best copy for assessment, dyslexic learners must be assessed alongside their peers. However, if the task is to do with identifying key issues, processing information to feed, then presentation/spelling, etc., is arguably not an issue. At GCSE, A level and GNVQ, the examination boards are very clear about the criteria for allowing special arrangements such as extra time, amanuensis and recognising the importance of sampling a wide cross-section of skills. They do this through the use of skill banks that value higher-order cognitive skills more than, say, spelling and grammar.

  Such clarity of objectives also permits work to be submitted in a variety of forms – evidence of research, for example, would be acceptable as bullet points, on a dictaphone, perhaps as a mind-map or even in cartoon/storyboard format. If the task is to do with an appreciation of a play, asking a dyslexic pupil for a written description is unlikely to produce ability appropriate results. However a mind-map may fit the bill just as well and may even be better.

Good practice

From the perspective of a teacher, the encouraging thing about developing 'dyslexia friendly' skills is that these skills also enhance the learning of non-dyslexic learners. This transfer occurs because the techniques are rooted in the psychology of learning and epitomise best practice. At its most simple, best practice can be defined as measures which:

- help rather than hinder;
- support rather than confuse;
- open doors rather than close them.

The initial role of the teacher is to set learning goals in such a way as to communicate, at both the conscious and unconscious level, the expectation that these goals will be met. This communication must also include the message that it is 'okay to be dyslexic' together with an explanation of the ways in which a given unit of instruction will be made accessible to dyslexic learners.

Setting achievable learning goals is a fundamental skill that is crucial to the self-esteem and self-belief of the learner. Because the goals are perceived to be achievable the learner will be able to operate in that optimum state for learning, a state of relaxed alertness. Success will inevitably follow, giving fresh opportunities for praise. Work in the field of neuro-linguistic programming (NLP) suggests a ratio of four positive comments ('strokes') to one negative to be the optimum for maintaining motivation and self-respect. To be able to operate at this ratio places a considerable demand on the skill and preparation of the teacher – to develop self-esteem tasks have to be largely 'error free' without being trivial, certainly in the early stages. As the learner gains in confidence, it becomes possible to challenge and pressurise, the opportunity for positive strokes coming from displays of tenacity, flexibility, determination and so on. *If the four-to-one ratio is found to be impossible to maintain, it may say more about the nature of the task than the ability and/or motivation of the learner.*

Making use of kinaesthetic, auditory, and visual preferences (KAV)

All learners have a preferred 'channel' through which to access and process information. Failure to provide opportunities to utilise preferred channels can be a significant handicap to effective learning. Research suggests that within a given population the distribution of preference will be:

37 per cent – kinaesthetic preference, typified by the use of phrases like 'That doesn't *feel* right';
34 per cent – auditory preference, 'That *sounds* good to me';
29 per cent – visual preference, 'I *see* what you mean'.

Identifying learning preferences

There are many definitions of learning. At its most simple, learning can be defined as 'The ability to do something new/different following a course of instruction.' This definition is particularly appropriate in the context of this chapter because it acknowledges the responsibility of the teacher to secure learning through the achievement, on the part of the learner, of the lesson objective(s).

Over a period of instruction there will be occasions when, for all sorts of valid reasons, objectives are not met. The key is for teachers to accept responsibility for securing learning and to adopt a multi-intelligence/multi-skill approach. The optimum culture has **zero tolerance of failure**.

Multiple Intelligences Theory

Effective teachers use every means at their disposal to secure learning. They also pay learners the compliment of empowering and persisting until learning objectives are met. The work of Howard Gardner (1983) suggests there to be at least seven intelligences, each with its preferred way of learning. We all possess varying degrees of each of these intelligences and it could be argued that true intelligence implies the optimum application of all of them. Intelligence can also be seen as a preferred learning style. If this is accepted, the definition has clear implications for teaching: successful teachers make sure that a majority of learning styles are utilised during a course of instruction and successful learners use different learning methods to suit the task in hand.

Putting it all together

1. *Supportive environment*
Dyslexic learners operate most effectively in an environment in which they feel safe and supported. However, just like any other learner, they do not appreciate condescension or 'dumbing down'. Once dyslexic learners feel secure they can be challenged, pressured, put under appropriate stress and be expected to cope: like most people they thrive under the pressure of high expectation once they believe themselves capable of delivering. Much of the art of the teacher, then, is to strike the balance between challenge and support, a balance that will change from learner to learner, from situation to situation and from day to day.

Key concepts

- Safe
- Stress free
- High expectations.

2. The Big Picture

Trying to learn anything without an overview or 'big picture' has been likened to trying to do a jigsaw puzzle without the picture on the lid – all the pieces obviously have meaning but, without insight into their relationship, it is impossible to perform the task.

All learners benefit from activities designed to give them the big picture and dyslexic learners find this particularly beneficial. Giving the theme or objective for the lesson together with small group activities to review the activities of the previous session are effective ways of establishing how the topic fits into past work. Similarly, 'prediction exercises' encourage learners to try to be one jump ahead, interacting with the topic and material in an involved way. Such activities are especially valuable to support learners to connect with long-term goals, to move away from passivity and towards independence.

Key concepts

- Establish purpose of the lesson – goals+objectives
- Participative review strategies
- Prediction exercises.

3. Target setting

Once the purpose of the instruction has been established, it becomes necessary to focus on teaching and learning. Another way to view this is to reflect on what the learners must be able to do at the end of the session. It is essential to place the learner at the centre of this reflective process because the sequence of instruction needs to focus on what they need to do in order to hit the targets.

Setting targets at the beginning of a session gives an immediate focus and sense of purpose. A typical introduction to targets could be, 'By the end of this session you will be able to . . .'. The teacher then continues to 'chunk down' the big picture until all the component parts are explicit and understood. It is also at this time that any assessment procedures should be introduced.

Key concepts

- Set learning objectives
- Set assessment criteria
- 'Chunk down'.

4. Accessing the content

While choice of content is inevitably determined by the syllabus, effective delivery is very much within the control of the teacher. Ideally, all input should include opportunities for the use of kinaesthetic, auditory and visual modes – this will benefit all learners, especially those who are dyslexic. Also, over a period of time (course of instruction, block of lessons, etc.), all seven intelligences should be accessed at some time, with planned opportunities to develop competencies in weaker skill areas. In particular, opportunities should be created to encourage learners to operate outside of their learning preferences. Taking them outside their 'comfort zone', in a safe environment, will reveal hidden depths and, perhaps, unexpected weaknesses.

Oracy is a powerful tool in the context of accessing content through learning preferences. Opportunities for structured talk in a variety of groups and settings encourage learners to think, reflect, acknowledge and then harness the intellectual capital of their group. Much of the skill of using oracy lies in the creation of different groups, one of the most effective, though often least popular, being 'mixed gender non-friendship groups'. Although not always a comfortable grouping for learners or teacher, it will often generate the 'change' of behaviour/approach that signifies real learning.

As a bottom line, the more senses (KAV) and intelligences that can be brought into play by the teacher, the more effective learning will be. Multisensory learning is the key to long-term changes in approach.

Key concepts

- KAV opportunities in every learning session
- Access all intelligences
- Oracy
- Multisensory approaches to secure long-term gains.

5. Demonstrate learning

Effective instruction focuses on what the learner is doing. To measure learning will require the learner to demonstrate knowledge and understanding, preferably throughout a lesson/block of lessons, rather than just at the end. While summative assessments have their place, it may be too late to take action if certain concepts are causing problems. Thus, opportunities for ongoing formative assessments help to keep learners up to the mark. This style of assessment is particularly 'dyslexia friendly' since it focuses on what they can do, rather than on what they can remember.

Formative assessment can be in the form of pen and paper exercises. However these inevitably discriminate against those who think faster than they can write. They also benefit those who write faster than they can think, which may give some cause for concern! The following techniques support learners to 'show what they know' without placing enormous demands on currently weak basic skills:

- peer presentations – ether individual or group;
- posters;
- instructional booklets;
- peer assessment – setting test questions, etc.;
- Mind-Maps (copyright) and storyboards (annotated cartoon strip presentations);
- models.

Key concepts

- Use of formative assessments
- Use of a variety of assessment techniques
- Link to targets.

6. Opportunities for reflection

Regular review is essential for long-term learning and recall. It has been suggested that adopting the following strategy could remove the need to learn for tests:

1. Read over all notes at the end of the day.
2. In the morning, read the previous notes for the lesson of the day.
3. At the end of the week, read all notes.
4. Re-process into another form – lists, key points, mind-maps, etc.

Key concepts

- Opportunities for systematic review
- Re-process – use different mode (KAV) and different learning preferences.

7. 'Hot tips'

Below is a collection of ideas that are particularly effective for dyslexic learners and actually enhance the learning of all.

- Consistently set high expectations – make it clear exactly how the learners will be empowered to meet them, especially those who are dyslexic.
- Use the jargon – refer to individuals learning preferences, etc.
- Be positive – say what you do want, rather than say 'don't'. Aim for the four-to-one positive strokes regime.
- Set targets, expectations and assessment criteria at the start of a course and at the start of each lesson.
- Constantly look for opportunities to utilise KAV and the seven intelligences.
- Always start with the big picture and then chunk down.
- Build in review opportunities to enable learners to 'show they know'.
- Use mind-maps.
- See learning problems as opportunities to try different approaches.
- Have fun!

8. Dyslexia friendly checklist

- Do you know your learners' preferred learning styles?
- How will you convey positive expectations regarding success?
- How are different learning preferences reflected in you lesson planning and delivery?
- How will you inform the learners of goals and targets?
- How will you utilise prior knowledge?
- How will you chunk down content from the big picture?
- How will your lesson incorporate KAV?
- Which multisensory techniques will you employ?
- How will you check learning throughout the lesson?
- Which intelligences/learning preferences are you using?
- How will you ensure you cover all seven intelligences over time?
- How will you ensure that success criteria are explicit and understood?
- How will you ensure a balance of individual, pair and group work?
- What opportunities will you create to allow learners to 'show they know'?
- How will you achieve success on behalf of all?

Summary

The ideas, techniques and methodology outlined above form the main elements of a dyslexia friendly approach to learning. They are particularly effective because they minimise literacy difficulties and empower the learner to operate at an ability appropriate level.

Making the changes necessary to become dyslexia friendly will, without doubt, enhance the effectiveness of instruction and the learning of all, whether dyslexic or not. Organising instruction in this way supports all to learn quickly and efficiently and to retain learning over long periods of time.

References

Basic Skills Agency (1998) *What Works In Secondary Schools.* London: Basic Skills Agency.

Ford, S. and Baxter, M. (1999) 'Key Skills For Citizenship', EIS, April, 10–12.

Gardner, H. (1983) *Frames of Mind*, 37–43. New York: Basic Books.

Harrison, B. and Butler, T. (1995) *Developing Effective Schools.* London: DfEE.

Scottish Education Office (1991) *Effective Schools.* Edinburgh: SEO.

CHAPTER 20

Dyslexia Across the Curriculum

Isobel Calder

This chapter:

- highlights policy, practice and provision issues in relation to a specific innovative approach in supporting dyslexic students in a mainstream setting
- discusses some key issues relating to inclusion and describes the practical aspects of including children with SpLD into different subject areas of the mainstream curriculum.

The aim of this chapter is to describe the experience of one school in supporting dyslexic pupils in accessing the secondary school curriculum. The intention is to discuss the decisions, which were taken with respect to the curriculum; the underlying assumptions and values, which informed these decisions, and the organisation and strategies, which were used to try to ensure access to the curriculum. It is hoped to demonstrate to the reader that it is possible to include pupils with dyslexia in a mainstream secondary school. There is evidence to suggest that this inclusion can be a highly satisfying experience for the pupils, their parents, specialist staff and classroom teachers.

The context

Denny High School, of which Northfield is a part, lies in central Scotland and is one of eight secondary schools within Falkirk Authority in Scotland. The school, which serves a diverse community, has a pupil roll of 1,200. The creation of the Northfield facility was partly motivated by the closure in the summer of 1998 of a nearby independent school, which provided for dyslexic pupils. The closure resulted in a need for Falkirk Education Authority to reconsider its facilities and resources to provide for pupils with severe specific learning difficulties. The provision, which was named Northfield, is located in an integrated setting located within the Denny High School building, opened in August 1998 with a roll of ten pupils, which spanned the first four years of secondary school. It has a maximum facility for 18 pupils from S1–S6 with severe specific learning difficulties. In the two years since opening, the roll has increased to 14 pupils. The accommodation comprises two teaching rooms and a large social area. The aim of Northfield is to include pupils, both socially and academically, in mainstream wherever and whenever possible.

Denny High School employs 2.4 Support for Learning teachers, 1.8 'Extended Learning Support' teachers, 2 Northfield teachers and 5.5 Supervisory Assistants (auxiliaries). A Principal Teacher, responsible to an Assistant Head teacher who also has a remit for Guidance leads the Support for Learning Department. The department has adopted a philosophy of integration and inclusion. This philosophy means that every teacher and every assistant in the department has duties which range across all three different types of learning support work in the school: that is general support for learning; support to pupils with Records of Needs, and work with the Northfield pupils. The teachers perform the roles for support for learning specialists outlined in the Scottish Office Report entitled *Effective Provision for Special Educational Needs* (SOEID 1994) which are: to offer consultancy to classroom teachers and other stakeholders, cooperative teaching, direct tuition to individual pupils and staff development.

Northfield

There are two classes in Northfield. The younger pupils follow a curriculum based on 5–14 guidelines while the older ones are engaged in Standard Grade courses. The teaching is shared between Northfield staff, subject staff and support for learning staff. A speech and language specialist works in the facility, either in collaboration with the teacher or individually with pupils when this is deemed necessary. The pupils are supported emotionally not only by the support for learning and subject teachers but also by guidance staff. One very important aspect of the Northfield curriculum is a weekly Circle Time session. The emphasis in the literature (Reid 1998, Westwood 1997) on using a multisensory approach to learning and teaching is evident in Northfield. The pupils are encouraged to use mind-mapping (Buzan 1993), already a well-established practice in the school, in order to capitalise on their global learning style. Alternatives to reading and writing have been supplied without totally ignoring the need to provide the pupils with strategies for tackling new words (Cooke 1993). Much emphasis is placed on discussion, the use of video and audio tape, on practical skills and on using the opportunities, which these offer to practise literacy skills. The pupils' impulsivity has been used in order to enthuse them into reading. For example, while fundraising for a national charity as part of an enterprise unit, they baked cakes, read recipes, made shopping lists and kept financial records and, in their enthusiasm, forgot that they were also in receipt of reading, writing and arithmetic lessons.

Assisted learning programmes already a feature of the school, are easily transferred to the facility with senior pupils employed in peer tutoring, mentoring and paired reading. The success of a mainstream metacognitive skills programme has been repeated in the facility and has made the pupils more aware of their thinking processes during learning. The school librarian also assists the pupils to gain access to the curriculum by allowing them practice in study skills such as research in the library and by encouraging them to use the mind-mapping skills already mentioned. For the older pupils, study skills also involve exam preparation, for example help in organising and actually undertaking revision and practice in using a reader and scribe. Careful consideration is always given to the choice of reader and scribe so that each pupil can have the same familiar adult for all assessment.

The process of Inclusion

Warnock (DES 1978: 8) reminds us that,

> The purpose of education for all children is the same; the goals are the same. But the help that individual children need in progressing towards them will be different.

The model, which is outlined here, echoes the description of Dyson and Skidmore (1996) as 'a flexible range of strategies in a customised package' and ensures that the pupils, in gaining their entitlement to the common curriculum, can still enjoy educational achievement and can look forward to a fulfilling adult life. This type of provision provides differentiation, the building of self-esteem, the encouragement of learner autonomy and the development of skills. It is based on an eclectic mix of strategies and approaches; pragmatism; customisation of the balance of the child's needs and preferences, and the reconciliation of a well-established collaborative approach with some specialised interventions to suit the needs of this client group. As far as is possible in a large and complex organisation such as Denny High School, the staff who are asked to accept these pupils into their classes are carefully chosen for their skills in dealing with children with learning difficulties and for their willingness to work with learning support teachers to support these pupils. The choice of staff is not made in a judgemental or negative way but rather in recognition of the fact that some teachers, because of personality, training, experience or inclination are more equipped than others to become involved in this kind of teaching. Those teachers who were willing to become involved with Northfield in its initial stages undertook the first module of the University of Edinburgh postgraduate masters programme in dyslexia. This training was financed by Falkirk Authority. Staff have also had training in handling confrontation and conflict, managing difficult groups, working with families and other agencies, characteristics of pupils with specific learning difficulties, teaching and management strategies. Discussion, case studies and workshops, contextualised for different subject areas were led by an external consultant and by support for learning staff.

Inclusion at Northfield

The inclusion of Northfield pupils begins long before they enter the doors of the school. Moore (1996) described the worries that all eleven year olds have when moving from primary school to secondary school and quite rightly pointed to the increased fears which a dyslexic child will have because of embarrassment about a lack of literacy skills and the fear of looking stupid. Early liaison with primary schools is a well-established strategy in Denny High School. Support for learning and guidance teachers gather information on pupil progress and strategies which have been employed and this is used to inform secondary teaching (Reid 1998). Pupils referred to Northfield do not necessarily come from the school's catchment area but can come from anywhere in the Falkirk Education Authority area. The main criterion for referral, laid down by the authority is that a pupil referred to Northfield must have a formal Record of Needs, which states a severe specific learning difficulty. Information is sought from the referring primary school as part of the admissions procedure and pupils and their parents are invited to visit Northfield before accepting a place. A recent evaluation of Northfield pointed to a need to tighten up the admissions criteria so that the challenges posed by behavioural difficulties did not threaten the effectiveness of the Northfield provision (Reid 2000).

From the very beginning there has been social inclusion of the pupils into the mainstream. The system in place illustrates the Inspectorate's assertion that 'Successful integration of pupils with special educational needs requires a high degree of teamwork between Guidance and Learning Support' (SOEID 1996: 37). This has been achieved by allocating the pupils to guidance houses and by including them in registration and personal and social development lessons as part of a mainstream guidance group class. Within this setting the pupils are encouraged to participate in all the inter-house competitions, activities days and other extracurricular activities offered within the school. So far Northfield pupils have taken part in the school sports day, European holidays and fun runs.

Inclusion in subject areas

There is curricular and social inclusion in Standard Grade English, History and Maths. In English four Fourth Year pupils share a classroom with eight others from mainstream. This small group of twelve follow a Standard Grade curriculum and are taught by an English specialist supported by a Learning Support teacher. It is expected that at least one Northfield pupil will attain at Standard Grade 3 next year. The success of this inclusion is due to several important factors. The two teachers involved were willing to spend time in the beginning clarifying roles and setting the ground rules. They agreed that:

- this should be an equal partnership;
- resources should be shared;
- consultation time must be built into the timetable;
- workload should be equal, so, for example, marking and setting of homework would be shared.

They also discussed the problems which were likely to arise. Mainstream and Northfield pupils might not want to cooperate, because of the very real anxiety on both sides. Basic literacy skills were weak in all the pupils and needed to be worked on. Both teachers were apprehensive about having to fulfil the requirements of a Standard Grade course with this group. Pupils might find it difficult to transfer skills learned in isolation to new situations.

During this past year the two teachers have worked towards their objective of obtaining five folio pieces from each pupil by adopting some useful strategies. A wall chart was produced which shows clearly what is expected of each pupil. Each time a folio piece was completed and graded the pupil would colour in a box. This has proved to be so motivating for the pupils that they have completed more folio pieces than was expected of them. All the pupils in the class had comprehension difficulties and therefore exercises specifically designed to build up this skill were incorporated into the course. One period per week was dedicated to vocabulary building in order to improve written work. The exercises were challenging but manageable and, importantly, the pupils could complete an exercise in one lesson period. Basic spelling and punctuation was worked into a homework programme, which was recorded on a chart to encourage pupils to complete work regularly and to be proud of their progress. 'Write on' sheets were provided to avoid having to ask pupils to perform too many copying tasks. Instructions, both oral and written were clear and unambiguous. Ensuring that everything that the pupils worked on was corrected and gone over with them was essential to boost morale. Finally a pattern of learning and teaching developed which was structured and well planned which ensured that the pupils knew what was expected of them at each lesson.

The same four pupils who are integrated in Standard Grade English are also integrated in Standard Grade Maths. This group of four are also being presented for Standard Grade Art, Craft and Design and Social and Vocational Skills in fourth year. They attend these last three subjects as a discrete group so that subject specialists cooperating with support for learning staff can give individual teaching. In addition one of the above pupils is studying Standard Grade History in a mainstream class of 31, where he is making excellent progress. The fact that the History teacher took time out to work with this pupil when there was difficulty in understanding an aspect of the course demonstrates the commitment from Denny High School staff to assist in the successful integration of Northfield pupils.

The first and second year pupils follow a curriculum similar to that experienced by the mainstream pupils. It consists of number and language work being taught within Northfield and art, computing, craft and design, geography, history, home economics, music, physical education, religious and moral education and science being taught by mainstream subject staff with support for learning staff assistance in appropriate mainstream accommodation.

Factors in an inclusive system

Individualised Educational Programmes have been prepared for all the pupils in Northfield. These detail the strengths of the pupils and their learning needs and set short- and long-term targets in language, number and behaviour. Subject-specific strategies designed to achieve the best results are also specified. These IEPs are negotiated and agreed with the pupils, parents and all the staff working with them.

Information technology is widely used by staff to increase curricular access for the pupils. For example software packages are available to augment language activities. The older pupils word process much of their work which helps to increase motivation and gives the boys confidence to improve the content when they see how good their well presented, accurately spelled work looks. The NCET team (1992) found that the language difficulties of pupils with dyslexia often stop them from writing at all, with the result that they have few opportunities to communicate in writing or to practise writing skills. Information technology can surmount this hurdle, and allow these pupils to become comfortable with this medium. Teachers too are encouraged to use technology in order to present information in new and exciting ways, which should interest and motivate all learners. Because there is a high involvement of support for learning staff in lesson planning and delivery, it is easier, because of the presence of two adults in the classroom, to organise this.

Consultancy is an essential part of the system, which has been set up to integrate the Northfield pupils into the mainstream. Support for learning staff are able to give advice on, for example, readability and on the particular needs of individual pupils. The support for learning team give subject teachers support by being in the classroom and by collaborating and cooperating outside the classroom. Reid and Hinton (1996) suggest this kind of support is needed when subject teachers are dealing with pupils with learning difficulties. As has already been stated, subject staff are carefully chosen and the timetable is negotiated to allow as much flexibility as possible. One important aspect which has been negotiated with senior management is that subject staff as well as learning support staff should be given time for liaison. Although this has been agreed in principle, it does not always happen in practice and much of the consultation, which takes place, is informal. This collaboration is crucial if the pupils are to be allowed a high level of curriculum access since a great deal of differentiation is always required. Simpson's (1995) suggests three key aspects of differentiation – the pupil, the course materials and the activity of the pupil. These fit neatly into Reid's (1998) model of the learning process explained as input, cognition and output. Dodds (1996) points to the need to concentrate on the area between input and output and in this case it is met by timetabling a support teacher to be with the pupils when they are being taught by mainstream staff. This allows discussion to play a large part in lessons and also allows subject staff to adopt more practical approaches when this is appropriate. Strategies such as DARTS (Directed Activities Related to Text) (Lunzer and Gardner 1979) can be more effectively employed so that the pupils can be more actively engaged with reading materials. Finally two adults can more easily motivate and organise this inherently disorganised group to prepare themselves to learn.

With the current trend of self-evaluation using performance indicators, it is important to keep in mind the importance of the distinctive features of effective provision outlined in the EPSEN Report (SOEID 1994). It is clear that the features relevant to curriculum access are demonstrated in this situation. For example, the attention that has been paid to staff development and the importance that has been placed on consultancy shows that a shared understanding of special educational needs exists in the school. Primary/secondary liaison is strong and the careful gathering of information both before and after the pupils arrive in Northfield demonstrates a thorough assessment of needs. The curriculum offered to the pupils within the constraints of the educational system is appropriate and the evidence of thorough assessment followed by a range of strategies to meet needs are indicators of provision which suits these pupils. The approaches to teaching and learning include specific strategies to address the particular needs of individual pupils. The provision is effectively managed at the levels of the facility, the support for learning department and the school. Parents are closely involved in the education of their children through the use of weekly progress reports and are encouraged to keep in contact with both Northfield and the wider school. Finally, by listening carefully and by creating an atmosphere of trust and respect it is possible to take into account the views of the pupils when decisions about provision are being made.

Conclusion

The features of good practice outlined in the Manual of Good Practice (SOEID 1998), which might lead to an inclusive school, are evident in this school. As Edwards (1999: 45) says, 'Access stems from the differentiation applied in whole-class work together with focused activities designed for some children to catchup'. Giangreco (1997) has also identified common features where inclusive education is thriving. These include collaborative teamwork, a shared framework, clear role relationships among professionals and the effective use of support staff. The importance of supportive teacher behaviour and attitudes and the fostering of peer acceptance in inclusive settings has been discussed by Westwood (1997).

The experience of the first two years of Northfield has highlighted several issues, which should be taken into consideration if successful inclusion is to be achieved. All levels of school staff must be prepared to allow the conditions for successful inclusion to exist. Small class sizes of around 12 to 15 pupils supported by a subject specialist and a learning support teacher can make functional inclusion a reality. This may seem expensive in staffing terms but the cost of this kind of system must be weighed up against the cost of educating these pupils in dedicated facilities. The economies of scale which are possible in a large comprehensive school can never be replicated in smaller specialist establishments. The social benefits of educating educationally vulnerable children with their peers are immense in terms of increased self-esteem and acceptance.

It is absolutely essential that consultation time is built into the timetables of both subject and support staff so that planning, development and evaluation of the curriculum can be achieved. This is a feature of Denny High School, which was negotiated before Northfield was created and has been extremely helpful during this initial time. It is hoped that, despite possible staffing restrictions, this can continue.

Subject departments must be willing to provide appropriate and adequate resources including texts at a suitable reading age and interest level. Subject teachers should be prepared to build up a bank of materials, which can be used with pupils who have literacy difficulties. It needs to be said here that the kind of materials which suit the needs of dyslexic pupils will often also be suitable for other pupils with learning difficulties. The teacher assigned to a class, which includes these pupils, should be willing, enthusiastic and committed. The teacher must be willing to work with a support for learning teacher and to share the preparation and correction load equally.

Finally, Reid and Hinton (1996: 399) point out:

> It is apparent [therefore] that within school factors such as school communication networks, interpersonal staff relations, organisational procedures, management concern for teachers' welfare, democracy in decision making and encouragement in relation to professional development are important considerations and need to be addressed.

Denny High School's demonstration of these 'within school factors' is undoubtedly the reason for the success of Northfield.

Acknowledgement

I wish to acknowledge the contribution to this chapter and to the success of Northfield made by all the staff of Denny High School but especially by Fiona Christie, Learning Support Teacher, Denny High School; Margaret McInally, Guidance/Learning Support Teacher, Denny High School; Marion McNicoll, Extended Learning Support Teacher, Denny High School, and Anne Motion, Assistant Principal Teacher, Northfield, Denny High School.

References

Buzan, A. (1993) *The Mind-Map Book – Radiant Thinking*. London: BBC.

Cooke, A. (1993) *Tackling Dyslexia: The Bangor Way*. London: Whurr Publishers.

DES (1978) *Report on the Committee of Enquiry into the Education of Handicapped Children and Young People* (the Warnock Report). London: HMSO.

Dodds, D. (1996) 'Differentiation in the secondary school', in Reid, G. (ed.) *Dimensions of Dyslexia: Vol. 1, Assessment, Teaching and the Curriculum*. Edinburgh: Moray House.

Dyson, A. and Skidmore, D. (1996) 'Contradictory models: the dilemma of specific learning difficulties', in Reid, G. (ed.) *Dimensions of Dyslexia: Vol. 2, Literacy, Language and Learning*. Edinburgh: Moray House Publications.

Edwards, S. (1999) *Reading for All*. London: David Fulton Publishers.

Giangreco, M. F. (1997) 'Key lessons learned about inclusive education: summary of the 1996 Schonell Memorial Lecture', in *International Journal of Disability, Development and Education* 44(3) 193–206.

Lunzer, E. A. and Gardner, K. (1979) *The Effective Use of Reading*. London: Heinemann.

Moore, K. (1996) *Home Help for Secondary School Pupils*. Scunthorpe: Desktop Publications.

NCET (1992) *IT Support for Specific Learning Difficulties*. Coventry: NCET.

Reid, G. (1998) *Dyslexia: A Practitioner's Handbook*. Chichester: Wiley.

Reid, G. (2000) 'An evaluation of the Northfield Facility at Denny High School'. Report commissioned by Falkirk Education Authority.

Reid, G. and Hinton, J. W. (1996) 'Supporting the system – dyslexia and teacher stress', in Reid, G. (ed.) *Dimensions of Dyslexia: Vol. 2: Literacy, Language and Learning*. Edinburgh: Moray House Publications.

Simpson, M. (1995) *Differentiation and Research: A Reader for Teachers*. Aberdeen: Northern College.

SOEID (1994) *Effective Provision for Special Educational Needs* (EPSEN). Edinburgh: HMSO.

SOEID (1996) *Effective Learning and Teaching in Scottish Secondary Schools – Guidance*. Edinburgh: HMSO.

SOEID (1998) *A Manual of Good Practice in Special Educational Needs*. Edinburgh: HMSO.

Westwood, P. (1997) *Commonsense Methods for Children with Special Educational Needs*, 3rd edn. London: Routledge.

CHAPTER 21

Inclusion and Dyslexia – The Exclusion of Bilingual Learners?

John Landon

This chapter:

- examines factors relating to linguistic and cultural diversity in education
- examines how the assessment and provision of needs for dyslexic bilingual learners can be met within the educational environment.

A number of studies in the UK (ILEA 1985, CRE 1996, Deponio *et al.* 2000) have revealed a relatively low percentage of bilingual learners diagnosed with dyslexia compared with the incidence of dyslexia in the population as a whole. Other studies (see the review by August and Hakuta 1997) show a high rate of reading failure among children acquiring literacy through a language other than their home language, specifically the recall of factual detail in information passages (Cline and Cozens 1999). What factors appear to lead to low rates of detection of dyslexia among bilingual learners? Could the same factors also explain the poor standards of literacy among many learners of English as an additional language (EAL learners)?

In recent years, the norms which operate in schools have been extended to include the needs of a wide range of children who were formerly either excluded from mainstream education or who found themselves unable to cross the barriers inherent in their mainstream schooling. The Macpherson Report (Macpherson of Cluny 1999) has raised the question of whether this policy of inclusion in public service provision has yet embraced people from minority ethnic and linguistic groups. The Report draws attention to the unconscious norms that continue to operate within our society to the exclusion and disadvantage of minority ethnic people. The Report (6.34) defines institutional racism as:

> the collective failure of an organisation to provide an appropriate and professional service to people because of their colour, culture and ethnic origin. It can be seen or detected in processes, attitudes, and behaviour which amount to discrimination through unwitting prejudice, ignorance, thoughtlessness and racist stereotyping ...

In other words, if the norms operating within a school and through the social and learning opportunities which it provides are predicated on the assumption of fixed power relations exercised to the detriment of a subordinated group and on the myth of cultural and linguistic homogeneity, then those who operate outside that power structure and whose cultures and languages are different will effectively be excluded from full participation in the life of the school. This type of exclusion is largely invisible in the discourse and research studies of inclusion (Diniz 1999). Inclusion of bilingual learners will require negotiation and restructuring of power relationships and the recognition and positive accommodation of differences in language and culture. Failure to include bilingual learners and their families within the school's definition of itself will inevitably affect their performance and sense of well-being and is likely to lead to poor standards of literacy development. This can either affirm the school in its exclusive self-definition and lead it to provide, at best, compensatory programmes for those bilingual learners who cannot meet its standards. If this is the case, the school need look no further to explain the literacy difficulties which bilingual learners have – by definition, they simply are unable to meet the standards. Concern as to whether a child is dyslexic is immaterial (Cline and Reason 1993). Alternatively, it can recognise the barriers which its perception of itself, and the practices which stem from that perception, present for the child and family who have low status and cultural and linguistic differences, and commit itself to dismantling them. This involves renegotiation with the whole school community of the school's self-definition and a restructuring and realignment of those perceptions and practices that the exclusive self-definition has distorted.

Let us consider how exclusive notions of power and status, culture and experience, and language affect understanding of bilingual pupil performance in reading and writing and how they might impact on the detection and support of bilingual learners with dyslexia.

Cummins (1996) has discussed what he calls 'coercive relations of power' or 'the exercise of power by a dominant group ... to the detriment of a subordinated group'. He contends that:

> Coercive relations of power ... usually involve a definitional process that legitimates the inferior or deviant status accorded to the subordinated group. In other words, the dominant group defines the subordinated group as inferior ... thereby automatically defining itself as superior. The process of defining groups or individuals as inferior or deviant almost inevitably results in a pattern of interactions that confines them, either psychologically or physically.
>
> (p. 14)

Smyth (2000) has further researched this definitional process in terms of the dominant cultural model of bilingual development which persists in schools. She has interviewed a number of teachers working in areas of low-incidence ethnic minority population and, on the basis of the teachers' views, has found that the dominant cultural model (or what she calls the 'Master Model') is: 'Bilingual Pupils need to become monolingual in order to succeed'. This model, she believes, 'helps to shape and organise the teachers' beliefs' and leads to a number of related cultural models:

> (1) Parents who do not speak English hinder the child's academic progress, by definition, their ability to become monolingual. (2) The role of schools and literacy events is to promote monolingualism. (3) There are two types of bilingual learner – those who fit the 'Master Model', that is those who operate monolingually in the dominant language and those who do not. (4) Those bilingual learners who do not fit the 'Master Model' are problematic and require learning support.
>
> (Smyth 2000: 7)

The exercise of the 'Master Model' in schools will encourage the process of subtractive bilingualism, or acquisition of a second dominant language at the expense of the first or home language. This leads to discontinuity in the process of learning between what has been learned through the first language and what can be learned through the second, once the child can effectively use the second language as a medium of learning. Since this discontinuity most seriously affects the early years of schooling, it is likely to have a serious detrimental effect on the acquisition of literacy. The process of acquisition of pre-reading concepts and skills which normally takes place in the preschool period within the sociocultural setting and interactions of the home cannot be drawn upon effectively by a child propelled, on entry to school, into a very different sociocultural setting mediated through an, as yet, unknown language. Baseline assessments standardised on native English-speaking populations and conducted in English at this stage in the child's linguistic development are likely to show depressed results. If these results are interpreted as measures of potential, they will merely legitimate the teacher's deficit view of the bilingual learner and confirm them in their insistence that as rapid a transfer to English as possible is the best way forward for the child. It is not surprising, therefore, in such a climate, that the school should fail to consider dyslexia as a possible cause of literacy failure.

The school's disregard of the bilingual child's different linguistic and cultural background is evident in the results of an audit of procedures to detect and support bilingual learners who are experiencing difficulties with reading carried out in Scotland (Deponio *et al.* 2000). In some ways, their reading difficulties were treated in the same way as a monolingual child's. Teachers seemed unaware of the difficulties of interpreting standardised assessment results for bilingual children, and were uninformed about tests like the Phonological Assessment Battery (PhAB) which have been standardised on particular minority linguistic populations (in this case, Sylheti speakers) (Frederickson and Frith 1997).They tended to interpret results in the same way as they would for monolingual English-speaking children. That is, they perceived low scores in comprehension tests generally as indicators of poor phonological awareness. However, in the case of bilingual children, who often gain good accuracy scores, it is likely that the cultural unfamiliarity of the content of texts and the complexity of their (English) language, and not poor phonic skills, contribute to low comprehension (Landon 1999). By and large, they failed to test hypotheses about possible underlying causes of reading failure by assessing the child in their first language. Practice did differ from approaches used with monolingual children in two respects. Underlying reasons for reading failure were not addressed immediately. They were left unresolved. The reason given was usually that teachers were waiting to see if reading difficulties would disappear as monolingualism in English was established. Secondly, parents of bilingual learners were almost never involved in discussion of their child's perceived difficulties. In other words, the legitimation of the child's 'problems' is linked to the school's self-definition as a monolingual establishment – an establishment from which, by definition, the other-language-speaking parent is excluded. There is no perception that the problem may, in reality, be the school's failure to accommodate to the reality of linguistic and cultural diversity both in its response to the child and to the child's family.

How can a school be transformed into an inclusive institution in which the corporate and individual diversity of all children – here, I will speak specifically about developing bilingual children – is positively accommodated? In this school, children will be described in terms of themselves, in all their diversity (expressed in terms of strengths and needs), and not, tacitly, in terms of their ability or inability to conform to the school's monolingual definition of itself. This description will include comprehensive profiles of the child's competence in the languages she/he uses. Where these descriptions reveal literacy difficulties, the hypothesis that the child is dyslexic will be considered alongside other hypotheses (including the hypothesis that the school is still excluding the child in some respects from full demonstration of his/her potential).

As with our discussion of the exclusionary tendencies of schools in terms of power, culture and language, these three aspects are central to a consideration of how the school might become inclusive. The school's definition of itself is often reflected in its policies and development plans, or lack of them. A school which is inclusive of linguistic and cultural diversity will need to reflect this inclusiveness in policies and actions (Corson 1999). I do not mean by this add-on policies or addenda to existing policies which deal with bilingual children separately from issues in the rest of the school. Each policy, and actions springing from them, will need to be written or reviewed, in collaboration with representatives of the whole school community. The reading policy, for example, will no longer be a monolingual reading policy, with a proviso added for bilingual children or dyslexic children. It will address reading styles, performance, needs and resources in terms of the wide range of diversity in the school and in terms of the multiple identities of individual children. Thus, the policy and its implementation will provide a structure, guidance and support to staff, other professionals and to parents for addressing the strengths and needs of all children, including, for example, the dyslexic bilingual boy from a Muslim background.

School development planning will also pay attention to the professional development of staff and support of parents in addressing the needs of children with reading difficulties, including bilingual and/or dyslexic children. Perhaps, the linguistic and cultural backgrounds of existing staff cannot adequately address the need to be fully inclusive. In this case, recruitment of, for example, bilingual and bicultural staff, will need to be prioritised. The recruitment of bilingual teaching assistants in Edinburgh schools has been a powerful instrument not only in addressing early reading failure, but also in providing a means of early detection of underlying processing difficulties (Landon 1999, City of Edinburgh Education Department 2000). The school will also need to investigate the child's literacy activities not only in school but at home and in the community and the perceptions which parents and community leaders have of reading and writing. Some studies of literacy practices in ethnic minority homes (for example, Gregory and Biarnes 1994) have tended to overgeneralise from single case studies. Others have revealed a richer and more diverse pattern of attitudes and attention to literacy across communities (Martin-Jones and Bhatt 1998, Hancock forthcoming).

Provision in schools of a range of texts written in different languages (dual language and single language texts) or translated from other languages, and representing different cultural backgrounds needs to be ensured. Where these texts are not available, as may happen for the less common languages of refugee groups, family literacy schemes can be developed to enable parents to work with the school to address these deficiencies. In cases where family literacy practices are very different from those found at school, the school will need to provide opportunities to introduce parents to school practice while affirming the very different approaches used in the home. Where the content and storylines of texts may themselves be exclusive, because they take for granted an understanding of a different set of cultural schemata and presuppose allegiance to a certain set of values, comprehension should not be seen merely in terms of retelling the story, and thereby endorsing it, but in terms of the ability to critique and challenge it from another cultural viewpoint (Ada 1988). If the complexity of the English language of the text is the issue, pre-reading discussion and the development of metacognitive skills to support the interpretation of complex sentence structures and unfamiliar vocabulary will be required (Chamot and O'Malley 1994).

Such inclusive approaches may support children from minority cultural and linguistic backgrounds who are finding difficulty in accessing written text. Amongst them there will also be those who experience more specific processing difficulties. According to Cummins' Interdependence Hypothesis (Cummins 1979), underlying processing difficulties experienced in the second language will also be evident in the first[1]. To investigate this in individual cases,

---

1   This may not be the case when the type of processing required for both languages is profoundly different, as, for example, the types of processing required to decode a logographic, as compared to an alphabetic, script (Wang, Inhoff and Chen 1999).

it is necessary to have access to trained assessors who are literate in the child's first language and to have research evidence of the normal patterns of literacy development for children learning to read that language in a multiliterate environment. If the child is not literate in the first language, we need to research perceptual indicators and indicators from oral/aural skills development which might facilitate early detection of dyslexia.

Having established a hypothesis that the child is dyslexic, the hypothesis needs to be tested against what we know of dyslexia and the development of bilingualism and biliteracy generally and the child's individual development (Hall 1995). Appropriate assessment instruments will need to be identified and their results corroborated by dynamic approaches to assessment. This will involve collaboration amongst professionals and with parents. A programme of intervention and support will also involve parents and an interprofessional team. The preferred medium of support will need to be established, since successful intervention in one language to address deep processing difficulties will transfer to the other language (see Holm and Dodd (1999), for intervention strategies in the case of a child with a phonological disorder). Many conventional intervention approaches will be appropriate, but cultural and linguistic issues must always be considered whatever resources are used. Finally, there must be constant reflection and vigilance by all staff concerned, to ensure that inappropriate professional or institutional norms and biased attitudes are not distorting perceptions and influencing decisions. M'gadzah, Saraon and Shah (1999) have produced a useful checklist of school internal steps (the class teacher in consultation with parents, pupil, bilingual support teacher, SEN coordinator and educational psychologist) and external steps (that is, involvement of external agencies) when testing hypotheses about the educational needs of a bilingual learner.

The move from exclusion to inclusion will require EAL and bilingual support staff to change their practice from a largely compensatory role to a strategic and transformative role across the school. They will create inclusive practices and policies which will affect the dyslexic bilingual child if they collaborate with senior management, the SEN coordinator and other support personnel. However, before they can effectively collaborate, traditional suspicions between EAL and SEN staff need to be broken down, the marginalisation of EAL staff needs to be addressed, and the realisation that a bilingual learner may have a specific learning difficulty needs to dawn.

References

Ada, A. Flor (1988) 'The Pajaro Valley experience: working with Spanish-speaking parents to develop children's reading and writing skills in the home through the use of children's literature', in Skutnabb-Kangas, T. and Cummins, J. (eds) *Minority Education: From Shame to Struggle*. Clevedon, Avon: Multilingual Matters.

August, D. and Hakuta, K. (eds) (1997) *Improving Schooling for Language-Minority Children: A Research Agenda*. Washington DC: National Academy Press.

Chamot, A. U. and O'Malley, J. M. (1994) *The CALLA Handbook: Implementing the Cognitive-Academic Language Learning Approach*. Reading, Mass.: Addison Wesley.

City of Edinburgh Education Department (2000) *Early Intervention with Bilingual Pupils 1998–2000*. Edinburgh: City of Edinburgh EAL Service.

Cline, T. and Cozens, B. (1999) 'The analysis of aspects of classroom texts that challenge children when learning to read in their second language: a pilot study', in South, H. (ed.) *Literacies in Community and School*. Watford: National Association for Language Development in the Curriculum (NALDIC).

Cline, T. and Reason, R. (1993) 'Specific learning difficulties (dyslexia): equal opportunities issues', *British Journal of Special Education* 20(1), 30–34.

Commission for Racial Equality (CRE) (1996) *Special Educational Need Assessment in Strathclyde: Report of a Formal Investigation.* London: CRE.

Corson, D. (1999) *Language Policy in Schools: A Resource for Teachers and Administrators.* Mahwah, NJ: Lawrence Erlbaum.

Cummins, J. (1979) 'Linguistic interdependence and the educational development of bilingual children', *Review of Educational Research* 49, 222–51.

Cummins, J. (1996) *Negotiating Identities: Education for Empowerment in a Diverse Society.* Stoke-on-Trent: Trentham/CABE.

Deponio, P. *et al.* (2000) 'An audit of the processes involved in identifying and assessing bilingual learners suspected of being dyslexic: a Scottish study', *Dyslexia* 6, 29–41.

Diniz, F. Almeida (1999) 'Race and special educational needs in the 1990s', *British Journal of Special Education* 26 (4) 213–17.

Frederickson, N. and Frith, U. (1997) 'The Phonological Assessment Battery: findings from the British standardisation'. Paper presented at Fourth International Conference of the British Dyslexia Association, York, 1–4 April.

Gregory, E. and Biarnes, J. (1994) 'Tony and Jean-Francois: looking for sense in the strangeness of school', in Dombey, H. and Meek-Spencer, M. (eds) *First Steps Together. Home-School Early Literacy in European Contexts.* Stoke-on-Trent: Trentham/IEDPE.

Hall, D. (1995) *Assessing the Needs of Bilingual Pupils: Living in Two Languages.* London: David Fulton Publishers.

Hancock, A. (forthcoming, research in progress) 'Literacy practices in Chinese families in Scotland'. Research being undertaken towards MSc., University of Edinburgh.

Holm, A. and Dodd, B. (1999) 'An intervention case study of a bilingual child with a phonological disorder', *Child Language Teaching and Therapy* 15(2), 139–58.

Inner London Education Authority (ILEA) (1985) *Educational Opportunities for All? Research Studies. Fish Report.* Vol. 2. London: ILEA.

Landon, J. (1999) 'Early intervention with bilingual learners: towards a research agenda', in South, H. (ed.) *Literacies in Community and Schools.* Watford: NALDIC.

Macpherson of Cluny, Sir William (1999) *The Stephen Lawrence Inquiry* (The Macpherson Report). London: The Stationery Office.

Martin-Jones, M. and Bhatt, A. (1998) 'Literacies in the lives of young Gujarati speakers in Leicester', in Durgunoglu, A. Y. and Verhoeven, L. (eds) *Literacy Development in a Multilingual Context: Cross-Cultural Perspectives.* Mahwah, NJ: Lawrence Erlbaum.

M'gadzah, S. H., Saraon, S. and Shah, T. (1999) 'Black and Asian consultants – working together to meet the cultural, linguistic and special educational needs of all children within a multicultural community: bridging the divide between LEA and community, *Education and Child Psychology* 16(3), 68–85.

Smyth, G. (2000) '"I feel this challenge and I don't have the background": teachers' beliefs about teaching bilingual pupils'. Paper presented at the Conference of the Association of Teacher Education in Europe (ATEE), Barcelona, 28 August–2 September.

Wang, J., Inhoff, A. W. and Chen, H-C. (1999) *Reading Chinese Script: A Cognitive Analysis.* Mahwah, NJ: Lawrence Erlbaum.

CHAPTER 22

Individualised Learning in a Group Setting

Janet Tod and Adele Fairman

This chapter:

- briefly reviews educational perspectives on individualised planning for dyslexic students within secondary schools contexts
- identifies critical issues and development opportunities.

Introduction

The specific aims of the chapter are to:

- examine developments in individual planning within the context of the Government's commitment to increasing inclusion (DfEE 1997, DfEE 1998a, DfEE/QCA 1999a, DfEE 2000);
- discuss the implications of the new National Curriculum (DfEE/QCA 1999a) and the draft revised SEN Code of Practice (DfEE 2000) for individual planning;
- appreciate the opportunities and constraints for individual planning within secondary school settings and illustrate how the principles of individual planning within group contexts can be applied to improving attainment and promoting participation.

Section 1: Individualised planning and inclusion

Planning for meeting individual needs within group settings has become of increasing concern to parents and students at a time when concern about educational outcomes, costs, societal inequalities, moral imperatives and political preferences has prompted the adoption of inclusion as the educational ideology for the new century (DfEE 1997, 1998a, DfEE/QCA1999a). While the draft Code of Practice (DfEE 2000) has retained the use of Individual Education Plans (IEPs) for those individuals who are deemed to require *additional to or different from* the differentiated provision which is in place for all pupils (p. 47) there is still debate about the principles and practices for individual planning within inclusive contexts (Mittler 2000). Obviously individual planning via IEPs addresses the needs of those students who are identified as having 'special educational needs' (SEN). However, many dyslexic students may not be designated 'SEN' by the Code of Practice criteria (DFE 1994, DfEE 2000) but still experience difficulties in learning which may be transient, longer-term or subject specific. The notion that all children would benefit from individual learning plans has been given ministerial support and has been taken on board by some schools (Kirkman 1999). Such plans are normally called 'Individual Learning Plans' in order to distinguish them from the Individual Education Plans described within the Code of Practice framework and differ in format, detail and time frame from IEPs. They do, however, share some features of effective IEPs in that they are integrated into whole-school planning and support student involvement in target setting and monitoring.

For many, the retention of IEPs for SEN students within inclusive settings is paradoxical:

> the principle of individualised and alternative pathways through the curriculum for all pupils would set IEPs for a minority of students in a broader and less exclusionary context.
>
> (Mittler 2000: 93)

Given that the government has recently (DfEE/QCA 1999a) opted for the term 'special educational needs' to be subsumed within 'diverse learning needs': 'boys and girls, pupils with special educational needs, pupils with disabilities, pupils from all social and cultural backgrounds, pupils of different ethnic groups including travellers, refugees and asylum seekers, and those from diverse linguistic backgrounds' (DfEE/QCA 1999a: 31), it could seem contrary to the spirit of inclusion and equal opportunities to offer resourced IEP provision to only one subset of individuals within this diverse learning needs grouping – albeit that these groupings are not mutually exclusive. However, it is recognised that while the debate about the role and realisation of individual planning continues, it is necessary for teachers to work within existing constraints and perceived paradoxes. Most teachers have become familiar with IEP procedures: 'Teachers working with pupils with special educational needs are familiar through the use of individual education plans (IEPs) with setting specific targets for students' (DfEE 1998c).

It seems therefore prudent to start with this experience of IEP planning and work forward to include other forms of individual planning rather than try and work with two separate systems: i.e., individual planning as prescribed for SEN pupils; and individual planning needed to support learners in inclusive settings.

While it can be argued that IEPs neither promote excellence or equality (Skrtic 1991) and their very existence can create segregation within the mainstream school unless skilfully managed (Ainscow 1999) it is true to say that many of the features of effective IEP provision mirror conditions cited as being important for inclusion (Tod 1999a). These include:

- a focus on pupil outcomes;
- provision for diverse needs embedded in whole-school practice;
- the need for formative reflection and analysis rather than merely summative reporting;
- student and parent involvement;
- the use of a variety of instruction;
- rigorous evaluation of the effectiveness of additional or otherwise extra support;
- sharing of responsibility for SEN support with other adults;
- peer involvement;
- collaborative multiagency planning.

So what more do schools need to consider if they are to continue to develop their provision for individuals within group settings? Firstly it is helpful for schools and their staff to openly discuss issues relating to 'the individual' and 'inclusion'. Many of the questions teachers and parents are asking about inclusion are particularly relevant to dyslexic students in secondary contexts. Inclusion has been something of a 'top down' initiative with limited opportunity for open discussion by stakeholders, parents and teachers. This has been to the extent that 'disagreement has been marginalised and individual doubts suppressed' (Garner and Gains 2000). As a consequence, although teachers have broadly welcomed a government commitment to inclusion there remain concerns about whether the ideologies of inclusion can be realised for individuals who are placed within competitive educational contexts 'with an almost exclusive emphasis on subject knowledge and standard forms of assessment' (Garner and Gains 2000). There is additional concern about whether teachers are sufficiently prepared for educational inclusion (Garner 2000), and whether a reduction in Statementing will decrease stakeholder rights to an appropriate education. Key questions that emerge in relation to *individuals* within inclusive contexts (Grainger and Tod 2000) include:

(1) Does an *individual* right to an appropriate education override an ideological commitment to inclusion? (Croll and Moses 2000). Is it justifiable to give an individual dyslexic pupil special education which may not be located in their neighbourhood school? Is it reasonable to 'withdraw' students from secondary classroom contexts? (SENCO-Forum 2000).

(2) The dominant educational model for inclusion in the UK is based on a social model of disability, which seeks to reduce barriers to learning and participation. For many students, including dyslexic students, learning difficulties arise from biological, psychological and sociological factors. Planning for provision within inclusive settings needs to be realistic about the complexity of barriers to learning experienced by dyslexic students and accept that a social model alone may not suffice to meet individual learning needs (Blamires 2001).

(3) Inclusion is currently framed within a political, rather than educational model, and is therefore likely to be subjected to inspection within a particular political agenda. One important question for individual stakeholders in education is whether the outcomes of inclusive provision will be measured in the long term or short term. Given that outcomes based evidence for inclusion remains limited (Hornby 1999), it is important that the impact of inclusion on the longer-term academic and social well-being of individual students is given due credence at times of inspection and evaluation of inclusion at the level of LEA and school policy.

(4) Can schools become inclusive while at the same time allowing specialist teaching and the use of LSAs to support individual pupils? Should learning support be organised to support all pupils? (Ainscow 2000).

(5) Will there be a true valuing of diverse outcomes for individuals in inclusive settings? Will dyslexic students simply be given increased opportunities to be 'normalised' via increased time and support to produce written evidence of attainment through examinations, etc., or will there be real opportunities to recognise and value the outcomes of diverse learners? Will other areas of achievement, e.g. creativity, be given due credence (DfEE 1999) as the country moves towards greater educational inclusion?

Although it is accepted that there is no *one* answer to these questions, they need to be aired if individual planning is going to be effective in terms of individual student outcomes. The history of special education suggests that individualised planning for 'diverse needs' should not be controlled by any one dominant policy or ideology. However some differences need to be taken on board if individual planning is to support both the process of inclusion and the personal and academic development of the individual within inclusive settings. Individual planning for dyslexic students in group settings does not start with the assumption that any one individual will need individualised planning simply because of their dyslexia. It might be helpful, in the context of inclusive practices, to consider the following principles, which apply to *all* learners:

(1) *Means–End principle:* The 'end' (teaching objectives, etc.) is usually given but the means of getting there can vary. While this is an acknowledged key feature of differentiation, effective teaching at secondary level should make this notion *explicit* to students by exploring alternative routes to particular ends at whole-class level. The realisation of this principle is not just the teacher's responsibility but is shared with the students themselves. Individual students should be guided and supported to choose the most effective routes for particular ends based on their response to the task and their unique knowledge about themselves as learners.

(2) *Relative–Unique principle:* Although any one dyslexic individual will have a unique bio/psycho/social make-up, his/her individual learning need in a group setting will be determined by that group. Norwich (1996) has drawn an interesting distinction between individual, exceptional and common needs, which provides a useful framework for considering individual planning within group settings.

- Individual needs – arising from characteristics which are unique to the child and different from all others.
- Exceptional needs – arising from characteristics shared by some (visual impairment, high musical abilities).
- Common needs – arising from characteristics shared by all (e.g. the emotional need to belong and to feel related).

Inclusive teaching strategies, either implicitly or explicitly, are often designed using this model. For example the literacy hour (DfEE 1998b) uses a whole-class format designed to address common needs; a small group format such that teaching can be focused towards the particular strengths/difficulties of individuals with shared needs; and individual planning for those pupils whose needs are sufficiently unique for them to require 'different or extra' provision to that given at whole-class/small group level. It logically follows that it is feasible to reduce the amount of individual planning needed in any one group by looking at pupil response and adjusting provision at whole-class and small group level (Tod 1999b).

(3) *Transient–Resistant principle:* While it is accepted that dyslexic individuals will experience some learning difficulties throughout their secondary school life (e.g. reading at speed while processing for essay writing, accurate spelling during generative writing, etc.), it is also true to say that dyslexic students will at times experience particular difficulties which may be, in some sense, 'constructed' by the learning context or subject-specific requirements. It follows that individual planning in inclusive settings must be able to address both resistant and transient learning needs. This is particularly important for dyslexic students who may need to 'revisit' areas of learning pertinent to an earlier Key Stage before they can advance with a current Key Stage learning objective. It is also important that individual planning should be sufficiently flexible to support the early identification of learning difficulties – in advance of these difficulties having a pervasive effect on student progress. While the same principles apply to transient learning plans as

apply to IEPs they need to be initiated quickly without hindrance from excessive paperwork. Given that most students experience transient learning difficulties there is only a need to formulate a transient learning plan if a student needs provision which is *additional to* or *different from* other students in the class.

> For the vast majority of pupils it is the action taken by their class teachers in ordinary settings which are the key to helping them make progress and to raising achievement.
> (DfEE 2000)

(4) *Skills–Strategies principle:* In practice, the individual planning which emerged from the IEPs of the 1994 Code of Practice has tended to focus more on student weaknesses than on their strengths. At secondary level there is often a need to consider 'strategies' rather than just skills and knowledge learning. In exam contexts teachers will also need to make some form of 'risk analysis' assessment based on their specific-subject requirements in order to prioritise action, e.g. if a student handed in a Chemistry homework which reflected that he/she did not know how to calculate how many moles in a certain amount of substance and he/she had also misspelled 'conical flask' then the teacher would prioritise the mole calculation for 'additional/different' tuition. While this is obvious it needs to be made explicit to students so that they can prioritise their individual learning needs and capitalise on their particular strengths.

Many learners only have recourse to their own strategies, some of which may be unsuccessful. In inclusive settings, where collaborative learning is encouraged, there are opportunities to examine 'learning' as a cross-curricular area for discussion. Peer generated strategies can be used to address particular areas of learning. Strategies can be targeted for action on individual learning plans and encourage a focus on using strengths to address difficulties – a feature not often used sufficiently in IEPs.

(5) *Enabling–Empowering principle:* Individual planning provides a focus for mediating learning based on the work of Vygotsky (1978). Using this model the teacher prompts the student to draw on their relevant knowledge and skills and gradually transfers the responsibility for problem solving to the individual student. The key element is to 'enable' – i.e. achieve something that could not be achieved alone at that stage in the student's learning. Education, in this model is 'an act of participation' and is not something that is 'done to' the learner (Marshall 1998). It follows that in using this model for individual planning that there is an 'enabling' stance to teaching and an 'empowerment' stance to learning.

The strength of individual planning is that it allows for the monitoring of an individual's progress within group settings. This is an important consideration during a period when national targets and league tables are the primary measure of school effectiveness. If students can be encouraged to take increasing responsibility for monitoring the effectiveness of their additional individualised provision it is hoped that the unequal balance between paperwork planning and impact on progress, which has dogged IEPs, can be redressed.

Section 2: Curriculum contexts and individual planning

There is optimism from the new National Curriculum (DfEE/QCA 1999a) that social and emotional learning should be linked to academic aspects of learning to provide a more coherent and balanced educational experience for all learners. Whereas policies for integration were concerned with 'access' to learning, inclusion is concerned with access *and* engagement, learning *and* social participation.

The implications of the new National Curriculum for individual planning is in relation to:

(1) *Diversity:* Individualised provision is undertaken within a context where teachers are being encouraged to plan for diversity. Suffice is to say that if schools can develop effective inclusive practices the chances are that the need for individual 'different or extra' provision and its accompanying paperwork should be reduced.

(2) *Engagement and participation:* Individual planning will need to reflect the importance of these two elements of learning. Whereas 'access' skills such as reading are clearly important, the need to target and nurture the development of skills that encourage involvement in task and class, are likely to emerge as key elements of individual planning (Tod 1999a): 'participation in education is a process that will necessitate all children being given the opportunity to make choices and understand that their view matters' (DfEE 2000: 14).

(3) *Combining of academic and social aims:* The new National Curriculum and the draft Code of Practice (DfEE 2000) emphasise the need for students to develop the independence and social skills necessary to become active and contributing members to society: 'pupils who play an active part in assessment and in monitoring agreed targets will also have greater self-esteem and feel confident that they are making progress' (DfEE 2000: 14).

As an example one of the key skills within the Citizenship curriculum is '"improving learning and performance" through reflecting on their own and others ideas and achievements and setting targets for future involvement and improvement' (DfEE /QCA 1999a, Citizenship – Key Stages 3–4, p. 7).

There is, in the new curriculum, a recognition that factors other than knowledge and subject-specific skills need to be prioritised if individual students are to develop the independence, motivation, metacognition and collaborative working skills needed to enhance their performance and prepare them for lifelong learning. Dyslexic students are likely to welcome the emphasis on the use of language and ICT to support the development of Citizenship skills. The requirement that students should become responsible for their own learning should help to minimise the learned helplessness and reduction in self-esteem, which characterise many students who experience dyslexia in the fast paced environment of the secondary school.

Section 3: Planning for action

Within the secondary school context there are both opportunities and constraints for individual planning. The Government guidance on IEPs within the draft new Code of Practice stresses the need to reduce the cumbersome paperwork that has been associated with IEPs. The guidance suggests 'crisply written action based IEPs which focus upon three or four targets'. Given that inspection evidence is likely to be looking at 'action based' IEPs there may be a need to rethink traditional formats and look at the possibilities for having IEPs fully integrated into pupil and teacher planners via MAPS (Monitored Action Plans) (Tod and Blamires 1998).

They [IEPs] are unlikely to be successful if they are not part of the school's overall arrangements for assessment and record keeping.

(OFSTED 1999, section 92, p. 22)

While the problems of time, coordination, paperwork and monitoring are far from resolved within secondary schools contexts, there are opportunities emerging from inclusion for IEPs to become more influenced by school culture and less subject to external accountability (Pearson 2000).

Figure 22.1 illustrates a framework for individual planning within secondary contexts – the example taken relates to raising attainment as measured by external examination performance at GCSE.

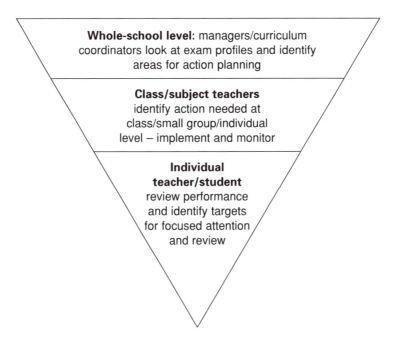

Figure 22.1 Contexturalised individual planning – raising attainment within the whole school context

Enhanced performance is the objective of all schools, class teachers and individuals, and it can be achieved through informed analysis and planning. The purpose of the planning exercise is to address *What* action needs to be taken? *Why* does this action have to be taken? *Who* is responsible for taking and monitoring the effectiveness of this action?

Individualised planning for improving attainment as measured by exam performance

School managers examine performance tables and identify key areas for development. Analysis identifies areas where there are opportunities to impact upon achievement. This may highlight a need for staff training; there may be resource implications; there may need to be organisational changes such as allocating time for thinking skills to be taught across a year group. Changes at this level should impact on all students.

Subject-based coordinators also analyse results and identify areas of strength and weakness. Performance can be improved by focusing on particular areas in which a significant proportion of marks have been lost, or by identifying particular topics that underperformed. Careful consideration of examiners' comments will highlight areas for action planning by the subject teacher.

The **class/subject teacher** needs to enable the students to understand what is required from them in order to achieve certain grades. Frequent monitoring of the group allows the class teacher to react by supplementing the original lesson plan with something 'extra or different' for either the whole class or a small group. Occasionally a specific individual may require further reinforcement to address a particular shortfall.

The **student** needs to be involved in evaluating their performance, sharing their unique knowledge about their own learning with the subject teacher and/or peers. They need to be involved in identifying areas for action and in monitoring response to any extra or different provision allocated via individualised learning plans. They will need to identify additional resources which can be brought to bear such as time, self, parental, sibling, peer support, additional tutoring or, ICT.

In essence the process for individual planning follows this sequence:

What examiners require needs to be understood by the teachers → this is then made explicit to the students → strategic responses are planned in order to maximise whole-group performance → observed student performance profiles are compared with expected profiles → strengths and weaknesses are identified and a risk analysis undertaken with a view to optimising group attainment → individual planning is undertaken in collaboration with the student → outcomes from this cycle of planning are regularly monitored and responsive adjustments made.

Table 22.1 describes how individual planning to raise attainment is compatible with action to improve exam grades at whole-school level.

The following part of this chapter provides more detailed information concerning particular emphasis which might be needed for dyslexic students.

It is difficult for some dyslexic students to understand whether topics are compartmentalised or interlinked until they understand how the whole syllabus is laid out. Revision Guides used at the *start* of the GCSE programme are often useful to dyslexic students. Diagrammatic representation of the syllabus set in a time frame showing core and interlinking features are also useful to keep as a reminder of 'where we are at'. Students who experience problems with organisation or in conceptualising time often panic simply because they do not have 'the whole picture' and do not know how much still has to be covered. If dyslexic students have a clear understanding of the relative importance of these aspects then they can prioritise. It is also useful to know how to study strategically – it is obviously worth expending more energy on reading a book that could be 'double entered', for both English Language and English Literature. The student who finds algebra very difficult might prioritise it for action if he/she has understands that it constitutes 20 per cent of the marks and that by ignoring that section his/her performance is likely to drop by up to three grades. Because dyslexic students are prone to discrepant performance it is more important for individual students to understand the weightings given to sections of the syllabus.

Dyslexic students need to understand subject-marking schemes. Many students struggle to understand why they only get a 'D' grade because they do not realise *what* they could have included to get more marks. Higher-level answers require examples, comparisons, reasons – even when not specifically requested. If a higher-level answer is known to require clear sentence construction it can be provided, or if bullet points are sufficient they can be used to save time. In some courses markers seek for key words and students need to know this. When the student is clear about the marking scheme he/she can be supported to produce a match between what is required and what is produced. In English Literature exams, questions do not ask for quotations to be used to illustrate the point being made but by doing so candidates score many

Table 22.1

What	Why	How (Group)	How (Individual)
Need to understand the syllabus structure.	To allow energy to be expended efficiently and facilitate time planning.	Give students a visual summary of the syllabus – ask them to highlight areas of key importance; check match between student and teacher perceptions.	Ask individual student how he/she thinks each section fits into the whole. Mediate understanding as to rationale for syllabus design and ordering. Peruse revision guide.
Explicit analysis of the marking scheme.	To capitalise on areas needed to boost grade attainment – prioritise areas for action.	Look at marking schemes produced by the examination boards.	Ask student to identify from his/her work what he/she often omits, e.g. diagrams and quotes.
Metacognition, understanding of what 'the examiner is looking for'.	Facilitate a match between what is required and what students produce.	Look at perfect answers. Identify strengths. Self-assess work in peer support groups.	Ask individual to identify where he/she could make improvements based on 'model answer exemplar'. Action plan to improve performance.
Improve understanding of vocabulary as used in subject areas.	It is possible to misinterpret questions and lose marks.	Give subject vocabulary list – with definitions.	Reinforce, help learn or reduce list.
Clarify use of language.	Impacts on marks.	List key examples, show examiner's reports.	Highlight problem areas. Prioritise for extra practice under exam conditions.
Motivation.	To complete work.	Extrapolate a grid of grades.	Explain how 'additional' effort on coursework elements can compensate for exam performance and influence overall grade.

more marks. Thus all students will need to develop the technique of using quotations. This may need to be individualised for some dyslexic students.

All students, but particularly dyslexic students, benefit from developing metacognition. If they understand what the examiners want as evidence of learning they can set appropriate targets for themselves. For example, students need to know that in 'three mark' questions three clear sentences written on separate lines are more likely to get three marks rather than a rambling paragraph from which information has to be extracted. When shown an 'exemplar' answer most students can get closer to reproducing it. Students working together reinforce what needs to be included and can remind each other to include what tends to be omitted. Peer marking, handled responsibly, can be very useful in enabling students to mark objectively using marking schemes.

Language is a problematic area for many dyslexic individuals and candidates who misread or misinterpret what is required lose many marks unnecessarily. Students can often be forgiven for their misinterpretation. The word 'illustrate', in a Geography exam, may mean that examples should be explained in detail, whereas in Art it may mean that a picture has to be drawn. By giving students a list of commonly used command words like 'comment on', 'describe', 'define', 'discuss', 'illustrate', 'explain', and identifying exactly what the examiner means by them, all students can be clearer about what is required of them. Strategies for addressing this important area of performance may have to become individualised if significant extra help or effort is required to remember the definitions or to help with sequencing. The vocabulary requirement in answers is as problematic as that in questions and similarly needs clarification to students. By reading examination board documentation it is possible to analyse the specific language requirements. Candidates can be penalised for using words like 'all' instead of, 'most of', or, 'the majority' (EDEXEL 1998).

All students need motivating, but particularly dyslexic students, who constantly need to use their strengths to overcome their weaknesses. In subjects that have a practical component, course work can contribute to up to 60 per cent of the total mark. It is possible to compile a grid (see Figure 22.2) based on an extrapolation of previous years' results to demonstrate what grades are likely to be achieved by what marks. For example, if an A grade normally requires 151 marks and a C grade 104 marks, and 90 marks can be gained from the practical, a student can clearly see why it is worth finishing off their practical to a good standard. If they can manage to get 70 marks in the practical they can get a grade C even if they only get 20 marks in the final exam. Placing a chart on the classroom wall allows all students to motivate themselves by clearly understanding the value of each course work mark and how this contributes to the final grade. This type of chart, while supplied to the whole class, is an example of individualised action because each student is able to compare their own marks with expected grades and action plan accordingly.

The emphasis throughout is not on what the individual cannot do but how they can be empowered, how they can help themselves, and what they specifically need to target in order to improve their grades. Exams still carry some mystique for which 'luck' is needed. Students who are empowered to 'achieve success' rather than 'avoid failure' are less likely to experience the learned helplessness and anxiety associated with exam preparation and performance.

Conclusion

This chapter promotes the view that the purpose of individual planning within inclusive settings is to optimise the chances of catering for diverse needs by mediating different routes to achieve prescribed ends. Although the context for individual planning since the introduction of IEPs (DFE 1994) has developed from that of integration to one of increased inclusion the key principles have remained stable. These are:

- Individual planning should be **contextualised** in order to identify 'additional or different provision' to that given to all pupils.

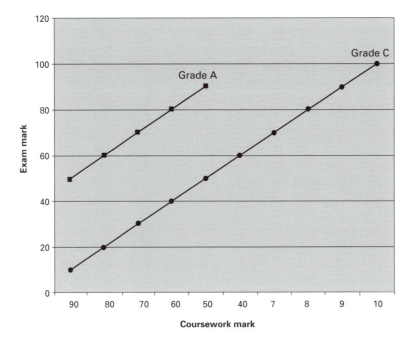

Figure 22.2 Graph to show relationship between coursework and exam grades in electronics

- Individual planning needs to be managed at whole-school level. Roles and responsibilities need to be identified at the different levels of planning to ensure that **outcomes are monitored** and responsive adjustments made.
- Schools will need **flexible arrangements** that support individual provision for all pupils, including IEPs for SEN pupils. Most schools already seek to meet individual learning needs but there needs to be a **strengthening of student involvement** in planning and monitoring.
- Individualised targets should reflect the need to develop **academic and social** aspects of development; should build on pupil strengths; should be concerned with both access and participation in education; and should address both **skills and strategy** aspects of learning.
- Individual planning in secondary settings should be both **enabling and empowering**.
- Individual planning should be **purposeful and motivating**. In secondary contexts there needs to be an emphasis on responsive and responsible planning, with a sharp focus on what the student *can do* to achieve higher grades.

While government seeks to balance equity and excellence within education, teachers strive to balance their responsibilities towards their class group and individual students. The introduction of IEPs prompted class and subject teachers to become more involved in provision for special needs pupils in their school. The seeds have therefore been sown to conceptualise outcomes-monitored individual planning as a necessary addition to whole-school strategies for raising attainment. No one denies the extent of this challenge. It is hoped that attention to the *principles* of individual planning, rather than to paperwork procedures, will empower schools, their staff and students to capitalise on the individual diversity that characterises dyslexia.

References

Ainscow, M. (1999) *Understanding the Development of Inclusive Schools.* London: Falmer Press.

Ainscow, M. (2000) 'The next step in special education: supporting the development of inclusive practices', *British Journal of Special Education* 27(2), 76–80.

Blamires, M. (2001) 'Is a social model sufficient to enable inclusive educational practice?', in O'Brien, T. (ed.) *Enabling Inclusion: Blue Skies–Grey Clouds.* The Stationery Office.

Croll, P. and Moses, D. (2000) 'Ideologies and utopias: education professionals' views of inclusion', *European Journal of Special Needs Education* 15(1), 1–12.

DFE (1994) *Code of Practice on the Identification and Assessment of Special Educational Needs.* London: DFE.

DfEE (1997) *Excellence for All Children: Meeting Special Educational Needs.* London: HMSO.

DfEE (1998a) *Meeting Special Educational Needs: A Programme of Action.* Sudbury: DfEE Publications.

DfEE (1998b) *The National Literacy Strategy Framework for Teaching.* London: DfEE Publications.

DfEE (1998c) *Supporting the Target Setting Process.* Nottingham: DfEE.

DfEE (1999) *All our Futures: Creativity, Culture and Education.* Report of the National Advisory Committee on Creative and Cultural Education. London: DfEE.

DfEE (2000) *Draft SEN Code of Practice on the Identification and Assessment of Pupils with Special Educational Needs.* London: DfEE.

DfEE/QCA (1999a) *The National Curriculum Handbook for Primary Teachers in England Key Stages 1–2.* DfEE and QCA.

DfEE/QCA (1999b) *Citizenship – The National Curriculum for England Key Stages 3–4.* DfEE/QCA.

EDEXEL (1998) London Examinations GCE AS/A Level Geography A (8201, 9201, 9202) Mark Schemes and Examiners Comments, Section A, p. 5. Nottingham: Edexel Publications.

Garner, P. (2000) 'Pretzel only policy? Inclusion and the real world of initial teacher education', *British Journal of Special Education* 27(3), 111–16.

Garner, P. and Gains, C. (2000) 'The debate that never happened', *Special!* Autumn, 8–9.

Grainger, T. and Tod, J. (2000) *Inclusive Educational Practice: Literacy.* London: David Fulton Publishers.

Hornby, G. (1999) 'Can one size fit all?', *Support for Learning* 14(4).

Kirkman, S. (1999) 'Under the Same Roof', *TES 'Special', Times Educational Supplement,* Summer, 7.

Marshall, B. (1998) 'What they should be learning and how they should be taught', *English in Education* 32(1).

Mittler, P. (2000) *Working Towards Inclusive Education: Social Contexts.* London: David Fulton Publishers.

Norwich, B (1966) 'Special needs education or education for all: connective specialisation and educational impurity', *British Journal of Special Education* 23(3), 100–104.

OFSTED (1999) *The SEN Code of Practice Three Years On: The Contribution of Individual Education Plans to The Raising of Standards of Pupils with Special Educational Needs* (HM1 221). London: OFSTED.

Pearson, S. (2000) 'The relationship between school culture and IEPs', *British Journal of Special Education* 27(3) 146–9.

SENCO-Forum (2000) (Darren Mayes@becta.org.uk) '"To withdraw or not" in secondary schools – report of SENCO-Forum debate', *British Journal of Special Education* 27(3) September, 160.

Skrtic, T. M. (1991) *Behind Special Education: A critical analysis of professional culture and school organisation.* Denver, Col.: Love Publishing.

Tod, J. (1999a) 'IEPs Inclusive Educational Practice?', *Support for Learning* 14(4), 184–8.

Tod, J. (1999b) *IEPs – Dyslexia.* London: David Fulton Publishers.

Tod, J. and Blamires, M. (1998) *IEPs – Speech and Language.* London: David Fulton Publishers.

Vygotsky, L. S. (1978) *Mind in Society.* Cambridge, Mass.: Harvard University Press.

CHAPTER 23

Examining the Challenge: Preparing for Examinations

David Dodds and David Lumsdon

This chapter:

- discusses key factors in examination preparation such as course choice, appropriate strategies and examination techniques
- examines the nature of the support for students undertaking examinations
- raises issues relating to special examination arrangements.

Examinations are an ever increasing event in the life of secondary school pupils. There is an increase in the number of public examinations taken and many of these are reported on nationally. As well as public examinations there are also internal school tests which provide students with challenges that require thorough preparation.

In this chapter course choice and special examination arrangements will be discussed as well as supporting course work, preparing for examinations through time management, structured planning, teaching and support from those adults close to the student.

Course choice and assessment method

There is a need for everyone; management, subject staff, learning support staff, outside agencies, parents and learners to have a clear picture of the strengths and needs of the learner, and the assessment demands of particular subjects. It is important students choose subjects that develop their own strengths and aptitudes.

School management needs to monitor option choices carefully to ensure that groupings of subjects do not force learners into inappropriate choices. Subject teachers, and particularly heads of departments, have a responsibility to provide accessible accurate information about the content and assessment requirements of courses on offer. Subject teachers with previous knowledge of dyslexic learners should highlight areas of strength in the learner's past performance and also areas of the course that are likely to pose particular problems.

Teaching staff should be able to produce an accurate learner profile based on a range of assessment approaches such as those outlined in Reid (1998). If an outside agency such as psychological services is involved with the learner, the school should ensure they provide accurate, up to date information on which to base any recommendation. Involvement of parents and the learner at this point is vital. Information should be shared and their views sought, taking into account their preferences for particular subjects and their aspirations. Tod (1999: 36) shows how this can be used in developing an appropriate IEP.

In addition to the individual subjects that constitute the learner's curriculum it is important to consider the whole picture and to make an assessment as to the appropriateness of the learner following courses leading to certification in every area. There may be advantages in offering an alternative in one area of the curriculum, allowing the learner extra support in the subjects studied and the opportunity to develop skills such as word processing or note-taking.

It would be helpful to mention to students, before they make choices for GCSE or S grade exams, the routes they could follow later and other types of qualifications which may be more suited to their particular skills.

There are a vast number of courses available. It may be helpful to discuss with staff whether specific elements of courses can be individually designed. Some subjects have a high practical content and a lot of course work. These subjects may be favoured by pupils who have difficulty with literacy skills.

The exact format of individual examination tasks and the type of answers required need to be considered. A format where questions consist of one or two sentences requiring multiple choice, single word or short sentence answers, will make different demands from one where the candidate needs to examine a range of source materials before writing paragraph or short essay responses. Whichever method is used it should be selected to best suit the student's needs.

Consideration of the contents of the examination syllabus is often useful and it may well be that pupils want to follow particular courses to help them in their likely chosen careers. Exploring a syllabus set by another examining board, rather than the one usually used by the school, where this is possible, might be more suitable for a particular pupil. An interesting breakdown of the similarities and differences of A/S level English papers was addressed in the *Times Educational Supplement*, 16 October 2000.

Subjects such as English and Mathematics are often compulsory entry requirements for many future courses so it is important to find the most suitable syllabus.

Modular course work often allows individuals to study at their own pace. Selecting all courses with a high proportion of continuous assessment might not always be advisable as it could place undue pressure on the student throughout the year. Students following courses with a high degree of continuous assessment benefit immensely from tutorial and planning support. Continuous assessment is not always easier than dealing with set examinations and this needs to be taken into account before a student embarks on a course.

Special examination arrangements

In some cases it is possible for students to have special examination arrangements. In England and Wales The Joint Council for General Qualifications produce a booklet entitled *GCE, VCE, GCSE and GNVQ; Regulations and Guidance relating to Candidates with Particular Requirements* and can be obtained from The Joint Council for General Qualifications, 1 Regent Street, Cambridge CB2 1GG. This booklet supports Heads of Centres, allowing them to make application for special arrangements for students. It outlines the needs of the pupils who are entitled to these arrangements and the procedures required for making the request.

The request should be made well in advance of the examination, along with a documented history of need which can be supported by professional reports as well as evidence of the pupil being able to manage the content of the curriculum.

The booklet contains a variety of application forms which, when completed, should be sent to the particular Examination Board which then makes the judgement on the special arrangements allowed. Centres should obtain this booklet each year, as special examination arrangements can change.

Recently, teachers with specific qualifications have been able to write the necessary reports to support the special examination arrangements application. These qualifications need to be checked with The Joint Council for General Qualifications, which usually produces a list in the booklet.

In Scotland, the SQA publish an annual guide to special examination arrangements which also gives details of available arrangements and the application procedures. In many areas local authority guidelines will also exist. Staff with responsibility for special examination arrangements need to be conversant with procedures that apply locally.

Where a candidate's difficulties are severe it is likely these will have been identified at an early age and the candidate will have experienced the types of arrangement likely to be offered. For others, the situation will be less clear, and experience gleaned from the early stages of the course will be important as evidence when making the case for a particular arrangement. In these circumstances close liaison between the SENCO/PT Support for Learning and subject teachers is essential.

Special examination arrangements raise a number of important issues, discussed at length by Pumfrey and Reason (1991), Duffield *et al.* (1995), Reason *et al.* (1999), but these relate mainly to aspects of policy and particularly equity at authority, examining body and national levels.

Discussions should take place, not only with the parents but the students themselves, about their special examination arrangements. Woods (2000) has shown that student's own views on their examination arrangements can be highly informative. When they are agreed then the student will need to be trained to gain the maximum benefit from this support. If an application is made for spelling to be set aside for a candidate who either agonises over the correct spelling of unfamiliar words or simply omits them in favour of a simpler alternative then it is vital that he/she is given opportunities to write without considering spelling. Equally, allowing a candidate additional time will not necessarily enhance performance unless he/she is shown how to use the time This may either be to spend more time reading questions or to take more time making notes before answering, or any other specific strategy that meets their needs. The Centre should ensure the student is able to experience special arrangements at other times rather than just the examination.

Supporting course work

The learner's IEP may indicate the type and level of support likely to be required in each area of the curriculum, and also the responsibilities of all of the individuals involved, including parents and the learner.

The learner needs to have a clear picture of assessment deadlines, and the nature of assessment tasks for every area of the curriculum. This could take the form of a colour-coded chart or wall planner, showing not only deadline dates but appropriate dates for completing stages in the process.

It is sometimes helpful to tape lessons where there is a high content of spoken information, especially when the student finds it difficult to take notes. The teacher needs to be in control of the tape and then the student can take it away and, with support, select the most important features.

It is useful to provide pupils with writing frames so they can locate key areas, key words and how these help access and organise information. They can help identify the main areas or events, which helps the student develop a particular way of thinking.

Dyslexic students often have a poor 'sense of audience'. They know what they want to say but cannot express it on paper. A writing frame can often help clarify thoughts. 'SQ3R' (Survey,

Question, Read, Review, Recall) is a structured way of combining skimming, scanning and detailed reading when approaching unfamiliar texts.

The use of different highlighter pens to emphasise distinct topics or events can help, but students often need adult input to help them with this task.

Direct activities related to texts

DARTS (Direct Activities Related to Texts) can be valuable in helping pupils to cope more effectively with reading tasks. These include a variety of activities such as:

- cloze procedure
- sequencing
- prediction
- table and diagram completion
- text marking
- labelling
- using pictures and models
- graphs, diagrams and tables
- pupil devised questions.

In many subjects, subject-specific words need to be taught and staff can help by exploring examination papers to find the type of text and language structure used.

The use of ICT

ICT is an important area and can be extremely beneficial to students in their secondary phase of education. It is also a huge area which develops quickly and is covered in more detail in Chapter 25.

Programs for the computer can be useful as they may allow the students to work at their own pace. Using the computer can motivate individuals. Even dyslexic pupils who are predicted to get A*s can benefit from this sort of work as it increases their confidence. It is often comforting for them to know someone has noticed their difficulties and is allowing them opportunities to reinforce their skills.

Whenever ICT solutions are considered it is important to assess their suitability for the individual learner concerned. Failure to do so may simply impose another burden on the learner in terms of using a new set of skills. The advice of experts, in school and beyond, should be sought at all times.

There are many constraints about using computers in examinations. Reference should be made to The Joint Council for General Qualifications' Handbook, or actually contact the Examination Board for guidance.

ICT helps the legibility and the presentation of work and generally enhances course work. Where possible, students should be encouraged to exploit the technology which is available to them.

Learning and teaching styles

Student's learning styles need to be considered and where possible staff should take the student's learning style into account in structuring lessons. Pupils need to be able to identify their preferred learning style and work to develop it, as well as learning to cope effectively in learning situations that do not suit their preferred style. This can help them to develop and exploit their opportunities when preparing for examinations.

There is a tendency when taking notes for students to try to write down every word. Depending on their particular learning style, it might be more useful to write down selective words, draw pictures, mind-maps, spider diagrams or charts. However, the student needs to identify which is the most successful method for them to learn and develop their skills in these areas. If students are unclear about this discussions with staff and parents might be beneficial, as well as thinking through the issues.

Staff need to look at different ways of presenting the curriculum and where possible produce lots of visual or concrete examples so that pupils can gain different experiences and experience information in different formats, e.g. reading evidence, looking at drawings or listening to tapes. As stress on the learner is reduced, self-confidence and self-esteem are increased.

Homework planning

Homework planners or diaries can be used and in some cases special needs staff, support teachers, or pupil mentors can support students by helping them write tasks and work out with the student when is the best time to tackle their work. Many schools now give homework tasks which do not have to be in the next day and if students are not good organisers they may be left with three or four tasks to complete in one evening because they have not planned efficiently.

Forward planning for homework and course work is vital. Cramming everything into the last few hours results in chaos and panic which raises stress levels in the student, parents and teaching staff. It is often helpful to have a timetable both at home and at school and use it to plan not only what is needed for lessons but to time homework and revision tasks and monitor course work completion.

Time management

Many dyslexic students have difficulty with time and organisation, therefore adult intervention is helpful. Over the duration of the course the syllabus needs to be broken down into component parts so it can be studied and revised systematically.

Students need to know when their examinations are to take place to enable them to plan accordingly so that all their work and revision is complete before the examination. This will reduce their own stress.

Thomson and Watkins (1990) pointed out that many dyslexic students find it difficult to appreciate time as a concept, they also find it difficult to estimate how long activities take. This becomes an increasingly important skill in terms of completing course work, finishing homework tasks, revising and also completing examination questions. Efficient use of time can be encouraged and specifically taught.

Tracking student progress

Structured tracking provides the opportunity for a member of staff to help the student approach their work positively by setting up interviews so that progress can be monitored as they tackle their revision work. Staff can also make sure that notes are concise so that there is not a lot to look at when revision takes place.

Opportunities need to be made available for students to think about their performances in internal and external examinations. They should examine the effectiveness of their approach and what could be improved. They may need adult support to do this.

Staff can also help students produce revision cards and case studies covering particular events, topics or issues, and help the student to work through these in a systematic way. This is also a wonderful opportunity for teachers to praise and reinforce the work the student is undertaking which can be fed back to parents who similarly can offer praise and support.

Essay planning

Many students need to be taught the skill of planning and writing essays. They require the opportunity to rehearse these outside the examination room without the pressure of having to submit the work as course work. Techniques such as draft and redraft also need to be developed. Writing frames, already referred to, are another approach to essay planning.

A useful way of preparing for essay writing is to obtain copies of previous examination papers to construct model answers. Northedge (1990) stated that this was probably the most useful revision technique. Initially these can be constructed with adult support. It may be beneficial for staff to provide topic headings and bullet points, areas to be investigated and ways of approaching revision so that a student can revise more effectively when they are at home.

If the learner has short-term memory difficulties then 'chunking' information can be helpful. This involves breaking down or reorganising information in a way which makes recall easier. Either the student or the teacher can engage in chunking information but often the pupil's own chunks or mnemonics can be more helpful than having them imposed. Students can break up text into chunks, read it onto tape or have somebody tape for them. Adult support can be very helpful in this process.

Preparing for the examination

For the dyslexic learner preparation for examinations is likely to be stressful, and ultimately ineffective unless essential study skills are taught explicitly. These include time management and study, and how to create a revision timetable and an appropriate environment in which to study. Many schools provide after-school sessions to allow students to revise key areas of the curriculum and the examination syllabus. Sometimes these may even take place during the school holidays.

A range of publications are available to support these areas. These include:

Learning Matters (Carel Press 1993), photocopiable masters. Covers a wide range of topics, but requires good reading skills.

Super Student (Carel Press 1989), worksheet based, contains a lot of useful information.

Strategies for Studying (Carel Press 1997). Aimed at post-16 learners, and again demanding on literacy skills.

Learning to Learn (Incentive Publications 1990). American, good self-assessment materials and checklists, but perhaps not all relevant.

Learning Made Easy (The Learning Game 1999). Group work based, attractively produced, includes an interactive CD, but expensive.

The Learning File (Jordanhill Publications 1998), for younger learners. Colourful OHTs backed up with resource sheets. Well produced but expensive.

Get Better Grades (Piccadilly Press 1995). Written in teen magazine style, contains useful ideas, inexpensive but wordy at times.

With the number of publications ever increasing it pays to be critical.

Dyslexic students will often need support to learn how to use the library and engage in research not only from books but looking for information from other sources, e.g. the Internet, interactive software.

Revision

Students need to plan ahead and be encouraged to make revision notes as early as possible. Eventually these will need to be condensed into a simple enough format so that they can be reviewed the night before the examination. Pupils with good aural skills may want to dictate these onto an audio tape. Others may use the opportunity to create mind-maps, diagrams, charts, cartoons, drawings or other suitable stimulating material which suits their learning style.

Students need to be encouraged and helped to set realistic targets during revision so they will accomplish certain pieces of work each day or week. They should also build in reward systems for themselves.

Students should be encouraged to study for short periods of time, e.g. 30 to 40 minutes, with regular breaks during which they should move away from the study area if possible.

Buzan (1986) suggests students should review work the day after a topic has been studied, recall what they covered the previous day, write down all they can remember about their study and check it with the notes they had made previously. They also need to think about what type of questions could be asked and what would be expected in a good answer.

Revision timetables should be constructed in consultation with parents and teachers but students need to find methods which work most effectively for them. Revision needs to cover all topics and not just the subjects which the student enjoys most.

The examination

Exam technique needs to be taught. Reid (1998) suggests students need to be encouraged to:

- read the paper quickly to get the general idea of what is being asked;
- read the whole question paper, including instructions;
- check how many questions have to be answered and decide in which order they are going to do them;
- check over individual words they may not be sure of;
- answer the question set, not the one they would like to be asked;
- read the question to gain understanding;
- ask themselves 'what is this question asking?';
- jot down all the words, names and ideas, dates or issues associated with that question and order them in hierarchy;
- look at a first key word and write simple sentences around it and link it to the second key word and so on;
- sum up and then check through their work, carefully examining their punctuation, common errors in grammar and general presentation.

If they have had plenty of practice this will come naturally to them. Dyslexic pupils in particular need to be taught to leave themselves the appropriate amount of time to answer each question. They also need to be given skills to answer questions in note form if they run out of time.

Self-esteem

Student self-esteem is extremely important and needs to be maintained and enhanced at all times. This can be achieved by helping students set realistic targets and providing praise and reward when these are achieved. Teachers need to look for evidence of strengths and use these to praise and encourage.

Ott (1997) comments that often students will experience a loss of self-esteem, self-doubt and self-criticism. It is important they are allowed to discuss what they are feeling with those close to them, and are supported through what can be a difficult time.

Parents

Parents are key players in preparing students for exams by helping their child with organisational skills and structuring their time. However, it is important they don't let their own anxiety transfer to the pupil. They need to support and encourage their child to build in specific rest and recreation times as well as study times. They need to liaise with staff at school and work closely together for the benefit of the student.

Some parents themselves may have difficulties and so lunch time and after-school support from subject teachers can be helpful. In some circumstances parents could be invited to these sessions. For those students whose parents can help it is useful to obtain a detailed checklist of what is needed so that parents can guide the pupils through their course.

It has often been a long time since parents themselves have studied, so school run evenings for parents on 'how to help your child study'; 'how to help your child to be successful with course work' or 'how to support your child in exams' are often welcomed.

In conjunction with staff, it is often helpful for parents or support workers to look through information students have collected in the lesson and help them make sense of it or interpret it in a particular way. In certain circumstances, where staff produce the information prior to the lesson, students can be briefed before attending that session and so be aware of what will be expected.

Parents should look at the work the student has completed and find areas to praise and support by developing areas in which they are struggling.

Parents should not compare their child with other students in their class group, siblings, relatives or neighbours. These are often negative motivators and tend to draw attention to the student's weaknesses rather than their strengths.

Other parents may be a lot less interested in their children's performance and for them it is sometimes helpful to receive guidance from school. Parents should be supportive, be aware of their child's preferred learning style, help them to work in that mode and generally encourage rather than criticise.

Conclusion

This chapter has identified the importance of course choice and outlined how to obtain special examination arrangements if they are appropriate. It has emphasised the importance of the relationship between pupil, parents, school and other agencies in supporting course work and preparing for examinations. Helping the student with time management and organisation skills, looking at structured planning, providing appropriate teaching and support from those close to the student all help this difficult time to pass smoothly.

References

Buzan, A. (1986) *Use Your Memory.* London: BBC Books.

City of Edinburgh Council (1997) Special Examination Arrangements: The identification, preparation and presentation of candidates who may require special arrangements for examinations for certification by the SEB and SCOTVEC.

Duffield, J., Riddell, S. and Brown, S. (1995) *Policy and Provision for Children with Specific Learning Difficulties.* Aldershot: Avebury.

The Joint Council for General Qualifications (2000) *GCE, VCE, GCSE and GNVQ: Regulations and Guidance relating to Candidates with Particular Requirements.* Cambridge: JCGQ.

Northedge, A. (1990) *The Good Study Guide.* Milton Keynes: Open University Press.

Ott, P. (1997) *How to detect and manage Dyslexia.* Oxford: Heineman.

Pumfrey, P. and Reason, R. (1991) *Specific Learning Difficulties (Dyslexia): Challenges and Responses.* London: Routledge.

Reason, R. *et al.* (1999) *Dyslexia, Literacy and Psychological Assessment.* Leicester: British Psychological Society.

Reid, G. (1998) *Dyslexia: A Practitioner's Handbook.* Chichester: Wiley.

Scottish Qualifications Authority (1998) *Guidance on Special Assessment. Arrangements and Certification Arrangements for Candidates with Special Needs; Candidates Whose First Language is Not English.* Dalkeith: SQA.

Tod, J. (1999) *IEPs – Dyslexia.* London: David Fulton Publishers.

Thomson, M. E. and Watkins, E. J. (1990) *Dyslexia: A Teaching Handbook.* London: Whurr Publishers.

Woods, K. (2000) 'Assessment needs in GCSE examinations: some student perspectives', *Educational Psychology in Practice* 16(2), 131–40.

CHAPTER 24

The use of Learning Styles and Thinking Skills to Access Success

Learning Styles – *Gavin Reid*
Thinking Skills – *Lindsay Peer*

This chapter:

- outlines the need to consider both learning styles and thinking skills in the mainstream classroom
- provides some suggestions on how this may be achieved
- highlights the benefits of this for dyslexic students.

LEARNING STYLES

Background

The aim of this chapter is to highlight the potential of learning styles and thinking skills for dyslexic children. Often these factors are overlooked in the development of a programme for dyslexic children as it is perhaps too easy to focus on the presenting and obvious difficulty of literacy. Literacy is however much more than acquiring print skills. The different sub-skills of literacy, the cognitive and processing components of literacy aquisition suggest that literacy should be seen as a vital component of the learning process with transferable skills. This chapter therefore suggests that literacy skills and understanding of text can be enhanced through the use of structured thinking skills and this can be made possible through acknowledgement of the individual's learning styles.

The process of learning

The process of learning is essentially processing information and this depends on attention to the brain's input, the type of input, how the brain and mind sort incoming data for interpretation and storage, and what is required to prompt information recall. Some proceed in a step-by-step manner through this process while others go about it in a randomly ordered fashion. Each of these styles can be used successfully but it is important to identify the individual's preferred style.

Information processing

In several research studies, when information was introduced and reinforced in ways most comfortable for them, students remembered significantly more than when they were provided instruction through their least preferred modalities (Dunn and Dunn 1992).

Information from the environment is so massive that the brain decides what to attend to and what to ignore. Attention, therefore, is the first step in processing information. Attending long enough for the brain to sustain focus or dismiss the information is often the point where students check out of what the teacher is saying and think their own thoughts. Sustained focus is required for the brain to search for something already known for comparison. If nothing is found, the brain goes on to something else unless, novelty, colour or movement generate interest and sustained or focused attention (Zeaman and House 1979).

Some persons find attending to sensations from one modality far more meaningful and powerful than attending to input from other modalities. Thus, when interest is generated in something that stimulates their senses, they begin constructing interpretations of the input based on past experiences and modality strengths. If enough connections and meaningful interpretations are made, the information is stored for later recall. But first, the information must be attended to and received. There is evidence that dyslexic students may have difficulty in the processing of information particularly if the information is not presented to their preferred modality.

Generally the left hemisphere deals with sequential information such as language, reading, mathematical formula, spelling, and the analysis of input, while the right hemisphere approaches tasks in a more simultaneous or all at once manner. The right hemisphere responds more to non-verbal input, such as colour, patterns, facial expressions and body language. Sequential, step-by-step, left-brained learners generally prefer instructions to progress in an orderly fashion until a conclusion is reached (Carlson 1988, Dunn and Dunn 1992, 1993).

Random, right-brained learners, by contrast, prefer knowing what outcome is expected before they begin a task. Then, they may begin in the middle and work in different directions until the task is complete. Analytic or sequential learners tend to analyse or take apart information to study its details while global learners prefer gathering information from various sources and building understanding by synthesising bits of information into a new whole (Carlson 1988). Accountants and mathematicians are good examples of analysers while architects and theorists posses strong abilities to synthesise.

The whole brain, however, processes information in both rather than just one hemisphere. Nevertheless, it is helpful to remember that each hemisphere processes information differently, and that each has primary responsibility for processing certain kinds of information. Children who have acquired effective learning skills often have difficulty in processing using both hemispheres and particularly if information is presented to their weaker hemisphere. The actual learning cycle is therefore important to note, particularly as there is evidence that children with dyslexia can have difficulties at various stages of the learning cycle. The learning cycle diagram (Figure 24.1) represents this process.

Learning style

Learning style is therefore important in order to identify the students' learning preferences. There are many instruments available to identify style, most of which are based on self-report. For example, Kolb's (1976) Learning Style Inventory, which is a derivative of Carl Jung's (1977) psychological types, combined with Piaget's (1955) emphasis on assimilation and accommodation of information for knowledge construction and Dewey's (1966) purposeful,

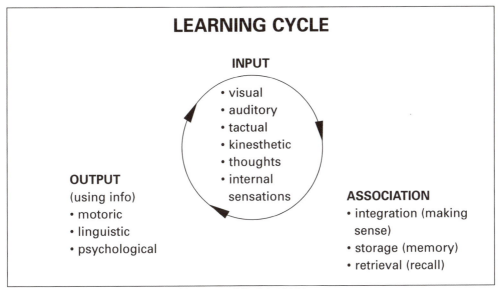

Figure 24.1 Learning cycle (Given and Reid 1999)

experiential learning, yields four types of learners: divergers, assimilators, convergers, and accommodators. His instrument and approach focus primarily on adult learners, as does the Gregorc Style Delineator (Gregorc 1997). By contrast, the Dunn, Dunn and Price (1975, 1978, 1984, 1987, 1989, 1990, 1996) Learning Styles Inventory contains 104 items that produce a profile of learning style preferences in five domains (environmental, emotional, sociological, physiological, and psychological).

The Interactive Observational Style Identification was developed by Given and Reid (1999) to attempt to allow the classroom teacher to use their knowledge of the children to identify specific styles.

It may be argued that observation in itself may not be sufficient to fully identify learning styles, but the use of a framework for collecting observational data can yield considerable information to supplement a formal assessment. An extract from the Interactive Observational Style Identification (IOSI) is provided in Figure 24.2.

It is useful therefore to consider learning styles through classroom observation since the student's style may vary in different classrooms.

Nevertheless possessing some knowledge of the student's preferences for learning can help access subject matter in many subjects and learning styles and indeed thinking skills both have cross-curricular implications.

THINKING SKILLS

Times have changed! The arrival of the technological age has brought with it great opportunities for major change in our education system. We need to be providing a process of education that will offer our children a way forward, a way of living, working and developing themselves in a fast changing society, the likes of which have never been seen or even dreamt about before. Preparing our children for the same old repetitive jobs in the industrial age, the very jobs that are disappearing daily, is totally inappropriate. Instead we should be preparing them for the jobs of the future – jobs that will require thinking skills and creativity, not rote memorisation and repetition. This plays most definitely to the strengths of the dyslexic person.

Cognitive

- Modality Preference
  - What type instructions – written, oral, visual – does the child most easily understand?
  - Does the child respond more quickly and easily to questions about stories heard or read?
  - Does the child's oral communication include appropriate variations in pitch, intonation, and volume?
  - In their spare time, does the child draw, build things, write, play sports, or listen to music?
  - When working on the computer for pleasure, does the child play games, search for information, or practice academic skill development?
  - Does the child take notes, write a word to recall how it is spelled, or draw maps when giving directions?
  - Given an array of options and asked to demonstrate their knowledge of a topic by drawing, writing, giving an oral report, or demonstrating/acting, what would the child choose?
  - Under what specific types of learning (reading, maths, sports, etc.) is tension evident such as nail-biting, misbehaviour, distressed facial expressions, limited eye contact, and so forth?
- Sequential or Simultaneous Learning
  - Does the child begin with step one and proceed in an orderly fashion or have difficulty following sequential information?
  - Does the child jump from one task to another and back again or stay focused on one topic?
  - Is there a logical sequence to the child's explanations or do the child's thoughts 'bounce around' from one idea to another?
  - When telling a story, does the child begin at the beginning and give a blow-by-blow sequence of events, or skip around, share the highlights, or speak mostly in how the movie *felt*?
  - When asked to write a report, does the child seek detailed directions or want only the topic?
  - What type of tasks are likely to be tackled with confidence?
- Impulsive versus Reflective
  - Are the child's responses rapid and spontaneous or delayed and reflective?
  - Does the child return to a topic or behaviour long after others have ceased talking about it?
  - Does the child seem to consider past events before taking action?

Figure 24.2 Extract from IOSI (Given and Reid 1999)

There is much research and optimistic thinking internationally pointing to Cognitive Development and Mediated Learning Experiences as major components to the success of individuals. In the world of business and education many are of the opinion that to be effective, people need to be developing the skills of *how* to learn – particularly those who are 'at risk'.

Feuerstein, the originator of many current theories of thinking world-wide, promotes the notion of 'plasticity' of the mind. We would agree with him that rather than seeing intelligence as a 'fixed' concept, *all* people have the innate ability to develop their thinking, their confidence, their skills and their intelligence. Plasticity of the mind implies flexibility, the ability of the mind to extend and reach out in all directions. There is no doubt whatsoever, that dyslexic people have this innate ability and should be encouraged to explore this positive side of themselves rather than focusing on their weaknesses and the aspects that are perceived to be 'wrong' with them as measured by traditionalist values within a rigid examination system.

Potential is currently measured by psychometric testing in many cases. This is limited as the results portray the results of past learning, acquisition of skills and knowledge, but show no indication of future potential. Cognitive tests are of great use as starting points: of immense value in highlighting the strengths and the weaknesses of the dyslexic profile and therefore of great value when constructing appropriate education plans to be fulfilled within an inclusive education system. However, there are dangers when there is too much of a reliance on this one measure. Results may be misinterpreted if the reader sees the child's potential as limited because of the results quoted in these tests. We know that this misunderstanding may lead to a great misrepresentation of an individual's capabilities and an acceptance of low expectation – a perception that needs to be changed. Once teachers see themselves as 'mediators' and have a firm and optimistic belief that they are able to change their students' thinking and perceptions, then that is just what happens. That immutable belief will transfer itself to the child, who will immediately receive a great boost to his or her confidence and self-esteem by moving along a continuum of learning in a way previously unknown. If one were to add to this a 'dyslexia friendly' environment and specialist teaching if and where necessary, success would be the inevitable outcome. Education is not about teaching the 'what' – remembering chunks of information or learning to carry out specific tasks, it should be about the 'how' people learn. While important, education is more than the three R's – reading, writing and 'rithmetic. Subject knowledge is important, but will only be useful in further and higher education or employment if specific skills are developed alongside the information giving. Clearly if all that could be achieved was that which was learned in school in the past, future prospects would be severely limited. Skills need to be transferable to new situations if people are to be adaptable; it is this adaptability that is so highly regarded by educators and employers alike.

Dyslexic adults are often able to learn that which is necessary to do a job well, but often undergo great stress when the job description changes and they are asked to fulfil a role that is different to that which they are used. They needed to have been given the skills to cope with such changes when they were in the secondary school system. It is clear that if we are to function effectively and make best use of our developable potential, thinking skills development is the key.

In the book *Changing Children's Minds*, Sharron (Sharron and Coulter 1994) looks at an historical perspective of change, linking the renowned psychologist, Reuven Feuerstein, responsible for the birth of many Thinking Skills programmes in the West, with Vygotsky. A theoretical move away from mainstream psychological educational opinion about intelligence initially left Feuerstein vulnerable in the 1950s. At the Oxford Schools Council, one senior British educationalist praised his 'practical' teaching technique, but found the theory of

Structural Cognitive Modifiability (SCM) and Mediated Learning Experience (MLE) 'hard to swallow'. Today this is no longer an issue, as the work of the development of thinking skills based on Feuerstein's original work has now traversed Europe, the USA and reached parts of Asia to great success.

In work with dyslexic learners it has been shown that great strides can be made in thinking, use of language and confidence levels when young people go through a process of MLE in addition to their dyslexia provision. I myself worked with several classes of dyslexic boys with this combined package and produced much enhanced results. Interestingly the reactions of inspectors in the lessons was amazement that boys who were so significantly 'impaired' in their literacy skills could work to such a high level of competence in areas which highlighted their abilities in their developing thinking capacities and use of spoken language. The individual parts of the programme, called instruments, which all started with 'Just a Minute...Let me Think' also reduced 'impulsivity' – an area known to be problematic for dyslexic learners. There were therefore noticeable improvements in both learning and behaviour. This in turn reinforced the sense from staff and parents that they were at last 'trying'!

The intellectual roots of Feuerstein's thinking skills programmes are based on the original thinking of Piaget. In his move away from traditional western psychology he moved close to the educational traditions of Eastern Europe, particularly those of the great Russian psychologist, Lev Vygotsky. Both men had worked with children who had suffered terribly because of cultural deprivation or because of their social or national groups – and needed to have their level of functioning raised. Both Vygotsky and Feuerstein found that the application of standard psychometric tests on these communities produced results that were absurdly low – even when 'adapted' to their cultures. For example, in one Soviet Republic only 16.8 per cent of children were found to be 'normal', 63.4 per cent mildly retarded and 19.8 per cent severely retarded. Whole communities were being intellectually placed at the level of 5 to 7 year old children. This is clearly not a measure of fixed intellectual competence. Both men independently came to the conclusion that low functioning, culturally deprived children can assume the skills of culturally sophisticated people in a matter of years through appropriate education. Both emphasised the overriding influence of the cultural environment on human development and the possibility of dramatic intervention. We can learn great lessons in relation to our dyslexic learners from this when we look only to psychometric testing for answers. These children too may have been through their own traumas in their educational lives. Sometimes stress and panic about consistent failure will lead them to do poorly in psychometric tests. If someone who does not know the child is placed in the position of deciding potential based on possibly a 90-minute assessment and that is the only measure used, there is more of a risk of under-assessment of the child's actual abilities. This remains as a permanent testament to 'supposed' intellectual ability and ultimately, future career. Many people believe that when the assessor puts a child at ease, he or she will actually perform to the best of their ability. This, as we know, is not always true. It might be said that the child at best works to the median of the range of potential scores. Ideally the child's progression within the education system should be closely monitored to see whether assumptions made by the measures and interventions are accurate. Educators are used to changing provision, but rarely question the result of the one-off psychometric test.

As a reaction to this both Vygotsky and Feuerstein looked to the future potential of the child rather than accepting a fixed IQ as the ultimate. Vygotsky developed a 'Zone of Next Development' (see Sharron and Coulter 1994 pp. 327–36) and Feuerstein a 'Learning Potential Assessment Device' (LPAD). Feuerstein (1980) asks:

- What is this individual?
- What is his level of functioning, not only in terms of his present repertoire?
- Does he function according to his age and education? Does his IQ permit him to go beyond the levels of functioning that he presents today?

Feuerstein strongly believes that human modifiability is accessible to the individual irrespective of age and aetiology.

All human beings have an option to become modified, for the better, to become modified in the direction of higher mental processes which are very important for their adaptation to the world. This is our belief system. (Conversation with myself in Israel, 1990).

He believes that cognitive systems can be divided into four strata, each representing a level:

1. **Conceptualisation:** Highest level of cognitive development; ability to clarify and categorise experience. Dependent on adaptive inner language. Abstract learning.
2. **Symbolisation:** Needed for coding, non-verbal, then verbal. Lead to generalisation on basis of similarities in meaning. Concepts not concrete – exist only in the mind.
3. **Imagery:** The dealing with sensory information after reception has ceased. Two parallel processes – working memory and reconstruction of experiences.
4. **Perception:** Basis of cognition – ability of central nervous system to attend to and decode sensory information.

In support of this idea Feuerstein developed his Instrumental Enrichment Programme (IE) – which is the basis of many thinking skills programmes in use today. The programme deals with multiple cognitive functions, which overlap for reinforcement and are graded for difficulty. As we read through them, we can see the direct benefit to all learners, especially those who have difficulty across the secondary curriculum in those particular areas dependent on accomplishment in literacy and numeracy. So many of the prerequisites of learning in which dyslexic children are traditionally weak can be 'mediated back in' to boost the learning process. The areas are as follows.

Non-verbal contents

1. Organisation of Dots – a multi-purpose task, emphasising a wide range spectrum of visuo-motor automatisms.
2/3. Orientation in Space – instruments which require lateral, directional various orientation tasks emphasising the training of reversibility and transivity in space.
4. Comparisons – an instrument essentially concentrating on the discovery of tiny and hidden details, which dominate between two adjacently presented forms of picture, originally used to train perceptual atomisations and visuo-spatial tasks.
5. Analytic Perception – an instrument that includes tasks requiring articulation of a given field, exercising field independence.
6. Representative Stencil Design – an instrument that manipulates visuo-spatial relationships and memories of sequences.
7. Illustrations – an instrument intended to produce an awareness of the existence of a problem based on humorous pictures close to real life situations.

Verbal contents

1. Categorisation – an instrument based on the abstraction of visually presented pictures, from elementary ones to complex dimensions, providing a convenient bridge to pass from visuo-spatial to verbal abstraction.

2. Family Relations – an instrument that defines family relationships, starting with simple ones and ending with complex dimensions giving opportunities to manipulate reversibility and reciprocity.

3. Temporal Relations – an instrument based on situations to train time orientation, with simple and complex time relations to explore solutions and comments enabling notions of causality.

4. Numerical Progressions – an instrument to extrapolate and interpolate numerical progressions, involving identical, inverted or different type of arithmetic operations.

5. Instructions – an instrument in which verbal factors play an important and central part in training the understanding of verbal instruction.

6. Syllogisms – an instrument of formal thought and manipulation of sets.

7. Transitive Relations – an instrument to train higher mental structure and knowledge organisation.

It could be said that cognition depends upon the participation and synchronisation of functional units, which process information. There are those that believe that they are responsible for the converting of concrete perception into abstract thinking. Any thinking skills programmes that are used for the benefit of dyslexic learners should reflect this need, basing the mediation and information giving in a way that reflects the use of as many senses as possible – a truly multisensory experience.

In such a way we are seen to be not merely remediating specific behaviours and skills but also changing the structural nature that alters the course and direction of cognitive development.

Feuerstein's now famous 'input–elaboration–output' model follows these functional processes as a guide to his Cognitive Map (Sharron and Coulter 1994).

INPUT	–	arousal, attention and perception.
ELABORATION	–	retention, iconic processing, symbolic processing and motor processing.
OUTPUT	–	planning, awareness of process, monitoring of process, prediction of consequences, evaluation of results, decision making, performance process, verification and responsiveness to feedback.

Many others have developed programmes, which are designed to support the learning process. Blagg's Somerset Thinking Skills programme, the University of Cambridge's Thinking Skills Programme, MENO, to name but two.

The MENO programme designed its higher education programme on three specific skills: (a) Communication, (b) Problem Solving and (c) Critical Thinking.

Adey and Shayer of the University of London produced a programme entitled the Cognitive Acceleration through Science Education Thinking Skills Programme (CASE). In this study, adolescents who had some of their Science lessons replaced by Thinking Skills lessons did considerably better than their peers, not only in Science but also in all of their GCSEs.

As we can see, Thinking Skills is of enormous value to the widest range of people – everyone! Programmes can be tailored to meet the needs of young children to adolescents to adults. They can be geared to those with a range of abilities and special needs. Teachers under great pressure are often asked whether or not Thinking Skills are not just another burden upon a system which is already crammed. The truth is that just as good dyslexia teaching is of value to all, so is the area of Thinking Skills. It is really a two-part process: (a) the notions of mediation ideally as a whole-school approach, and (b) a programme, which is fitted into the timetable that ultimately supports all learning. Children feel successful and valued; they are therefore motivated and willing to participate. It develops their skills and helps them achieve to a higher standard than anyone would have imagined. It is particularly noticeable among children who are 'failing' by common standards as their interest and behaviour improve dramatically. I therefore have to ask the following question. The question should not be 'Can the UK afford Thinking Skills Training for *all* learners?' It ought to be 'Can we not?'

References

Carlson, N. (1988) *Foundations of physiological psychology.* Needham Heights, Mass.: Allyn and Bacon.

Dewey, J. (1966) *Democracy and Education.* New York: Free Press.

Dunn, R. and Dunn, K. (1993) *Teaching elementary students through their individual learning styles: Practical approaches for grades 3–6.* Boston, Mass.: Allyn and Bacon.

Dunn, R. and Dunn, K. (1992) *Teaching secondary students through their individual learning styles: Practical approaches for grades 7–12.* Boston, Mass.: Allyn and Bacon.

Dunn, R., Dunn, K. and Price, G. E. (1975, 1978, 1984, 1987, 1989, 1990, 1996) *Learning style inventory.* Lawrence, Kan.: Price Systems.

Feuerstein, R. (1980) *Instrumental enrichment: An intervention program for cognitive modifiability.* Baltimore: University Park Press.

Given, B. K. and Reid, G. (1999) 'The interactive observation style identification', in Given, B. K. and Reid, G. *Learning styles: A Guide for Teachers and Parents.* Red Rose Publications, 20 St Georges Road, St Annes on Sea, Lancashire FY8 2AE.

Gregorc, A. F. (1982) *An adult's guide to style.* Columbia, Conn.: Gregorc Associates, Inc.

Gregorc, D. F. (1997) *Relating to style.* Columbia, Conn.: Gregorc Associates, Inc.

Jung, C. (1977) 'Psychological types', (trans. Hull, R. F. C.), *Collected works of C. G. Jung*, vol. 6. Bollingen Series XX, Princeton University Press.

Kolb, D. A. (1976) *Experiential Learning: Experience as the Source of Learning and Development.* Englewood Cliffs, NJ: Prentice Hall.

Kolb, D. A. (1984) *Learning Styles Inventory Technical Manual.* Boston, Mass.: McBer.

Piaget, J. (1955) *The Child's Construction of Reality.* London: Routledge and Kegan Paul.

Sharron, H. and Coulter, M. (1994) *Changing Children's Minds: Feuerstein's Revolution in the Teaching of Intelligence.* London: Condor Press.

Zeaman, D. and House, B. J. (1979) 'A review of attention in retardate discrimination learning', in Ellis, N. R. (ed.) *Handbook of mental deficiency*, 2nd edn. 63–120. Hillsdale, NJ: Lawrence Erlbaum.

Useful books and further information

Instrumental Enrichment. Feuerstein, R. in collaboration with Rand, Y., Hoffman, M. B. and Miller, R., University Park Press, USA, 1980.

Mediated Learning Experience (MLE):Theoretical, psychosocial and learning implications. Feuerstein, R., Klein, P. S. and Tannenbaum, A. J., Freund Publishing House, 1991.

The Hope Foundation (sole UK distributor of IE).

The Independent Centre for Mediated Learning. Info@ThinkingSkillsUK.org

Cognitive Acceleration through Science Education Thinking Skills Programme (CASE). Adey and Shayer. Kings College, University of London.

MENO Thinking Skills Programme (For Higher Education). University of Cambridge, 1993.

CHAPTER 25

ICT Across the Curriculum

Part 1 – *Victoria Crivelli*
Part 2 – *Colin Lannen*

Pupils should be given opportunities to apply and develop their ICT capability through the use of ICT tools to support their learning in all subjects.

(National Curriculum 2000 Document KS3 and 4)

Included in this chapter are:

Part 1:
- the impact of ICT for dyslexic learners
- ICT as a generic tool
- access to information
- presentation and recording
- teaching and learning
- organising and planning
- meeting individual needs
- additional technological aids
- what the future holds.

Part 2:
- self-esteem – the key reason for introducing IT
- IT and learning styles
- technology – rate of change

PART 1

The impact of ICT for dyslexic learners

There can be few people who have not been affected by the impact of Information and Communication Technology (ICT) in their daily lives, during the last few years. Computers are now commonplace in schools, in the workplace and in many homes. In most schools teachers and pupils will find that ICT has become an integral part of their working day, be it in the classroom, or preparation for lesson, or homework tasks.

The impact for dyslexic learners has been even greater. For them ICT has unlocked doors to previously inaccessible information and has removed many barriers to learning. It has become for many, the much-needed lifeline to independent learning and an essential tool to overcoming many of their difficulties in relation to reading, writing, organisation and memory skills.

Older pioneering technology has been refined and made accessible to all. On screen texts that are spoken when needed, word processors that speak what has been typed and enable easy editing, programs that read web pages, applications that help learn and practise essential skills are all examples of how ICT can empower dyslexic people.

Where writing an essay was a daunting and often frustrating task dyslexic learners now have in ICT a variety of tools to support them and help them organise their ideas and get them down on paper. Computers are endlessly patient and will repeat words and instructions as many times as required, assisting those with difficulties in sequencing, memory and reading. Computers are usually encouraging and non-judgemental in their suggestions and corrections enabling discreet help and self-correction. They are motivating, confidence-building and can help raise self-esteem. Many dyslexic pupils are able to shine in ICT and display their true abilities. ICT helps to create a level playing field.

There are a few that may reject the opportunities ICT can offer. There is usually an underlying reason for this rare occurrence when investigated, such as early failure due to lack of training or use of inappropriate software or visual discomfort. With appropriate support many of these initial and discouraging problems can be overcome.

It is essential to demonstrate to all dyslexic pupils the power of ICT and the effect it can have not only in their education but their life and future.

ICT as a generic tool

ICT is a tool that can be used right across the curriculum in a variety of ways. Many programs are open-ended and content-free, enabling them to be adapted to specific subjects. For example, an onscreen wordbank is a useful aid to writing when used in combination with a word processor. Subject-specific words can be added to the bank, enabling easier recording of information; it removes the barriers to spelling difficult words and saves keystrokes of those who are slow at typing. It allows the user to concentrate on the content and use appropriate vocabulary rather than choosing words that are perhaps limited to their spelling skills.

Searching for information on the Internet and the World Wide Web (www) saves dyslexic pupils hours of time wearily scanning difficult textbooks to locate the information they need. Specific programs can be used in tandem with their research that will then read aloud the desired texts for them if required. Selected texts can be copied and pasted into notes for future reference. Useful sites can be bookmarked and added to personal favourites to enable speedier access when revisiting a subject and help users remember where they found the information.

Presentation of work is another area of concern for dyslexic learners. While many dyslexic pupils have recognised graphic and artistic strengths, getting written ideas down on paper without making several drafts, corrections and final copies has often been their greatest difficulty with the end result not being a true reflection of their ability and effort. The computer offers a range of presentation tools to use such as graphs, charts, tables and word processing that can be edited with ease and give pleasing results. Anyone familiar with the undo and redo buttons, cut, copy and paste or search and replace will identify immediately with the advantages.

Access to information

At KS3/4 and beyond pupils are faced with additional or new subjects areas, each with a specific vocabulary to read and spell. The essential lists of subject words for KS3 in the current Literacy Strategy are confirmation of this. Dyslexic learners will need support in helping them read, understand and write such words. Longer and more complex texts in subject books and literature in English can be an added burden.

While written glossaries are helpful as a source of reference for pupils and their supporters, if dyslexic learners are unable to decode the words or read the definitions they are equally frustrating. There are several ways using ICT can assist in this area. For example:

- Onscreen wordbanks that can have the text and a definition recorded in addition to the written word.
- Abridged texts of novels to read onscreen. Users can follow the highlighted words or phrases as they are spoken or scan the texts for themselves and highlight any unknown words to be spoken. This enables pupils to revisit and read curriculum texts at a pace that suits their needs.
- Study Guides for literature in CD format provide users with the whole text, helpful ways through themes and the opportunity to focus on specific characters.
- Information offered in word processed format on screen can be accessed either through a talking word processor or used with an additional text reader program.
- Whole textbooks and teacher support materials are now being produced in CD format so teachers can differentiate the content but equally they can be used with a text reader by the pupils onscreen. Information from the Internet can be downloaded and accessed in the same way.
- Many texts of novels are also available online. Relevant sections can be studied and used directly for quotes, highlighting key points and passages with the text being spoken.
- Many multi-media CDs such as encyclopedias or subject-specific information and revision CDs offer partial speech support, spoken explanations and animated diagrams that provide visual support to subjects such as Science and Geography. Many have live video footage or eye witness descriptions to listen to. Many of the text reading programs mentioned earlier work well with such applications too.
- Many web sites and information CDs offer virtual tours and explorations of subject-specific materials with spoken and written commentary.
- Several of the latest information CD programs come with interactive dictionaries, glossaries and help screens offering speech-supported explanations.

Presentation and recording

Using a computer is a popular and often preferable choice for many dyslexic students when recording and presenting any information, in class or for homework.

Many music departments offer pupils the opportunity to use compositional software. The relative ease of being able to score and edit musical notes visually and aurally is as liberating for the would be composer as it can be for the dyslexic user of a talking word processor, trying to compose thoughts and ideas.

Many word processors offer extra features beyond plain text input, such as tables or columns, while data and spreadsheet software enable more complex charts and graphs to be produced with relative ease. Dyslexic pupils enjoy using desktop publishing packages to present tasks such as posters, brochures or designs for technology subjects. While access to desktop or full laptop computers is not always possible in many subject classrooms there are alternatives for dyslexic pupils who wish to wordprocess in this situation. Portable writing aids that offer wordprocessing facilities are a popular solution, allowing notes to be typed and downloaded to desktop at a later or more convenient time. Many pupils use small cassette recorders and write to their own dictation later.

Becoming a confident user of ICT has to include efficient keyboard and typing skills. Touch typing is desirable but not always realistic so pupils need to aim for two-handed efficiency and accuracy that is at least faster than their handwriting. However touch typing does allow the confident keyboard user to maintain eye contact with the teacher and/or type notes while watching a visual presentation.

Talking word processors allow the user to hear all that is being typed, be it a word, sentence or selected passage. This can be reassuring to dyslexic learners who need auditory feedback.

Many pupils find an onscreen wordbank with subject specific vocabulary very helpful as it cuts down keyboard strokes and allows the writing process to continue unhindered by spelling and typing speed. One mouse click on the desired word will enter it into the text. Most talking word processors have this facility, allowing users to hear the words in the list before selection. Word lists can be created easily and saved to support a variety of subject or individual needs. More sophisticated programs can be used in tandem with the word processor offering multiple wordbanks with phrases as well as words.

Predictive lexicons take this support a step further by offering the majority of commonly used words in the predictor window following an initial keystroke. For example, if the user types 't', a choice of common words beginning with 't' is offered. The choice can be refined further by entering a second or third letter such as 'th' or 'thr' if the desired word does not appear. The choices can be spoken before and after selection to help accurate choice.

The real bonus for pupils and teachers is that subject-specific words can be added and saved to these lexicons ready to use for specific writing tasks. This enables the pupils with the greatest of spelling difficulties the opportunity to write at length using appropriate vocabulary. Many of these predictive programs have additional features, as mentioned earlier, that enable any text onscreen to be spoken. Some will enable words and sentences to be spoken as they are typed, effectively creating a talking word processor within standard programs such as Word. Another useful feature that is particularly popular with dyslexic people, is an onscreen keyboard as it reduces the eye movements away from the screen to the manual keyboard. Other useful features may include a talking spellchecker.

Further support in getting information down at speed may be found in voice recognition software. Many of the problems experienced in early programs have been refined and adjusted in the later versions released. However voice recognition is not an easy option in terms of the time, training and the technology involved, for both user and trainer. Serious consideration to all the issues needs to be given before choosing this support route. Some of the alternatives mentioned earlier may be more successful and accessible. Many users find it particularly useful at home for homework and extended study, if it is available for them. Pupils at KS4 and beyond will use it well once they have mastered the technology. However those dyslexic pupils who continue to find reading difficult may find the proof reading of voice recognition texts frustrating even with a speech facility. The lack of accuracy, however well trained, can often create more difficulties. It has been found to be an aid to reading and spelling in the long term in some instances. There is no doubt that with the current pace and developments in technology, voice recognition will be regarded as the norm in the not too distant future.

There are additional programs available to support writing in a variety of subjects through onscreen writing frames for specific subjects. These offer a selection of structures and presentations using appropriate style and genre with wordbanks to enable appropriate technical vocabulary. The user then types directly into the text. A similar approach can be created easily using the wordbanks and talking word processors mentioned above to make a talking writing frame.

Many of the ICT programs and tools described above are a matter of preference and will not be appropriate for all dyslexic individuals. However, potential users will need to know what works for them, what meets their needs and learning styles and what may be more useful in the future. Teachers will need to be aware of the options, and SEN Coordinators (SENCOs) will need to provide guidance and review them with staff and pupils to make the optimum use of ICT.

Teaching and learning

While the benefit of ICT is widely accepted for pupils, it is equally useful for those teaching and supporting them.

Many teachers now use ICT in their lesson planning, as an aid to differentiation and in their own presentation of information hand-outs, worksheets, overhead transparencies (OHT), wall displays and notices.

Teachers can create word processed OHTs enabling easier reading. The use of colour to highlight specific words on OHTs or emboldening key texts in a hand-out are just two examples of making a difference. Producing information sheets in a larger font size or in double-spaced text is preferable to small, dense type. A careful choice of font is also helpful to a dyslexic pupil who can find certain fonts uncomfortable or impossible to read. Sassoon or Comic Sans are useful choices.

Some schools have interactive whiteboards or LCD projectors that enable the teacher to work directly from the computer for all to see.

Any documents produced by teachers for their pupils could be saved as text files and used in any talking word processor or with a predictive lexicon. This would give instant access to pupils enabling them to complete any tasks directly into the 'talking worksheet'.

Many schools now have their computers networked, making such documents available for pupils at study, learning support or library centres or directly in the classroom. Those with Internet facilities at home may even be able to access them via school web sites and complete their homework tasks online.

Dyslexic pupils find ICT a great tool to support their learning. It provides a multisensory environment that will suit a variety of learning styles. Dedicated software to help practise specific literacy and maths skills can be a rewarding and motivating task. Many programs provide excellent record-keeping options so that both pupil and teacher can monitor progress. Several programs are now available for revision in all subjects. There are dedicated interactive web sites to support learning and revision, often providing online marking and help, providing a refreshing alternative to books and notes.

Organising and planning

Many dyslexic learners find their lack of organisational skills a major problem especially with the increased curriculum demands at secondary school. Many requirements are made, from remembering books and equipment to deadlines to be met and tasks set. They often require extra support and strategies to help them organise their school work, homework and the day to day demands of a busy life.

Some of the portable writing aids have personal organisers which can be used to help pupils remember and plan on a daily, weekly or even termly basis. Some pupils find small memo microphones useful for daily important tasks or information. A micro cassette or small cassette recorder can assist this way as well, providing verbal prompts or a way of recording information quickly and accurately.

Timetables created on computers can be printed many times (if lost), and colour coded with symbols and clip art as visual reminders of days, subjects and equipment. They can be edited or added to on a weekly basis with relevant information regarding deadlines and extracurricular events. Tables created as planners can also provide pupils with a visual reminder of the progress of a major project or piece of work.

There are several programs available that help pupils (and teachers), plan, draft and organise their work. Many provide a flexible, visual planner similar to brainstorming on the screen. The use of colour, pictures and shapes can help illustrate the themes and ideas. Similar programs can be used for revision sheets. As well as the visual plan many programs offer a text view with the sequence or format of the plan, providing written headings for essays or chapters. The various templates provided in some of the programs offer pre-set structures to help with specific tasks such as comparisons or processes.

Meeting individual needs

ICT can be used by many pupils to support all areas across the curriculum. It can also be adapted to meet individual needs and learning styles.

Screens can be adjusted to meet specific requirements of individual users. These may include text and font size, colour of background and text. Many dyslexic learners prefer alternative settings that are visually more comfortable for longer periods of writing or reading. When an optimum screen setting has been created it can then be saved and recalled whenever required. Sometimes just increasing the zoom facility is enough and easily done when wordprocessing, for example.

Many of the dedicated programs for literacy and maths can be pre-set to meet specific targets for individual users so that they match their learning needs.

Many programs are a matter of preference and according to individual strengths and weaknesses some programs will be more suitable than others. For example, confident readers may not need a talking word processor's speech facility but would prefer an onscreen wordbank if spelling is their particular difficulty. Pupils with good keyboard skills may not want a predictive lexicon but would prefer a talking word processor to read back each sentence or word typed to help them spot typographical or spelling errors.

Dyslexic pupils need to know what is available and use what best suits their needs and learning style. These needs may well change as they progress from Year 7 into KS4 or as greater demands are made in the content of curriculum tasks. Their limited experience of ICT may make it inappropriate to introduce some software to start with. They will need time for training in the use of specific programs or hardware that are not included in the core curriculum.

As with any learning tool, strategy or prop, there is always the danger of overload or offering so much that none of it is used to any real effect. Teachers need to help pupils make the best and most appropriate choices. To do this they will need to do a regular needs analysis of any particular difficulties and see how using ICT may possibly help. It is also important to recognise that many pupils do not wish to appear different and/or special in their groups or classes and the greater use of ICT as the norm for discreet support or regular choice of activity should be encouraged in all subjects.

Additional technological aids

There are several resources that come within the wider technological context but are not computers or software as such. Portable writing aids, mentioned in an earlier section as an accessible wordprocessing tool, are one example.

Portable writing aids or laptop word processors have proved very popular for dyslexic learners who use word processing as their usual or chosen form of recording in most or selected curriculum areas. They are particularly useful where availability of desktop computers is limited or unavailable. Text that has been started in class can be continued at home, downloaded to desktop, printed or saved. The simplest models carry basic wordprocessing functions; the more sophistiacted models have a range of full wordprocessing options and additional features or functions.

These are several such resources to choose from, all offering a range of options. Considerations need to be made before selecting the best for an individual user, such as:

weight and portability;
power source and durability;
memory, file saving and transfer options;
screen, font and keyboard size;
additional features such as organisers and calculators;
home and/or school use, individual or multi-user options;
printing arrangements;
costs, warranty and repair.

Handheld cassette recorders can be a useful aid for both classroom and home use. Those with variable speed and voice activated options are popular.

Micro cassettes are useful for space saving but standard size tapes that can be accessed on any cassette recorder at home or school may be a better option. Users find them useful for a variety of tasks such as note-taking, recording information (directly from teaching staff or themselves), homework details, reminders, revising, writing from their own spoken notes, recordings of key texts, recordings to support homework tasks.

Handheld spellcheckers, in particular the range from Franklin, can often be more effective than the usual computer spellchecker and can offer a thesaurus and personal wordlist facility. They are more accessible and less frustrating to use than a dictionary for many dyslexic learners. They offer more realistic suggestions to the spellings entered and will endeavour to interpret phonic alternatives such as 'circle' for an entry of 'sercl' as opposed to the first two letter match of standard spellcheckers. (The latest version of Write Out Loud (Don Johnson) word processor includes a Franklin spellchecking facility.)

What the future holds

The current drive for total inclusion, together with the philosophy and expectations of Curriculum 2000, make the opportunities for using ICT to support dyslexic learners a reality for the immediate and foreseeable future.

It is widely recognised that many of the ICT strategies and programs used for dyslexic pupils are equally useful for others with special educational needs and are generally recognised as good practice. The use of ICT as an access tool and a support to learning in all subjects with all pupils will become the norm. This will be most beneficial to dyslexic pupils and the overall use of ICT will not single them out as different to their peers.

While accessibility to computer hardware and appropriate software may still be an issue in many schools today, the emphasis on using ICT in all subject areas and the continuing funding for provision should increase the provision both in dedicated ICT areas and in the classroom.

Many schools are networking their hardware so that software is available to all pupils wherever they are in the school. Many schools are developing and planning so that ICT can help deliver the whole curriculum whenever appropriate. Increasingly homework tasks are being made available on school networks and/or web pages.

The investment in NoF (New Opportunities Fund) ICT training for all teachers is helping to bridge the knowledge and training gap. It will raise awareness regarding the possible use of ICT in their subjects and enable teachers to acquire the skills and confidence in using ICT to support pupils.

BECTa (British Educational Communications and Technology agency) are looking at ways to help influence and encourage software publishers to write or adapt future programs to include access tools, formats and speech support as standard options, making them acceptable to all users including dyslexic learners.

The BDA Computer Committee (BDACC) are continually researching and reviewing software and hardware particularly appropriate for dyslexic learners and are in direct contact with many of the key software houses and publishers.

ICT is an empowering tool for dyslexic people, offering them opportunities to learn, access and record information independently in a risk-taking, interactive and multisensory environment they can control to meet their individual learning styles and needs. The current rate of growth and development in ICT is sometimes overwhelming but dyslexic learners can harness the opportunities it offers to help them achieve and realise their goals.

Case Study 1

Sean, Y7 High School

Using a writing aid and Franklin spellchecker

Sean was having difficulty sustaining a legible script and was finding all written recording difficult. He has a wide vocabulary, a reading age of 10 years but a spelling age of 8 to 9 years. He found it frustrating not being able to spell the words he wanted to include in his work.

He avoided most writing tasks and was losing confidence when even his most careful and best efforts appeared to go unnoticed and did not truly reflect his knowledge and ability.

He had used Talking First Word on the desktop computer in his primary school for longer pieces of writing and used Word on his home PC for some home work tasks.

His keyboard skills were not much faster than his writing speed but word processing enabled pleasing results and easy editing.

The SENCO loaned him a Dreamwriter 200 portable writing aid to use at school. He shared it with one other Y8 pupil, each having it timetabled for specific subjects. Sean liked the large screen and the fact he could save his work to disk and continue at home if he needed to. He found the spellchecker of the Dreamwriter frustrating so loaned a Franklin Bookman from the local support services to use for spellings. He mastered this quickly and added his own list of personal words and some key curriculum vocabulary he needed to learn.

He now has his own personal Franklin Bookman and the school will provide more Dreamwriters next year so he can have one for personal use in all lessons in Y8.

The school have asked him to attend regular typing skill sessions at the learning support centre for half a term to improve his typing speed and efficiency.

His History and RE teachers have been providing the SENCO with some homework tasks on disk in text file format to transfer to the Dreamwriter enabling Sean and others in his year to answer tasks directly on to the Dreamwriter.

Sean is now able to fulfil many written tasks and is willing at least to have a go. Many staff have noticed the difference in his attitude and confidence.

Sean is keen to use the organiser part of the Dreamwriter to help him remember plans and deadlines for projects and homework.

Case Study 2

Jenny, Y8 Middle School

Penfriend and Word

Jenny is a keen and hardworking Y8 dyslexic pupil who was identified as having specific learning difficulties in Y7.

She has a reading and spelling age more than three years below her chronological age. She finds most reading and writing tasks very demanding and is often frustrated by her inability to read subject texts, especially in Science which is of personal interest.

She uses a computer at home and her parents purchased Penfriend with speech for her PC to help with her homework when writing. Jenny had used an Acorn version of this successfully at primary school in Y6. She is delighted to be able to get text down almost as quickly as she thinks and that it makes her PC 'talk'. She prefers to use the onscreen keyboard in Penfriend as she is not very familiar with the keys and gets tired looking up and down from the screen.

Her subject teachers have provided lists of words to add to specific subject lexicons for Science and History.

The school has recently purchased a new suite of computers for the school that will be networked. They will have Word and Penfriend available on them. Jenny will soon be able to use PCs in some lessons as the older PCs have been put in several classrooms.

She is now learning to use Penfriend to help her access onscreen texts via the clipboard. She has already accessed information from an encyclopedia CD for Biology homework and from two web sites.

She will need to learn to use the keyboard more efficiently in future. Several members of staff are hoping to offer information and task worksheets they have produced in Word, on screen for Jenny to access. The ICT department have developed a school web site with several subject information and homework tasks already online for KS4 pupils or on the school Intranet. They are now developing materials for KS3. Jenny will be able to use these with Penfriend so she can have any difficult passages or words read for her.

Case Study 3

Daniel, Y10

Inspiration and Wordbar for course work

Daniel has a statement of SEN and attends a high school that is resourced by the local support services to support pupils with SpLD including dyslexia.

He is a pupil of above average ability and has excellent skills in graphic design and ICT. He is very interested in History and despite the demands of the course in reading and writing he has chosen this as an option for GCSE.

He would like to study it at A level too. His reading has improved but his spelling is still a difficulty. He has good keyboard skills.

Danny uses Wordbar, an onscreen multiple wordbank, when he is wordprocessing any homework tasks.

He uses the screens that came with the program for Science and the writing frames for short essays and technology evaluations.

His History teachers have provided his SpLD learning support teacher with vocabulary for his History GCSE modules. A wordbank for each module has been created. Difficult terms have been recorded in real speech with additional explanation added where necessary. Three other pupils are finding this useful for longer essays and homework tasks.

Danny was shown Inspiration in Y9 to enable him to plan projects for Design and Technology and prepare for course work in Y10. Danny has found this a really useful tool and intends to use it to help him plan essays for History and use specific templates to help develop a good argument in one task set.

He is intending to create a kind of mind-map for one topic to help him with revision later on.

He has been able to show other Y10s and some Y12s how to use Inspiration which has really raised his self-esteem.

Suppliers

There are too many software suppliers and hardware manufacturers to list in full, however further details can be found in many BDA publications. Brief details of suppliers of some of the products mentioned in this chapter are listed below.

Crick Software (Wordbar) 01604 671691

Don Johnston (Word Processor, Predictive Lexicon, Talking stories, planning software) 01925 241642

Dreamwriter Solutions (Portable Writing Aids) 01902 423111

Fisher Marriott (Curriculum spelling and planning software) 01203 616325

Folens (Writing Frames on CD) 01582 472788

Iansyst (Inspiration and Franklin spellmasters/casettes) 01223 420101

Longman (GCSE literature guides) 01223 425558

Macmillan (Heinemann Readers, abridged novels on CD) 01256 302699

Penfriend Ltd (Predictive Lexicon) 0131 668 2000

REM (REM deal in most educational software) 01458 253636

Sherston (Punctuation, grammar and spelling software) 01666 840433

Softease (Textease talking word processor) 01335 3433421

TAG (Portable Writing Aids) 01474 357350

Texthelp Predictive Lexicon 0800 328 7910

White Space (Literacy and Numeracy) 020 874 85927

Xavier (Spelling and Punctuation) 01248 382616

PART 2

Self-esteem – the key reason for introducing IT

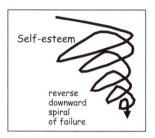

There is no doubt that IT is an essential tool for the dyslexic learner. However, before launching into what are perceived to be the normal 'ins and outs' of IT, there is one key reason for introducing IT to the dyslexic which is so very often forgotten or lost in the rush to compare one software program against another – self-esteem. The dyslexic learner's first sense of failure or bullying at school nearly always results in the inevitable downward spiral of self-esteem or self-concept. Indeed the older the dyslexic becomes without appropriate intervention and gaining an understanding of their learning difficulties, the worse their self-esteem becomes. In many cases the heart-felt frustrations lead to the dyslexic pupil either becoming introverted or starting to show 'behavioural difficulties'. Using IT provides the dyslexic with a stimulating media within which they can achieve immediate success, so starting to reverse this downward spiral of failure.

IT and learning styles

The true wonder of using IT is that it provides the only state-of-the-art media which facilitates all learning styles: physical, visual, cognitive, auditory, social and tactile. Indeed, IT is now so pervasive to Western culture that it could be argued that it adds a new learning style – 'motivation'.

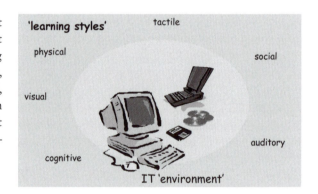

Technology – rate of change

IT technology is changing at such a rate that it is a difficult, if not impossible, challenge to provide guidelines which keep abreast with the changes. For example, although it may seem to be a good idea to give readers a hardware minimum specification list, this list will be redundant before this book is published. Moreover, it has to be recognised from the outset that the rate of change of technology is such that any IT capital expenditure will only have a limited useful 'shelf-life'.

Within these parameters, it is recommended that within each setting prospective IT buyers should establish their IT provision as follows:

- Determine minimum student access requirements (this will point the buyer towards either individual PCs/laptops or Intranet via server with linked PCs and laptops for individual use).
- Determine the application software required (this will highlight the minimum hardware requirements).
- Determine minimum hardware requirements:
    processor speed
    RAM
    Windows environment
    hard drive
    video
    CD/DVD
    sound card
    modem.
All computers generally come with Internet access software.

It is important that IT requirements and provision should be planned and not merely selected on an ad hoc basis depending on budget availability. The planning should be long-term and should also consider the need to update and replace some items of hardware. With sufficient planning and funding IT can provide the dyslexic child with achievable goals, success and a positive self-concept.

CHAPTER 26

Self-esteem and Counselling

Gerald Hales

This chapter:

- discusses the secondary school context in relation to situations which can confront dyslexic students
- examines the importance of self-image
- discusses the hidden effects of dyslexia
- considers the nature of counselling and mentoring in the secondary school.

Aims

This chapter does not aim to provide a miniature training course on counselling, nor to outline the deep psychological constructs of self-esteem. That would take far more space than is available here and in any case there are many books and training courses that are appropriate. It aims to provide explanations of the situations in which dyslexic pupils find themselves within secondary schools, together with examples of how low self-esteem can be engendered by what happens to them. It is good to establish procedures to 'rescue' young people when things go wrong, but it is much better to prevent them going wrong in the first place. Children cannot change the way a school works, although they often have highly informative ideas about what is wrong and why (if asked!).

Teachers reading this chapter might well come to the conclusion that dyslexic children are not favourably placed by some of the ways schools operate. If so, some careful consideration of what you do, why you do it and whether it would be better to do it some other way may pave the way for the development of a more human, rational and supportive approach. That will need careful thought, dispassionate planning and the need to attract the cooperation of others. So this chapter is designed to make you think in order to facilitate planning and cooperate in beneficial ways. Anyone doing those will make the effort of writing it more than worthwhile!

Into the deep end

Most people recognise that self-confidence can fall, self-esteem may diminish and depression might develop in dyslexic children, but most have only the haziest ideas of why these should happen. Some feel that it is some form of inadequacy in the individual affected, others believe that it requires merely the application of strength of character, offering suggestions like 'You'll just have to snap out of it' and 'Why don't you pull yourself together?'. It is rarely understood that it is often the result of actions by others, not the affected person. Many teachers would be distressed to find that such states may actually be caused by their school – and especially with pupils with disabilities or special educational needs.

It is not difficult to understand that the comment below might damage a child. You would never expect to see something like this, would you?

St Albert's High School
Annual Record of Achievement
Dennis Fidget, Year 7

Year Tutor's comments

Dennis is not a cooperative boy, using blindness as an excuse for not doing work. He must realise that this is a visual world and in the end he will have to learn to see. He is messy in art, blaming the fact that he cannot see what to do and he will not make any attempt to improve his writing. Dennis frequently claims he cannot see things and makes his own life worse by turning up without the correct books.

The reaction to this would be considerable; everyone would find it offensive, including teachers, Dennis's parents, Dennis himself, the Education Authority, teachers unions, the courts. This type of statement is just impossible, isn't it? Well, let's reconsider that paragraph with some of the nouns and verbs changed so that it's a different disability. It then looks like this:

St Albert's High School
Annual Record of Achievement
Dennis Fidget, Year 7

Year Tutor's comments

Dennis is not a cooperative boy, using dyslexia as an excuse for not completing work. He must realise that this is a literate world and in the end he will have to learn to read and write. He is inadequate in English, blaming the fact that he cannot write down what to do and he will not make any attempt to improve his timekeeping. Dennis frequently claims he cannot find things and makes his own life worse by not being properly organised.

How horrifying is this? Would this lead to action by the Education Authority, protests by teachers' unions, proceedings in court? Experience suggests that it is much less likely to do so. Many professionals working with dyslexic children have seen and heard comments like this;

they have also seen that there is often little understanding of the effect on the personal strength of the dyslexic individual.

This is not just a thought-provoking exercise. Imagine *how Dennis would feel*. The first victim of this scenario would be Dennis, his self-confidence, his self-esteem and his self-image.

The secondary school context

There are many conflicting emotions in entering secondary education. It is exciting and everyone tells you that it is an important step. It is also grown up, the first step out of childhood. You ought, therefore, to be able to cope with your problems and take responsibility for your progress. There are difficulties, naturally. Having risen to the top of the tree in junior education you are now one of the smallest and youngest again. You are not aware of the procedures and protocols that affect everyday life and this is especially important in terms of the *unwritten* procedures and protocols which have a profound effect on the way life is organised. No one teaches you these. You are expected to assimilate them as you go along, together with learning about the layout of the buildings, the large number of teachers, different subjects and new terms like 'Life Sciences' and 'Humanities' – a myriad of items, large and small, which are essential to survival in a new context.

This is hard work and a source of temporary anxiety, but not impossible or amazingly stressful – unless you are dyslexic. Most secondary education is designed to work for the majority of pupils who are not dyslexic. The dyslexic child already has difficulties with aspects such as reading, spelling, writing, mathematics, but now are added place, relationships, social acceptance and participation. The dyslexic child's self-image may be seriously affected within days, if not hours, of entering a secondary school.

Self-image

Everyone has an 'image' within their own perceptual framework – that something that each of us recognises as 'myself'. That image is often out of step with reality, for this is how we manage to cope with our imperfections on a day-to-day basis. It is important that it is possible to live with our image, though. If people begin to believe that they are inherently inadequate, they will ultimately behave as if that were true. The damage done to a child by destroying self-esteem may well be far greater than neglecting education, for it undermines all those elements that provide the motivation for succeeding in life.

This is particularly important at the secondary stage, as children pass through adolescence. Adolescence encompasses the vital period when the individual matures from child into adult and everyone has many tasks to accomplish. We learn to sort out confusions, to distinguish truth from fiction and to cope with emotional development; all made much more difficult by being dyslexic. The development of increasing personal independence is balanced by requirements to internalise and utilise intellectual concepts and social skills. This is the foundation of values which lead to behaviour which is regarded as socially responsible and any child failing to grasp and manage these fully is at a great disadvantage. The presence of support may be the lifeline that maintains a dyslexic child steadily through the trauma of adolescence set against the difficulties of dyslexia. The absence of support may do untold damage to individuals and their belief in themselves.

It is not widely recognised that these will not be the first experiences like this. Children are reminded of the past, reinforcing the idea that they are not like others. Much that happens to dyslexic children reinforces the message that they are different, but they are damaged by negative memories. This is not the first time they have started at a new school. Everyone has done it at least once before and some will have been through it several times. What happens when dyslexic children are first introduced to the concept of 'school'? When young dyslexic children first start to participate in school and learning there is no reason for them to suppose that they are different from others. They may have difficulties in some spheres – reading and writing, maybe speech and articulation, perhaps fine motor control or coordination – but young children develop at amazingly different rates and many of the others are not fantastic at some of these things either! The experience is somewhat traumatic and involves a number of new experiences such as:

- separation from family, relatives, friends and neighbours;
- having to cooperate with other children;
- having to conform to the teacher's routine.

These are also true for many other children: there is no reason for dyslexic children to suspect that they have any different problem. The realisation of something 'different' comes slowly, as the learning process unfolds and tasks become more difficult. Particularly with tasks like reading, writing and arithmetic dyslexic children slowly realise that they find some items are not as easy as (apparently) they are for the others. At first the difference may be perhaps no more than a slight discrepancy in speed of working, but as the others begin to develop new skills and lose early difficulties the gap between the dyslexic children and their peers widens and become more obvious. Some tasks may eventually become impossible to do at all. Thus, the dyslexic children themselves are the first to realise that there is something wrong. Parents and teachers may not, so at an early age the child acquires a 'dark secret' which others neither recognise nor understand.

It is unlikely that the children will mention their fears and worries to anyone. There is a risk in asking a question which amounts to 'Is there something odd about me?'. That risk is that the answer might be yes! So the young dyslexic children keep it to themselves, regress into themselves, hide their fears, and begin the retreat that can lead to many emotional and personal difficulties. This is the historical backdrop to their first impression of secondary school. It is why everything should be done to support them and smooth their path, especially during the early days in a new secondary school, for a negative affect acquired at that stage is difficult and slow to eradicate later.

The hidden effects of dyslexia

Much research has gone into developing methods of addressing the obvious practical effects on skills such as reading, writing, spelling. Those effects that impinge on the individual, not his or her skills, are less visible and therefore more likely to be ignored. These are the personal aspects of anxiety, loss of confidence and low self-esteem. The tendency is to pay regard to the 'mechanics' of the difficulty. This is understandable, as the mechanical factors are the most directly problematical in day-to-day life and many dyslexic people feel that these elements are most important. If only they could solve the practical problems of not reading, or not spelling well, they would be in a better position to tackle the way they felt.

In reality these aspects are better conceived the other way round. Research shows that among the variations in the effects of dyslexia on people one consistency is a high level of anxiety and frustration. In 1972 Klasen reported that anxiety was the one stable difference between her dyslexic group and control group, while in 1974 the major report of the British Royal Society for the Rehabilitation of the Disabled stated:

> A substantial number of individual workers who have given evidence to us have referred to cases in which the emotional repercussions of dyslexia have begun to manifest themselves before the age of seven.
>
> (Kershaw 1974)

By the mid-1980s the distinction between the mechanistic and the personal was beginning to become clear. Ravenette (1985) wrote:

> the dyslexic model . . . is mechanistic. The child is seen as a learning machine in which some of the parts are either defective or inefficient. Even when human feelings are acknowledged it is rather as though they were bits of extraneous matter clogging the works.

Two years later Manzo noted that a sizeable proportion (he suggested 15 to 20 per cent) of problems in the areas of reading and learning have their foundations in emotional difficulties (Manzo 1987). There is relatively little to be gained by trying to treat the dyslexic *condition*, but failing to support the dyslexic *person*. As children develop, the uncertainties and disorientations that arise when dyslexia is present affect the individual in profound ways. This situation demands empathy, understanding, support and assistance in a manner that is capable of addressing the inner, personal, demands of dyslexic young people (Hales 1990). It is vital to remember that we are dealing with *people*, and it is vital to recognise that we must consider the overall health of those we support. The difficulties of dyslexia cannot be addressed in isolation from other factors. The way someone learns affects the sort of person he or she is and the sort of person someone is affects the way he or she lives and learns.

We have already seen that many of the seeds of low self-esteem are sown before children enter secondary education. This, however, means that secondary schools must recognise and cope with the needs that the dyslexic children bring with them. There is a risk that the assumption will be made that the state in which dyslexic children arrive is simply the way they 'are', but the need to consider the effects of being dyslexic on the person is supported by research results, which show that even children as young as six years old are concerned about being rejected. One defence against this is to make sure that they reject others before they have any opportunity of being rejected themselves (Hales 1994b). Teenage dyslexic boys, in particular, have a need to be accepted, coupled with a fear of rejection and they are likely to defend themselves by rarely giving others any opportunity to reject them. This defence tends to work so well that people are seldom aware that they actually have any concern over rejection. If someone does manage to reject them, they find someone else with whom to associate quite quickly (Hales 1994a).

The effect on dyslexic children of participating in school produces an almost immediate drop in self-confidence. The pattern indicates that dyslexic children (and particularly female dyslexic children) are in quite a pessimistic state during the period of their lives just before they transfer to secondary school (Hales 1994b). Their self-confidence begins to fall almost from the start of formal education and does not return to even approximately its original level until school-days are nearly over (see Figure 26.1). This is significant because it means that they are in the worst condition at the time when decisions are being made about their transfer to secondary education, which may include some form of assessment procedure, test or examination. It is vital to recognise that the dyslexic children are entering secondary education in this condition and unless it is taken into account they have less likelihood of success.

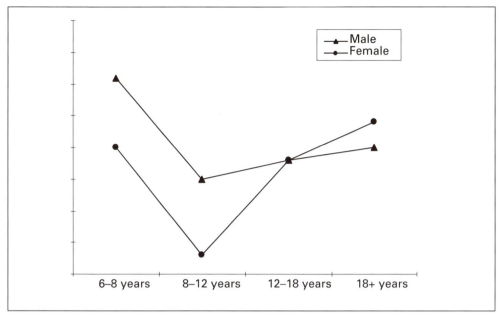

Figure 26.1 Self-confidence level (Hales 1994b)

The message contained in what happens

A major difficulty in understanding the situation, both for dyslexic children and everyone else, is that the problems 'spill over' into aspects of life that might easily be thought to be quite separate from dyslexia. The general inability to organise can develop into an untidy and chaotic lifestyle; having no spare capacity to 'cope' can extend to problems with relationships and coping with people. This can easily make a dyslexic child seem to be rude or unconcerned, instead of stressed and in need of help. It is important to remember two particular points:

- Dyslexic children frequently find the demands of conforming to society's rules all the time a substantial burden of effort, making them appear to be uncooperative or antisocial.
- They are *unable* to rectify matters (at least, not completely), rather than *unwilling* to do so, rendering encouragement and patience essential in dealing with them. Adverse reactions, and especially punishment, are often of no use as they make the child more aggrieved and more likely to think that whatever they do is valueless.

It is important that they receive praise and credit when they *do* succeed. Life composed of a large proportion of failure will depress anyone and reduce the ability to cope. Dyslexic children are not immune from normal reactions! When considering such things as untidiness, poor relationships or apparent rudeness, a calm approach, gently explaining what is wrong *and what to do about it* are beneficial. Remember that dyslexic people find difficulty in aspects of learning *that everyone else finds perfectly easy*. Indeed, there may well be some matters, apparently quite simple and self-evident to most, where dyslexic children simply do not know what to do, or how to do it, unless someone explains it to them. We must not make the assumption that dyslexic children know how to be polite, tolerant, or to express themselves in socially-acceptable ways unless they have been told in a fashion which they can understand, internalise and use. Problems here cannot be corrected unless they are given the information in a style which they can operationalise.

This pattern of coping also matters in academic work and progress. Dyslexic people effectively 'divert' some of their ability into coping strategies, whether these are formal strategies they have been taught, or informal ones they have worked out for themselves. This enables them to cope better in day-to-day situations, but it also means that they are less likely to achieve at the level commensurate with their real potential – giving the impression that their potential is lower than it actually is. This occurs because at any one time they are only working with the mental capacity that is (so to speak) 'left over' from their coping. Since the amount of effort needed to cope varies from situation to situation and depends on other factors like fatigue level at the time, this leads to academic performance being highly variable and frequently unrepresentative of their ability.

This experience is especially telling on those who are towards the ends of the ability spectrum. Intelligent dyslexic children find that people do not believe their work is affected by dyslexia. Suggestions for work difficulties include such things as

- they are not of high intelligence after all;
- they are lazy;
- they are uncooperative or naughty;
- they have a behaviour difficulty.

These upset and anger them, partly because they are unfair, but especially because they indicate a belief that their difficulty is caused by some inadequacy in them, over which (if they wished) they could establish control.

Children with lower ability levels also find that less importance is attached to their dyslexia, but for different reasons. To the uninformed the errors produced because of dyslexia are not dissimilar from those produced by people who have low ability. This means that often the difficulties are attributed solely to the intelligence pattern, without the dyslexic tendencies being taken into account. This can mean that dyslexic children with lower academic potential are often not diagnosed as dyslexic. Any support and help may be designed solely to address the pattern of intelligence, without the dyslexic tendencies being taken into account. It is considerably less effective than it might be and reinforces in the minds of the children that they are 'just thick'.

Anxiety

We all become anxious at times. This is natural and sometimes it is positive; it can even aid survival. However, because everyone experiences it to a relatively small degree it is easy to fail to understand the level of debility created in those whose reaction is more significant. For some the anxiety created by certain situations becomes paralysingly frightening, so that they will go to extraordinary lengths to avoid the situation. Not being able to 'cope' to this extent depresses self-esteem considerably. In any case, avoidance is not always possible. If, for example, the anxiety-inducing item is 'taking part in school' this is something that cannot simply be avoided. Dyslexic children, also, have a particular aspect of this type of difficulty, for they do not necessarily find the concept of 'school' frightening per se, but rather they suffer anxiety from the requirement to participate in particular tasks. This means that they do not fit the pattern of the school phobic, although there are cases in which such a phobia has developed if no support is provided. Equally it is not usually a reticence because of poor understanding of what is taking place, as can be the situation for children of low ability who become anxious because they are always 'out of their depth'. Dyslexic children expect to take part in what schools do and find it distressing when they cannot meet the expectation of themselves and others.

It is natural for adults to wish to offer all children as much opportunity to learn and experience as is possible. However, for the dyslexic child repeated opportunities to participate – normally regarded as a good thing – are often repeated opportunities to get things wrong and make a fool of yourself, possibly in public. Therefore the very actions taken to help the child can contribute to the exacerbation of the difficulty.

The perception of others

The ways in which dyslexia is perceived by others affects the manner in which help is provided (or not). Dyslexic children often develop the symptoms of a range of difficulties which arise as a result of being dyslexic. They may develop a raised anxiety level, or become negatively oriented towards school, or exhibit increasingly aggressive symptoms through frustration. This does not mean, however, that the underlying cause of the problem is anxiety, school-phobia or behavioural difficulties. Many children suffer from these types of conditions without being dyslexic but in dyslexic children they are the *symptoms* of the underlying problems and not the *causes*. Behavioural problems are not always what they seem: difficulties with communication can easily appear to be 'bad behaviour' in the school situation. This arises where children are trying to communicate using different rules from everyone else – and certainly different ones from what the teacher expects. This leads to them blamed for being awkward and uncooperative when in fact they are trying very hard to do what is expected of them – or at least, the nearest they can get!

In circumstances like this help may be offered that addresses only the symptoms, so perhaps a child is placed in a school for emotionally and behaviourally disturbed children, or therapy for school-phobia is arranged. Such experiences are unfortunate in many ways:

- they confuse and upset parents;
- they provide a situation which may make things worse for the child;
- they do not provide any help for the underlying dyslexia;
- they utilise expensive, but inappropriate, resources in a way which will achieve little or nothing.

Children who have received inappropriate help like this may well end up in an even worse state of anxiety or depression than they were at first, so the descent into the realms of low confidence and poor self-esteem is accelerated.

How do we learn skills?

Most of us learn the skills for travelling through life from parents, relatives, teachers, friends and so on. Dyslexic people often find that they have been presented in a way that is difficult to understand. Teachers with a piece of work not as good as expected may tell a child to 'Go and do it again'. This is not what is meant. The teacher means *Go and do it differently* – exactly the opposite of what was said! If the child does what was asked they are likely to get into more trouble for doing as they have been told! This leads both to reduced self-esteem and a sense of resentment because it is unjust. If we think someone has done something the wrong way we have to show them what we expect.

If dyslexic children are put in a position to succeed, the very experience will be a support for them. One aspect where it is often crucial to assist is in ensuring that care is taken in arranging workload. For many dyslexic children in the secondary school there is often no point in insisting on languages, for example. To do so only gives them considerable work for little gain. However, even in planning examination courses more flexibility may be required than is often realised, even to ensuring that the whole time-scale is thought through. For example, there are many dyslexic individuals who could achieve, say, six GCSEs or three 'A' levels, *but not if they do them all together*. Consideration of the possibilities of them doing some subjects one year and others later on can be a great relief.

Many dyslexic children find that the fact that they may do something very well one day and terribly the next is extremely trying. The situation is especially enhanced when people constantly ask them 'Why can't you do it?', for they do not know either! This is something over which they have no conscious control, so it is just as frustrating for them as for others. They become despondent as their self-worth diminishes and they tire of constantly competing without being able to tell whether they will succeed or not. In these situations they need considerable support, especially if there is a risk of them being teased or bullied. Particular vigilance is required to prevent this happening.

Counselling

Counselling involves *treatment of the person* not *remediation of the difficulty*. For many dyslexic people *reading, writing and spelling* are the elements which present greatest difficulty and these are the areas in which help and tuition is frequently provided. Even problems in these areas are the *symptoms* of dyslexia, not the cause and dyslexic people have other substantial practical needs. Because they have difficulties, to a varying extent, with organising information they rarely assimilate instructions with the same degree of efficiency as others. They need to check things and ask for clarification much more than everyone else, especially when they are in pressured situations. This has a number of effects:

- It makes them appear strange, different or inadequate, especially to their peers.
- It frequently gives others the impression that they are 'dim' or not paying sufficient attention.
- It creates difficulties because they are often working with deficient or incomplete information – and if the question isn't right, it is most unlikely that the answer will be right!

This leads to a self-concept that is not what is desired, but the way to put it right is not obvious to the dyslexic individual. Various strategies may be adopted to allow for their position and they must be recognised before they can be addressed. Some examples of the more obvious are illustrated below (this list is by no means exhaustive!).

- *'It isn't there'* – People who have difficulties try to work out answers. Sometimes this is deliberate, sometimes it is unconscious. However, it is surprisingly easy to work out answers that don't work. Many people – and definitely most children – do not want to be 'different'. This means that, ideally, dyslexia should disappear and it is not far to the idea that 'if I take no notice of it, it isn't there'. This is *denial*, which can lead to a refusal to learn how to handle reality in many aspects of life. We must encourage the understanding that solutions must be based on reality. Wishing you weren't dyslexic is understandable, but behaving as if you weren't is counter-productive – and because, deep down, you know the situation is false, self-esteem drops.

- *'It is there, but it's everyone else's fault'* – Slightly different from denial is *denial of responsibility*. They are often on the receiving end of unfriendly interactions, which pushes self-esteem down. They can decide that therefore, whatever goes wrong, it's not their fault: everyone else is stupid, uncooperative, careless, rude, or unfriendly. This allows the dyslexic child to feel self-righteous inside but it does not promote an ability to make valid judgements, nor make friends. Children must be led to an understanding of basing decisions about how to get along in the world on an ability to share understanding, responsibility and benefits.

- *'I'm going to be perfect'* – One way of avoiding criticism is not to merit it. People who are perfect do not attract criticism, so this can easily become a valid goal. This has to be selective: because dyslexic people cannot excel at everything (as if everyone else could!) so they have to choose very carefully in which fields they work. This often includes many extracurricular areas including many minor, less important, fringe activities that do not underpin ultimate success and achievement. This can lead to good popularity and success, but it is not usually productive in the long term and, as the individual becomes older, it is increasingly recognised as an avoidance tactic and so self-esteem is gradually reduced.

- *'I'm going to be a clown'* – Many children appear to admire those who flout authority. They support, encourage and lead them, assuring them of their admiration – but they don't copy them. Dyslexic children often only see part of this equation. They discover how to obtain popularity, support and friends in ways that never even bring up the question of whether or not they are 'different'. This often produces difficulties with authority, but this does not damage the picture they create. Being part of the group is better than being odd, but as the other children mature and develop, the dyslexic children remain obstinate rebels. Eventually that is all they know, for they do not possess the skills of more conventional behaviour. Eventually it becomes apparent that the group is moving away from them and they are no longer the leaders – or even a member. Once again, self-esteem diminishes.

- *'If you can't beat 'em . . . don't even try!'* – Many dyslexic children lose out in three ways:

> They work harder than the others, just to keep up.
> Even though they work harder, they don't keep up and their position deteriorates.
> During all this they are berated for not working hard enough!

One of the most damaging effects at school is when children know they have the ability and understand what is required, but cannot deliver it. A perfectly understandable reaction is to stop trying. These children learn that giving up is the easy route. Of course, it leads to failure, but most of the time they reach failure even when they do try, so logic is on their side! Unfortunately, sometimes this does not just mean 'stop trying' in school, but 'stop trying' in many aspects of life. They become withdrawn, unwilling to participate in anything, moody, morose and 'loners'. In later life they run the risk of being told that they 'suffer from depression', without realisation that this was created by their situation. Underneath they may well be aware of the truth – which does nothing good for their self-esteem.

Mentoring

In the structured and wide-ranging setting of secondary education a procedure known as *mentoring* is often very valuable. Mentoring is where a specified member of staff is available to the dyslexic person for them to seek answers to questions they suspect might be awkward or embarrassing in a confidential manner. This is not the same as providing 'an opportunity to ask'. Many schools comment on pupils in terms like 'Tom must learn to ask for help when he needs it'. Tom, of course, may not believe that he needs it, but we must consider why Tom doesn't ask? He often suspects that everyone else already knows the answer to that question and they will only laugh; sometimes there is the fear, which experience tells is not entirely unfounded, that the answer might not be understood; occasionally there is the worry that instead of an answer the question may only invite castigation for asking it. Dyslexic pupils learn to be very wary of who, when and where they ask.

This places the responsibility for corrective action onto the child. It is satisfactory to build the procedure into the structure of the timetable by specifying one or two moments in the week (maybe only five or ten minutes) when the dyslexic child and the mentoring teacher meet in order to discuss whatever is required. Dyslexic children then know that they can ask, safe in the knowledge that they will receive help and support, not an unsympathetic reply. The mentor will not always know all the answers and might have to seek assistance, but there is a source of providing support for all the information that the dyslexic person would otherwise find hard to find out and therefore difficult to know. Additionally, learning that adults and teachers are not all-wise and all-knowing is one of the lessons, too!

We must be careful that we do not train our pupils to be entirely reactive and only reliant on others. It is easy for significant adults to establish an expectation of failure in the dyslexic person's mind. This will not be deliberate nor justified, but once established it is difficult to rectify. Although 'nothing succeeds like success', it is salutary to remember that 'nothing fails like failure', either. It is important for dyslexic people to have some experience of success. There must be some moments when they can take pride in the thought 'I did that!'. If there is no other way for a dyslexic child to have some occasional experience of success, it doesn't truly disrupt any great plan for adults to fiddle it occasionally!

Conclusion

Two aspects of dyslexic people's situation are important:

- their disability is frequently not recognised, or is misunderstood;
- they frequently feel a degree of powerlessness in improving their own position.

The feeling of powerlessness creates a need for help, so dyslexic individuals must be assisted in taking more power over their own life. However, the situation lays the foundation for complicating conditions to arise, such as anxiety, low self-esteem, poor concept of self-worth and panic responses. These interfere with the practical requirements of study and work, of course, but they also permit the creation of a personal world in which individuals become of less and less value in their own eyes. This in turn creates the conditions where success becomes less likely, even when the person has the knowledge, skills and ability which would normally lead to a successful outcome.

One of the less obvious outcomes of low self-esteem or poor confidence is suppressed risk-taking behaviour. Risks are an essential part of learning: we learn where boundaries are by assessing risk. Dyslexic children must be able to try, for only by trying will they learn to be successful – but the road to success is often paved with some failures as well. In the failures we must be supportive, offering love, inclusion and practical advice. It is essential, therefore, that we address the needs of the personal support required by dyslexic individuals. This will achieve a number of goals, all good, which will include:

- happier children;
- more successful children;
- more confident children;
- children with more power over determining their own paths through life;
- children confident that they have techniques within *their* control that will assist them;
- higher levels of self-esteem and growing confidence.

References

Hales, G. W. (1987) 'The educational experience of disabled people: irresistible force or immovable object?' Paper presented to the conference 'Education as Challenge and Emancipation', The Open University.

Hales, G. W. (1990) 'Personality aspects of dyslexia', in Hales, G. W. (ed.) *Meeting Points in Dyslexia*. Reading: British Dyslexia Association.

Hales, G. W. (1994a) 'Little fish in big ponds: how do dyslexic people interact with the world around them?' Paper presented to the Third International Conference of the British Dyslexia Association, Manchester, April.

Hales, G. W. (1994b) 'The human aspects of dyslexia', in Hales, G. W. (ed.) *Dyslexia Matters*. London: Whurr Publishers.

Kershaw, J. (1974) *People with Dyslexia*. London: British Council for the Rehabilitation of the Disabled.

Klasen, E. (1972) *The Syndrome of Specific Dyslexia*. Lancaster: Medical and Technical Publishing Company.

Manzo, A. V. (1987) 'Psychologically-induced dyslexia and learning disabilities', *Reading Teacher*, 40, 408–13.

Ravenette, A. (1985) *Specific Reading Difficulties: Appearance and Reality*. London: Newham Education Authority.

SECTION 5: Professional Perspectives

CHAPTER 27

Assessment and Support in Secondary Schools – An Educational Psychologist's View

Chris Ashton

This chapter:

- examines the varied thinking of educational psychologists regarding their role
- examines the concept of inclusion
- discusses factors relating to assessment and support.

Aims

The main aim of this chapter is to help teachers, especially SENCOs, to make good use of their educational psychologists. This is not a straightforward matter, since EPs vary enormously in their views, skills, experience and practices. The same is also true of teachers and SENCOs. It follows that a good working relationship between a SENCO and an EP has to be based on a level of mutual understanding which can only be reached by a joint exploration of what the SENCO (and the school) need and what the EP can offer. It is reasonable for a teacher to expect every EP to have certain core skills, but is also realistic to expect EPs to vary a lot one from another (some might prefer all EPs to offer much the same service, but that is another matter). To take an obvious example, EPs who have recent experience of teaching in a secondary school have certain advantages over their colleagues who lack such experience.

Educational psychology – origins

Every LEA has its own Educational Psychology Service (EPS). These for the most part appeared in their present form and grew quite rapidly in the 1970s, but their earliest precursor was Sir Cyril Burt, who was employed by the Greater London Council (GLC) several decades earlier. In Burt's work we can identify three broad strands of practice which are still important today. Firstly, he saw himself as a scientist whose job it was to develop psychological knowledge and apply it objectively. Secondly, he saw his scientific activities as serving to help children. Thirdly, he had a role as an employee of the GLC it helping to develop its services. All three of these stands are apparent in his work on developing criteria for the placement of low ability pupils in special schools. Even as recently as twenty or thirty years ago, it was widely accepted that children with IQs below about 70 were better off in special schools than in the mainstream, though this practice was beginning to be questioned. Nowadays, the influence of IQ in the making of such decisions is much reduced, and the practice of segregation in special schools is of course subjected to much more scientific criticism and political challenge. Nevertheless, it is still of interest to look back and see why the IQ figure of 70 was thought to be about right. Given that special schools for low ability pupils existed, and were thought to be the best way of educating some pupils, the question put to Burt by his employers was how to ensure as far as possible that the right children were placed in these schools. His answer was in part scientific and in part administrative.

He started from the belief that IQ was a good objective measure of a child's ability to cope with the academic demands of school. Whether right or wrong, this was a scientific approach – there is a sad history, especially in the USA, of large-scale pseudo-scientific abuse of IQ testing (Gould 1981), especially when applied to blacks and recent immigrants from non-English speaking countries. But it should also be remembered that a key purpose in the original development of IQ testing by Binet was to identify potential in children from relatively deprived backgrounds who might otherwise be wrongly regarded as dull or uneducable (Medawar 1996). This has a parallel later in the use of IQ testing to prevent dyslexic children being similarly mislabelled as stupid or lazy.

Starting from the position that IQ was a useful measure (indeed a key measure) in this context, Burt then looked at the distribution of IQ scores in the school population and at the total number of places available in the GLC's special schools at the time. He then calculated the IQ score below which there would be just enough pupils to fill the places available – this, of course, is the administrative part of the work. It turned out that if those pupils with IQs below about 72 were selected, then there would be just about the right number of places available for them.

Whether this was good science serving the best interests of children, or a cynical abuse of power in the interests of administrative convenience is not the issue here. My aim is simply to show how right from the start the role of the EP has entailed three key elements:

(a) the application of science;
(b) serving the needs of pupils;
(c) serving the employer (the LEA).

Educational psychology in practice

In practice, every EP has his or her own way of combining these three strands and reconciling the competing demands contained within them. Some are more comfortable than others with working to implement LEA policy on, for example, statementing or inclusion. Some have a stronger need than others to see themselves as scientists, or as psychologists with professional skills in assessment, counselling, etc. Some are much less concerned with scientific standards or LEA policy than with doing whatever they can to help the individuals with whom they are working. For the SENCO to get the best out of their own EP, it is useful to know how they feel about these issues and what really motivates them. This does not mean that you should be content to let your EP work in whatever way they wish, regardless of your wishes and the needs of the pupils and teachers in your school, but it does mean that if you assume all EPs do much the same job in much the same way, you may miss opportunities.

With this in mind, it is interesting to look at some of the views 'outsiders' have about EPs. Tim Brighouse, Chief Education Officer for Birmingham has observed that EPs 'have very strong views about things and those very strong views rarely seem to coincide with one another'. In the same interview he paid tribute to EPs' intelligence and their familiarity with up to date research, but he also observed that they 'are very adamant about their position and whenever I've met them, above any other group, I've always thought they are the most reasonable and then after I've worked with them for a while I've discovered that I was completely wrong!'

Another education officer, Alan Wood, presents a more critical picture of EPs. He is unhappy that 'many EPs believe their main task to be supporting pupils and their families... Schools, they feel, need consultancy on whole-school issues.' He is very dismissive of EPs' reports, which he sees as being characterised by a tendency to repeat what others have said while giving little by way of diagnosis or new insights; he finds these reports full of 'incredibly banal targets' and 'very generalised proposals'. There is no doubt some truth in these criticisms, but many EPs might argue that the production of reports like this is a consequence of their administrative role within their LEA's 'statementing machine', which results in relatively routine assessments done under severe time pressure with relatively little freedom to assess, observe and consult in-depth. While some LEA officers may resent EPs putting support of the child first, there are probably many parents who fear that the EP who assesses their child is going to be too concerned about LEA policy at the expense of their child's best interests. In my experience, EPs caught between these two sets of expectations are usually doing their best to satisfy the legitimate pressures from both sides, while also adhering to scientific standards of procedure. As if this were not enough, some of them are also trying to persuade their schools that they have far more to offer (by way of consultancy, INSET and systems work) than just individual assessments.

Educational psychologists and dyslexia

Wood makes an interesting comment on dyslexia. He says that 'Some EPs proudly denounce tests as unhelpful... and never use them... But there needs to be an approach which combines a level of testing and in-context assessment... This issue is clearest when considering children described as dyslexic. Increasingly, LEAs are recognising that they have egg all over their faces for accepting so readily the prejudicial dismissal of the condition.' I suspect that only a small proportion of EPs 'proudly denounce tests... and never use them'.

Nevertheless, Wood no doubt has a point. The British Psychological Society has recently consulted psychologists in an attempt to establish an accepted definition of dyslexia. It has suggested:

> Dyslexia is evident when accurate and fluent word reading and/or spelling develops very incompletely or with great difficulty. This focuses on literacy learning at the 'word level' and implies that the problem is severe and persistent despite appropriate learning opportunities. It provides the basis for a staged process of assessment through teaching.

(BPS 1999)

Of 141 EPs who responded to a questionnaire, 59 per cent supported this definition of dyslexia, 15 per cent preferred a slightly different definition and 26 per cent did not support either. Overall, only 71 per cent supported the use of the term 'dyslexia' (although 74 per cent had supported a particular definition of the term!); 22 per cent thought that the term 'dyslexia' should be used synonymously with 'SpLD' while 66 per cent thought that dyslexia was one type (subset) of SpLD. It is striking that the profession is still so split about such basic questions. Even the 74 per cent support for the two suggested definitions is less significant than it seems when one considers that the definition was put forward as a 'working definition', the implication being that while it is far from being an ideal definition, it is good enough to serve for practical purposes.

In effect, if the BPS definition is taken as anything more than a pragmatic 'working definition' then it tends to define dyslexia out of existence by reducing it to a literacy problem of a particular kind while neglecting broader approaches such as those of Nicolson and Fawcett (1995), Shaywitz (1996) and Stein (1993), which place the literacy difficulties within the context of a broader consideration of individual cognitive functioning. The BPS definition also tends to dismiss the notion that underachievement is an important consideration in determining which pupils should be considered to have special educational needs which require extra provision. This issue is discussed in Ashton (1997) and Stanovich and Stanovich (1997).

Inclusion

The common theme of this book is 'inclusion', but this is an idea which must be applied with care to the education of dyslexic pupils, since it can easily work against their best interests. In a press release on 7 July 2000, the Schools Minister, Jacqui Smith said, 'There is a lot of nonsense talked about the Government's approach to special needs. We support a more inclusive approach to meeting the needs of the pupils with SEN when they are in mainstream schools, including many blind children and wheelchair users. We have always recognised that for some special needs such as Emotional and Behavioural Difficulties, special schools will often be most appropriate.'

This statement shows an awareness that some SEN pupils are relatively easy to 'include' while others are not. It shows also a political awareness that there is great resistance in schools to the idea that they should be prevented from excluding pupils who are severely disrupting the education of others. The degree of disruption in any particular case depends, of course, not just on the pupil in question but upon school policies, the resources available and many other factors. Few, if any, schools nowadays would resist taking in a pupil in a wheelchair, so long as they have the necessary ramps, lifts, etc., but all schools set limits on how much disruption they are prepared to tolerate. In this context inclusion is essentially part of the terminology of 'human rights' and is closely related to the American concept of 'least restrictive environment' (LRE) (Hegarty *et al.* 1981, Lerner 1993). Inclusion as an ideal means, essentially, that all children have a right to be appropriately taught in a mainstream school; more specifically, in the terminology of LRE, each child should be taught as near as possible to the normal end of the 'continuum of alternative placements' (Lerner 1993). This continuum begins with normal education in the 'regular classroom' and goes through support within the classroom to withdrawal provision, special schools and finally education in a hospital or at home for pupils unable to attend classes.

Under human rights legislation, it will no doubt be up to the courts to decide in particular cases whether schools or LEAs have made reasonable efforts to include pupils and whether the sort of continuum used in the USA is appropriate.

Apparently, Jacqui Smith said nothing about dyslexic pupils in her statement. This is understandable. The drive for inclusion has come from concern about the fate of pupils with other categories of need, and especially those who have often been put into segregated special provision – the physically handicapped, the blind, Down's syndrome children and so on. The situation of dyslexic pupils is quite different. It is rare for dyslexic pupils to be excluded from mainstream schools, but they are often subject to treatment within the school which fails to recognise and develop their potential. So far as dyslexic pupils are concerned, a good number of parents have found themselves pushing for less inclusion rather than more; they often find themselves arguing for more specialist provision for their children, and in practice this often entails some withdrawal from the classroom. This proposal may be resisted on the grounds that every pupil should have access to a 'broad and balanced curriculum'.

These parents are clearly not rejecting inclusion as an ideal, but they find that their children are victims of the misapplication of the ideal. In most cases they are happy for their child to attend a local mainstream school and take part in the same lessons and other activities as their non-dyslexic friends. But (and it is a big 'but') they also want their children to be placed in teaching groups appropriate to their ability, they want them to be given tuition to improve basic literacy skills and they want them to have appropriate support in coping with the complexities of life in a secondary school. All too often, however, the dyslexic child of high or average ability is placed in teaching groups where pupils of below average ability predominate. Schools do this from the best of motives – they see that the dyslexic child needs support in class and it is often only in the lower sets or bands that this support in available, but the effects on self-esteem, academic progress and social integration can be devastating, especially when compounded by a failure to provide effective tuition in basic skills.

The irony is that such situations are often justified in the name of inclusion! This is the result of muddled thinking. The implied reasoning seems to go roughly as follows: (1) all pupils are entitled to access to a broad and balanced curriculum; (2) therefore they should follow the full National Curriculum; (3) therefore they should not miss any lessons in any National Curriculum subjects; (4) and they should certainly not have any National Curriculum subjects disapplied (except perhaps one foreign language in schools where pupils normally take two). The gaps in reasoning are fairly obvious at every step. The key point is, of course, that a National Curriculum 'entitlement' was put in place in an attempt to protect pupils who might otherwise receive a second best curriculum, but in the case of dyslexic pupils this entitlement is turned into an obligation. The pupils themselves and their parents have little difficulty seeing that compulsory exposure to a 'broad and balanced curriculum' is not in the interests of these pupils if the practical outcome is that they do not receive the tuition in basic skills and other forms of support which they so desperately need, and which can only be effectively provided out of class. This is not, it should be stressed, an argument against in-class support. In-class support may be very helpful but, especially in the case of severe dyslexic learners, much more is needed (OFSTED 1999).

Assessment

Lannen and Reid (1996) cite studies showing a 'mismatch between the perceptions of teachers and educational psychologists regarding the role of the psychologist in assessment'. Teachers in these studies 'perceived psychologists as a group of professionals with the skills and remit to provide informative, child-focused cognitive assessment [to give] a clearer explanation of the child's difficulties. Educational psychologists, however, ... [preferred] to adopt a consultancy and advisory role.'

As a broad generalisation, this is probably still true, though it is also the case that individual views vary considerably within both groups. Educational Psychology Services and EPs vary enormously. Some carry out a cognitive assessment (usually including WISC-III or BAS-II) in all or most cases, while at the other extreme some are opposed in principle to the use of IQ tests and rely on consultation, observation and curriculum-based assessment.

These debates and disagreements will no doubt continue, and no attempt will be made to resolve them here, beyond reiterating the obvious, but often neglected, point that EPs and SENCOs should sit down together to discuss the purpose of assessments. It is often the case that assessments take place primarily to determine whether or not the pupil in question should have a Statement of SEN. Most (though not all) LEAs have issued increasing numbers of Statements throughout the 1990s. In recent years, those involved have come increasingly to realise that this exponential growth cannot continue and it now seems likely that there will be radical changes over the next few years. The future of educational psychology is actively under review (DfEE 2000).

What this will mean for the future role of EPs is not yet clear. The result could be an increasingly narrow role assessing fewer children, though perhaps in more depth. Another outcome could be that they spend less time on individual assessments and use the increased freedom from the demands of 'statementing' to develop a broader role. One only has to glance through the profession's own journal *Educational Psychology in Practice* to see that even while the profession has been on the 'statementing' treadmill, there has been sustained interest in many other ways of working. Most of these come under the broad headings of 'consultation', 'projects', 'systems work', etc.

Some SENCOs will prefer the narrower role for EPs either because this is what they are comfortable with or because they have doubts about how well-equipped EPs are to do other things. However, I would argue that it is of central importance for SENCOs and EPs to sit down together from time to time to discuss what they are doing together and why. It is all too easy to carry on with a familiar routine. Both SENCOs and EPs can easily find that they 'don't have time' to reflect together on what they are doing. SENCOs are increasingly burdened with paperwork and increasingly distracted by a whole range of day-to-day concerns and crises, which they may or may not see as relevant to what they should really be doing. Leyden (1999) was talking about EPs when he said, 'What do we do?... It is not that we are not hard-working, nor that we are doing a bad job. We are doing the wrong job.' There are probably many SENCOs who feel the same with equal justification.

It may be that now is a particularly opportune time for both sides to help each other to break free from the grip of unproductive ways of working. The government says that it wants to reduce the administrative burden on teachers, the role of EPs is actively under review and LEAs (under pressure from central government) are making serious attempts to reduce the number of Statements of SEN.

In this context, there is an opportunity to discuss the purpose of assessment. If assessment of individual pupils is no longer routinely required as part of an ever expanding system of statutory assessment, then what else is it for?

Assessment for what?

If one has a thoughtful approach to assessment and some freedom in deciding what to do, then it no longer makes sense to limit oneself to individual assessment. This is not to say that individual assessment is a waste of time – it can be extremely valuable. A few years ago, a head teacher of a primary school explained to me that she knew by Year 2 at the latest which children were 'SpLDs' and 'MLDs'; it was then just a case of waiting for the EP to make the assessment so that a Statement could be issued. My first assessment in this school was one of the 'MLDs' who, it turned out, had an IQ of 102 on the WISC-III! This is an extreme example, but it is still not uncommon for children with quite specific difficulties to be dismissed as low ability or lacking in motivation. More targeted diagnostic assessment can also be helpful in identifying more accurately the specific difficulties a pupil has. In the case of dyslexic pupils, one can commonly identify weaknesses in phonological processing which call for structured literacy tuition with an emphasis on 'phonics'; it is also quite common to find visual processing difficulties which call for optometric assessment.

However, individual assessment is of limited value if one does not also spend time considering what comes before the assessment and what happens after it. 'Before assessment' refers to the information already available in schools – what assessment information is already available, what help has the pupil already had and what effect has this had? 'After assessment' refers to the consequences that flow from the assessment – is the pupil taught differently in subject lessons, is he or she offered more support in or out of class, is he or she withdrawn for individual or group tuition, is he or she offered counselling, support with organisation and homework, are parents involved?

As soon as one starts to consider these issues, the boundaries between assessment, consultation, systems work, INSET, etc., start to break down.

The logical starting point is to consider the information schools already have on their pupils. In addition to KS2 SATs results, many secondary schools systematically collect data on all their pupils at the time of secondary transfer, often using NFER tests of verbal and non-verbal ability, as well as normative tests of reading and spelling. These tests can be misleading – some SpLD pupils obtain deceptively low scores on written, group tests of ability and only show their true ability on individually administered tests. Nevertheless, careful consideration of data of this kind, as well as feedback from subject teachers, provides an obvious starting point. From this starting point we need to do much more than identify a small number of pupils with severe difficulties who are then 'seen by the psychologist' and allocated a share of that fabled prize, 'one to one teaching'. There may indeed be some pupils for whom individual assessment and 'one to one' tuition is appropriate, but while all pupils are unique, few have difficulties which are so unique that individual tuition is the only answer. This may not be the best use of skilled SEN teachers. It is usually possible to identify groups of pupils who can be withdrawn together in groups for extra help in specified areas. Properly planned group work can be just as effective as individual tuition if the right pupils are in the group. A good example is SRA Corrective Reading, which is just as effective with dyslexic pupils as with any others. Other examples would be intensive courses (for perhaps half a term or a term) in essay planning (mind-mapping, etc.), reading comprehension, use of word processors, handwriting, spelling, etc.

Such an approach should be a much more effective use of teacher time than 'one-to-one' teaching. As soon as we start to think in this way we are into 'systems work', whether we know it or not. We are looking at the information we have about the needs of a whole range of pupils and trying to set up a range of provision to match those needs. As soon as we start to do this it becomes obvious that we need to think about the quality of the information we have. Are there better tests? Shouldn't we be more systematic in asking pupils themselves about their difficulties and needs? Could we devise a simple questionnaire for all pupils midway through their first year to find out what problems they have and what help they would like? Could subject teachers be encouraged, on the basis of questionnaire results and other evidence, to make more use of hand-outs so that less time is wasted on copying or writing notes, thus freeing up time for lecturing, discussion and demonstration?

In this way, assessment (whether by SENCOs, EPs or others) becomes an integral part of a whole system of screening, problem identification and provision. Instead of the EP 'seeing' a pupil in order to 'get a Statement', psychological assessment would be concerned more with matching children to available forms of provision. In practice, there would probably be little need for this kind of work once the appropriate range of provision was in place. Most of the necessary 'assessment' would be built into the school systems and would be done by teachers. The EP could then either go home or find something else more useful to do! Although there might still be a residual need for in-depth assessment of a few children, more time could be spent on counselling pupils, or on consultation with teachers who felt the need for ideas and advice from a relatively detached 'outsider', and on a range of other activities.

An interesting example of what can happen when one explores openly what can be done is provided by the work on 'emotional intelligence' and 'anger management' which is being developed by Southampton EPS and others. An important part of this work involves EPs working over a period of about six sessions with groups of pupils who need help in dealing with their anger. This work is mainly targeted at the extreme end of the 'EBD spectrum' but there is no reason why it should not be adapted for dyslexic pupils and others who are experiencing anger, frustration, depression and other strong reactions to their learning difficulties. Such work retains the main principles of counselling but lets go of the idea that 'one-to-one' is best.

Support

Clearly, assessment without support is of little or no use. The main purpose of assessment is to ensure that the support given is appropriate. Assessment and support are inseparable in practice, and therefore most of what is to be said about support has already been said during the discussion of assessment. In a sensible system we do not reinvent support for each individual case – we start the assessment knowing what forms of support are available or could be made available.

In this section, I will try to sketch out extremely briefly the basis for a systematic approach to support. There are three questions. What is support for? What kind of support should there be? And who is it for?

What is support for? In the case of dyslexic pupils, the key purpose of support is to enable pupils to (a) survive and (b) prosper both academically and socially in a system which all too often fails to recognise and develop their full potential. The purpose of support (and ultimately of assessment) is to show them what they can do, motivate them and provide them with the means to fulfil their potential despite their difficulties.

What kind of support? Key elements of support will be built into subject teaching procedures, and where this is insufficient pupils will need additional 'in-class support'. In addition, many pupils will need support in skill development in order to increase the pupil's capacity to learn independently, and much of this will have to take place outside the normal range of subject lessons. Some pupils will need supplementary sessions to keep up with their work. In the more severe cases, this will not work without effective measures to reduce 'curriculum overload', which will sometimes include disapplication of a National Curriculum subject. Otherwise, the attempt to cram in too many 'extras' at break times or after school will fail because neither the teachers nor the pupils will be sufficiently rested and clear headed to work effectively.

Who is support for? There is just one point I would like to make here. At the risk of stating the blindingly obvious, support is for any pupils who need it. When we use labels (whether 'dyslexia' or others such as 'dyspraxic', 'MLD', 'ADHD', etc.) there is always a risk of confusing labels with needs. Labels are useful if they help us to understand children better, but if a child's handwriting is illegible, the important question is not whether the child is 'dyspraxic' (whatever we think that means) but whether the child would benefit from a handwriting course, a motor skills training course, a wordprocessing course, a Dictaphone or some other provision. SENCOs do not do 'their' children any favours if they draw a line between SEN pupils and other pupils. The proposed BPS definition of dyslexia, which I criticised earlier, is attractive to many psychologists because it highlights a difficulty which is common both to dyslexic learners and to other poor readers. Similarly, the British Dyslexia Association is increasingly recognising that many of the needs of dyslexic pupils can be met by good teaching procedures which can be used appropriately with all children (BDA 1994, 1996 and 1999).

References

Ashton, C. J. (1997) 'SpLD, discrepancies and dyslexia', *Educational Psychology in Practice* 13(1), 9–11.

British Dyslexia Association (1999) *Achieving dyslexia friendly schools.* Reading: BDA.

British Psychological Society (1999) *Dyslexia, Literacy and Psychological Assessment.* Leicester: BPS.

DfEE (2000) *Educational Psychology Services (England): Report of the Working Group.* London: DfEE.

Gould, S. J. (1981) *The Mismeasure of Man.* London: Penguin.

Hegarty, S. *et al.* (1981) *Educating Pupils with Special Needs in the Ordinary School.* NFER-Nelson.

Lannen, S. and Reid, G. (1996) 'Psychological assessment', in Reid, G. (ed.) *Dimensions of Dyslexia*, vol. I. Edinburgh: Moray House Publications.

Leyden, G. (1999) 'Time for Change: the reformulation of applied psychology for LEAs and schools', *Educational Psychology in Practice*, 14(4).

Lerner, J. (1993) *Learning Disabilities: Theories, Diagnosis and Teaching Strategies.* Boston and Toronto: Houghton Mifflin.

Medawar, P. (1996) *The Strange Case of the Spotted Mice.*

Leyden (1999) 'Time for change' *Educational Psychology in Practice*, 14(4) 222–27.

Nicolson, R. I. and Fawcett, A. J. (1995) 'Dyslexia is more than a phonological disability', *Dyslexia* 1(1), 19–36.

OFSTED (1999) *Pupils with specific learning difficulties in mainstream schools.* London: OFSTED.

Peer, L. (1994) *Dyslexia: the Training and Awareness of Teachers.* Reading: British Dyslexia Association.

Peer, L. (1996) *Winning with Dyslexia. A Guide for Secondary Schools.* Reading: British Dyslexia Association.

Shaywitz, S. E. (1996) 'Dyslexia', *Scientific American*, November, 78–84.

SRA *Corrective Reading.* Henley-on-Thames: Science Research Associates.

Stanovich, K. E. and Stanovich, P. J. (1997) 'Further thoughts on aptitude/achievement discrepancy', *Educational Psychology in Practice* 13(1), 3–8.

Stein, J. F. (1993) 'Visuospatial perception in disabled readers', in Willows, D. M. *et al.* (eds) *Visual Processes in Reading and Reading Disabilities*, 331–46. New Jersey: Lawrence Erlbaum Associates.

CHAPTER 28

Dyslexia and the Careers Service

Madeleine Reid

This chapter:

- examines the role of careers advisers
- discusses influential factors associated with their role such as assessing needs and dealing with career obstacles
- considers the tendency to underestimate the potential of dyslexic young people
- discusses key factors which can help young people with dyslexia find the most appropriate career or course.

The aim of this chapter is to look at existing good practice within both the mainstream secondary school and the small independent specialist school and to try and highlight the best and most successful methods of guidance and ongoing help for dyslexic students. One dictionary definition of 'Career' is 'Pathway through life' and throughout this chapter I shall be referring to that pathway and the guidance process, which helps that pathway lead to a happy and successful working life. I see my role, and that of other professional advisers involved with Careers as trying to make that pathway as clear and free from debris as possible. It must be kept clear and we must ensure that the exit roads from it are also kept clear and that they are clearly marked. If there are long straight and smooth parts to that pathway we need to make doubly sure that no sudden potholes appear or that it does not suddenly turn from an inviting pathway to an overgrown impassable track. Dyslexic students are used to overcoming rough terrain but when the going gets too tough some may decide that the gain is not worth the pain and they simply give up.

Background

I have been a Careers Adviser with Somerset Careers Ltd for over twenty years and a simple geographical quirk of fate gave me my legacy of two independent schools both specialising in dyslexia. I was very cynical about dyslexia, and part of me believed it was a 'middle class' euphemism for sons or daughters who were not as bright as parent's had hoped. It was a good example of Chairman Mao's theory about starting with a completely blank sheet of paper, and my aim was to research as much as I could on careers and dyslexia before going into these school in a professional capacity.

It was then I began to realise that there was, in fact, very little written on careers for dyslexic learners and that although I found reams on diagnosis, strategies for dealing with a variety of subjects, IT help for dyslexic pupils, I could find nothing at all on Careers. There seemed to be nothing that would help me as a total novice to understand dyslexia and give guidance for future options. I could not even find anything that talked about dyslexia and careers at all. I was at a loss where to start and decided that I ought to spend a week in both my schools to get more of a 'hands-on-picture' of the problems these young people were facing. I was to discover during this time that there were so many extra aspects to dyslexia of which I was unaware, added problems of organisational skills, short-term memory and probably the most limiting factor for a Careers Adviser to overcome – very low self-esteem. It highlighted to me that dyslexia was a continuum and that like any other group of Year 9, 10 or 11 pupils there was a very wide range of abilities.

Assessing the need

There was not going to be one easy answer or one easy method to deal with these pupils. Although the label was the same for all of them each one posed different problems. In discussion they appeared very self-confident and self-assured, but it did not take a great deal of probing and digging to break through this thin layer of protection. Many told me that they were aiming at careers in the great outdoors such as farming, gamekeeping or fishfarming but for a lot of these clients they were only looking at careers they considered to have a minimum of reading and writing.

I felt that I needed some extra way to help me assess the true strengths and weaknesses of these students. I am not in favour of psychometric testing for all pupils but I hoped it might be helpful to highlight strengths that our exam system does not. For instance, a lowish grade at GCSE English or Maths does not necessarily mean a low verbal or numerical reasoning ability. I had been trained to use psychometric tests and Somerset Careers were piloting the Morrisby test in their mainstream sector schools so I decided that I would try it on my dyslexic clients. Although some dyslexic students had been tested with this test there had not been extensive testing of large groups of dyslexic individuals and so the results could have been not only a disaster but also an inaccurate picture of the dyslexic student. I just felt that these pupils were mostly of average or above average intelligence and anything that helped me arm them with higher aspirations must be worthwhile

It was with a great deal of apprehension that I undertook the testing of the whole year groups in Year 10 of both my schools. I asked if the results could be ipsatised in the case of very low scores. (This is done by comparing strength with strength rather than comparing individual scores against the equivalent UK age group norm.) There would have been no point in feeding back low scores as this would simply have compounded the problems and sent the low self-esteem plummeting out of sight. I was almost afraid to open the box when the results were returned.

They were an amazing set of results, far higher than I had anticipated, far higher than the schools had anticipated as well. Many scores were 'off-the-scale' and even the verbal reasoning scores were good, many very high. So at last I was in a position to say 'Look, here you are compared with the rest of your age group in the UK and you can see how good you really are'. Parents were delighted as it proved for many that they had been right about their children's abilities and several of that year group got offers on college courses on the strength of those tests rather than predicted grades which were not high enough. I have now tested four year groups in my schools with similar results to prove the first one was not just a fluke. It is another tool in the assessment battery that I can use to help my clients aim for the right level of course and not to under-aspire. Appendix 1 at the end of this chapter includes a short summary of some results I have had during the testing period and a little about the candidates who undertook that test.

Overcoming the obstacles

It may be worth looking now at some specific problems I have had during my ten years working with dyslexic students and present some quotes from students and parents which might enable mainstream schools to develop strategies for overcoming these problems.

> I feel I am getting the right kind of schooling now and that my GCSE grades are going to be good, but I feel that I've lost my family.

This student came from a very poor inner city area and arrived in school as a boarder in Year 10. There were huge adjustment problems for him and he displayed quite difficult behavioural problems towards fellow pupils and staff. He was severely dyslexic but with a lot of common sense and very streetwise. He has now settled into school life, works hard and enjoys lessons but he told me that his siblings and father teased him when he went home because he now had different manners and behaviour. Also his peer group at home became distant and so it was as though one set of problems had just been replaced by another and he still had to wrestle with mixed emotions and extra stresses. It shows that if an inclusion within mainstream had been successful in his home area he would have had a more ideal base for moving forward. It is often a double-edged sword to just take a young person away from the environment they know in order to get the educational side right.

> I felt as though I had a permanent babysitter. I got fed up with all my classmates taking the mickey all the time.

This comment was from a boy who had been provided with an assistant to take notes during lessons and be with him during all lessons. The idea was excellent but this dimension of singling him out from his peer group had not been addressed. He told me he felt very stupid and he also said that his classmates did not understand the nature of his disability so perhaps more education on dyslexia may be necessary.

> We were told over and over again that Chris was remedial but I knew he was not. It has been such a battle to get teachers to accept that he is dyslexic and not just plain thick.

How many times have we all prejudged a young person and not listened to parents. We all know that parents can be difficult and we think we know best but we must not just dismiss them without further investigation, they are often proved right but the struggle for this diagnosis can be very destructive to that family. Both my small schools are full of such parents whose whole life has been a battle to get authorities to recognise dyslexia. These parents come from the whole of the UK, mostly they do not want their son or daughter taken away into a residential school miles from their home. But they do want real help with the problem and see a specialist school as the only way forward.

> They put on this brilliant presentation to persuade me and my parents to take up the offer of A levels there but when I arrived there the reality was very different. It was very obvious that they only wanted the Local Authority money. I was so unhappy that I left after the first term.

This was a very bright girl who had done well with GCSEs and was looking to do A level English, Drama and Sociology at further education. A sixth form agreed to take her for this but when she arrived said they felt she needed to rethink her choices and look at something she could cope better with, certainly not English. This highlights the problem of getting the whole process right, not just the secondary school part. We must ensure that guidance leads the student onto the right place and course and that we liase closely with colleges and sixth forms to make sure they can provide.

It is easy to assume that I am in favour of the small specialist school and it is true that I do enjoy working in both of them. I readily admit that I tend to deal with students whom the system has already failed rather than the ones who have had a successful inclusive education. There are many problems of guidance and careers that need to be addressed not only by schools but guidance services themselves in order to make the inclusion ideal work well in all schools, but many more schools are listening and trying to make changes. My main advantage in being a Careers Adviser in a small specialist school is the flexibility to try new methods, the flexibility to see students at short notice and a very close working relationship with staff and parents. If this could be the case in the mainstream secondary school I think guidance could be a much 'safer' process for the students.

We must also recognise that for a few pupils the small specialist school is still the best option and allow for this individuality. I see both sides of the story as a guidance worker in a large mainstream school as well as the small independent sector. I hope the improvements I have seen over the past years towards a better inclusive system continue and that neither side dismisses the other as second rate.

Inclusion in practice

Good inclusion cannot count the cost and must never be the cheap option. This is as true for the guidance within school as it is for any other area of the curriculum. Schools must liase closely with guidance workers and mentors to ensure its success. It has to live up to its promise to the dyslexic pupil. In order for the best guidance to be given within this ideal, guidance must have a more 'holistic' approach than is needed for the mainstream non-dyslexic pupil. We need to involve all the strongest influences at the centre of the young person. Parents need to be consulted and enlisted as helpers in that process. I still write to all the parents of my dyslexic clients to tell them what we have talked about and ask for their opinion on that advice. Is it appropriate? is it feasible?; is it what they want for their child? Parents may give reasons we did not know as to why that advice is not right for their child. They may be unsure about the further education package that has been suggested. We all need to listen and not assume we know best.

Post-Secondary guidance

Good guidance to the secondary pupil cannot be given in isolation of the school years. The career process does not stop when they leave secondary school. We must look longer term and certainly a lot more research needs to be undertaken on tracking past students. I have done a mini survey on students from my independent schools but it is not so easy to get data from mainstream and so it is difficult to compare success in later life between the two groups.

Research needs to be carried out into further education courses and the help that is offered there to dyslexic pupils. I know many dyslexic learners who have done well in my small schools and gained high grades to subsequently fail at the next hurdle of further education and drop out completely. Often the reason is that the course did not offer the right level of support, the mainstream college tutors did not understand dyslexia or the level of the course was wrong. Sometimes grades for dyslexic students may be high and indicate that a high level course is suitable but these grades are gained with much support and a gentler, less stressful introduction to college may be better.

Some key factors

- *Assessment* – Research needs to be carried out on psychometric tests available. What is the most approriate form of assessment and test which can be used?

  Tests can be expensive and it might be more cost effective to get a group of dyslexic students from several mainstream schools in an area and test them together. This would have to be carefully planned however, so as not to single them out or make them feel uncomfortable. The results must be carefully fed back to candidates and time must be built into the guidance process for this. Also the briefing session must boost self-esteem and give sound reasons for the test to both students and parents.

- *Interviewing* – Interviews must be shorter and more frequent and follow-up is vital. We must never assume that when a dyslexic pupils smiles at the end of an interview and agrees to carry out certain tasks that they will even remember or be able to organise the application procedure. They are masters at the art of deception and I do not mean this unkindly. For most of them they have been successfully fooling the world at large for a number of years and covering up problems in order to avoid looking foolish. It is easier for them to agree than to admit they are unsure or that they have not understood. Once again Careers Services and schools must allow the right time for this guidance process for there may be a series of interviews and access to students for this is vital.

- *Self-esteem* – Self-esteem with dyslexic students is a fragile veneer and can easily be cracked or removed at the next stage after school if that stage is not the right one. Dyslexic students hate to be singled out from their peers but are still in need of support and colleges must be careful to offer this support in a discreet way and in the amounts needed.

- *Training in guidance* – Training must be given to students on guidance courses. I take a couple of students with me when I do a session on Dyslexia and Guidance for the students on the Careers Guidance Course at University West of England. Many say this is one of the best sessions and I cannot take the credit for this. These pupils paint a clear picture of the problems and obstacles they faced during school. They are happy to answer questions and to talk freely about their disability. They speak candidly on what they expect from professionals and schools should encourage their dyslexic students to talk about their problems to the rest of their peers if possible.

- *Stigma and disclosure* – Schools must make efforts to educate other pupils about dyslexia and remove its stigma and this also applies to other members of staff, especially new ones. Guidance courses must include dyslexia; it is after all the disability that most generic Careers Advisers will come in contact with more than any other. And perhaps for many of us we do not realise we are dealing with a dyslexic person until it is too late.

  Guidance workers and mentors must stop searching for 'suitable' careers and realise that almost all careers are as open to dyslexic individuals as to anyone else. However to achieve them it may need twice the level of motivation and struggle.

- *Employers and employment* – Finally we must somehow educate industry and employers about dyslexia and remove their fears that they may be employing a second rate person for a first class job. School work experience and Industry days at schools can help address this but there is a still a long way to go on this issue.

It is easy for us to hold up the high achievers who have dyslexia but they are not the norm, anymore than high achievers with ordinary mainstream students. For many small achievements are arduously won and are equally worthy of merit. For some, a lowish grade at GCSE may be a real success and can indicate a level of determination that would make this person an excellent employee.

Conclusion

My fervent hope is that inclusion within the mainstream secondary school lives up to its promise and that it offers the same rounded package for disabled students as it does for all the others. It may be easier to quantify success or failure however for other curriculum areas. The problem with guidance is that we do not find out if we won or lost until several years down the line and by that time a young person's life may be totally ruined.

My small scale survey sadly found several pupils who had succeeded well in the specialist school but had failed once again when they were forced back into the mainstream system. One of my saddest replies was from a Mum of a lad I had dealt with several years ago:

> He did so well at school, we were all so optimistic but college was an unmitigated disaster. The support was wrong, they would not listen to him and he felt he was put into groups with people with learning difficulties. The tutors at College did not really understand dyslexia. He's totally given up now, he's on medication for depression and I'm afraid to answer the phone in case it's the Police to tell me he's been found dead in some remote spot.

It just serves as a tragic reminder that we do not always get it right and if we get complacent and do not follow up our guidance we will never know how successful it was!

Appendix 1: Profiles from psychometric tests

Some profiles from my psychometric tests over the past four years.

Test type	Low	Fair	Average	High	Very High
Reasoning					
Verbal					
Numerical					
Perceptual					
Spatial					
Mechanical					
Manual Speed					
Manual Skill					

This was a boy who had failed in his mainstream school and dropped out completely in Year 9. His expectactions were low and his self-esteem was at rock bottom. Convinced he was doomed to fail at every educational hurdle it was a very difficult process to convince him that he was extremely bright. He is now in the second year of a Maths Degree and doing well.

Test type	Low	Fair	Average	High	Very High
Reasoning					
Verbal					
Numerical					
Perceptual					
Spatial					
Mechanical					
Manual Speed					
Manual Skill					

This is the profile of the young lady who wanted to do English at A level although her predicted grade was only D/possible C. She restarted the course at college and succeeded in gaining a B at A level.

Test type	Low	Fair	Average	High	Very High
Reasoning					
Verbal					
Numerical					
Perceptual					
Spatial					
Mechanical					
Manual Speed					
Manual Skill					

This is the profile of a young man who had bullied at school because of his inability to read and write and was predicted low GCSE grades. His grades were not brilliant but this profile persuaded the college to offer him a place on the Advanced GNVQ in Electronics and Computing and he succeeded in gaining a Distinction and moved onto a Degree course.

Appendix 2: The guidance process

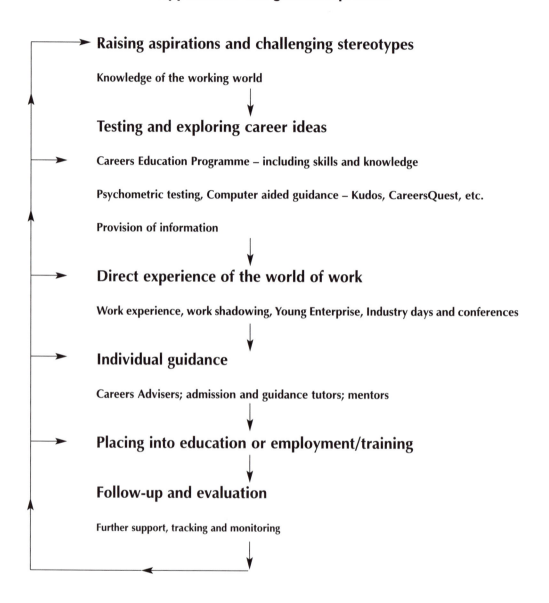

Raising aspirations and challenging stereotypes

Knowledge of the working world

Testing and exploring career ideas

Careers Education Programme – including skills and knowledge

Psychometric testing, Computer aided guidance – Kudos, CareersQuest, etc.

Provision of information

Direct experience of the world of work

Work experience, work shadowing, Young Enterprise, Industry days and conferences

Individual guidance

Careers Advisers; admission and guidance tutors; mentors

Placing into education or employment/training

Follow-up and evaluation

Further support, tracking and monitoring

CHAPTER 29

Dyslexia and the Law

Carol Orton

This chapter aims to:

- explain the different legal definitions of special educational needs and disability
- explain who holds responsibility for meeting children's needs
- offer a broad sweep of the administrative processes involved in monitoring special educational provision and the people responsible for them.

The 1996 Education Act provides the main legislative framework underpinning provision for children who have special educational needs. It applies to England and Wales; the law is different in Scotland.

The Act defines special educational needs (SEN) and details the duties of those responsible for meeting them. In practice these duties are the same as first laid out in the 1981 Education Act.

Definitions

A child has special educational needs if he has **a learning difficulty** which calls for **special educational provision** to be made for him.

A child has a learning difficulty if:

a) he has a significantly greater difficulty in learning than the majority of children of his age,

b) he has a disability which either prevents or hinders him from making use of educational facilities of a kind generally provided for children of his age in schools within the area of the LEA.

Special educational provision means:

educational provision which is additional to or otherwise different from the educational provision made generally for children of his age in schools maintained by the LEA (other than special schools) in the area.

(Section 312, 1996 Education Act)

There are continuing arguments about just how 'significant' a difficulty must be and how large the majority of children.

The symptoms of dyslexic difficulties – difficulty acquiring literacy skills, are too often supposed to be the sum of the learning difficulty. Attainment scores are frequently used to establish whether a child qualifies for special educational provision rather than an in-depth investigation into and understanding of underlying cognitive weaknesses causing individual barriers to learning.

The definition of a learning difficulty relates to a 'difficulty in learning', not low attainment. An astute teacher can identify these difficulties at an early age. The dyslexic child should not have to fall behind his peers before his needs are investigated. The House of Lords have ruled (July 2000) that educational professionals, including teachers, have a common law duty of care to children they are responsible for. Failing to investigate the nature of possible difficulties a child may be experiencing, or failing to ask advice, may constitute a breach of such a duty. Most teachers are keen to ensure that children in their class are learning effectively and so have nothing to fear.

A child does not have special educational needs by virtue of the fact that he is, or may be dyslexic – only if as a result he requires special educational provision. Dyslexic children can and do learn effectively and achieve alongside children without special educational needs of similar ability if they are taught in the way they learn best. Some schools have adopted whole-school policies which address many of the needs of dyslexic pupils across the curriculum. What may be special educational provision in other schools becomes the norm. 'Dyslexia friendly schools' find these methods help all children but understand that prevention of SEN is dependent on an understanding of individual strengths and weaknesses as well as an understanding of the principles underpinning specialist teaching for dyslexic pupils. (The British Dyslexia Association has produced a resource pack, *Achieving dyslexia friendly schools*.)

Special educational provision is therefore not a fixed concept, but this 'can if' aspect of dyslexia does not fall neatly into the type of local authority or school SEN policies that seek to ration provision. Parents naturally become frustrated when their child is denied help because 'he is not far enough behind'.

The definition of SEN, above, swept away the concept of categorising children with disabilities and learning difficulties and there was a trend against labelling children in any way. Both children and adults identified as dyslexic find the label helps. They often say it is a huge relief to know they are not stupid, something they have invariably thought themselves to be.

The BDA expects the SEN and Disability Rights in Education Bill to pass through Parliament in the session beginning November 2000. Its purpose is to bring education within the philosophical framework of the Disability Discrimination Act (DDA).

Under the DDA a person has a disability if they have a:

physical or mental impairment which has a substantial adverse effect on his ability to carry out normal day to day activities.

Employers and providers of goods and services have a duty to make 'reasonable adjustments' to avoid discriminating against disabled people. If challenged the onus is on the employer or provider to demonstrate that to make adjustments would be unreasonable.

The DDA definition may become another hoop to jump through to obtain support. Is dyslexia a mental impairment? What are its adverse effects on everyday activities? (Ask any parent!)

However when schools consider the adjustments they need to make to avoid discriminating against disabled children, either on entry or in the delivery of the curriculum, whole-school policies such as 'dyslexia friendly schools' could become more widespread.

Existing guidance associated with the DDA accepts severe dyslexia as a disability and the draft guidance during the early consultation of the SEN Bill contained examples relating to dyslexic students in higher education.

Duties and responsibilities

School governors carry responsibility for all but a small minority of children with SEN. They have specific duties towards students with SEN under Section 317 of the 1996 Education Act. These are to:

(a) use their best endeavours to secure that, if any registered pupil has special educational needs the special educational provision that his learning difficulty calls for is made;

(b) secure that (for a student with a statement) his needs are made known to all those who teach him; and

(c) secure that teachers in the school are aware of the importance of identifying, and providing for, those registered pupils who have special educational needs.

In addition, governors have to have regard to the Code of Practice for the Identification and Assessment of Special Educational Needs. They must publish information about their school policy for Special Educational Needs which must comply with The Education (Special Educational Needs) (Information) Regulations 1994.

While governors must plan and make policies for all students in their school, including all the students with special educational needs, the duty under the Act is to secure that appropriate provision is made for individual students which will meet their individual needs. Under the SEN and Disability Rights in Education Bill there will be a stronger duty and schools may be called on to explain why they cannot make adjustments to avoid discriminating against a pupil with disabilities.

Understanding the student is the key to tackling his difficulties in learning. This process of identification, assessment and considering provision should be detailed on the student's Individual Education Plan (IEP), and all teaching staff should be responsible for meeting the student's needs within their department.

Containing a student's difficulties is not the same as meeting his special educational needs. 'Meeting' is a more ambitious concept. Schools need to balance facilitating access to the immediate curriculum and addressing underlying cognitive difficulties. If all a student's needs are fully met he can become an effective learner and achieve his potential. This should be the long-term aim of all special educational provision, a philosophy endorsed in the Government's 1997 Green Paper *Excellence for all children*. The aims of education for pupils with difficulties and disabilities are the same as those for all students. The help they need in progressing towards these aims will be different.

The Code of Practice for the Identification and Assessment of Special Educational Needs places much emphasis on the need to review all students with special educational needs by regular monitoring and evaluation. If the provision is not resulting in measurable progress it must be changed. No one expects schools to get it right first time – if they could then special educational needs might not exist at all! The willingness to search for the solution and employ specific and appropriate methodologies represents the main hope for students who find it, for whatever reason, so hard to learn. (The Code of Practice is under review and the new Code is due to come into force in 2001. It is unlikely that the fundamental principles described in this chapter will alter significantly.)

The local education authority (LEA) becomes responsible for children living in their area, wherever they go to school, when they have SEN and 'it is necessary' for them to 'determine the provision' a child needs. They fulfil this duty by carrying out a statutory assessment to identify needs and then by making a statement of those needs – the statementing process.

The LEA must review the statement at least every 12 months. The LEA initiates the review and considers the report. The school makes all the arrangements but must follow Regulations, printed at the back of the Code. The school invites reports from all parties, including the parents. These reports must be circulated two weeks before the meeting.

The LEA may cease to maintain the statement but should only do so after extensive consultations with the parents. The parents have a right to appeal to the Special Educational Needs Tribunal.

If the LEA ceases to maintain the statement the school again becomes responsible for meeting the special educational needs of the student, usually at Stage 3/School Action Plus.

The legislative framework and its associated guidance is intended to ensure that any child with special educational needs is identified and gets the right sort of support. It is silent on many issues – adequate provision, resources, and professional expertise, to name a few. However there is much that can be done to build on its foundation and to ensure that children with SEN, including dyslexia, have equal opportunities to reach their potential alongside their peers.

References

DFE (1994) *The Code of Practice on the Identification and Assessment of Special Educational Needs.* DfEE.

HMSO (1996) *Education Act.* London: HMSO.

HMSO (1997) *Excellence for All Children* (Green Paper). London: HMSO.

CHAPTER 30

Inclusion – A Parent's Perspective

Angela Fawcett

This chapter aims to:

- provide coping strategies for parents
- promote issues of independent learning
- raise issues of self-esteem.

Introduction

The issue of inclusion remains one of the most controversial aspects of education as far as parents of dyslexic children are concerned. Is it a better educational experience for the child to be included in mainstream schooling, or to attend a school or unit designed to address their specific needs? The current thinking in education is that inclusion is the right policy to adopt. In this chapter, I shall set out the issues involved in inclusion from a parent's perspective, illustrating my points with anecdotal evidence drawn from the experience of my son Matthew, and from the many dyslexic children who have formed part of my research panel for many years. I have followed these children from the age of seven, until they reached their mid-20s, and in the process befriended both them and their parents. This places me in a relatively unique position, in that I can not only represent their viewpoint, but also interpret the outcomes from the point of view of a psychologist. So in this chapter, rather than adopting my usual role as a researcher examining objective evidence, I am interested in the subjective experience of education which dyslexic children receive, as well as the objective analysis of the outcomes of that experience. Here I am acting as an advocate for dyslexic children whose lives are affected by the policy to include or not include. It is important to note that my views may differ from other commentators in the field, some of whom adopt a more emotive approach to the issues here. I should state at this point that I am a strong advocate for inclusion wherever possible, not least because of the stress which can be engendered for the child by placement in special educational classes

In my analysis, I draw on the work of Riddick (1996), who identifies good practice in supporting dyslexic children in mainstream school. Her work advocates the following approach: direct help with specific difficulties to improve basic skills; improving curriculum access; encouraging coping strategies and independent learning; and building up confidence and self-esteem. It seems to me that direct help with basic skills may be more easily delivered in special needs placements, and considerable care is needed to ensure that it is adequately achieved in mainstream school. Conversely, in my view, the remaining examples of good practice would be difficult to deliver via special education, and are naturally represented in mainstream. The key issues here, in my experience, have been coping strategies and independent learning and self-confidence and esteem. These are the issues I seek to illustrate in my anecdotal account of the comparative strengths and weaknesses of inclusion. I also consider the recommendations of the DfEE (1997) report of the *Excellence for All Schools* on inclusion and special needs, and their impact on future educational practice, and conclude the chapter with my thoughts on the way forward.

Parenting a dyslexic child in secondary education 1986–1993

From an historical viewpoint, my experience of parenting a dyslexic child at secondary level spans a period when withdrawal via special schools and special units was favoured for children with dyslexia. In my role as Chair of the Sheffield Dyslexia Association, the support group and the Parent Helpline, I have spent many hours in discussion with distressed parents who felt that the mainstream system was failing their child, and sought further specialist provision addressed to the specific needs of their child. They argued that their children's opportunities to succeed were restricted by the paucity of special needs units dedicated to dyslexia, and the high costs of private provision. It is perhaps hardly surprising that some parents have brought actions against their LEA for failing to provide the support they feel their children need, and have pushed for placements in private units at the LEA's expense. Naturally, I am also familiar with a range of private specialist schools, which provide support tailored to the individual needs of dyslexic children, and have been impressed by the caring environment they provide. However, in my view, resources are better allocated in providing support for as wide a range of children as possible, as advocated more recently under the 1994 Code of Practice.

As you will realise, my original interest in dyslexia was stimulated by the difficulties experienced by my son Matthew, who was first diagnosed as dyslexic at the unusually early age of five and a half (for a full acount see Fawcett 1995). As a small child, Matthew was clearly bright and enquiring, with a challenging mind, great confidence in himself, and tremendous enthusiasm for life. However, when he started school, he became withdrawn and introverted, to the extent that his first teacher questioned whether or not he could speak. At this stage he had been at school for around nine months, in a fairly formal environment, where the children were expected to be able to write their name on arrival. Matthew could not even hold the pen, and was still undecided whether to use his right or his left hand! Matthew's problems were relatively easy to identify, because the discrepancy between his intelligence in the top one per cent and his inability to recognise a single letter was particularly striking.

Following the diagnosis of dyslexia, Matthew's life was transformed, and his relief was palpable. He had been particularly concerned by the flash cards which the teacher held up, which other children read easily, and had therefore assumed that he must be stupid. The unexpected breakdown in communication between Matthew and his teacher meant that he had no opportunity to reveal the discrepancy between his spoken and written language. Matthew's need to hide his difficulties and appear the same as the other children, only increased his feelings of anxiety and fear of failure.

I had foolishly assumed that a diagnosis of dyslexia would in many ways alleviate the stress in itself. Certainly, Matthew had become aware that there was a reason for his difficulties, and no longer saw himself as stupid. However, as any parent can tell you, the identification of the problem is just the beginning of a long slow battle for recognition. The first stage for the family is coming to terms with the problem and the acceptance that the child you thought was perfect in every way has difficulties. The key here is insight for all concerned, the dyslexic child, the family and the school all need to understand the phenomenon of dyslexia, in order to build on the strengths of the child and minimise the weaknesses. My involvement in the Dyslexia Association brought me into contact with a group of families at different stages in their experience of the problem. I met strong-minded women who had fought for their sons, but I noted that in the process many of these sons, even as adults, had not developed the autonomy I would wish for my own children. I was aware of my own instincts to protect Matthew, and deliberately set out to ensure that his difficulties in organisation did not preclude him from developing independence. The first step here was to make sure that Matthew's experiences in school were as normal as possible.

Interestingly enough, in the context of inclusion, the issue of special school arose for Matthew even at junior school level. The infant school had been particularly successful in developing Matthew's self-concepts, allowing him to tell stories to the rest of the class, one of his particular strengths. However, they were concerned for his welfare at junior school. By this stage, when prompted with the letter 's' at the beginning of a word such as 'says', he still failed to recognise the letter 's' at the end. His written performance was even worse, so that his infant school teachers described him as the brightest boy in the class, but able to write less than the little Chinese boy who could not speak English. At this time, a placement in a local special school for language and literacy difficulties was considered, but the local junior school decided they were prepared to take Matthew, despite his difficulties. It must be said that as parents we were somewhat relieved by this decision. We had visited the special school, a delightfully supportive environment where the head teacher knew each child by name, and we were impressed by the confidence it engendered in the children. Nevertheless, the ethos of the special school was more that of a nursery or infant school, and it was clear that the curriculum delivered was not designed to stimulate the children, but to ensure success for children of all abilities. This did not seem to us to be appropriate for Matthew, who even at this stage was well aware of instances when he felt patronised by a 'watered-down' approach to learning.

Nevertheless, despite the decision to accept Matthew at the local school, in the first year his slowness in producing the work he was set and his difficulty in following instructions nearly undid all the good work which had been achieved in infant school. Following a difficult term with his first teacher at junior school, who was naturally enough irritated by Matthews vagaries, he developed a stammer. During this year, the educational psychologist came into school to attempt to resolve a situation which was becoming increasingly stressful for Matthew. Matthew's problems were compounded in the second year of junior school by a very pleasant but over zealous teacher, who sent home nine pieces of homework some nights, in her efforts to ensure that Matthew had completed as much work as the rest of the class. Matthew became anxious, and started trying to get up very early in the morning in order to complete the work. At this stage, we decided that it might be appropriate to change schools, and send Matthew to a school that was a little less academic and formal. However, the situation was defused by intervention from the head teacher, who dictated the work to Matthew and wrote down his response, thus completing the allocated work in 30 minutes. There then followed two of Matthew's happier junior school years, with teachers who understood and liked him. By the time he reached secondary school, his reading was adequate but slow, but he needed a further year in the special needs class to improve his writing and spelling skills.

This year in the special needs class proved to be particularly traumatic for Matthew. He had always struggled with his work, but had built-up excellent relationships with his peer group, including among his friends the brighter, more able children. Placement in the special needs class destroyed this for Matthew, who was ostracised by his former friends. This seems to me to be an important and often overlooked aspect of the dyslexic problem. Intellectually, Matthew belonged with the able children, but if categorised on his literacy alone, he clearly grouped with the special needs class. This was a devastating year for Matthew. The work he undertook was easy, possibly even too easy for him. The special needs teacher did an excellent job of convincing him that he could achieve good results, but at the expense of his self-concepts. In retrospect, he may have needed this boost for his skills, but it certainly had a negative effect overall, and left him feeling very depressed. Interestingly, a mythology had developed about the special needs classroom, which was held to be a place of torture, and therefore not only to be feared but also strictly avoided by the 'normal' children. Fortunately, at this stage Matthew became friends with a dyslexic girl in his special needs class, a child of intellectual ability and spirit. They became inseparable and spent many hours discussing politics, ethics, morality and life in general, laying a firm foundation for Matthew's lifelong understanding of women. This friendship became the envy of all his former friends, and the associated kudos restored him to his rightful place, as someone people would wish to call a friend. This group of friends have remained in touch with Matthew and our family over the years, and many of them volunteered to join the control group for my research, and remain members to this day. This period was not only painful for Matthew, but also for me as his parent, who was very well aware of the difficulties he was experiencing, at a time when the transition to secondary school proves stressful for most children, including those without any specific difficulties at all. It may well be that my viewpoint on inclusion stems in part from my memories of this experience.

In the first year of secondary school, of course, Matthew had been in the sheltered environment of the special needs class. In the second year, Matthew exasperated his teachers with his forgetfulness, until they realised that this was just one manifestation of a more generalised memory problem. I should emphasise again here that this understanding of the impact of dyslexia outside the field of literacy is the key to successful inclusion, and one of the more difficult aspects for teachers (and parents!) to grasp. The school operated a fortnightly timetable. Matthew, however, could never work out whether it was week one or week two, and anyway he had lost his timetable before we could copy it. At this stage, of course, pupils no longer have desks, and need to bring the appropriate books daily. Matthew's response was to fill his large bag to overflowing with every book he possessed, and then delve fruitlessly in its depths for the appropriate books. Moreover, he would spend many hours completing his homework, only to leave it crumpled in the bottom of his bag, because he could not find the pigeon holes to hand the work in. A memorable instance was the occasion when, having been sent home for a forgotten book, he simply forgot that he had put some sausages under the grill and set fire to the house. Strangely enough, Matthew's response to this near disaster endeared him to his teachers, and from that stage forward he had reached a turning point. The special needs teacher, a woman with a very clear understanding of dyslexia, set up a support system for Matthew, which for the first time allowed him to do himself justice. He simply reported to her each morning, and she checked that he had handed in his homework. At the end of the day, she checked that he had copied down his homework correctly. This is an excellent illustration of a support system designed to provide autonomy and independence for a dyslexic child, with a coping strategy to ensure success. This recognition that his efforts to achieve were hampered by his memory difficulties transformed the situation for Matthew. Just how much progress we had made became evident during his GCSEs, when one of the more resistant members of staff exclaimed 'That boy has difficulties – he does tremendously well!', in response to my query about the regularity of presentation of his homework. This is not to say that everything became perfect, and Matthew now admits to the odd day where he pretended to be sick, presenting me with a mixture of orange juice and flour, to justify his claims. It seems to me that it is simply not possible for even the most motivated child to constantly maintain the degree of effort and concentration necessary to become a successful dyslexic.

On the other hand it was also clear that perceptions of dyslexia, unfortunately, remained very much dependent on the viewpoint of the observer. This is illustrated by a series of vignettes on the dyslexic child, drawn from interviews with parents and teachers and from school reports on the progress of secondary school children.

Exasperated (but supportive) teacher (of 14 year old)

This year Mark has put in the very minimum of effort. He arrives at lessons ill-prepared, his homework is rarely, if ever, handed in and his work is scrappily presented. He is his own worst enemy!

The parents

Baffled parent (me!)

Matthew just keeps losing things – he put his coat in the locker so it wouldn't get lost, but then he lost the key, and now he can't even remember which locker it was – he'd lose his own head if it wasn't joined on!

Depressed parent

The depressing thing is that although we've gone over the words 20 times this weekend, he still doesn't seem to be any better at spelling them!

Desperate parent

He's been in the remedial reading group for five years now, but I'm sure he's reading worse now than when he was eight years old.

Inclusion in adolescence

With considerable support from school and home, Matthew had largely overcome his reading difficulties by the time he reached GCSE level. His spelling remained relatively poor, and the speed of his written work significantly slower than other children of similar ability. Nevertheless, with extra time allowances for GCSE, he achieved laudable grades, and went on to tackle A levels. Here he chose subjects which place an unacceptable burden of written work on the majority of students, not simply those who are dyslexic. He decided to take English Literature, History and Sociology, despite the fact that he was still considerably slowed down by the effort required in reading and writing.

However, because his reading skills were improved, the issue of whether or not extra time should be allowed in his examinations was less clear-cut. The school put him in for extra time, on the grounds that they recognised his dyslexia. A short questionnaire was sent out to all the teachers, who agreed that, although his performance was not always exemplary, he was generally a conscientous student who should be allowed extra time because he was still slow to complete his work, and continued to have considerably more difficulty than others of similar ability. Again, it could be argued that Matthew benefited here from the knowledge which his teachers held about his personal characteristics, strengths and weaknesses. It seems likely that this knowledge would not have been so freely available to staff had he spent longer within the special needs class.

Nevertheless, Matthew did not receive the extra time to which he should have been entitled as a dyslexic. Not only this, he had completed half his exams before a decision was reached, and each day faced the uncertainty this failure to reach a decision engendered. Overall, however, the story has a happy ending, with Matthew achieving grades which allowed him to take up a place at university to study Politics. Space precludes a full discussion of Matthew's decision to take up a place in Russian Studies, which would lead to an MA, and a year in the Kremlin, writing a dissertation in Russian. Suffice it to say that this plunged him into a nightmare scenario, where he proved just as resistant to acquiring the Russian alphabet as he had the English at age five! Neither shall I give you the full details of Matthew's handing in his dissertation in May when the deadline was March, because he had mixed up the months! Despite the penalties applied, Matthew finally graduated with a 2.1 in Politics from a reputable university. Much of his success to my mind, could be attributed to his development as an autonomous learner, prepared to take responsibility for his own development. Moreover, his educational experiences overall, coupled with the support he received at home and at school, had given him the confidence in his own abilities necessary for a positive outcome.

Of course, not all dyslexic learners are quite so successful – which brings me to my second case study of inclusion and special education in adolescence, Paul.

Paul

I have worked with Paul since 1985, when he became one of the first members of my research panel following a referral via the Parent Helpline. At ten years old, Paul presented as a pleasant outgoing boy, with extensive difficulties in the area of language and literacy. His score of good average on the WISC test was probably an underestimate, because he was slowed down somewhat by his tendency to verbalise when completing each task. His reading was around four years behind his chronological age, which meant that he had barely started. Paul was a boy who was extremely distressed by his difficulties, and devastated by the decision to place him in a unit for children with special needs when he reached secondary level. Following two years of special placement, where Paul was transported to the Unit twice weekly, Paul had made no gains in his literacy skills, constantly struggled to establish that his literacy scores were not representative of his overall ability, and had developed lowered self-concepts. He had always had a good measure of support from his parents, who even became involved as officers in the local branch of the British Dyslexia Association, and his school and most of the individual teachers were sympathetic. However, it was less clear what could be done to support him. Indeed, some of his teachers felt that Paul made unreasonable demands on their time when he was in class, because he needed everything to be read or written down for him. Eventually, the gap between his chronological and reading age became so wide, with his reading age never progressing beyond the six year level, that Paul was awarded a statement of special educational needs. From this stage onwards, the support Paul received became more systematic and structured, and Paul had a teaching assistant with him at all times. Paul was much happier in himself under this system, and it soon became evident when he was feeling stressed, because he would start to twist his ankles together and wriggle in his seat, a warning sign to all concerned to provide some further direct support.

By the time he reached GCSE level, the system developed by the school to assist Paul enabled him to obtain a good set of GCSE grades, including an 'A' in Geography, using his teaching assistant as amenuensis. Paul's school eventually accepted that he would leave school without being able to read, because he was reluctant to expose himself to failure, and lacked the motivation or belief that he could succeed. Interestingly, many children remember the words they can manage on standardised tests of reading, and simply will not attempt anything beyond that, because they are afraid of showing themselves up. However, we undertook a short intervention with him at age 16, delivering a paired and speeded technique with familiar high interest material via a group of female students. This proved most effective in improving his skills, to the extent that his parents complained that he refused to go to bed, and lay on the floor reading at midnight!

It may be seen from these illustrations that inclusion largely proved more appealing to secondary children, because they felt less stigmatised if they were able to cope within the mainstream classroom. This seems to hold true for many children in my experience, ranging from the high achievers, such as Matthew, to children like Paul who were still struggling with their basic literacy skills. It seems to me that the main issues here are the pride and self-concepts of the children involved. It must be clearly evident that in order to succeed with dyslexia at any level, it is necessary to develop an inner strength and determination to succeed, which can carry you through the daily round of frustrations. This is certainly true of the two members of my panel who went on to become medical and nursing students, who fought one of the more unsupportive systems at all stages to convince the authorities that they were competent and capable. Alternatively, some children simply opt out of the competition in school, and can be encouraged to develop their strengths in areas outside the educational arena. This held true for another of my panel, Chris, whose consuming passion for motor bike scrambling overflowed into proficiency with technical journals and manuals which lay far beyond his real level of reading ability. The common factors here are confidence, motivation and autonomy in the development of skills.

Inclusion – current practice and legislation

In terms of inclusion, it must be emphasised that the success of support for children with dyslexia is critically dependent on a whole school understanding of dyslexia. In my view, this is one of the main benefits of inclusion, in that it becomes the responsibility of the whole school to make the adjustments necessary to ensure success. Potentially, this is very different from the situation some years back, when Matthew and his contemporaries were in secondary school, when the knowledge of dyslexia was largely restricted to the special needs teacher.

Current legislation in the UK supports the UNESCO Salamanca World Statement on Special Needs Education, 1994 (DfEE 1997). The current aims of special needs education are to extend the capability of provision within the mainstream sector, working within a framework that recognises that special needs can generally be met in this way, with more complex literacy problems requiring only short-term attendance in specialist provision, if any. Current thinking advocates the full inclusion of children with special needs in all aspects of the curriculum with their peers. Nevertheless, it is recognised that there are sensitive issues at stake here, and that some parents feel their children would be better served by special placements, which they are still entitled to request. Practical steps can be taken to facilitate inclusion, including the preparation of plans, the integration of younger children with special needs, registration for all children on the mainstream roll, increasing funding and grants to enable mainstream schools to adapt to special needs, and developing a 'kite mark' for appropriate standards. These issues have been discussed in previous chapters of this book, and priority measures are in preparation, based on a new statutory Code of Practice.

Inclusion – the way forward

Changes brought about by the existing Code of Practice since it was introduced in 1994 have facilitated the early identification of dyslexia and other learning disabilities. Placing the onus on the school and the infant school teacher to identify and support children with special needs in the first instance has in my view revolutionised the situation for young children with difficulties. It has now become possible for problems to be identified before children try (and fail!) to learn to read. This has the potential to break into the cycle of disadvantage which previously characterised children with dyslexia. Providing early prophylactic help, via early screening tests (Nicolson and Fawcett 1996, Fawcett and Nicolson 1996, Fawcett *et al.* 1998), and cost-effective short-term interventions (Nicolson *et al.* 1999) has the potential to transform the future for children with dyslexia, allowing them to express their strengths and overcome their weaknesses. As a parent and advocate for dyslexia, I am optimistic that this combination of early identification and support should ensure that the majority of children with dyslexia can move towards full inclusion and achieve their full potential within the mainstream school environment. Mainstream and special schools will work in partnership to ensure the most successful outcomes for children with special needs. In the IT generation, as Tom West (1991) would argue, dyslexic children will have the opportunity to demonstrate their creativity and visual strengths.

Let me finish this chapter by returning to the story of my son Matthew, who is currently researching for an ethical journal. Remember that Matthew went through the education system at a time when dyslexia was less widely recognised, when methods of teaching such children were less widely available and when the advantages of inclusive education had not yet been appreciated. Like many adults, his experience of education was likely to be less satisfactory than children in the current school system. In my view, Matthew's is surely a success story, moving from the seven year old child whose writing skills were worse than a non-English speaker, to become a dyslexic journalist whose work has recently been nominated for an award! My final message for parents is this – work with the system to develop the confidence and independent learning of your dyslexic child in order to achieve the most positive outcome.

References

DFE Welsh Office (1994) *Code of Practice on the Identification and Assessment of Special Educational Needs.* London: HMSO.

DfEE (1997) *Excellence for All Schools.* London: The Stationery Office.

Fawcett, A. J. (1995) 'Case studies and some recent research', in Miles, T. R. and Varma, V. (eds) *Dyslexia and Stress* 5–33. London: Whurr Publishers.

Fawcett, A. J. and Nicolson, R. I. (1996) *The Dyslexia Screening Test.* London: The Psychological Corporation.

Fawcett, A. J., Singleton, C. H and Peer, L (1998) 'Advances in early years screening for dyslexia in the UK', *Annals of Dyslexia* 48, 29–60.

Nicolson, R. I. and Fawcett, A. J. (1996) *The Dyslexia Early Screening Test.* London: The Psychological Corporation.

Nicolson, R. I. *et al.* (1999) 'An early reading intervention study: evaluation and implications', *British Journal of Educational Psychology* 69, 47–62.

Riddick, B. (1996) *Living with dyslexia.* London: Routledge.

West, T. G. (1991) *In the Mind's Eye.* New York: Prometheus.

Index